A CATALOGUE OF MANUSCRIPTS IN LAMBETH PALACE LIBRARY

A CATALOGUE OF MANUSCRIPTS IN LAMBETH PALACE LIBRARY

MSS. 1222–1860

E. G. W. BILL
LAMBETH LIBRARIAN

WITH A SUPPLEMENT TO
M. R. JAMES'S *Descriptive Catalogue of the Manuscripts in the Library of Lambeth Palace*
BY N. R. KER

OXFORD
AT THE CLARENDON PRESS
1972

Oxford University Press, Ely House, London W. 1

GLASGOW NEW YORK TORONTO MELBOURNE WELLINGTON
CAPE TOWN IBADAN NAIROBI DAR ES SALAAM LUSAKA ADDIS ABABA
DELHI BOMBAY CALCUTTA MADRAS KARACHI LAHORE DACCA
KUALA LUMPUR SINGAPORE HONG KONG TOKYO

PRINTED IN GREAT BRITAIN
AT THE UNIVERSITY PRESS, OXFORD
BY VIVIAN RIDLER
PRINTER TO THE UNIVERSITY

CONTENTS

INTRODUCTION

THIS catalogue of manuscripts in Lambeth Palace Library continues the numerical series terminated at MS. 1221 in the first published catalogue of the library, that by H. J. Todd, entitled *Catalogue of the archiepiscopal manuscripts in the Library at Lambeth Palace*, London, 1812.

The provenance and date of accession of much of the material contained in the catalogue is unknown, perhaps owing to the destruction of library records by enemy action during the Second World War. But, with the exception of most of the fragments and of some other manuscripts for which there is presumptive evidence that they were previously at Lambeth, if not actually in the library, accessions have taken place since 1812.

The Carlyle MSS., which are included in Todd, were the only acquisition of any magnitude during the nineteenth century, and few manuscripts at all were acquired during this period. It is unlikely that a catalogue ever existed of post-1812 accessions, but there are grounds for believing that in a few cases subsequent numbers in the manuscript sequence were allotted to rare printed books. Where such evidence has been found, the numbers so allotted have been left blank. Since 1953, when the library was restored after the war, the quantity of manuscript accessions has increased, and papers relating to the history of the Church of England or supplementing the older collections have been received by gift or purchase.

In this catalogue the manuscripts have in most cases been described summarily, but papers of the eighteenth century or earlier and isolated documents of later date have been described in more detail. A list of correspondents will be found in the index. The main series of official papers of the Archbishops of Canterbury, which begins with Archbishop Longley (1864–8), is not included in this catalogue, nor are the various archives deposited at Lambeth.

The descriptions of MSS. 1229–41, 1681, are by Mr. N. R. Ker, who has also contributed an account of the rebinding of manuscripts undertaken by Archbishop Sancroft (1617–1693). This account forms a supplement to Todd's volume and more particularly, since it deals mainly with mediaeval manuscripts, to M. R. James's *Descriptive Catalogue of the manuscripts in the library of Lambeth Palace*, published in 1932.

The publication of the catalogue has been made possible by generous assistance from the British Academy, the Friends of Lambeth Palace Library, the Greater London Council, the Corporation of London, and Kent County Council.

E. G. W. B.

ARCHBISHOP SANCROFT'S REARRANGEMENT OF THE MANUSCRIPTS OF LAMBETH PALACE

THE manuscripts of Lambeth Palace which made the journey to Cambridge in 1647 and came home again in 1664 are in their present state a remarkably neat collection, arranged by size,[1] mostly of a fairly uniform thickness, and mostly bound in lightish late-seventeenth-century calf. The effect is, of course, artificial. Much work has to be done to get a collection of manuscripts to look like this. At Lambeth, Archbishop Sancroft was primarily responsible for their present arrangement and he did a lot of the work himself. His aims, apart from rebinding, were, it seems, to eliminate the thinner volumes by binding them up with one another, and to make homogeneous volumes by moving pieces from one volume to another, so that like came to be with like.

The collection catalogued at Cambridge in the Commonwealth time[2] consisted of 515 shelved volumes, ninety-three pieces kept in what were called bundles or fasciculi,[3] and one unclassified item. The same collection (almost) catalogued by Sancroft consisted of 459 volumes.[4] The reduction in numbers from 609 to 459 is chiefly because items which had been separate previously were now put together.

A. THE COLLECTION BEFORE SANCROFT'S TIME

The collection consisted of manuscripts acquired by Archbishops Bancroft (†1610) and Abbot.[5] Our first clear view of it as a whole

[1] MS. 1 is the largest, MS. 564 the smallest.

[2] Oxford, Bodleian Library, MS. Tanner 268 ff. 137–70.

[3] Some of the bundled books were thin books in limp covers. Others show signs that they were once coverless. Others may have had bindings that were falling to bits.

[4] Bodleian MS. Tanner 270.

[5] Cf. Ann Cox-Johnson, 'Lambeth Palace Library 1610–1664', *Transactions of the Cambridge Bibliographical Society*, ii (1955), 106–8, and M. R. James, 'The History of Lambeth Palace Library', *Trans. Camb. Bibl. Soc.* iii (1959),

is in a catalogue drawn up after Abbot's death in 1633.[1] The catalogue is a bad one, which lists the manuscripts alphabetically by authors, or, if anonymous, by subjects, and assigns a pressmark to each. The marks run from A.1 to V.34. Presumably the letter denotes the shelf and the number the position of the book on the shelf. Some of the manuscripts still bear these marks on a flyleaf or at the head of the first leaf of the text.[2]

In 1647 another poor alphabetical catalogue was produced, no doubt in a hurry, with a view to the transfer of the collection to Cambridge University Library.[3] It lists 241 folios, 212 quartos, and 59 octavos or duodecimos. After the books arrived in Cambridge a shelfmark was put inside each volume at the top of the first available leaf and, if possible, in the top left corner of the pastedown,[4] and a new and admirable catalogue was drawn up in shelf order.[5] The Cambridge shelfmarks are in series with those assigned to the manuscripts of the University Library, and like them are preceded by the sign #.[6] The newcomers from Lambeth have class-marks beginning with the letters C, E, G, I, L, N, and T. In # C they were on four shelves (γ, ζ, η, θ), in # E, G, I on eight (α, β, γ, δ, ε, ζ, η, θ), in # L on five (γ, ε, ζ, η, θ), in # N on three (ζ, η, θ) and in T on one (α). In addition to the 514 books on these thirty-seven shelves, the new catalogue lists on f. 168 a book kept in the oriental section and an unclassified item,[7] on ff. 162^{v}–5

1–3, 19, 28–9. Four hundred and seventy-two manuscripts are listed in the two duplicate copies of the catalogue of Bancroft's books in Lambeth Palace Library Records f.1. ff. 68–73^{v} and L.R.f.2 ff. 79–85. Some fifty manuscripts are listed among the printed books in the duplicate copies of the catalogue of Abbot's books, L.R.f.3 and L.R.f.4.

1 L.R.f.6 ff. 268–310. MS. 1047 is a copy corrected by Sancroft.

2 For Sancroft's use of these marks see below, p. 8. M. R. James has usually noted them in his catalogue.

3 Copies in Bodleian, Arch. Seld. B.5 (*Summary Catalogue*, 3335) and in C.U.L., Oo.7.51 ff. 72–84. Cf. Cox-Johnson, loc. cit., pp. 115–17. Oo.7.51 is in the hand of Jonathan Pindar.

4 The shelfmarks are recorded in Oo.7.51, but not in Arch. Seld. B.5. For the manuscripts in which they are still to be seen, see below, Concordance I.

5 Bodleian MS. Tanner 268 ff. 137–70, a copy by an ignorant scribe, s. xvii^{2}, not before 1658, since it includes six manuscripts returned in that year by D'Ewes's executors and put in as # C.γ.2–7). The original must have been finished before three manuscripts borrowed by Selden were returned in 1656. Two of them were placed at the end of # C.η and one in an empty shelf as # C.γ.1. In the catalogue they are listed out of order after # C.θ.48.

6 Mr. J. T. C. Oates, to whom I owe much, suggests that the sign represents a lock.

7 Both now missing: see below, p. 4.

the contents of three bundles kept in # C.ζ,[1] where there was only one book with a shelfmark, and on ff. 168ᵛ–9 the twenty-four manuscripts (and printed books with manuscript additions) scattered among printed pieces in the large collection of pamphlets kept in bundles marked with letters from A to R and T.[2] Three manuscripts in class B are omitted in Tanner 268, but recorded among Lambethana in Oo.7.51.[3]

In addition to the full shelfmark inside the cover, each shelved book probably carried a number outside it which showed its position on the shelf. The number was written in the middle square of a small paper label ruled with horizontal and vertical lines. In bound books with sufficiently thick boards the label was pasted either to the fore-edge of the lower board, as often in seventeenth-century libraries, or to the upper edge of this board, a position in which it can be read if the book lies on its fore-edge with the head facing outwards. In these positions labels appear to survive on the bindings of MSS. 346 (?) and 353 (fore-edge) and of MSS. 376, 401, 436, 464, and 474 (upper edge). They are hard to see because later labels have been pasted over the top of them. A complete label bearing the number '6' is pasted to f. 22 of MS. 425, formerly # C.θ.6, a complete label bearing the number '11' is on the outside leaf of MS. 806, no. 21, formerly # C.θ.11, and a complete label with '16' on it is pasted to f. i of MS. 217, formerly # N.η.16.[4]

At some point in its mid-century history the collection was rearranged in a slightly different order making for more exact sizing,[5] and marked afresh, not with shelfmarks, but with a straight numeration of folios, quartos, and octavos. The new numbers were entered after or below the Cambridge shelfmarks, and a new catalogue giving the new numbers was made, in the order folios (1–247), bundle 2 (1–12), quartos (1–204), bundle 1 (1–42), bundle 3 (1–15), bundle 4 (1–24), and octavos (1–66). Bundle 4 consisted of the manuscripts (or printed books with manuscript additions) formerly mixed in with the bundles of printed books marked A–R

[1] Listed also in Oo.7.51 ff. 71(2)–71(3)ᵛ.

[2] Oo.7.51 has a full and careful list of the contents of Bundles A–R and T on ff. 157–60ᵛ.

[3] See below, p. 4.

[4] Similar labels survive on a few books at Cambridge, as Mr. Oates tells me, for example on MSS. Mm.1.22 and 23, bequeathed in 1658.

[5] See pp. 35, 36 (Concordance II).

and T.[1] The descriptions are the same as in Tanner 268, but shortened now and then. The surviving copy of this catalogue, Bodleian MS. Tanner 274, is in a good educated hand, that of William Crowe, and is without the scribal errors of Tanner 268.[2] Sancroft's use of it gives it special importance.

Six items previously catalogued at Cambridge are not recorded in this new catalogue: (1) Tanner 268 f. 167ᵛ, # C.θ.24 (*miswritten* 4), 'Statuta Collegii Reginalis Cantab. vetera et recentiora. De fundatione collegii Reginalis et benefactoribus. De prefectis Alumnis etc. huius collegii';[3] (2) Tanner 268 f. 168, 'Three loose sheets of paper containing a relation of Jesuiticall conversation by one who lived amongst them 9 yeares';[3] (3) Tanner 268 f. 168, K.β.35, 'Evangelium secundum D. Iohannem Hebraicè interprete ignoto';[4] (4) Oo.7.51 f. 80ᵛ, # B.β.2, 'Persici Idiomatis libellus viz: quatuor Evangelia Persicè; (5) Oo.7.51 f. 73, # B.γ.1, In Chinesi charactere liber; (6) Oo.7.51 f. 126ᵛ, # B.α.24, 'Epistola ad Coloss: Arab: et lat'. per Beduellum'.[5]

When the collection went back to Lambeth at the end of 1664, it appears to have been put back on the shelves in the same order as it was in before 1647. The evidence for this comes partly from Sancroft's use of the pre-1647 shelfmarks,[6] and partly from the numbers on the new labels pasted on the covers, presumably at this time since they lie on top of the Cambridge labels. These numbers are printed within square brackets. They coincide, where legible, with the numbers recorded in the pre-Cambridge catalogue in L.R.f.6. Thus, for example, '[18]' is on the label of MS. 410 and '[19]' on the label of MS. 536: these manuscripts were I.18 and D.19 respectively before 1647.

[1] See below, Concordance I.

[2] William Crowe, 1616–75; see *D.N.B.* Mr. Oates made this discovery. In a letter of 4 January 1967 he told me that Cambridge Univ. Libr. MS.Ff.4.47 and part of MS. Dd.8.45 are in the same hand as MS. Tanner 274, that there is evidence from the university accounts for 1663–4 that the hand is Crowe's, and that the question of hand could be settled one way or the other by reference to an autograph letter by Crowe in MS. Tanner 162 f. 80. The letter proved to be in the same hand as MS. Tanner 274.

[3] Not found.

[4] Not found. The description in Oo.7.51 f. 127, is 'Codex MSS. hebraicè in fol. in pergameno deaurato'.

[5] The Persian manuscript, the Chinese printed book, and the Arabic manuscript of William Bedwell are still at Cambridge, MSS. Gg.5.26, Ll.5.14, and Dd.15.4, as Mr. Oates tells me.

[6] See p. 8.

B. THE COLLECTION CATALOGUED BY SANCROFT

Sancroft's work on the manuscripts is not to my knowledge datable, but the catalogue written in his own hand, Bodleian MS. Tanner 270, shows that he duly completed it. This catalogue lists 243 folios, 170 quartos, and 46 octavos.[1] The folios are the present MSS. 1–16, 18–243, 324. The quartos, save two, are the present MSS. 325–488, 496, 510, 519, 567. Quarto 165, item 2, is now MS. 1042; item 1, not found, is described as 'Concio ad Synodum in Act. xv. 6. Convenerunt Apostoli et Presbyteri ut despicerent etc.' Quarto 168, not found, was 'The Sclavonian Psalter': it is marked as 'wanting' in the same bracket as Q.169 and Q.170, both of which are, however, still in the library (MSS. 510, 519). The octavos, save one, are the present MSS. 489, 522–7, 529–46, 548–65, 861, 873. Octavo 46, not found, was # C.θ.36 at Cambridge: Sancroft describes it as 'I. M. priest's Daily Exercise privately of devout persons to be used'.

The two Cambridge catalogues, Tanner 274 and 268, on the one hand, and Sancroft's catalogue, Tanner 270, on the other, are such careful catalogues that we are able to specify exactly the respects in which they differ, or in other words we are able to see exactly what Sancroft did with the collection of manuscripts he had inherited. (I) He left 357 volumes in their old bindings, or rebound them without changing the contents. (II) He made ninety new volumes out of 203 previously separate items. (III) He did not catalogue thirty-six items which had had shelf-numbers or bundle-numbers at Cambridge, nor a number of single items from volumes with shelf-numbers. (IV) He added nine items. I take these four categories in turn.

1. *Manuscripts left in their old bindings or rebound without change of contents*

(*a*) *Manuscripts now in pre-Sancroft bindings*

MSS. 1–4, 19, 20, 23, 33–5, 49, 51, 62, 65, 89–91, 160, 167, 169, 211, 225, 234, 324, 333, 340, 341, 343, 346, 349, 350, 353–5, 358, 361, 362, 369, 370, 376, 381, 386, 401, 403–7, 410, 415–22, 424, 426(=1112), 433, 440, 441, 446, 450, 461–8, 470, 474, 476, 482, 487, 510, 524–6, 529, 531–3, 535–7, 544, 546, 548, 549, 551–4, 560, 562–4, 566, 873.

[1] See Concordance III.

Most of the later pre-Sancroft bindings are of limp parchment, plain or with gilt ornament, sixteenth and seventeenth century, or are in dark calf with the arms of Archbishop Bancroft (MSS. 19, 23, 34, 358, 361, 415, 416, 418, 424, 552–4).

The older bindings are classifiable as:

White skin over thick wooden boards cut flush with the edges of the leaves, twelfth or thirteenth century: MSS. 343, 346, 349, 353, 440.

White or red skin over wooden boards, fourteenth or fifteenth century: MSS. 3, 4, 8, 33, 350, 354, 355 (red), 370, 376, 401, 404 (red), 410, 420, 433, 436 (red), 536 (red).

Red leather slip case: MS. 873.

Stamped calf over wooden boards, fifteenth century: MS. 450.

Stamped calf over new boards: MSS. 340 (Oxford), 341.

Calf with fillets forming a pattern of lozenges over wooden boards, fifteenth/sixteenth century: MS. 62.[1]

Calf decorated with gilt rope-pattern over wooden boards, Italian binding, late fifteenth century: MS. 529.

Black velvet over wooden boards (for Henry VIII): MS. 49.

Calf decorated with rolls over wooden boards or pasteboards, sixteenth century: MSS. 2 (HM.a.3 and gilt centrepiece and cornerpieces), 20 (AN.b.1 and Orn.A.1: Reynes), 386 (HE.h.1), 421 (FP.g.5), 422 (CH.a.1), 532 (FL.a.8), 562 (a narrow roll of RP or FP type not recorded by Oldham).[2]

Calf decorated with panels over wooden boards or pasteboards, early sixteenth century: MSS. 466 (HE 28, RO20), 482 (a 'Flemish animals' and +IHESVS MARIA roll, as on Leicester Museum, Wyggeston Hospital, MS. 34.D.10/16), 535 and 546 (both, AN 8 and AN 23), 560 (AN 24 and AN 3).[3]

(*b*) *Manuscripts now in bindings done for Sancroft*

MSS. 5, 9–14,[4] 16, 21, 25, 26, 28–32, 36–48, 52–4, 56–8, 60, 63, 64, 66–8, 70, 72, 74, 75, 77–9, 81–6, 88, 92–5, 97, 99–103, 106–11, 117–22, 128, 130–3, 135–7, 141, 146, 148, 150, 152, 154–8, 161–4,

[1] Three other Christ Church, Canterbury, manuscripts are bound in the same style: MSS. Bodley 214 and 379 and University College, Oxford, MS. 68.

[2] For these rolls see J. B. Oldham, *English Blind-stamped Bindings*, 1952.

[3] For these panels see J. B. Oldham, *Blind Panels of English Binders*, 1958.

[4] The order was changed: in MS. 12, so that the first nine leaves became ff. 248–56; in MS. 216, so that the first two leaves became ff. 110–11. For other changes in order, see Concordance IV, MSS. 221, 392, 395.

166, 168, 171–5, 177, 180, 183–7, 189–91, 193–8, 198b, 199, 201–5, 207–10,[1] 212–16,[2] 219, 220, 222–4, 226–33,[1] 235, 236, 238–40, 325–9, 332, 334, 336, 337, 339, 344, 347, 348, 351, 352, 359, 364, 366, 367, 371–3, 375, 377, 382, 384, 385, 387–91, 393, 394, 396–400, 412, 413, 428, 431, 432, 434, 435, 442, 443, 448, 449, 452, 453, 455, 458–60,[3] 471–3, 477, 479–81, 483, 486, 519, 522, 523, 527, 530, 538–40, 542, 543, 550, 555–9, 567.

Sancroft's bindings are all just the same, a lightish calf, plain except for a double fillet all round the edges and two double fillets vertically down each cover a bit out from the spine; also, on folios only (MSS. 1–240), Sancroft's arms as Archbishop in gilt on each cover. The binder inserted paper pastedowns and flyleaves, usually two at each end. Sancroft wrote the cost of binding at the top of the front pastedown. The range is from 6*s.* 6*d.* for a large folio (MS. 5) to 10*d.* for a small octavo (MS. 556). Fortunately M. R. James recorded these prices in his catalogue, for many of them have since been lost or covered over in the process of re-backing. The same style of binding, sometimes priced, is on MSS. 241–4, 246–9, 251, 253, 257, 490–5 and on Bodleian MS. Tanner 119 (2*s.* 6*d.*). The binder took some care to preserve old paste-downs and flyleaves, even if they bore no writing.

(*c*) *Manuscripts rebound since Sancroft's time*

MS. 489 was in a pre-Sancroft binding when catalogued by M. R. James, but it has been rebound since. Most of the following were probably in pre-Sancroft bindings before they were rebound in the nineteenth and twentieth centuries: MSS. 7, 73, 330, 363, 368, 383, 430, 438, 484, 496, 534, 541, 545, 561, 861, all rebound by John Tuckett, 66 Great Russell Street, between 1869 and 1873;[4] MSS. 6, 69, and 427, rebound before 1931, MS. 6 by Lamacraft and Lawrence.

II. *Newly made up manuscripts*

The ninety volumes which Sancroft made from 203 separately catalogued items of the old collection were formed either by

[1] MSS. 209 and 233 have been rebound, but with the old covers preserved.

[2] See note 4 on page 6.

[3] MS. 459 was 'repaired and armed', that is to say stamped with the archi-episcopal arms in gilt, by Tuckett in 1872.

[4] Tuckett's receipted bills are in LR.A.4. He also rebound MSS. 65 and 535, but preserved the old covers.

putting together two or more volumes or bundled pieces or by breaking up single volumes and distributing their contents in two or more volumes. Putting together presents no difficulties: the manuscripts concerned, old and new, may be seen in Concordance IV. Breaking up requires detailed discussion: thirty volumes of the old collection are in question.

In attempting the reconstruction of the thirty broken-up volumes I have been helped by the concordance of old and new numbers in Sancroft's hand in the margins of Tanner 274, and even more by the pre-1647 shelfmarks, also in his hand, in the manuscripts themselves. The concordance is useful, but not reliable.[1] The pre-1647 shelfmarks are a better guide. Sancroft entered them only in manuscripts which he put into new bindings, and not in all of these. Their place is the bottom right corner of the first leaf, and in thirteen of the broken-up volumes they are also to be found in the same position on the first leaf of separated parts.[2] Probably they are memoranda put in by Sancroft when he decided to disbind and rebind. His large programme of rebinding will have taken some years to complete. With the manuscripts off the shelves, and until new numbers had been assigned, it would be important to preserve old shelfmarks for finding purposes. The reason why Sancroft did not enter the old shelfmarks in all the rebound manuscripts may be because new numbers had been assigned before all the rebinding was done.[3]

In five manuscripts, 452, 459, 530, 538, 542, we find a row of horizontal dots instead of the old shelfmark, because Sancroft was unable to discover what the old shelfmark had been. In MS. 452 the dots are followed by the number 3 and in MS. 530 by the number 36. These numbers were probably on a label on the old bindings:[4] MS. 452 was I.3 before 1647 and MS. 530 may have been K.36 or V.36.[5] Sancroft used dots in the same way in

[1] For example, Sancroft marked the Bibles wrongly, 90 instead of 89, 190 instead of 90, and 89 instead of 190. Cf. also nos. **4, 7, 9, 12, 20, 24, 30.**

[2] Nos. **3, 4, 7, 8, 9, 10, 18, 21, 22, 25, 26, 27, 30.**

[3] The new numbers, those now in use, are in an early hand, not Sancroft's, in MSS. 162–3, 166, 168, 171–2, 175, 184–7, 189, 193, 194, usually at the foot of the first leaf on the left. Sancroft did not put the pre-1647 shelfmark in any of these volumes.

[4] Cf. above, p. 4.

[5] K and V were the shelves with the largest number of books, but the Bancroft–Abbot catalogue records nothing beyond K.32 and V.34. Nor does it record either of the two copies of Petrus Riga, *Aurora*, now at Lambeth, MSS. 530 and 531.

the margins of Tanner 274. Many of his numbers there are in fact written over dots, or, in the folio series, a dash.

1. T.1, #I.γ.2. T.2, Fol. 84:[1] five items, the first four marked '22'[2] and the last, 'Commentatio brevis et mutila in Aristot. metaphysica', marked '55'. Now **MS. 22+MS. 55 ff. 157–61.**

Scala mundi and other historical texts, followed by a single quire in a similar hand containing a brief commentary on the *Metaphysics*. This quire was taken out and placed with a copy of the *Metaphysics*, MS. 55 ff. 1–156, 162, after worms had made a pattern of holes through ff. 156 and 162.

2. T.1, #L.γ.4. T.2, Fol. 18: two items, the first, 'Casus Codicis Iustiniani', marked '27' and the second, 'Decisiones anonymi; in fine desiderantur nonnulla', marked '18'. Now **MS. 27 ff. 231–96 +MS. 18 ff. 123–82.**

The same hand of the fourteenth-century wrote marginalia in both the now separated parts. Sancroft saw that the second item was 'Annot. in 5 libros Decretalium' (his emending title in T.2) and therefore removed it to a volume of canon law. MS. 27 f. 231 is marked 'A.9'.[1]

3. T.1, #E.α.3. T.2, Fol. 204: forty items, the first seven marked '59' and the rest '50'. Now **MS. 59 ff. 191–278+MS. 50.**

Works of Anselm and Augustine. The former, occupying the first eleven quires—88 leaves, foliated 1–88—were taken out and placed after the Christ Church, Canterbury, copy of Anselm's letters. MS. 50 now consists of 112 leaves, foliated 89–200. Both MS. 50 f. 1 and MS. 59 f. 191 are marked 'L.1'.

4. T.1, #N.η.2. T.2, Fol. 5: two items, 'B. Gregorii Homiliæ 40. Origenis et Beda Homiliæ quædam', both marked '96'. Now **MS. 96 ff. 113–243+MS. 145 ff. 257–64+MS. 96 f. 244.**

MS. 145 ff. 257–64, a quire containing three homilies, one ascribed to Origen and two to Bede, are in the same hand as MS. 96 ff. 113–243. MS. 96 f. 244, a flyleaf, bears the rust-mark from the pin of an old strap-and-pin closure. A similar mark is on MS. 145 f. 264. Both MS. 96 f. 113 and MS. 145 f. 257 are marked 'B.13'; Sancroft when marking up T.2 failed to notice that the last quire had been taken out and put with his 'Fol. 145'.

[1] I refer to MS. Tanner 268 as T.1 and to MS. Tanner 274 as T.2: see above, pp. 2–3 and 3–4. Titles are from T.2.

[2] For these marks in Sancroft's hand see above, p. 8.

5. T.1, #G.δ.4. T.2, Fol. 163: seven items, the first four marked '104' and the last three, 'Quoto anno Britanni susceperunt Fidem. De Constitutione Episcopatuum, . . . Historia contractior de Regibus . . .', marked '188'. Now **MS. 104 ff. i, 1–208+MS. 188 ff. 168–74.**

MS. 104 ff. i, 1–208 is a copy of Higden, *Polychronicon* (etc.), part of which belonged to John Grandison, Bishop of Exeter (†1369). A quire of English historical collections, early thirteenth century, inserted at the end, belonged with the *Polychronicon* already in the fourteenth century, if I am right in thinking that a hand on f. 170^{v} is Grandison's. This quire was taken out and put after *Flores historiarum* (MS. 188 ff. 1–167).

6. T.1, #G.η.17. T.2, Fol. 132: two items, the first, 'Edwardi 1^{mi} Regis Angliæ Literæ' marked '104' and the second, Higden, *Polychronicon*, marked '112'. Now **MS. 104 ff. 227, 225, 226+MS. 112 ff. 130–5+MS. 112 ff. 1–129.**

Of nine leaves originally in front of the *Polychronicon*, the first, a paste-down, and the second and third, containing Edward I's letters on his claim to Scotland, written in the same hand as the *Polychronicon*, were taken out and placed in MS. 104 (cf. no. 5). The other six leaves were transferred to the end of MS. 112. Their original position appears from the ruling and from worm-holes.

7. T.1, #I.η.5. T.2, Fol. 54: 'Dictata D. Isamberti, Professoris Regii in alma Acad. Paris. 1628.[1] in 1^{am} 2^{æ} Diui Thomæ. De Iudice Controuersiarum', marked '123'. Now **MS. 123 pp. 235–352+MS. 124 ff. 1–132+MS. 126 ff. 246–95.**

These lectures on the *Summa* of St. Thomas—not only on 1^{a} 2^{ae}—were joined to three of six volumes of Louvain lectures copied at Douai in 1577 (I.ζ.16–21 at Cambridge), according to the part of the *Summa* they were concerned with. MS. 123 p. 235, MS. 124 f. 1, and MS. 126 f. 246 are all marked 'S.8'.

8. T.1, #G.ζ.19. T.2, Fol. 114: sixteen items, the eleventh, 'Petri Lombardi liber Sententiarum cum indice copioso' marked '115' and the rest '129'. Now **MS. 129+MS. 115.**

An unhandy Lanthony volume of 516 leaves, now divided in two. The unlikely presence of a copy of the *Sentences* and an index to the *Sentences* in the middle of patristica (after f. 183 of MS. 129) is vouched for not only by T.1 and T.2, but also by two medieval tables of contents in MS. 129. Both MS. 115 f. 1 and MS. 129 ff. i, 1, 184 bear the mark 'B.8'.

[1] *Sic* for 1618. The date 17 March 1618 is on p. 351 of MS. 123.

9. T.1, #G.η.20. T.2, Fol. 135: five items, the first, second, and fifth, Jeremiah, Lamentations, and Isaiah, all glossed, marked '134', and the third and fourth, 'Sermo de Latrone crucifixo' and 'Passio Domini secundum Nicodemum', marked '200'. Now **MS. 134 ff. 97–245+MS. 200 ff. 168–75+MS. 153 ff. 7–88.**

A Lanthony book, no. 21 in the medieval Lanthony catalogue and 'R. 22' in the '1633' Lambeth catalogue. Items 3 and 4, on a single quire in the middle, were taken out and put in a miscellany volume, MS. 200 (cf. nos. 12, 13). Reasons for supposing that item 5 is MS. 153 ff. 7–88 and not MS. 134 ff. 1–96 are the mark 'R.22' on 153 f. 7 and the Lanthony provenance of 153 ff. 7–88, deducible from the traces of chapter-numbering at the foot of the pages, like that in 134 ff. 97–245.[1] This chapter-numbering does not occur in the margins of 134 ff. 1–96.[2]

10. T.1, #E.ζ.17. T.2, Fol. 181: Two items, Bede and Gregory, the first marked '147' and the second '144'. Now **MS. 147 ff. i, 1–59+MS. 144 ff. 164–314.**

From Lessness, with ex-libris on MS. 147 f. 1. The Bede was put with another Bede and the Gregory with another Gregory. Both MS. 144 f. 164 and MS. 147 f. 1 are marked 'Q.5'.

11. T.1, #G.η.15. T.2, Fol. 130: five items, the first, 'Præfatio ampla in libros canonicos S. Scripturæ', marked '153' and the rest marked '114'. Now **MS. 153 ff. 1–6+MS. 114.**

The point of moving this 'Præfatio' from its old position in front of Judges, etc., glossed, to a new one in front of Isaiah, etc., glossed, is not obvious, but there is no reason to doubt Sancroft's identification, and ff. 1–6 of MS. 153 are evidently not in their original position (cf. no. **9**). Sancroft followed the Cambridge description in calling item 1 in MS. 153 'Præfatio in libros canonicos S. Scripturæ', both in the table of contents on the flyleaf and in his own catalogue.

12. T.1, #L.ζ.11. T.2, 4° 46: two items, the first, 'Evangelii secundum Lucam pars glossata', marked '153' and the second,

[1] I did not know of this Lanthony marking in time for the second edition of *Medieval Libraries of Great Britain* (1964). It numbers books, chapters, psalms, and sometimes leaves, and is always at the foot of the pages in pencil or ink and sometimes in both pencil and ink. The scratchy style and light-brown colour of the ink numbers is distinctive. At Lambeth the numbers are in MSS. 29, 56, 61 ff. 1–117, 77, 81, 85, 102, 110, 119, 134 ff. 97–245, 153 ff. 7–88, 161, 164, 335 ff. 1–228, 343; at Oxford in Bodleian MS. Auct. D.2.1; Corpus Christi College MS. 139; Trinity College MSS. 39, 40, 69; in London, in B.M. Royal MS. 5 B.i ff. 20–41.

[2] The medieval catalogue records only one copy of Isaiah glossed, no. 21, so MS. 134 ff. 1–96 is unlikely to be from Lanthony. Sancroft's error in T.2 may be because he wrote 'R 22' on f. 96 instead of on f. 97 of MS. 134.

[12 *cont.***]**
'Sermones varii, etc.', not marked. Now **MS. 153 ff. 156–79 + MS. 200 ff. 176–217** (*and perhaps further*).

There is no certainty that the sermons now in MS. 200 are those which once followed the glossed St. Luke in MS. 153 (from Lanthony), but they and arts. 11, 12 (ff. 218–25, 226–9) of this miscellany volume are not identifiable with anything else in the Tanner catalogues. The former contents of the volume which began on f. 156 of MS. 153 are noted in the hand of Morgan of Carmarthen on that leaf: 'In isto volumine continetur Lucas glosatus. Item diuersi sermones cum aliis etc.'

13. T.1, #N.η.23. T.2, 4° 24: two items, 'Psalmi cum glossa et litania in fine', the first marked '170' and the second '200'. Now **MS. 170 + MS. 200 ff. 164–7.**

The litany was detached and put into the miscellany, MS. 200 (cf. nos. **9**, **12**). Notes on MS. 170 f. 1 are in the same hand as MS. 200 f. 164[rv].

14. T.1, #G.δ.3. T.2, Fol. 162: four items, the first three marked '181' and the fourth, 'John Hartgills words . . .', '159'. Now **MS. 181 ff. i, ii, 1–223 + MS. 159 ff. 276–83 + MS. 181 f. 224.**

MS. 181 is Higden, *Polychronicon*. At the end, f. 223[v], a hand of the sixteenth century wrote the words 'Ane epytaphe vpon the death of John Hartgill'. Sancroft seems to have thought that Hartgill's verses and the verse epitaph on him, mid sixteenth century, would be better placed after the early sixteenth-century verses at the end of MS. 159.

15. T.1, bundle 2, no. 4. T.2, bundle 2, no. 4: four items, the first and last marked '182' and the other two '137'. Now **MS. 182 ff. 185–206 + MS. 237 ff. 107–45 + MS. 182 ff. 173–84.**

A fragment in French (two quires) was followed by Augustine, *De caritate* (four quires) and the first quire of a 'Tractatus de penitenciis et remissionibus'. The Augustine was taken out and put with other works of Augustine (MS. 237 ff. 1–106 and ff. 146–208), and the two fragments were bound up in a miscellany. The written space is the same throughout, but the lower margin of the Augustine has been reduced by about 15 mm. to make it fit into a smaller volume.

16. T.1, #I.ζ.28. T.2, Fol. 49: three items, the first two marked '192' and the third, 'De episcopis Norwicensibus a Felice Burgundo usque ad Thomas Browne', marked '188'. Now **MS. 192 ff. 1–44 + MS. 188 ff. 175–9** (misnumbered **165–9**).

The five leaves now removed from MS. 192 were probably put there by Bale, whose hand is on f. 177 of MS. 188 as well as in MS. 192. The leaves came from the beginning of the Norwich *Polychronicon*, now British Museum, MS. Add. 15759. The pressmark of Norwich cathedral priory is in the form O.xcviii on f. 175ᵛ of MS. 188 and in the form O.lxxxxviii on f. 2 of Add. MS. 15759. The histories of Norwich bishops are no doubt less out of place where they now are after *Flores historiarum* than where they were after *Speculum carmelitarum*. The mark of a chain is at the head of f. 175. As M. R. James noted, 'quod R [. . .]' on f. 44 of MS. 192 is in the same hand as 'quod R. Gorst' on f. 175 of MS. 188. MS. 192 f. 44, a singleton, belonged therefore, originally, with the Norwich manuscript and not with *Speculum carmelitarum*.

17. T.1, #E.η.2. T.2, Fol. 186: thirteen items, the first and the last eight marked '221' and the rest marked '142'. Now **MS. 221 ff. 262–309+MS. 142 ff. 124–204+MS. 221 ff. 158–261+ MS. 104 ff. 228, 229.**

The red-pencil pagination on rectos shows the order of the leaves as they were assembled for Archbishop Matthew Parker: 1–31 (MS. 221 ff. 262–77); 33–191 (MS. 142 ff. 124–203); 193–325 (MS. 221 ff. 158–224); 327, 329 (MS. 104 ff. 228, 229); 331–73 (MS. 221 ff. 225–46); 375–439 (MS. 221 ff. 278–309); 441 (MS. 142 f. 204); 443–71 (MS. 221 ff. 247–61). The eighty-three leaves now in MSS. 104 and 142 had no connection originally with the eighteen quires of Oxford interest in MS. 221. The leaves in MS. 142 are of theological and those in MS. 104 of historical interest. The inference to be drawn from a note in Parker's hand in the margin of f. 228 of MS. 104 is that this leaf and f. 229 came from a book which Parker had lent to Sir William Cecil, later Lord Burleigh.

18. T.1, #L.ε.3. T.2, 4° 78: seven items, the first three marked '18' and the last four '32'. Now **MS. 356 ff. 125–75+MS. 380 ff. 1–120.**

A Lanthony book of twenty-one quires, 1–5 Jerome, 6 Comestor, 7–20 Isidore, 21 Bede. The division was made after quire 6. The first six quires were put with works of Jerome (MS. 356 ff. 1–124) and the other fifteen with a volume from Lanthony containing Isidore, etc. (MS. 380 ff. 121–228). Both f. 125 of MS. 356 and f. 1 of MS. 380 are marked 'G. 8'.

19. T.1, #L.ζ.18. T.2, 4° 53: eleven items, the first ten marked '33' and the eleventh, 'Galfridus Monemuthensis de gestis Britonum', marked '55'. Now **MS. 357+MS. 379 ff. 1–68.**

Item 11 was removed. Sancroft identified it with MS. 379 ff. 1–68 in T.2 and on a flyleaf of MS. 379, but with evident hesitation, since he marked f. 1 at the foot with a row of dots[1] and on a flyleaf wrote and then cancelled the mark 'F.3.5' in favour of '55'. Fasciculus 3,

[1] See above, p. 8.

[**19** *cont.*]

no. 5 is, as Sancroft saw, MS. 457 ff. 133–92, and not MS. 379 ff. 1–68. The latter is the only Geoffrey of Monmouth now at Lambeth which can be identified with the Geoffrey formerly at the end of L.ζ.18.

20. T.1, bundle 3, no. 14. T.2, bundle 3, no. 14: three items, the first two, 'S. Bibliorum Summa . . .' and 'Iniunctiones . . .', marked '36' and the third, 'In 7tem Epistolas Canonicas Glossæ et Annotationes', not marked. Now **MS. 360 ff. 119–58+MS. 335 ff. 229–77.**

Item 3 was removed. If still at Lambeth, it can only be identified with the otherwise unaccounted for copy of the glossed Catholic Epistles now forming part of MS. 335. There is something to be said for the identification, since scribbles on f. 235^{v} of MS. 335 name Roger de Tykessover (Tixover in Rutland) and the 'villa de Wermygton' (Warmington, Northants.). The names fit well with the presence in MS. 360 of Bishop Russel's injunctions to the monks of Peterborough.

21. T.1, #L.η.20. T.2, 4° 70: six items, the first, 'Divi Augustini Confessiones', marked '41', the last, 'De diversis Significationibus verborum variorum in S. Scriptura', marked '68', and the four others marked '107'. Now **MS. 365 ff. i, ii, 1–119+MS. 431 ff. 161–82+MS. 392 ff. 11–131.**

A Lanthony book, with a medieval table of contents, MS. 365 f. ii^{v}, which lists the six items recorded in T.1 and T.2. Sancroft put the *Confessions* with *De doctrina christiana* and the rest into two miscellany volumes: cf. nos. **22–5, 27.** Both MS. 365 f. 1 and MS. 431 f. 161 are marked 'O.7'. MS. 392 f. 131 shows marks of exposure.

22. T.1, #E.θ.22. T.2, 4° 166: five items, the third and fourth marked '132' and the others '68'. Now **MS. 392 ff. 1–28+MS. 456 ff. 127–46+MS. 392 ff. 59-115.**

A miscellany. A single quire of twenty leaves, written by the same scribe as MS. 392 ff. 59–111, was taken out and put with other bits of books in a philosophical miscellany, MS. 456: cf. nos. **29, 30.** MS. 392 ff. 1, 59 and MS. 456 f. 127 are all marked 'K.28'.

23. T.1, #I.θ.14. T.2, 4° 96: five items, the first, 'Liber cui titulus in fronte est Viaticus, siue medicinalis, scil. animæ; continet Summam Theologiæ', marked '68' and the rest '85'. Now **MS. 392 ff. 29–58+MS. 409.**

A Lanthony book, in which medical texts were preceded by the priest's guide Qui bene presunt. Qui bene presunt was removed to a theological miscellany: cf. nos. **21, 22.** MS. 392 f. 29 and MS. 409 ff. 1, 53, 88 are marked respectively, in medieval hands, 'iii quaterni i°', 'vii quaterni ii°', 'ii quaterni iii', and 'i quaternus iiii'.[1]

24. T.1, #E.θ.3. T.2, 4° 147: five items, the fourth, 'Divus Augustinus de differentia Spiritus et Animæ', marked 'q.' (for 'quære'), and the rest marked '80'. Now **MS. 404 ff. i–v, 1–154+MS. 431 ff. 8–15+MS. 404 ff. 155–60.**

The old table on f. ii^v of MS. 404 shows that the Pseudo-Augustine was already here by the thirteenth century, following canon-law texts. It was taken out and put with another copy of the same text in the miscellany volume MS. 431: cf. nos. **21, 27**. MS. 404 ff. 155–60 and MS. 431 ff. 8–15 are in the same hand and the text runs on from f. 15^v of MS. 431 to f. 155 of MS. 404, ending on f. 155 at the end of chapter 33 in *PL* xl. 803.

25. T.1, #I.θ.17. T.2, 4° 99: two items, the first, 'Sermones in Dominicas et Festa', marked '84' and the second, 'S. Leo Papa de conflictu vitiorum et virtutum', marked '107'. Now **MS. 408 ff. 20–141+MS. 431 ff. 146–60.**

Both MS. 408 f. 20 and MS. 431 f. 146 are marked 'F.14' by Sancroft. MS. 408 is identifiable in the Lanthony catalogue, and the Lanthony *ex libris* is on f. 160 of MS. 431, but there is no evidence, apart from T.1. and T.2 and Sancroft's markings, that they were once bound together.

26. T.1, #E.θ.7. T.2, 4° 151: three items, the first not marked, the second, 'Causæ, siue Casus aliquot in foro Ecclesiastico, Auth. Anon.', marked '87' and the third, 'Divus Bernardus de Consideratione', marked '113'. Now **MS. 411+MS. 437 ff. 43-73.**

A Lanthony book, no doubt, since item 1, not now to be found, is described in T.1 and T.2 as 'Fructus siue pensiones quas Hibernia soluere tenebatur Monasterio Lanthoniæ'. The Bernard was removed and put with other works of Bernard in MS. 437. Both MS. 411 f. 1 and MS. 437 f. 43 are marked 'H.9'. MS. 437 f. 73 was the end paste-down, and a bit of the old paper label still adheres to it.

27. T.1, #L.θ.1. T.2, 4° 75: eight items, the first six marked '75' and the last two, 'Cicero de Amicitia; Item de Senectute', marked

[1] An example of the common medieval use of 'quaternus' to mean simply a quire in our modern sense, without regard to the number of leaves. Only seven of these thirteen quires are actually quaternions, that is quires of four sheets or eight leaves.

[27 *cont.*]
'101'. Now **MS. 431 ff. i, 1–7, 16–65+MS. 425 ff. i, 1–21+ MS. 431 ff. 66–88.**

A miscellany which belonged to Walter Hay, prior of Lanthony 'prima', and was later transferred to Lanthony 'secunda'. MS. 431 ff. 50v–51 and MS. 425 f. 1 are in the same hand; so too are faces in the margins of MS. 431 and of MS. 425 f. 1. The contents show where MS. 425 ff. 1–21 originally came: the subject of 'prudentia' runs on from 431 f. 65v to 425 f. 1. Both MS. 431 f. i and MS. 425 f. 1 are marked 'K.16'.

28. T.1, Classis A, H.10. T.2, bundle 4, no. 11: four items, the first three marked '121' and the last, 'Three loose sheets of paper, one concerning Reformation, The other two concerning a Controversie between Tho. Whetenhall, and his wife', marked 'f. 113'. Now **MS. 445 pp. 436–507+MS. 113 ff. 235–40.**

The leaves in MS. 113 are folio size and show marks of having been folded across the middle to fit in a quarto-size volume.

29. T.1, #E.θ.4. T.2, 4° 148: two items, the first, 'Dicta moralia philosophorum Gallicè per Guil. de Cignoville', marked '132' and the second, 'Horatii sermones' marked '101'. Now **MS. 456 ff. 147–220+MS. 425 ff. 74–116.**

The identification is confirmed by the medieval foliation, which runs on from 'lxxiiii' on MS. 456 f. 220 to '75' on MS. 425 f. 74. The second leaf (MS. 456, f. 148) has 'Sum Roberti pantheri' in the margin, early sixteenth century.

30. T.1, #N.θ.15. T.2, 4° 29: seven items, the first three marked '164', the fourth, 'Excerpta varia per Epiphanium', marked 'q' (for 'quære'), and the last three marked '132'. Now **MS. 488 ff. 89–126+MS. 457 ff. 193–254+MS. 456 ff. i, 1–126.**

A miscellany from Buildwas on twenty-seven quires numbered in pencil by a medieval hand in a continuous series: I–VIII (MS. 457 ff. 193–254); IX–XI (MS. 456 ff. 107–26); XII–XXIV (MS. 456 ff. 1–106); XXV–XXVII (MS. 488 ff. 89–126). The order was changed and MS. 488 ff. 89–126 put at the beginning by the early fourteenth century, when a table of contents was entered on the flyleaf (MS. 488 f. 90v). The section now in MS. 457 contains mainly excerpts from letters of Jerome and Seneca and is called 'Seneca ad Lucillum' in the medieval table. Why T.1 and T.2 call it 'Excerpta varia per Epiphanium' I do not know, but the title goes back to the pre-Cambridge Lambeth catalogue which has 'Epiphanii varia' (MS. 1047 f. 14): it defeated Sancroft. The title of the first item in T.1, T.2, 'Homiliæ Willelmi de

Lafford de muliere chananea', is taken from the explicit on f. 106 of MS. 488: James does not notice the ascription. Both MS. 488 f. 90 and MS. 456 f. i are marked 'K.1.'

III. *Items omitted from Sancroft's catalogue.*

(*a*) *Lost manuscripts and parts of manuscripts*[1]

The move from Cambridge to London, and Sancroft's large-scale reorganization, seem to have done remarkably little damage. Three shelved manuscripts and twenty-two bundled manuscripts described in the Cambridge catalogue, MS. Tanner 274 (T.2), are not described by Sancroft and are not now at Lambeth. Nor, apparently, are some loose papers, flyleaf notes and the like which, to judge from T.1 and T.2, should be now in MSS. 79, 137, 144, 204, 394, 437, 448, 467 and 488.

M. R. James included # G.ε.5, # C.θ.11, # N.θ.9, # L.γ.2, # C.η.11, # L.γ.6, # G.η.17, # G.η.5, and # C.θ.46 in his list of missing books ('History of Lambeth Palace Library', p. 31), but these are respectively MSS. 385, 806 no. 21, 459, 38, 113 ff. 179–86, 30, 112, the printed Summa Rosellæ (**H1 938), and MS. 861. Over # G.ε.5 he was misled by the incorrect description in Oo.7.51: 'Acta Apostolorum cum glossa'. The description in T.2 and T.1 is correct.

The leaves formerly at the end of #L.η.14 (= MS. 372) have been found recently among loose fragments and are now MS. 1229, nos. 14, 15.

The most important missing piece is not described in the Cambridge catalogues or by Sancroft. The Old English 'Finnesburh fragment' was a single leaf found by Hickes, apparently in MS. 487, and printed by him in 1705: cf. N. R. Ker, *Catalogue of Manuscripts Containing Anglo-Saxon*, Oxford 1957, no. 282.

C.θ.29. Sir John Perrott's Arraignment.

C.θ.47. Prayers sett forth by command of Qu. Elizabeth and the Ladie Margarett in King Henry the 7th his time.

E.θ.11. Anthem, etc.

Bundle 1, no. 1. Robert Hill's Sermon att St Pauls Crosse *Jan. 20* 1605.

Bundle 1, no. 3. A Sermon preached before the King att Charterhouse *May ye 12th* 1603.

[1] Titles are from T.2. Superior oblique strokes ` ' mark additions in Sancroft's hand. Words in italics are derived from the rather fuller descriptions in T.1.

Bundle 1, no. 4. The B[p] of Bristoll's Sermon preached in S[t] Pauls London, *16th of December* 1591 att the funerall of S[r] Christopher Hatton.

Bundle 1, no. 7. Concio ad Clerum in Synodo.

Bundle 1, no. 14. A Sermon on Matthew, 9. 38.

Bundle 1, no. 15. A Sermon on Psalme 106 v. 29, 30 att S. Paul's Crosse 1604 *June 10*.

Bundle 1, no. 18. D[r] Walker's Sermon at Chemlsford [*sic*] in Essex att the Assizes *2 Aug.* 1592.

Bundle 1, no. 21 M[r] Rudd's Sermon Matth. 5. 14.

Bundle 1, no. 25. D[r] Robinson's Sermon att S. Maries 2 May 1591.

Bundle 1, no. 27. Another Sermon of the same D[r].

Bundle 1, no. 30. Concio habita in Aula Regia *die veneris 13 Martii* 1578.

Bundle 1, no. 32. Demonstration of the Severall revenues of England, France, Spaine, D. of Tuscany, and Venice.

Bundle 1, no. 34. A Sermon on Jeremy 29. 7.

Bundle 1, no. 37. Annotations MS. vpon Dr Soames's Treatise touching Ministry, Sacraments, Church etc.

Bundle 1, no. 38. Thomæ Mortebois Concio in Matth. 3.

Bundle 4, no. 1. A Treatise that the Traditions, for wch Controversy is in our Church att this day, are abominable etc.

Bundle 4, nos. 6, 12, 14, 15.

Manuscript pieces bound with printed books. See III (*c*).

Bundle 4, no. 17. Petri Smith Pembrochiensis Epigrammata. Lat. Græc.

Bundle 4, no. 24. Catalogus librorum in Bibliotheca Coll. Petrens. ante obitum D[ris] Perne.

C.γ.7 (= MS. 448), last item. Descriptio Convivii in Aula Westmonasterii cùm Catherina, Henr. 5[ti] uxor, diademate insignita fuit. Gallicè. Libellus Cartaceus sex foliis comprehensus, huic libro insertus, non adsutus nec compactus. 'q.'

E.η.1 (= MS. 137), last item. Distinctiones Anon.

E.θ.7 (= MS. 437), first item. Fructus siue Pensiones, quas Hibernia tenebatur soluere Monasterio Lanthoniæ.

G.δ.6 (= MS. 79), last item. Præfixa cernitur bulla Innocentii 7[mi] Papæ. 'q. de Bullâ'.

G.θ.9 (= MS. 394), item 1. Excerpta quædam mutila circa administrationem S. Eucharistiæ. Item Constitutiones quædam Ecclesiast.

I.η.10 (= MS. 144 ff. i, ii, 1–163), item 1. Compendiosissima Explicatio Orationis Dominicæ, et Symboli Apostol.

I.η.12 (= MS. 204), item 1. Fragmentum de ministris Ecclesiast. eorumque Officiis, utrinque imperfect.

I.θ.9. (= MS. 467), last item. A Relation of a fight between the Portingall's and 4 English Shipps 1616. This Relation is putt loose att the end of Terry's Relation 'and so is lost'.

Bundle 1, no. 8 (= MS. 488 ff. 43–72), item 2. Richard Butler's Letter to the Archb^p^ of Cant. 'y^e^ Letter wanting'.

(*b*) *Manuscripts omitted in error or for unknown reasons*

C.θ.11. Now MS. 806, no. 21.

Bundle 1, no. 2. Now MS. 806, no. 8.

Bundle 2, no. 1. A Bible in old English, very imperfect. 'I have it unbound.' Now MS. 1033, bound in s. xviii (?).

Bundle 3, no. 13. Now MS. 1042, rebound in 1873.

Bundle 4, no. 10. Now MS. 842. Pre-Sancroft binding.

Bundle 4, no. 19. Aliæ Constitutiones illarum Ecclesiarum . . . 'Habeo'. Now MS. 744.[1] Pre-Sancroft binding.

(*c*) *Printed books*

Sancroft turned out from among the manuscripts all but two of the printed items listed in Tanner 268 and Tanner 274. The two he kept back are his Fol. 15, formerly # L.γ.7 and now MS. 15, the New Testament part of the 42-line Bible, and his Fol. 7 ff. 189–94, formerly # Bundle 2, no. 6, and now MS. 7 ff. 189–94, a calendar from a printed Sarum missal, *STC* 16179. On the other hand, he brought in one printed book and put it among the manuscripts: his Quarto 145, now MS. 469.[2]

C.η.16. La Dance Macabre Historeè et augmenteè, Gallicè. 'Habeo' 'printed'. Now MS. 279. Paris, sine anno: on parchment.

G.η.5. Summa Rosellæ de Casibus Conscientiæ. Liber impressus. Now **H 1938. Strassbourg, 1516.

N.θ.18. Eadem [*sc.* M. T. Ciceronis Officia] rursus scitè scripta, vel potius typis excusa . . . 'Habeo'. Now MS. 765. Mainz, 1466. *GKW* 6922.

[1] The hand is that of MS. 470, formerly Bundle 4, no. 18.

[2] According to M. R. James, Sancroft's Quarto 145, now MS. 469, was never at Cambridge. This is wrong. At Cambridge it was counted rightly as a printed book and bore the mark, still partly visible, N.δ.35.

Bundle 4, no. 2. The thirty-nine Articles wth some marginal notes written, noting the difference from King Edward the 6th his Articles. Now 1537. 1/9. *STC* 10051.

Bundle 4, no. 6. A forme of Prayer appointed vpon occasion of an Earthquake 1580 wth one Prayer written. Not found. *STC* 16512.

Bundle 4, no. 9. A large Examination of George Blackwell. London 1607, wth notes written in the margin. Not found. 1607. 41 has no notes. *STC* 3104.

Bundle 4, no. 12. Henry Jacob's 4 Assertions concerning Reformation printed . . .[1] Now 1599. 18/2. *STC* 14338.

Bundle 4, no. 14. Thomas Whetenhall's discourse of the abuses now in question in the Churches etc. printed 1606 . . .[2] Now 1588. 11/2. *STC* 25332.

Bundle 4, no. 15. Dr Soame of certaine questions touching the ministry, wth a written Confutation. The printed part is perhaps 1570. 4/4. *STC* 22910.

Bundle 4, no. 16. 8vo A forme of Common Prayers and administration of Sacraments etc. agreable to the vse of the best Reformed Churches, wth a Preface or Bill, for further Reformation etc. written.

According to the description of this item in Oo.7.51, the printer was R. Walgrave, so this is *STC* 16567. 1598. 27 is a copy without a preface in manuscript.

IV. *Items added by Sancroft*

The nine manuscripts listed by Sancroft in his catalogue, Tanner 270, but not in the Cambridge catalogues, are presumably additions to the collection made by Sancroft himself. (1–3). Folio MSS. 241–3, the present MSS. 241–3.[3] (4, 5). Quarto MSS. 165 (item 1), 168, now missing.[4] (6, 7). Two items in the composite volume, Fol. 113, now MS. 113: ff. 203–22 An answere to Mr Cartwrights letter, for Ioyninge with the English Churches; ff. 223–6 Anti-Cami-Tami Categoria. (8, 9). Two items, the first and second,

[1] Bundle 4, no. 12, also contained Jacob's 'papers', now MS. 113 ff. 242–54.

[2] Bundle 4, no. 14, also contained a manuscript treatise by Whetenhall, now MS. 445 pp. 313–90.

[3] MS. 244 is also listed in Sancroft's catalogue, but as an addition in another hand.

[4] See above, p. 5.

in the composite volume Quarto 130, now MS. 454 ff. i, 1–27, and 28–123. Both are marked 'W: Cant.', showing that they belonged to Sancroft himself.[1]

CONCORDANCE I

Pressmarks of Tanner 268 (T.1) and Tanner 274 (T.2) equated with those now in use.

An asterisk in the first (*T.1*) column shows that the manuscript still has in it the mark given in T.1. An asterisk in the second (*T.2*) column shows that the manuscript still has in it the mark given in T.2, but not the mark given in T.1. Numbers in bold type, 1–30, in the third column refer to the numbers in the list of broken up manuscripts on pp. 9–17, above.

The T.1 pressmarks are here arranged in alphabetical order of classes, C–T, and within classes in alphabetical order of shelves, α–θ. The Bundles come at the end. The actual order of T.1 is: T.α.1–4; N.ζ, η, θ; L.ζ, η, θ, γ, ε; I.ζ, η, θ, α, β, γ, δ, ε; G.ζ, η, θ, α, β, γ, δ, ε;[2] E.ζ, η, θ, α, β, γ, δ, ε; C.ζ.1; Bundles 1–3; C.η.1–16; C.θ; C.η.17, 18; C.γ.1; 'Three loose sheets . . .';[3] K.β.35; the 24 items which later formed Bundle 4;[4] C.γ.2–7. I owe to Mr. Oates an explanation of the back-to-front order of T.1. The cataloguer began with # T, the press furthest from the door, and worked back to # C, the press nearest the door. He went through the shelves on the far sides of the presses (ζ–θ) before the shelves on the near sides (α–ε).

T.1	*T.2*	*Now*
C.γ.1[5]*	F.241	23
2	242	73
3*	243	118
4*	244	179 ff. 1–98
5	245	183
6	246	225
7	Q.204	448
C.ζ.1*	F.247	24 ff. 49–58
C.η.1	F.227	140 ff. 98–224
2	228	178 ff. 1–91
3	229	113 ff. 101–78
4*	230	178 ff. 142–207
5*	231	178 ff. 92–141
6	232	138 ff. 290–315

1 Cf. 'W: Cant.' in Bodleian, MS. Tanner 348.
2 The leaf containing G.α.5 to G.ε.7 is misbound after E.α.4.
3 See above, p. 4. 4 See above, p. 3.
5 All pressmarks entered in the manuscripts in this form are preceded by the mark #: see above, p. 2.

T.1	*T.2*	*Now*
7	233	138 ff. 213–89
8	234	138 ff. 113–78
9*	235	138 ff. 77–112
10	236	179 ff. 197–244
11	237	113 ff. 179–86
12*	238	104 ff. 209–24
13*	239	182 ff. i, 1–12
14	240	179 ff. 245–318
15	Q.175*	209
16*	176	279 (printed book)
17*	177	364
18*	202	383
C.θ.1*	O.45	473
2*	Q.178	434
3*	O.46	496
4	47	478 ff. 92–145
5*	48	482
6*	Q.179	425 ff. 22–73
7*	180	443
8	181	397
9*	182	446
10*	183	464
11*	184	806, no. 21
12*	185	487
13	O.64	525
14*	65	524
15*	49	526
16*	Q.186	379 ff. 69–130
17	187	374 ff. 21–90
18*	188	427
19*	203	435
20	189	439 ff. 144–210
21	190	
22	191	402[1]
23	192*	
24	—	—
25*	193	461
26	194	426
27*	195	462
28*	196	392 ff. 148–218, 132–47
29	197	—
30*	O.66	548
31	50*	565 ff. 16–70
32	Q.198	447 pp. 101–67

[1] C.θ.21–3 are called 'Dr Reynold's Disputation wth Hart in 3 vols.' or (T.1) '3 parts', but MS. 402 seems never to have formed more than one volume.

T.1	*T.2*	*Now*
33*	O.51	873
34	52*	475 ff. 111–79
35	53	555
36	56	566
37*	54	565 ff. 1–15
38*	Q.199	463
39	O.55*	539
40*	57	529
41*	58	527
42*	Q.200	488 ff. 149–98
43*	O.59	549
44*	60	551
45*	61	537
46	62	861
47	Q.201	—
48	O.63	559
E.α.1*	F.202	20
2	203	6
3	204	59 ff. 191–278+50 [3]
4	205	13
E.β.1	206	66
2	207	59 ff. i, ii, 1–190
3	208	58
4*	209	29
5*	210	67
6*	211	32
E.γ.1*	212	35
2	213	16
3*	214	19
4	215	324 ff. 3^v–34
5	216	324 ff. 37^v–68
6	217	7 ff. 1–188
7*	218	55 ff. i, ii, 1–156, 162
8	219*	39
E.δ.1*	220	72
2*	221	42
3*	222	24 ff. 1–48
4*	223	99
5	224	36
6	225	100
7	226	61 ff. 1–117
E.ε.1*	Q.168	353
2	169*	224
3	170	406
4*	171	352

T.1	*T.2*	*Now*
5*	172	329
6	173*	371
7	174	396
E.ζ.1*	143	235
2*	F.166	165 ff. 102–90
3	167	131
4*	168	205
5*	169	71 ff. i, 1–118
6	170	210
7*	171	70
8	172	143
9	173	74
10	174	127 ff. 1–77
11*	175	75
12*	176	158
13*	177	121
14	178	150
15	179	111
16	180	148
17	181	147 ff. i, 1–59+144 ff. 164–314 **[10]**
18	182	147 ff. 60–179
19	183	149 ff. 1–138
20*	184	163
E.η.1*	185	137
2	186	221 ff. 158–309+142 ff. 124–204+ 104 ff. 228, 229 **[17]**
3	187	159 ff. i, ii, 1–275, 284, 285
4	188	200 ff. 66–113
5	189	211
6*	190	164
7	191	97
8*	192	340
9*	Q.144	386
10	F.193	212
11*	194	105 ff. 1–133
12*	195	89
13*	196	90
14*	197	233
15*	198	186
16	199	190
17*	200	162
18*	201	198b
E.θ.1	Q.145	413
2*	146	401
3*	147	404+431 ff. 8–15 **[24]**

T.1	*T.2*	*Now*
4	148	456 ff. 147–220+425 ff. 74–116 [**29**]
5*	149	433
6*	150	442
7	151	411+437 ff. 43–73 [**26**]
8	152*	451 ff. 83–192
9	153	452
10*	154	422
11	155	—
12*	156	378 ff. i, ii, 1–56, 125–65
13	157	384
14*	158	375
15*	159	362
16*	160	419
17	161	439 ff. 1–143
18*	162	449
19	163	431 ff. 183–242
20*	164	465
21	165	412
22		392 ff. 1–28, 59–115+456 ff. 127–46 [**22**]
23*	O.43	531
24*	44	476
25		348
G.α.1*	F.139	5
2*	140	8
3	141	25
4	142	9
5*	143	37
6*	144	14
G.β.1*	145	69
2	146	65
3*	147	91
4*	148	49
5	149	53
6	150	54
7	151	140 ff. i, 1–97
G.γ.1	152	47
2*	153	103
3*	154	31
4*	155	128
5	156	18 ff. i, ii, 1–122
6	157*	60
7	158	21
8*	159	45
G.δ.1	160	106
2*	161	160

T.1	*T.2*	*Now*
3	162	181+159 ff. 276–83 **[14]**
4*	163	104 ff. i, 1–208+188 ff. 168–74 **[5]**
5	164	48
6	165	79
G.ε.1*	Q.134	327
2*	135	346
3*	136	218 ff. 90–208
4	137	192 ff. 45–153
5	138	385
6	139	358
7*	140	343
8*	141	350
9	142	387
G.ζ.1	113	331 ff. 1–117
2	F.97	84
3*	98	156
4*	99	176 ff. i, ii, 1–120
5	100	185
6	101	172
7	102	101
8	103	93
9	104	92
10	105	176 ff. 121–96
11*	106	87 ff. i, ii, 1–136
12	107	116 ff. i, 1–131
13*	108	136
14*	109	135
15	110	108
16*	111	184
17*	112	175
18*	113	77
19*	114	129+115 [8]
20	115	107
G.η.1*	116	154
2	117	110
3*	118	71 ff. 119–222
4	119	85
5	120	Printed book
6*	121	174
7	122	153 ff. 89–155
8*	123	157
9*	124	180
10*	125	173
11*	126	200 ff. 114–63
12*	127	119

T.1	*T.2*	*Now*
13	128	177
14	129	134 ff. 1–96
15	130	114+153 ff. 1–6 [**11**]
16	131	133
17	132	112+104 ff. 225–7 [**6**]
18	133	120
19*	134	171
20	135	134 ff. 97–245+200 ff. 168–75 [**9**]+ 153 ff. 7–88
21	136	127 ff. 78–198
G.θ.1	Q.114	423 ff. 115–208
2	115	431 ff. 89–144
3*	116	428
4*	117	399
5	118	438[1]
6*	O.38	484
7	Q.119	395 ff. 53–138
8*	120	436
9	121	394
10	122	421
11	123	432
12*	124	344
13*	125	341
14*	126	354
15	127	395 ff. i, ii, 1–16, 19–52, 141–72
16*	128	389
17*	F.137	217 ff. 128–268
18	Q.129	338 ff. 1–96
19*	130	466
20*	F.138	188 ff. 1–167
21*	Q.131	356 ff. i, 1–124
22	O.39*	522
23*	40	474
24	Q.132	342 ff. 120–233
25*	O.41	567
26	42	472
27*	Q.133	388
I.α.1	F.71	10
2	72	11
3	73	12
4*	74	52
5	75	43

[1] The identification of Q.118 with the present MS. 438 is Sancroft's. He corrected the title in T.2, 'Portiforium' to 'Imò Processionale'. Presumably his identification is based on now missing pressmarks.

T.1	*T.2*	*Now*
I.β.1	76*	46
2	77	81
3	78	63
4	79*	80 ff. 1–167
5*	80	102
6*	81	68
7*	82	122
I.γ.1*	83	28
2*	84	22+55 ff. 157–61 [1]
3*	85	33
4*	86	51
5*	87	40
6	88	61 ff. 118–42
7*	89	116 ff. i, 1–131
I.δ.1*	90	78
2	91	86
3	92	117
4	93	155
5*	94	34
I.ε.1*	Q.107	400
2*	108	367
3*	109	370
4*	110	382
5	111	339
6*	F.95	333
7*	Q.112	420
8	F.96	223
I.ζ.1*	F.22	83
2	23	140 ff. 225–333
3	24	139 ff. 101–77
4	25	142 ff. 1–123
5*	26	82
6	27	234
7	28	132
8*	29	41
9	30	189
10	31	130
11*	32	193
12	33*	87 ff. 137–210
13*	34	138 ff. i, ii, 1–44
14*	35	167
15	36	138 ff. 45–76
16*	37	123 pp. ix, x, 1–234
17	38	124 ff. 133–483
18	39	125 ff. iv, 1–198

T.1	*T.2*	*Now*
19	40	125 ff. 199–332
20	41	125 ff. 333–520
21	42	126 ff. iv, v, 1–245
22	43	94
23	44	182 ff. 13–172
24	45	166
25*	46	194
26*	47	168
27	48	221 ff. 1–157
28*	49	192 ff. 1–44+188 ff. 175–9 **[16]**
I.η.1	50	222
2*	51	198
3	52	207
4*	53	57
5	54	123 pp. 235–352+124 ff. 1–132+126 ff. 246–95 [7]
6*	55	169
7	56	152
8*	57	109
9	58	96 ff. 1–112
10*	59	144 ff. i, ii, 1–163
11	60	64
12	61	204
13*	62	187
14	63	161
15*	64	80 ff. 168–244
16*	65	105 ff. 134–292
17*	66	145 ff. i, ii, 1–137
18*[1]	68	145 ff. 138–227
19	67*	146
20*	69	216
21*	70	330
I.θ.1	Q.83	460
2	84	453
3	85	455
4	86*	425 ff. 117–217
5	87	450
6*	88	429 ff. 1–105, 163–232
7*	89	408 ff. i, 1–19
8*	90	441
9*	91	467
10*	92	510
11	93	391
12*	94	417

[1] # I.η.18 and # Bundle 2, no. 8, originally one manuscript, were reunited by Sancroft.

T.1	*T.2*	*Now*
13*	95	376
14	96	392 ff. 29–58+409 [**23**]
15*	97	416
16*	98	390
17	99	431 ff. 145–60+408 ff. 20–141 [**25**]
18*	100	398
19	101	403
20	102	366
21	103	424
22*	105	373
23	106*	471
24*	O.35	489
25*	36	475 ff. i, ii, 1–110
K.β.35	—	—
L.γ.1*	F.15	56
2	16	38
3	17	44
4	18	27 ff. 231–96+18 ff. 123–82 [**2**]
5*	19	27 ff. 1–230
6	20	30
7*	21	15
L.ε.1*	Q.76	380 ff. 121–228
2	77	363
3	78	380 ff. 1–120+356 ff. 125–75 [**18**]
4	79	377
5	80	239
6*	81	369
7	82	328
L.ζ.1	36	199
2	37	200 ff. i, 1–65
3*	38	325
4	39	326
5*	40	349
6*	41	219
7*	42	236
8	43	195
9*	44	238
10	45	332
11	46	153 ff. 156–79+MS. 200 ff. 176–229 [**12**]
12	47	220
13*	48	179 ff. 99–196
14*	49	335 ff. 1–228
15*	50	347
16*	51	196

T.1	*T.2*	*Now*
17*	52	334
18*	53	357+379 ff. 1–68 **[19]**
19*	54	232
20*	55	227
21*	56	213
22	57	361
23*	58	451 ff. 1–82
24	59	415
25	60*	351
L.η.1	F.6	141
2	7	76 ff. i, 1–147
3	8	151 ff. i–v, 1–209
4	9	151 ff. 210–335
5*	10	149 ff. 139–240
6	Q.61	237 ff. 146–209
7	F.11	88
8*	12	76 ff. 148–238
9	13	95
10	14	201
11	Q.62	202
12	63	226
13	64	237 ff. 1–106
14	65	372
15	66	215
16*	67	437 ff. 1–42
17	104	414 ff. 1–80
18	68	203
19	69*	337
20*	70	365 ff. i, ii, 1–119+392 ff. 116–31+ 431 ff. 161–82 **[21]**
21	71	336
22	72	214
23	73	365 ff. 120–228
24*	74	410
L.θ.1	Q.75	431 ff. i, 1–7, 16–88+425 ff. 1–21 **[27]**
2	O.14	479
3	15	481
4*	16	541
5*	17	477
6*	18	478 ff. i–iii, 1–91
7*	19	538
8*	20	545
9*	21	480
10	22	486
11	23*	530
12*	24	534

T.1	*T.2*	*Now*
13*	37	533
14*	25	544
15*	26	532
16*	27	552
17*	28	553
18*	29	554
19*	30	536
20	31	546
21	32*	523
22	33*	483
23	34	558
N.ζ.1	Q.1	165 ff. 1–101
2	2	360 ff. 1–118
N.η.1*	Q.3	345 ff. i, ii, 1–96
2	F.5	96 ff. 113–244+145 ff. 257–64 **[4]**
3*	Q.4	240
4*	5	430
5	6	218 ff. 1–89
6	7	345 ff. 97–227
7*	8	381
8*	9	231
9*	10	229
10	11	228
11*	12	230
12*	13	206 ff. 1–81
13*	14	418
14*	15	355
15*	16	440
16*	17	217 ff. i, 1–85
17	18	378 ff. 57–124
18	19	338 ff. 97–214
19*	20	359
20*	21	407
21*	22	405
22*	23	368
23*	24	170+200 ff. 164–7 **[13]**
24*	25	197
25*	26	206 ff. 82–235
26*	27	208
N.θ.1*	O.1	542
2*	2	485 ff. i, 1–117
3	3	550
4*	4	563
5*	5	540
6	6	535

T.1	*T.2*	*Now*
7	7	543
8*	8	560
9	Q.28	459
10*	O.9	556
11*	10	564
12*	11	562
13*	12	561 ff. 1–145
14*	13	561 ff. 146–202
15*	Q.29	488 ff. 89–126+456 ff. i, 1–126 [30]
16*	30	458
17	31	342 ff. 1–119
18*	32	765 (printed book)
19	33	423 ff. 1–114
20*	34	457 ff. 1–132
21*	35	393
T.α.1	F.1	1
2*	2	2
3*	3	3
4*	4	4
Bundle 1		
no. 1	Nos. 1–42,	—
2*	as in T.1	806, no. 8
3		—
4		—
5		447, pp. 292–319
6*		374 ff. 91–110
7		—
8*		488 ff. 43–72
9*		374 ff. 111–252
10*		488 ff. 1–42
11*		488 ff. 73–88
12*		113 ff. 63–8
13*		113 ff. 99, 100
14		—
15		—
16*		113 ff. 69–78
17*		113 ff. 79–86
18		—
19		374 ff. 253–72
20*		113 ff. 53–62
21		—
22		178 ff. 208–29
23		447 pp. 204–91
24		113 ff. 35–44
25		—
26		113 ff. 87–98

T.1	*T.2*	*Now*
27		—
28		447 pp. 320–99
29*		113 ff. 1–34
30		—
31		113 ff. 45–52
32		—
33*		447 pp. 73–100
34		—
35*		565 ff. 71–6
36		447 pp. 400–15
37		—
38		—
39		445 pp. 391–423
40		374 ff. 1–20
41*[1]		113 ff. 227–34
42*[1]		113 ff. 255–60
Bundle 2		
no. 1*	Nos. 1–12,	1033
2*	as in T.1	188 ff. 180–213
3*		139 ff. 1–100
4*		182 ff. 185–206+237 ff. 107–45 +182 ff. 173–84 **[15]**
5*		61 ff. 143–7
6*		7 ff. 189–93
7*		138 ff. 179–212
8*		145 ff. 228–56
9*		331 ff. 118–57
10*		191
11*		62
12		26
Bundle 3		
no. 1*	Nos. 1–15,	557
2*	as in T.1	444 ff. 25–68
3*		485 ff. 118–287
4*		444 ff. 1–12
5*		457 ff. 133–92
6		454 ff. 124–204
7*		444 ff. 13–24
8*		444 ff. 69–186
9*		429 ff. 106–62
10*		437 ff. 74–107
11*		217 ff. 86–127
12		414 ff. 81–159
13*		1042

[1] In Oo.7.51 nos. 41, 42 are added in another hand.

T.1	*T.2*	*Now*
14*		360 ff. 119–58+335 ff. 229–77 [20]
15*		356 ff. 176–283
Classis A	Bundle 4	
A.17	no. 1	—
A.18	2	Printed book
D.20*	3	113 ff. 187–202
E.2	4	445 pp. 508–681
E.3	5	113 f. 241
F.2	6	Printed book
G.11	7	519
G.12	8	445 pp. i–iv, 1–312
G.13	9	Printed book
H.1	10*	842
H.10	11	445 pp. 436–507+113 ff. 235–40 [28]
H.14	12	Printed book and 113 ff. 242–54
H.15*	13	445 pp. 424–35
H.21*	14	Printed book and 445 pp. 313–90
K.7	15	Printed book and —
M.4	16	Printed book and —
T.25	17	—
T.26*	18	470
T.27	19	744
T.28*	20	468
T.29	21	447 pp. 168–203
T.30	22	447 pp. ix–xii, 1–72
T.31	23	98
T.32	24	—

CONCORDANCE II

Pressmarks of Tanner 274 (T.2) compared with those of Tanner 268 (T.1)

The actual order of T.2 is Folios, Bundle 2, Quartos, Bundles 1, 3, 4, Octavos. The back-to-front order of T.1 (see Concordance I) is preserved, but concealed by the new terms. The changes as compared with T.1 make for more exact sizing. The shelves most affected were C.θ, G.θ, L.θ, and N.η. Elsewhere a dozen books, larger or smaller than others on the same shelf, were downgraded or upgraded: C.η.15–17, E.ζ.1, E.η.9, E.ε.23, 24, G.ζ.1, I.ε.6, 8, N.ζ.1, N.θ.1.

T.2	*T.1*	*T.2*	*T.1*
F.1–4	T.α.1–4[1]	11–14	L.η.7–10
5	N.η.2	15–21	L.γ.1–7
6–10	L.η.1–5	22–49	I.ζ.1–28

[1] See p. 21 n. 5.

T.2	*T.1*	*T.2*	*T.1*
50–70	I.η.1–21	131	G.θ.21
71–5	I.α.1–5	132	G.θ.24
76–82	I.β.1–7	133	G.θ.27
83–9	I.γ.1–7	134–42	G.ε.1–9
90–4	I.δ.1–5	143	E.ζ.1
95	I.ε.6	144	E.η.9
96	I.ε.8	145–66	E.θ.1–22
97–115	G.ζ.2–20	167	E.θ.25
116–36	G.η.1–21	168–74	E.ε.1–7
137	G.θ.17	175–7	C.η.15–17
138	G.θ.20	178	C.θ.2
139–44	G.α.1–6	179–85	C.θ.6–12
145–51	G.β.1–7	186–8	C.θ.16–18
152–9	G.γ.1–8	189–92	C.θ.20–3
160–5	G.δ.1–6	193–7	C.θ.25–9
166–84	E.ζ.2–20	198	C.θ.32
185–92	E.η.1–8	199	C.θ.38
193–201	E.η.10–18	200	C.θ.42
202–5	E.α.1–4	201	C.θ.47
206–11	E.β.1–6	202	C.η.18
212–19	E.γ.1–8	203	C.θ.19
220–6	E.δ.1–7	204	C.γ.7
227–40	C.η.1–14	O.1–8	N.θ.1–8
241–6	C.γ.1–6	9–13	N.θ.10–14
247	C.ζ.1	14–24	L.θ.2–12
Q.1–2	N.ζ.1, 2	25–34	L.θ.14–23
3	N.η.1	35, 36	I.θ.24, 25
4–27	N.η.3–26	37	L.θ.13
28	N.θ.9	38	G.θ.6
29–35	N.θ.15–21	39, 40	G.θ.22, 23
36–60	L.ζ.1–25	41, 42	G.θ.25, 26
61	L.η.6	43, 44	E.θ.23, 24
62–7	L.η.11–16	45	C.θ.1
68–74	L.η.18–24	46–8	C.θ.3–5
75	L.θ.1	49	C.θ.15
76–82	L.ε.1–7	50	C.θ.31
83–103	I.θ.1–21	51–3	C.θ.33–5
104	L.η.17	54	C.θ.37
105, 106	I.θ.22, 23	55	C.θ.39
107–11	I.ε.1–5	56	C.θ.36
112	I.ε.7	57, 58	C.θ.40, 41
113	G.ζ.1	59–62	C.θ.43–6
114–18	G.θ.1–5	63	C.θ.48
119–28	G.θ.7–16	64, 65	C.θ.14, 15
129, 130	G.θ.18, 19	66	C.θ.30

CONCORDANCE III

Pressmarks of Sancroft's catalogue, Tanner 270, equated with those now in use

Tanner 270	*Now*
F.1–16	1–16
17	324
18–243	18–243
Q.1–164	325–488
165	—
166	496
167	567
168	—
169	510
170	519
O.1–6	522–7
7	489
8–25	529–46
26	861
27–43	548–64
44	873
45	565
46	—

CONCORDANCE IV

Pressmarks now in use equated with those of Tanner 268 (T.1) and, for Bundle 4 items only, Tanner 274 (T.2)

The old numbers are noticed in M. R. James's catalogue at the head of each description. Numbers printed there out of brackets are usually reliable. For the rest James appears to have made his identifications with the help of the unsatisfactory Cambridge catalogue Oo.7.51, and not Tanner 268, with the result that he was often uncertain about them. Thus he was unable to distinguish between one Bracton and another (MSS. 92, 93) or one Burley and another (MSS. 74, 143) and queries his (correct) identification of MS. 66 (Mimalis) with E.β.1. The descriptions in Tanner 268 leave no doubt about what is what, here and elsewhere. Those in Oo.7.51 are often so brief that they are useless: there the two Bractons are listed together in a one-line entry, and likewise the two Burleys, and the Mimalis is called 'Annales Anonymi'.

Now	*T.1*
1	# T.α.1[1]
2	T.α.2
3	T.α.3

[1] See p. 21 n. 5.

Now	*T.1*
4	T.α.4
5	G.α.1
6	E.α.2
7 ff. 1–188	E.γ.6
ff. 189–94	Bundle 2, no. 6
8	G.α.2
9	G.α.4
10	I.α.1
11	I.α.2
12	I.α.3
13	E.α.4
14	G.α.6
15	L.γ.7
16	E.γ.2
17 *vacant*	
18 ff. i, ii, 1–122	G.γ.5
ff. 123–82	Part of L.γ.4
19	E.γ.3
20	E.α.1
21	G.γ.7
22	I.γ.2
23	C.γ.1
24 ff. 1–48	E.δ.3
ff. 49–58	C.ζ.1
25	G.α.3
26	Bundle 2, no. 12
27 ff. 1–230	L.γ.5
ff. 231–96	Part of L.γ.4
28	I.γ.1
29	E.β.4
30	L.γ.6
31	G.γ.3
32	E.β.6
33	I.γ.3
34	I.δ.5
35	E.γ.1
36	E.δ.5
37	G.α.5
38	L.γ.2
39	E.γ.8
40	I.γ.5
41	I.ζ.8
42	E.δ.2
43	I.α.5
44	L.γ.3
45	G.γ.8
46	I.β.1

Now	*T.1*
47	G.γ.1
48	G.δ.5
49	G.β.4
50	E.α.3
51	I.γ.4
52	I.α.4
53	G.β.5
54	G.β.6
55 ff. i, ii, 1–156, 162	E.γ.7
ff. 157–61	Part of I.γ.2
56	L.γ.1
57	I.η.4
58	E.β.3
59 ff. i, ii, 1–190	E.β.2
ff. 191–278	Part of E.α.3
60	G.γ.6
61 ff. 1–117	E.δ.7
ff. 118–42	I.γ.6
ff. 143–7	Bundle 2, no. 5
62	Bundle 2, no. 11
63	I.β.3
64	I.η.11
65	G.β.2
66	E.β.1
67	E.β.5
68	I.β.6
69	G.β.1
70	E.ζ.7
71 ff. i, 1–118	E.ζ.5
ff. 119–222	G.η.3
72	E.δ.1
73	C.γ.2
74	E.ζ.9
75	E.ζ.11
76 ff. i, 1–147	L.η.2
ff. 148–238	L.η.8
77	G.ζ.18
78	I.δ.1
79	G.δ.6
80 ff. 1–167	I.β.4
ff. 168–244	I.η.15
81	I.β.2
82	I.ζ.5
83	I.ζ.1
84	G.ζ.2
85	G.η.4
86	I.δ.2

Now	*T.1*
87 ff. i, ii, 1–136	G.ζ.11
ff. 137–210	I.ζ.12
88	L.η.7
89	E.η.12
90	E.η.13
91	G.β.3
92	G.ζ.9
93	G.ζ.8
94	I.ζ.22
95	L.η.9
96 ff. 1–112	I.η.9
ff. 113–244	Part of N.η.2
97	E.η.7
98	Bundle 4, no. 23
99	E.δ.4
100	E.δ.6
101	G.ζ.7
102	I.β.5
103	G.γ.2
104 ff. i, 1–208	Part of G.δ.4
ff. 209–24	C.η.12
ff. 225–7	Part of G.η.17
ff. 228, 229	Part of E.η.2
105 ff. 1–133	E.η.11
ff. 134–292	I.η.16
106	G.δ.1
107	G.ζ.20
108	G.ζ.15
109	I.η.8
110	G.η.2
111	E.ζ.15
112	G.η.17
113 ff. 1–34	Bundle 1, no. 29
ff. 35–44	Bundle 1, no. 24
ff. 45–52	Bundle 1, no. 31
ff. 53–62	Bundle 1, no. 20
ff. 63–8	Bundle 1, no. 12
ff. 69–78	Bundle 1, no. 16
ff. 79–86	Bundle 1, no. 17
ff. 87–98	Bundle 1, no. 26
ff. 99, 100	Bundle 1, no. 13
ff. 101–78	C.η.3
ff. 179–86	C.η.11
ff. 187–202	Bundle 4, no. 3
ff. 203–22	—
ff. 223–6	—
ff. 227–34	Bundle 1, no. 41

Now	*T.1*
113 ff. 235–40	Part of Bundle 4, no. 11
f. 241	Bundle 4, no. 5
ff. 242–54	Part of Bundle 4, no. 12
ff. 255–60	Bundle 1, no. 42
114	G.η.15
115	G.ζ.19
116 ff. i, 1–131	G.ζ.12
ff. 132–236	I.γ.7
117	I.δ.3
118	C.γ.3
119	G.η.12
120	G.η.18
121	E.ζ.13
122	I.β.7
123 pp. ix, x, 1–234	I.ζ.16
pp. 235–352	Part of I.η.5
124 ff. 1–132	Part of I.η.5
ff. 133–483	I.ζ.17
125 ff. iv, 1–198	I.ζ.18
ff. 199–332	I.ζ.19
ff. 333–520	I.ζ.20
126 ff. iv, v, 1–245	I.ζ.21
ff. 246–95	Part of I.η.5
127 ff. 1–77	E.ζ.10
ff. 78–198	G.η.21
128	G.γ.4
129	G.ζ.19
130	I.ζ.10
131	E.ζ.3
132	I.ζ.7
133	G.η.16
134 ff. 1–96	G.η.14
ff. 97–245	Part of G.η.20
135	G.ζ.14
136	G.ζ.13
137	E.η.1
138 ff. i, ii, 1–44	I.ζ.13
ff. 45–76	I.ζ.15
ff. 77–112	C.η.9
ff. 113–78	C.η.8
ff. 179–212	Bundle 2, no. 7
ff. 213–89	C.η.7
ff. 290–315	C.η.6
139 ff. 1–100	Bundle 2, no. 3
ff. 101–77	I.ζ.3
140 ff. i, 1–97	G.β.7
ff. 98–224	C.η.1

Now	*T.I*
140 ff. 225–333	I.ζ.2
141	L.η.1
142 ff. 1–123	I.ζ.4
ff. 124–204	Part of E.η.2
143	E.ζ.8
144 ff. i, ii, 1–163	I.η.10
ff. 164–314	Part of E.ζ.17
145 ff. i, ii, 1–137	I.η.17
ff. 138–227	I.η.18
ff. 228–56	Bundle 2, no. 8
ff. 257–64	Part of N.η.2
146	I.η.19
147 ff. i, 1–59	Part of E.ζ.17
ff. 60–179	E.ζ.18
148	E.ζ.16
149 ff. 1–138	E.ζ.19
ff. 139–240	L.η.5
150	E.ζ.14
151 ff. i–v, 1–209	L.η.3
ff. 210–335	L.η.4
152	I.η.7
153 ff. 1–6	Part of G.η.15
ff. 7–88	Part of G.η.20
ff. 89–155	G.η.7
ff. 156–79	Part of L.ζ.11
154	G.η.1
155	I.δ.4
156	G.ζ.3
157	G.η.8
158	E.ζ.12
159 ff. i, ii, 1–275, 284, 285	E.η.3
ff. 276–83	Part of G.δ.3
160	G.δ.2
161	I.η.14
162	E.η.17
163	E.ζ.20
164	E.η.6
165 ff. 1–101	N.ζ.1
ff. 102–90	E.ζ.2
166	I.ζ.24
167	I.ζ.14
168	I.ζ.26
169	I.η.6
170	N.η.23
171	G.η.19
172	G.ζ.6
173	G.η.10

Now	*T.1*
174	G.η.6
175	G.ζ.17
176 ff. i, ii, 1–120	G.ζ.4
ff. 121–96	G.ζ.10
177	G.η.13
178 ff. 1–91	C.η.2
ff. 92–141	C.η.5
ff. 142–207	C.η.4
ff. 208–29	Bundle 1, no. 22
179 ff. 1–98	C.γ.4
ff. 99–196	L.ζ.13
ff. 197–244	C.η.10
ff. 245–318	C.η.14
180	G.η.9
181	G.δ.3
182 ff. i, 1–12	C.η.13
ff. 13–172	I.ζ.23
ff. 173–206	Part of Bundle 2, no. 4
183	C.γ.5
184	G.ζ.16
185	G.ζ.5
186	E.η.15
187	I.η.13
188 ff. 1–167	G.θ.20
ff. 168–74	Part of G.δ.4
ff. 175–9	Part of I.ζ.28
ff. 180–213	Bundle 2, no. 2
189	I.ζ.9
190	E.η.16
191	Bundle 2, no. 10
192 ff. 1–44	Part of I.ζ.28
ff. 45–153	G.ε.4
193	I.ζ.11
194	I.ζ.25
195	L.ζ.8
196	L.ζ.16
197	N.η.24
198	I.η.2
198b	E.η.18
199	L.ζ.1
200 ff. i, 1–65	L.ζ.2
ff. 66–113	E.η.4
ff. 114–63	G.η.11
ff. 164–7	Part of N.η.23
ff. 168–75	Part of G.η.20
ff. 176–229	Part of L.ζ.11
201	L.η.10

Now		*T.1*
202		L.η.11
203		L.η.18
204		I.η.12
205		E.ζ.4
206	ff. 1–81	N.η.12
	ff. 82–235	N.η.25
207		I.η.3
208		N.η.26
209		C.η.15
210		E.ζ.6
211		E.η.5
212		E.η.10
213		L.ζ.21
214		L.η.22
215		L.η.15
216		I.η.20
217	ff. i, 1–85	N.η.16
	ff. 86–127	Bundle 3, no. 11
	ff. 128–268	G.θ.17
218	ff. 1–89	N.η.5
	ff. 90–208	G.ε.3
219		L.ζ.6
220		L.ζ.12
221	ff. 1–157	I.ζ.27
	ff. 262–309, 158–261	Part of E.η.2
222		I.η.1
223		I.ε.8
224		E.ε.2
225		C.γ.6
226		L.η.12
227		L.ζ.20
228		N.η.10
229		N.η.9
230		N.η.11
231		N.η.8
232		L.ζ.19
233		E.η.14
234		I.ζ.6
235		E.ζ.1
236		L.ζ.7
237	ff. 1–106	L.η.13
	ff. 107–45	Part of Bundle 2, no. 4
	ff. 146–209	L.η.6
238		L.ζ.9
239		L.ε.5
240		N.η.3
241		—

Now		*T.1*
242		—
243		—
279		C.η.16
324		E.γ.4, E.γ.5
325		L.ζ.3
326		L.ζ.4
327		G.ε.1
328		L.ε.7
329		E.ε.5
330		I.η.21
331	ff. 1–117	G.ζ.1
	ff. 118–57	Bundle 2, no. 9
332		L.ζ.10
333		I.ε.6
334		L.ζ.17
335	ff. 1–228	L.ζ.14
	ff. 229–77	Part of Bundle 3, no. 14
336		L.η.21
337		L.η.19
338	ff. 1–96	G.θ.18
	ff. 97–214	N.η.18
339		I.ε.5
340		E.η.8
341		G.θ.13
342	ff. 1–119	N.θ.17
	ff. 120–233	G.θ.24
343		G.ε.7
344		G.θ.12
345	ff. i, ii, 1–96	N.η.1
	ff. 97–227	N.η.6
346		G.ε.2
347		L.ζ.15
348		E.θ.25
349		L.ζ.5
350		G.ε.8
351		L.ζ.25
352		E.ε.4
353		E.ε.1
354		G.θ.14
355		N.η.14
356	ff. i, 1–124	G.θ.21
	ff. 125–75	L.ε.3
	ff. 176–283	Bundle 3, no. 15
357		L.ζ.18
358		G.ε.6
359		N.η.19
360	ff. 1–118	N.ζ.2

Now	*T.1*
360 ff. 119–58	Part of Bundle 3, no. 14
361	L.ζ.22
362	E.θ.15
363	L.ε.2
364	C.η.17
365 ff. i, ii, 1–119	Part of L.η.20
ff. 120–228	L.η.23
366	I.θ.20
367	I.ε.2
368	N.η.22
369	L.ε.6
370	I.ε.3
371	E.ε.6
372	L.η.14
373	I.θ.22
374 ff. 1–20	Bundle 1, no. 40
ff. 21–90	C.θ.17
ff. 91–110	Bundle 1, no. 6
ff. 111–252	Bundle 1, no. 9
ff. 253–72	Bundle 1, no. 19
375	E.θ.14
376	I.θ.13
377	L.ε.4
378 ff. i, ii, 1–56, 125–65	E.θ.12
ff. 57–124	N.η.17
379 ff. 1–68	Part of L.ζ.18
ff. 69–130	C.θ.16
380 ff. 1–120	Part of L.ε.3
ff. 121–228	L.ε.1
381	N.η.7
382	I.ε.4
383	C.η.18
384	E.θ.13
385	G.ε.5
386	E.η.9
387	G.ε.9
388	G.θ.27
389	G.θ.16
390	I.θ.16
391	I.θ.11
392 ff. 1–28, 59–115	Part of E.θ.22
ff. 29–58	Part of I.θ.14
ff. 116–31	Part of L.η.20
ff. 148–72, 132–47	C.θ.28
393	N.θ.21
394	G.θ.9
395 ff. i, ii, 1–16, 19–52, 141–72	G.θ.15

Now	*T.1*
395 ff. 93–138, 53–92	G.θ.7
396	E.ε.7
397	C.θ.8
398	I.θ.18
399	G.θ.4
400	I.ε.1
401	E.θ.2
402	C.θ.21–3
403	I.θ.19
404	E.θ.3
405	N.η.21
406	E.ε.3
407	N.η.20
408 ff. i, ii, 1–19	I.θ.7
ff. 20–141	Part of I.θ.17
409	Part of I.θ.14
410	L.η.24
411	E.θ.7
412	E.θ.21
413	E.θ.1
414 ff. 1–80	L.η.17
ff. 81–159	Bundle 3, no. 12
415	L.ζ.24
416	I.θ.15
417	I.θ.12
418	N.η.13
419	E.θ.16
420	I.ε.7
421	G.θ.10
422	E.θ.10
423 ff. 1–114	N.θ.19
ff. 115–208	G.θ.1
424	I.θ.21
425 ff. 1–21	Part of L.θ.1
ff. 22–73	C.θ.6
ff. 74–116	E.θ.4
ff. 117–217	I.θ.4
426	C.θ.26
427	C.θ.18
428	G.θ.3
429 ff. 1–105, 163–232	I.θ.6
ff. 106–62	Bundle 3, no. 9
430	N.η.4
431 ff. i, 1–7, 16–88	Part of L.θ.1
ff. 8–15	Part of E.θ.3
ff. 89–144	G.θ.2
ff. 145–60.	Part of I.θ.17

Now		*T.1*
431	ff. 161–82	Part of L.η.20
	ff. 183–242	E.θ.19
432		G.θ.11
433		E.θ.5
434		C.θ.2
435		C.θ.19
436		G.θ.8
437	ff. 1–42	L.η.16
	ff. 43–73	Part of E.θ.7
	ff. 74–147	Bundle 3, no. 10
438		G.θ.5
439	ff. 1–143	E.θ.17
	ff. 144–210	C.θ.20
440		N.η.15
441		I.θ.8
442		E.θ.6
443		C.θ.7
444	ff. 1–12	Bundle 3, no. 4
	ff. 13–24	Bundle 3, no. 7
	ff. 25–68	Bundle 3, no. 2
	ff. 69–186	Bundle 3, no. 8
445	pp. i–iv, 1–312	Bundle 4, no. 8
	pp. 313–90	Part of Bundle 4, no. 14
	pp. 391–423	Bundle 1, no. 39
	pp. 424–35	Bundle 4, no. 13
	pp. 436–507	Part of Bundle 4, no. 11
	pp. 508–681	Bundle 4, no. 4
446		C.θ.9
447	pp. ix–xii, 1–72	Bundle 4, no. 22
	pp. 73–100	Bundle 1, no. 33
	pp. 101–67	C.θ.32
	pp. 168–203	Bundle 4, no. 21
	pp. 204–91	Bundle 1, no. 23
	pp. 292–319	Bundle 1, no. 5
	pp. 320–99	Bundle 1, no. 28
	pp. 400–15	Bundle 1, no. 36
448		C.γ.7
449		E.θ.18
450		I.θ.5
451	ff. 1–82	L.ζ.23
	ff. 83–192	E.θ.8
452		E.θ.9
453		I.θ.2
454	ff. i, 1–27	—
	ff. 28–123	—
	ff. 124–204	Bundle 3, no. 6
455		I.θ.3

Now	*T.1*
456 ff. i, 1–126	Part of N.θ.15
ff. 127–46	Part of E.θ.22
ff. 147–220	Part of E.θ.4
457 ff. 1–132	N.θ.20
ff. 133–92	Bundle 3, no. 5
ff. 193–254	Part of N.θ.15
458	N.θ.16
459	N.θ.9
460	I.θ.1
461	C.θ.25
462	C.θ.27
463	C.θ.38
464	C.θ.10
465	E.θ.20
466	G.θ.19
467	I.θ.9
468	Bundle 4, no. 20
469	Printed book, N.δ.35 at Cambridge
470	Bundle 4, no. 18
471	I.θ.23
472	G.θ.26
473	C.θ.1
474	G.θ.23
475 ff. i, ii, 1–110	I.θ.25
ff. 111–79	C.θ.34
476	E.θ.24
477	L.θ.5
478 ff. i–iii, 1–91	L.θ.6
ff. 92–145	C.θ.4
479	L.θ.2
480	L.θ.9
481	L.θ.3
482	C.θ.5
483	L.θ.22
484	G.θ.6
485 ff. i, 1–117	N.θ.2
ff. 118–287	Bundle 3, no. 3
486	L.θ.10
487	C.θ.12
488 ff. 1–42	Bundle 1, no. 10
ff. 43–72	Bundle 1, no. 8
ff. 73–88	Bundle 1, no. 11
ff. 89–126	Part of N.θ.15
ff. 127–48	—
ff. 149–98	C.θ.42
489	I.θ.24

Now	*T.1*
496	C.θ.3
510	I.θ.10
519	Bundle 4, no. 7
522	G.θ.22
523	L.θ.21
524	C.θ.14
525	C.θ.13
526	C.θ.15
527	C.θ.41
528 (*given in 1680*)	—
529	C.θ.40
530	L.θ.11
531	E.θ.23
532	L.θ.15
533	L.θ.13
534	L.θ.12
535	N.θ.6
536	L.θ.19
537	C.θ.45
538	L.θ.7
539	C.θ.39
540	N.θ.5
541	L.θ.4
542	N.θ.1
543	N.θ.7
544	L.θ.14
545	L.θ.8
546	L.θ.20
547	—
548	C.θ.30
549	C.θ.43
550	N.θ.3
551	C.θ.44
552	L.θ.16
553	L.θ.17
554	L.θ.18
555	C.θ.35
556	N.θ.10
557	Bundle 3, no. 1
558	L.θ.23
559	C.θ.48
560	N.θ.8
561 ff. 1–145	N.θ.13
ff. 146–202	N.θ.14
562	N.θ.12
563	N.θ.4
564	N.θ.11

Now	*T.1*
565 ff. 1–15	C.θ.37
ff. 16–70	C.θ.31
ff. 71–6	Bundle 1, no. 35
566	C.θ.36
567	G.θ.25
744	Bundle 4, no. 19
765	N.θ.18
806, no. 8	Bundle 1, no. 2
no. 21	C.θ.11
842	Bundle 4, no. 10
861	C.θ.46
873	C.θ.33
1033	Bundle 2, no. 1
1042	Bundle 3, no. 13

Catalogues of Lambeth manuscripts referred to on pp. 2–5, in chronological order.

Pre-Cambridge.	Lambeth Palace, L.R.f.6 ff. 268–310	p .2
	Lambeth Palace, 1047	
Cambridge.	Bodleian, Arch. Seld. B.5	p. 2
	Cambridge, University Library, Oo.7.51 ff. 72–84	p. 2
	Bodleian, Tanner 268 ff. 137–70 (T.1)	p. 2
	Bodleian, Tanner 274 (T.2)	p. 3
Post-Cambridge	Bodleian, Tanner 270	p. 5

A CATALOGUE OF MANUSCRIPTS IN LAMBETH PALACE LIBRARY

1222. STATUTES OF ALL SOULS COLLEGE, OXFORD

Copy of the statutes of All Souls College, Oxford, with an appendix of precedents, finely written on vellum for Archbishop Sancroft, *c.* 1680. The last three items relate to the Visitation of 1710–11. All are printed in *Statutes of the Colleges of Oxford*, 1853, except pp. 114–19. The contents are as follows:

Statuta in 34 chapters (pp. 1–70).

De dispositione camerarum (p. 70).

Ordinatio Johannis Stafford Cantuariensis Archiepiscopi, de electione Vicecustodis, Bursariorum et Decanorum, 1445 (p. 71).

De disputationibus in Theologia ordinatio Willelmi Warham, Cantuariensis Archiepiscopi, et de Modo et Forma eligendi Rectorem earundem, 1519. Title partly in the hand of Sancroft (p. 73).

John Whitegift, Lord Archbishop of Canterbury, his Order For auoyding corruptions in Resignations (p. 77).

Iniunctio Domini Johannis Whitegifte Archiepiscopi, De Communiis in aula percipiendis, et puerorum numero moderando, 1592 (p. 79).

Whitgift's Injunctions, 3 August 1601 (p. 81).

Cranmer's Injunctions, 26 August 1541 (p. 104).

De Numero Medicorum Studentium, 12 March 1710 (p. 114).

Injunctions of John Bettesworth, Commissary to the Visitor, 12 October 1710 (p. 116).

Cover stamped on back and front with the college arms. Inside front cover the shelfmark C.6.12.30, and the signature J. Cantuar [Archbishop Moore].

xiii+120 pp.

1223. BIBLE: New Testament

Variant readings in Greek of the gospel of St. Mark [by Charles Burney, 1757–1817], by collation of Lambeth MSS. 1175–80 and 1192 with J. J. Griesbach's edition of the text. The variants have been transferred by Burney to his interleaved copy of Griesbach's New Testament printed in London, 1809. This book is now in the British Museum (1003.c.8–19). MS. 1180 was returned in 1817 to the Patriarch of Jerusalem, from whom it was borrowed by J. D. Carlyle. For Burney's work on the Carlyle MSS. now in Lambeth Palace Library, see H. J. Todd, *An account of the Greek manuscripts, chiefly biblical . . . deposited in the archiepiscopal library*. See also MSS. 1224, 1255.

243 ff.

1224. BIBLE: New Testament

Descriptions [by Charles Burney] of Lambeth MSS. 1175–80 and 1192. See also MSS. 1223, 1255. The descriptions occur as follows:

1175: ff. 1–11
1176: ff. 12–23
1177: ff. 26–30
1178: ff. 32–45
1179: ff. 48–51
1180: ff. 52–4
1192: ff. 57–60

61 ff.

1225–6. RECORDS OF CANTERBURY

Transcripts by Charles Sandys (1786–1859), antiquary and solicitor of Canterbury, with translations in parallel columns, of royal charters and other instruments concerning the liberties and boundaries of Canterbury, 1827. The documents are presented in the form of a legal brief, and are extracted from the archives of the city and of Christ Church, Canterbury, and from printed sources.

1225. RECORDS OF CANTERBURY

'Charters of Canterbury. Schedule No. 1.' This volume contains royal charters of confirmation, unless otherwise indicated, as follows:

2 August 1461 (*C.C.R., 1427–1516*, 138–41) (ff. 13–73).

29 November 1487 (f. 74).

24 April 1521 (*C.L.P. For. & Dom., 1519–23*, pt. 1, no. 1249) (f. 75).

8 May 1548 (f. 76).

20 October 1559 (f. 77).

13 June 1498 (*C.P.R., 1494–1509*, 136–8) (ff. 78–86).

Act of Parliament, 34 & 35 Henry VIII, Cap. 18 (ff. 87–9).

8 September 1608 (ff. 90–124).

8 November 1684 (ff. 125–51).

Proclamation, 17 October 1688 (Steele 3881) (ff. 152–4).

'Allowance of Liberties of Canterbury. In Exchequer. Trinity Term. 8 George III' (ff. 155–65).

A table of contents (f. 3), and 'A Breviate or Summary of All the Charters Granted to the City of Canterbury' (ff. 4–11).

168 ff.

1226. RECORDS OF CANTERBURY

'Charters and other Records relating to the Boundaries of the Counties of Kent and Canterbury. Schedule No. 2.' The volume is divided into three sections: (*a*) records relating to the Archbishop of Canterbury and to

Christ Church, Canterbury; (*b*) records relating to St. Augustine's; (*c*) records relating to the city of Canterbury.

Records relating to the Archbishop of Canterbury and Christ Church, Canterbury

Charter of Edward the Confessor (f. 5).

Notification (in English language) by William I of grant of liberties, *c.* 1070 (*Regesta Regum*, 1, no. 38) (f. 6).

Extract from Domesday Book (Somner, *Antiquities of Canterbury*, ed. 1703, appendix, no. I) (ff. 7–8).

Charter of William II, 1093 (*Regesta Regum*, i, no. 336) (f. 9).

Notification (in Latin and English) by Henry I of grant of liberties, ?1107 (*Regesta Regum*, ii, no. 840) (f. 10).

Charter in English of Henry II (f. 12).

Charter of Henry II (*Foedera*, ed. 1816, pt. 1, 40) (ff. 13–14).

Charter of Edward I, 14 June 1294 (*C.C.R.*, *1257–1300*, 435) (ff. 15–18).

Charter of Edward IV de libertatibus clericorum, 2 November 1462 (*Concilia*, iii, 583–5) (ff. 19–26).

Grant by Archbishop Reynolds to Christ Church of the manor of Caldecot near Canterbury, 1326 (f. 27).

Composition between Christ Church and the city of Canterbury, 20 May 1492 (*Literae Cantuarienses*, R.S., iii, no. 1105) (ff. 28–33).

Quo Warranto proceedings against the city of Canterbury, 27 Charles II (ff. 34–43).

'La Fraunchise Lercevesque de Cantebirs quil ad en Staplegate' (*Decem Scriptores*, 2204) (ff. 44–6).

Records relating to St. Augustine's

Donacio Regis Ethelberti de terra ubi scitum est Monasterium Sancti Augustini (*Monasticon*, i, 110) (ff. 47–8).

Charter of Cnut (*Monasticon*, i, 139) (f. 49).

Exemplification of composition between St. Augustine's and the city of Canterbury, 14 May 1402 (Partly printed. Somner. op. cit., appendix, no. LXVI) (ff. 50–9).

Placita de Libertatibus, 7 Edward I (*Placita de Quo Warranto*, 1818, 431–2) (f. 60).

Allocatio Libertatis Monasterii Sancti Augustini, 1313 (*Placita de Quo Warranto*, 1818, 318–19) (ff. 61–5).

Surrender of the Abbey of St. Augustine to the Crown [4 December 1537] (*Monasticon*, i, 123) (ff. 66–70).

An Act that all religious Houses under the yearly Revenue of Two hundred Pounds shall be dissolved and given to the King and his heirs, 27 Henry VIII, Cap. 28 (ff. 71–6).

[1226 *cont.*]

An Act for Dissolution of Monasteries and Abbies, 31 Henry VIII, Cap. 13 (ff. 77–87).

Records relating to the City of Canterbury

Exemplification of charters of liberties, 18 November 1395 (Somner, op. cit., appendix, no. VI) (ff. 88–95).

Extracts from Burgmote Books concerning the city charter and boundaries, 1683–6, 1688, 1728 (ff. 96–103).

Letter from James II to the Aldermen and Corporation of Canterbury, 17 December 1687 (f. 104).

Letter from C. Robinson, Recorder of Canterbury, returning the charter of 35 Charles II, 3 June 1775 (f. 105).

Extracts from the Chamberlains' accounts, 1683–5 (ff. 106–10).

Perambulatio antiqua, n.d. (ff. 111–14).

'Some Notes touching the Perambulacon of Canterbury Compared withe the Bounders of Longport' (ff. 115–16).

'Perambulatio ballivorum et communitatis civitatis Cantuariae facta per bundas libertatum civitatis predictae anno regni regis Edwardi tercii quadragesimo sexto' (*Decem Scriptores*, 2147) (ff. 117–18).

Perambulation of the bounds of Canterbury, 19 September 1728 (ff. 119–20).

Notes on a perambulation of Canterbury, 1745 (ff. 121–4).

Notes concerning Black Friars (ff. 125–35).

Grant by Henry VIII to Thomas Spilman, Receiver of the Court of Augmentations, of Grey Friars, Canterbury, 17 July 1539 (*C.L.P. For. & Dom., Jan.–July 1539*, no. 1354 (40) (ff. 136–7).

Notes on the city jurisdiction in Grey Friars (f. 138).

Notes on the same in White Friars (f. 139).

Notes on the same in St. Lawrence (f. 140).

Notes on the same in St. Gregory (f. 141).

Lease for lives granted by Robert Bacon, Master of the Hospital of the Poor Priests in Canterbury, to Stephen Thornherst of Canterbury, Agnes his wife and Stephen his son, of lands at Patrixbourne, 26 July 1561 (ff. 142–3).

Notes on the city jurisdiction in St. Martin (ff. 144–5).

Notes on the same in Nackington (ff. 146–9).

Presentment of court leet on the same in Patrixbourne, 2 November 1820 (ff. 150–1).

A table of contents (ff. 3–4).

153 ff.

1227. Not allotted.

1228. HOUSEHOLD BOOK OF ANNE, COUNTESS OF MIDDLESEX, 1622

Accounts of household expenditure on diet and inventories of furniture and equipment at the house of Anne Cranfield, Countess of Middlesex, at Chelsea, 1622. A finely engrossed copy, bound in leather, by Morgan Colman, pensioner of the Charterhouse, 'a poore cast-downe gentleman', and finished by him on 31 October 1622. The manuscript is a companion to another Household Book of the Earl of Middlesex in the Fulham Papers transferred to the Library in 1960. The present manuscript may have been brought to Lambeth from Fulham on Archbishop Howley's translation in 1828. It contains:

Daily statements, with weekly summaries, of the consumption of provisions, 15 February–14 March 1622, and (ff. 68–86) 4–18 July 1622. The names of those present at dinner and supper daily are stated (ff. 6–43).

Details of items purchased for banquets and festivities at Chelsea, 24, 26–7 December 1621 (ff. 46–9).

Inventory of household furniture, 1622 (ff. 51–9).

Inventory of plate, 1622 (ff. 60–1).

Inventory of linen, 1622 (f. 62).

Weekly summaries of expenditure for each department of the household, 25 March–24 June 1622 (ff. 68–86).

A blazon of the arms of the Earl and Countess of Middlesex has been removed from f. 4. The name Paul Haget occurs in the cover.

ii+94 ff.

1229. FRAGMENTS REMOVED FROM THE BINDINGS OF MANUSCRIPTS

Nos. 1–8, 10, 12–15, 18, 19 are bifolia and single leaves of unwanted manuscripts used by binders at, presumably, Bury St. Edmunds, Gloucester (Lanthony), and Canterbury. No. 11 is certainly from a medieval binding. No. 16 was used to wrap a sermon at the end of the sixteenth century. The manuscripts from which nos. 1–17 were taken were rebound in the time of Archbishop Sancroft (1678–90). MS. 793 (cf. nos. 18, 19) was rebound in 1873.

Nos. 1–4. Four bifolia. Second half of 13th century. From MS. 105 ff. 1–133.
Digestum vetus, part of bk. 16: as ed. 1576, cols. 1565–1619. No regular apparatus. Many untidy marginalia in ink and pencil, in English hands. 305×220 mm. Written space 168×98 mm. 2 cols. 37 lines.

The flyleaves and pastedown between f. 1 of MS. 105 ff. 1–133 (from Bury St. Edmunds) and the front board of the former binding. The

[1229 *cont.*]

Cambridge mark # E.η.11 is on the exposed side of the pastedown, now the verso of the first leaf of no. 1, and a chain mark shows at the head of this leaf.

Nos. 5, 6. Two bifolia. Second half of 13th century. From MS. 105 ff. 1–133.
Digestum vetus, part of bk. 10: as ed. 1576, cols. 1128–49. No regular apparatus. Notes in the margins in a neat textura and in current English hands. 305×215 mm. Written space 205×100 mm. 2 cols. 44 lines.

No doubt the flyleaves and pastedown between f. 133 of MS. 105 ff. 1–133 and the back board of the former binding. The sewing holes at the bands coincide with those of nos. 1–4.

Nos. 7, 8. Two single leaves. 10th century.[1] From MS. 119.
Two leaves of a commentary on St. Matthew, partly in Latin and partly in Irish. No. 7 covers Matt. 5: 5–7 and no. 8, Matt. 5: 20–2. Written space, not quite complete, 288+×188 mm. 2 cols. 64+ and 61+ lines. Written closely in insular minuscule.

Pastedowns of MS. 119 (from and probably written at Lanthony). The Cambridge mark # G.η.12 is on no. 7, so this leaf was at the front.

No. 9. A piece cut from a roll (?). First half of 14th century. From MS. 121.
Appointment of proctors by the prior of 'Moyllerone' (Mouilleron, O.S.A.), in the diocese of Luçon (Vendée), A.D. 1322. Imperfect at beginning and end, and damaged by pasting down. Written space 155 mm. in width. The dorse is blank.

A pastedown from the front board of the former binding of MS. 121. The Cambridge mark # E.ζ.13 is on the dorse, the exposed side. MS. 121 ff. 1–229 is in a French hand.

No. 10. A bifolium. 12th century. From MS. 148.
Two leaves of a copy of the earliest customs of the Cistercian order, agreeing nearly with the text printed from the only known manuscript in *Analecta Sacri Ordinis Cisterciensis*, xii (1956), caps. CVIII. 11–CXI. 6 and CXIII. 9–50. Written space 160×110 mm. 26 long lines. Written in England (?).

A pastedown. Conclusive evidence that it lined the back board of MS. 148 (from Lanthony) comes from the words 'Lanthon' and 'Beda', on the exposed side, the size, and the coincidence in position of a mark made by the pin of a former strap-and-pin fastening with a mark on f. 150 of MS. 148.

No. 11. A single leaf. Early 13th century. From MS. 216.
Vacarius, *Liber pauperum*, parts of bk. 3, tit. 45, beginning in D. 9. 2. 28, and tit. 46, ending in D. 9. 3. 5; ed. F. de Zulueta, Selden Society xliv, 1927, pp. 97–9. Written space 182+×100 mm. 43+ long lines. Written in England.

[1] The date has been supplied by Professor W. O'Sullivan.

A pastedown from the front board of the former binding of MS. 216, a copy of the *Oculus Sacerdotum* which belonged to someone in the diocese of Worcester. The exposed side bears the Cambridge mark # I.η.20 and in the wide margins of the Vacarius are notes in a hand of the 14th century which occurs also on ff. 108ᵛ–109. The writer begins with the verses on sins requiring episcopal absolution, 'Deditus usure . . .' and 'Qui facit incestum . . .' (6+6 lines; Hans Walther, *Alphabetisches Verzeichnis der Versanfänge mittellateinischer Dichtungen*, 1959, nos. 4210, 15482) and continues 'Hec colliguntur ex summa fratris Raymundi de penaforti hostienc' fratris bonauenture et ex quibusdam aliis vt asserit tamen ego non vidi omnes . . .'.

Nos. 12, 13. A bifolium and a single leaf. Second half of 13th century. From MS. 218 ff. 90–208.
Digestum vetus, parts of bks. 7 and 8: as ed. 1576, cols. 914–27, 963–75. 290×185 mm. Written space 170×95 mm. 2 cols. 43 lines. Written in England.

The flyleaves and pastedown between f. 90 of MS. 218 ff. 90–208 (from Bury St. Edmunds) and the front board of the former binding. The Cambridge mark # G.ε.3 is on the exposed side of the pastedown, now the verso of the second leaf of no. 12, and a chain mark shows at the foot of this leaf. 'W. Sadler', 16th century, is at the head of no. 13.[1]

Nos. 14, 15. Two bifolia. 12th century. Almost certainly from MS. 372. Four adjacent leaves of a text dealing with the significance of rites and observances of the church on Holy Thursday, Good Friday, and Holy Saturday, which begins and ends imperfectly. A section begins (no. 14, leaf 1) 'Noscat uestra caritas quod in diebus solemnibus quantum possimus altaria ornamus. in his autem tribus diebus a cena domini usque in sabbatum sanctum nudamus.'

The section beginning 'Noscat uestra caritas' occurs also in Salisbury Cathedral 135, Exeter Cathedral 3525, Cambridge, Fitzwilliam Museum, McClean 101, and B.M. Cotton Nero A.i. In these manuscripts it is part of a text beginning 'Legitur in ecclesiastica historia quod nabuchodosor' (Salisbury, ff. 7–23; Exeter, ff. 121–74; Fitzwilliam, ff. 169–174ᵛ; Nero A.i, ff. 106–108ᵛ). 242×172 mm. Written space *c.* 190×100 mm. 29 long lines. Ruling with a hard point. The two central bifolia of a quire. Written in a fine round hand like that used at Lanthony. Two-line initials, red or green.

The pre-Sancroft catalogues record as the last item of MS. 372 a now missing 'Tractatus Anonimus utrinque mutilus mystice exponens ritus quosdam ecclesiasticos'. This entry perplexed Sancroft, who wrote 'q.' (for 'quere') against it in MS. Tanner 274. It is a good description of nos. 14, 15. The verso of the second leaf of no. 15 is somewhat stained from exposure, and all four leaves bear the mark made by the pin of a former strap-and-pin fastening. A similar but fainter mark is to be seen in the

[1] I have also recorded in old notes 'W. Sadler 1573 Maij 20', with a wrong reference to a flyleaf of MS. 218. I cannot now find these words. N. R. K.

[1229 *cont.***]**

same position on ff. 138 and 139 of MS. 372. The leaves are the same size as the leaves of MS. 372.

No. 16. A single leaf. 14th century. From MS. 374 ff. 253–72.
Alphabetically arranged 'Distinctiones', as appears from the letter *T* as running title on recto and verso. The whole of this leaf is on the subject of 'Temptatio'. 350×245 mm. Written space 260×172 mm. 2 cols. 61 lines. Written in England.

Formerly folded in two as a wrapper. The mark 'Bundle y[e] first . . . 19' and the words 'M[r] Barnes his Sermon' in the margin show that it was the wrapper of MS. 374 ff. 253–72, a sermon of Thomas Barne, 13 June 1591.

No. 17. A bifolium. First half of 13th century. From MS. 378 ff. 57–121.
Apparently an abridgement of the *Digest* in subject order. Extracts here are, for example, from D. 33. 5. 16, D. 39. 2, D. 47. 111. A heading is 'Quedam dubia ex postfacto retroundi'. 245×170 mm. Written space 157×87 mm. Two narrow columns of 42 lines. Writing above top ruled line. Written in England (?).

The flyleaf and pastedown between f. 57 of MS. 378 ff. 57–121 and the front board of the former binding. The Cambridge mark # N.η.17 is on the exposed side of the pastedown.

No. 18. A bifolium. 14th century.
Planetary tables. Figures in 29 columns over a double opening headed 'Tabula martis prima'. Red figures run vertically from o to 29 and then recommence at o. Written space *c.* 245×195 mm. 60 lines. Written in England.

The outer of two thicknesses of parchment forming the wrapper of MS. 793, 'Rentale de Holyngborn', a Christ Church, Canterbury, manor, early 16th century (cf. no. 19). The label with printed number '793' still remains *in situ* on the 'spine' of the wrapper.

No. 19. A bifolium. Late 13th century. From MS. 793.
Two leaves of a commentary on Lamentations. The commentary on Lam. 4: 8, Denigrata est super carbones . . ., begins 'Et notandum quod in predictis describitur pulcritudo nazareorum'. Written space 215×140 mm. 37 long lines. Written in a current English hand.

The inner of two thicknesses of parchment forming the wrapper of MS. 793: cf. no. 18.

1230. FRAGMENTS

A bifolium. 11th century (?).

Two leaves of a Passionale for the month of June.

1. f. 1[r–v]. The end of a Life of St. Erasmus (2 June).

2. f. 1[v]. Incip' pas' sancti ciricii et matris eius iulitæ xiii kl' iul' una cum .xi. milibus et cccc[tis] iiii. Factum est in diebus alexandri impera*toris* agente preside alaxandro . . . locutus fuerit (*ends imperfectly*).

3. f. 2[r–v]. The end of a life of SS. Peter and Paul.

1) and (2) agree, but not at all closely, with Lives printed in *Acta Sanctorum*, Junius I, pp. 215E–216D, and Junius III, pp. 28–29A. (3) is as ed. Lipsius, *Acta apostolorum apocrypha*, i (1891), 165/16–169/3, 169/11–171/9, 171/16–175/10, 177/1–3, but the last words there are followed here by 27 lines on f. 2ᵛ col. 2, Hodie sancti apostoli suum certamen consummauerunt . . . regnabunt in æternis.

Written space 230+ × 150+ mm. 2 cols. 30+ lines. Written in insular minuscule, probably in Wales.

The pastedown and flyleaf inserted by a binder at the beginning or end of a book.

1231. FRAGMENTS

A bifolium (1, 2) and a single leaf (3). 9th century.

Parts of bks. II, VIII, IX, X of the collection of synodal canons known as Hibernensis, but differing in order and wording and to some extent in content from the collection in Bodleian MS. Hatton 42 and as printed by H. Wasserschleben, *Die irische Kanonensammlung*, 2nd edn., 1885. The text is very corrupt. No division into books or numbering of chapters.

f. 1ʳ⁻ᵛ. nullus presumat (ed. II. 17/7) . . . libras obtullit (ed. II. 24/2). The chapters after bk. II. 17 are 'De eo quod prespiteri nihil uendunt de rebus æcclesiæ sine episcoporum iussione. senon necyna ait . . .', bk. II. 11, 'De superfiluis [*sic*] sacerdotum æclesiam dandis. seno[n] agatensis ait . . ., bk. II. 23, 20, 22, 21, 24.

f. 2ʳ⁻ᵛ. qui communicant (ed. VIII. 2/7) . . . habuit neque illum. The chapters after bk. VIII. 2 are 'De acolita et psalmista. de nomine acolita . . .', bk. IX. 1, IX. 2b, IX. 2a, De clerico (as MS. Hatton 42 f. 12/21–9), [De eo quod n]on ordinantus est clericus qui uxores [. . . . .] habuit in lib' do`g´matis legitur maritum . . .

f. 3ʳ⁻ᵛ. qui uiduam . . . in matrimoniam sumpsit (*apparently in continuation of* f. 2ᵛ). De multis modis . . . si uero humilior. From 'De multis modis . . .' (f. 3ʳ/2–3ᵛ/10), except the last four lines, is as ed. pp. 28/1–29/12. Then come sections 'De eo quod omnes qui habent gradus . . . , De eo quod non debent clerici discordantes . . .', 'De caus. clericum episcopo', 'De uoce moderanda clerici' (cf. ed. p. 27, footnote, and MS. Hatton 42, f. 12/30–2, f. 12ᵛ/1–10, 22–4).

Three leaves of one quire. ff. 2, 3 appear to be adjacent leaves, and 3 was the last of a quire, since it has the signature 'III' at the foot of the verso. Written space *c.* 202 × 130 mm. 24 long lines. The script is rather untidy Caroline minuscule: *a* has the double-*c* form sometimes. Abbreviations include -t' for *-tur*, q; for *qui*, and q for *quam*. Two-line initials in the ink of the text, the shafts filled in red or in pale yellow dotted with red: a yellow ground and outline of red dots sometimes. Written in France (Brittany?).

Formerly pastedowns in a binding. Both were folded and the fold was pasted to the board. The fold is narrow on f. 3, the single leaf, and wide on the bifolium, ff. 1, 2, which lay sideways.

1232. FRAGMENT

A bifolium (ff. 1, 4) and two single leaves. 14th–15th century.

Damaged leaves from the end of a sacrist's book of Christ Church, Canterbury, with contemporary foliation XXV[.] (? XXVI) on f. 1, XXVII on f. 2, XXVIII on f. 3, XXXI on f. 4.

1. f. 1^{r-v}. (*Begins imperfectly*) Item de Ioseph ab Arimathia . . . Item de sancto Martino [. . .]

2. f. 2. Cert[. . . . .] pro sonitu communi [. . . .]s.

3. f. 2^v. Certa familia liberaciones ac solidata in officio sacristarie. Custos de Wexhous . . . de custode feretri.

4. f. 3. Directions about candles on feast days.

5. f. 3^v. Notes of the customary payments by the sacrist's tenants in Strete and Gedding on the death of a sacrist, and particulars of proceedings at courts on the death of John Molond, sacrist, in 1428.

6. f. 4. Dues of four bellringers at the anniversary of Archbishop Lanfranc and on other occasions, and duties of the bellringers and the aurifrigerius at the anniversaries of Archbishops Lanfranc and Winchelsea.

7. f. 4^v. Blank, except for a note of the weight of Archbishop Arundel's chrismatory, alone and with 'cassa' and 'zona'.

The book ended originally on f. 2^v. (2) and (3) were added to and (4–7) added in the first half of the 15th century. (1) and (3) agree closely with texts in B.M. Cotton MS. Galba E.iv ff. 126^v–127 and 97^v–98. (1), the end of the list of relics at Christ Church, is printed from the Cotton manuscript by Legg and Hope, *Inventories of Christ Church, Canterbury*, pp. 91–4. (2) lists payments for bellringing on seventy-one specified days from Michaelmas to St. Matthew and—out of order at the end—'Die animarum. Pro lamfranc'. Pro Willelmo bastard. Pro ediua regina. Pro procession' sancti Augustini in rogacionibus. Die oblacionis beate marie. Die concepcionis beate marie'. The range is from 3*s.* 6½*d.* on great feasts to 3*d.* (3) was drawn up in 1322 according to the heading in B.M. MS. Galba E.iv.

The best-preserved leaf, f. 2, measures 385 × 255 mm. Written space (f. 2^v) 315 × 220 mm. 2 cols. 42 lines. The marks of five bosses from the old binding show on ff. 3, 4.

1233. FRAGMENT

Part of a bifolium. 10th century.

Two consecutive leaves of Alcuin on the Creed, beginning 'miserere domine. quia misericordia tua liberauit nos' and ending 'magnitudo una bonitas'.

As *Patr. Lat.* ci. 56B–57C. One line of writing, probably, is missing from each leaf.

Written space 163+ × 103 mm. 19 (out of 20?) long lines. Written in Anglo-Saxon minuscule: bow of *g* closed; *i* occasionally tall in the word *in*; round *s* common in all positions. The punctuation includes the punctus elevatus (.').

In use as strengthening inside the limp parchment cover of Georgius Acanthius, *Partitiones* (Lyon, 1554).

1234. FRAGMENTS

Pastedowns removed from bindings by W. G. (no. 63), the Unicorn Binder (nos. 58–9), Spierinck (nos. 22–3, 34–5, 55–6), Godfrey (nos. 20, 25–9, 43–53), Siberch (nos. 31–2, 37–9), and later Cambridge binders (nos. 3, 6, 9, 10, 13, 16–17); also two paper pads, nos. 4, 7, and two covers, nos. 2, 12. Nos. 3, 4 came from the same binding as no. 2; no. 7 from the same binding as no. 6; no. 13 from the same binding as no. 12.

No. 2. Cover bearing Oldham's roll HM.h.29.

No. 3. Part of a leaf of Alexander Nequam, *Corrogationes Promethei* (cf. MS. Bodley 550, ff. 12ᵛ–13). 13th century. England.

No. 4 (i–x). Ten fragments of a canon-law book on paper. 15th century.

No. 6. Part of a leaf of Petrus de Vineis, *Epistolae* (bk. 2, letters 16–20). 14th century. Italy.

No. 7 (i–xii). Twelve fragments of a printed commentary on the Decretals (bk. 5) on paper.

Nos. 9–10. Two leaves and parts of two other leaves of the *Catholicon* of James of Genoa (letter D). 14th century. England.

No. 12. Cover bearing roll FF 3 and a small ornament used often on books bound in Cambridge, *c.* 1560.

No. 13. One leaf of a commentary on *Digestum Inforciatum* (bk. 37). 13th century. Italy.

Nos. 16–17. Two leaves of Aquinas, *Prima Secundae*. 13th–14th century. England. Written space 235 × 155 mm. 2 cols. 46 lines.

No. 20. One leaf of a commentary on *Decretum Gratiani* (De poenitentia, D.1). 13th century.

Nos. 22–3. Two leaves of a manuscript of sermons (?). Late 14th century. England.

Nos. 25–6. Parts of two leaves of a commentary on canon law. 13th century.

Nos. 28–9. Two leaves of a Bible (Gospels: 2 cols., 62 lines). 13th century. England.

Nos. 31–2. Two leaves of the commentary of Innocent IV on the Decretals (bk. 2), with marginalia in English hands.[2] 13th century. Written space 225 × 150 mm. 2 cols., 58 lines.

[1] A list of Cambridge bindings in the library containing manuscript pastedowns *in situ* is kept with MS. 1234.

[2] These leaves have been used as labels for stock by a bookseller: cf. S. Gibson in *The Library* xii (1932), 432 and N. R. Ker, *Medieval Manuscripts in British*

[1234 *cont.*]

Nos. 34–5. Two leaves of Aristotle, *De anima*, bk. 1. Second half of 13th century. Written space 150×102 mm. 40 long lines.

Nos. 37–9. Three leaves of a Psalter.[1] 14th century. England. Written space 235×145 mm. 24 long lines.

Nos. 43, 43*, 44–53. Twelve leaves of *Codex Justiniani*. With continuous apparatus. 14th century. England.

Nos. 55–6. Two leaves of *Codex Justiniani*. With continuous apparatus. 13th century. Written space (text) 225×130 mm. 2 cols. 56 lines.

Nos. 58–9. Parts of two leaves of *Codex Justiniani*. 13th century.

No. 63. Part of a petition in English 'To the King' (Henry VII) from the surviving heirs of Edmund Beaufort, Duke of Somerset, for the reversal of his attainder. Written space 260+×210+ mm. The dorse is blank.

1235. FRAGMENTS[2]

Fragments removed from books bound in Oxford.[3]

Nos. 1, 2. From **H 890 P3 M5, R. de Mediavilla, Venice 1509, in binding bearing roll IV in S. Gibson, *Early Oxford Bindings*, and roll FL.a.4 in J. B. Oldham, *English Blind-stamped Bindings*. Four leaves (the two central bifolia of a quire) from bk. 1 of Aristotle, *Analytica Posteriora*, 32 long lines. Written in the first half of the 13th century.

No. 3. From *H 2005, H. Helmesius, Cologne 1550, in binding bearing Gibson's roll XX. A bifolium of a lectionary: cf. N. R. Ker, *Pastedowns in Oxford Bindings*, nos. 728, 738, for other leaves probably from this manuscript. 2 vols. 32 lines. Written in England in the 13th century.

1236. FRAGMENTS

Twenty-three pieces.

No. 1. From MS. 35. A strip of a service book.

Nos. 2, 3. From MS. 1106. Two strips of one leaf.

Nos. 4, 5. From 1484. 1 (Capreolus: binding by Oldham's 'Binder D': see *English Blind-stamped Bindings*, p. 31). Two pastedowns. From accounts of a royal household (cf. 'pro expensis hospicii domini Regis predicti', no. 4, line 12). Second half of 15th century. England.

Libraries, i. 131. 'Paradisus heraclidis. Concordancie biblie' is written large along the length of no. 32 and 'De vita spirituali Io Gerson' large along the length of no. 31.

[1] Two more leaves are in the binding of **H 1970 (Clichtoveus).

[2] A list of Oxford bindings in the library containing manuscript pastedowns *in situ* is kept with MS. 1235.

[3] The fragment of *Digestum Novum* recorded by Ker, *Pastedowns in Oxford Bindings*, p. 6, no. 58a, as removed from *Psalterium Cisterciensis ordinis*, Paris, s.a. (now **H 2033 C5) has not been found.

Nos. 6–9. From 1485.2 (Alchabitius, etc.). Four leaves folded to form four thicknesses (pastedown and flyleaves) at each end. Well written in an Italian hand, 13th century. 2 cols. 74 lines. From a copy of a commentary on *Digestum Novum* (titulus 'De damno infecto').

No. 10. From **H 5142 M1506. Wrapper. 52 lines, some complete. Case at Ludlow, 5 Nov. 5 Eliz., between John Wyn ap Mered*ith* of the parish of Syllatyn, plaintiff, and Thomas Hulse Esq., defendant.

Nos. 11, 12. From SA 8501.1 (Erasmus, *Enchiridion*, Strasbourg, 1524, etc.). Two fragments of *Digest*. 13th–14th century, England.

Nos. 13–16. From **SA 2361 (Trebellius, 2 vols., Basle, 1545), in binding bearing Oldham's rolls HM a 17 and FP a 8. Pastedowns. Four leaves of *Digest*. 14th century.

Nos. 17, 18. From **SA 2361 (see above, 13–16). Two strips, with legal notes, perhaps from the same manuscript as nos. 13–16.

Nos. 19, 20. From KB 735 (G. a. Reychersdorff, Vienna, 1550). Pastedowns. Two leaves of a commentary on the *Posterior Analytics*. 14th–15th century. England.

Nos. 21, 22. From 'C.θ.10' and said to be 'Taken out of the fifth volume of the works of John Chrysostom 4. D. 4 Parisiis 1556 by W. Root and Son in repairing July 1936', but this edition of Chrysostom is not now at Lambeth. Pastedowns. 2 leaves. 2 cols. 36 lines. From a missal. 14th century. England.

No. 23. From '23.5.33': this mark on label and also '[. . . .] Simanc [. . . .] iscopus/[. . . . . .]sis de Republica/μ (?) 3.2'. Wrapper. 2 leaves. 3 cols. 51 lines. Dictionary of Hebrew names (so ? from a Bible). 13th century.

1237. FRAGMENTS

Fragments in French:

Nos. 1–2. Two small strips, 13th century, from the binding of John Fisher, *Opusculum de fiducia et misericordia dei* (Cologne, 1556) (f. 130). They contain parts of lines 1641–63 and 1672–96 of Bevis of Hampton, ed. A. Stimming, *Bibliotheca Normannica*, vii (1899).

Nos. 3–9. Five complete but damaged leaves (written space 10 × 17 mm.) and strips from one bifolium in better condition, 14th century, in an English hand. The text is from the *Roman des Sept Sages* in prose.

1238. FRAGMENTS

Fragments, mainly of a handsome missal (England, s. xv in.), removed from the bindings of the Plantin Polyglott Bible (Antwerp, 1589) (*E 1: 7 vols.).

1239. FRAGMENTS

Fragments of the early 13th century and earlier removed from the bindings of unidentified books.[1]

[1] For other fragments of this date, see MSS. 1229, nos. 7–8, 10–11, 14–15, 1233, 1241.

1240. FRAGMENTS

Fragments of the 13th–15th centuries, removed from the bindings of unidentified books.

1241. FRAGMENT

Part of a leaf of a large Bible written in England in the first half of the 12th century. It contains parts of 1 Ezra vi–vii. Cut into three strips and used in the binding of Reinerus Reineccius, *Syntagma de familiis*, Basle, [1574], now *K. 78. R. 3.

1242–9. Not allotted.

1250. KENT COLLECTIONS

Collections concerning the Hospital of St. Thomas the Martyr, Canterbury, and other places in Canterbury and its environs, by Nicholas Battely, Vicar of Beaksborne and Rector of Ivechurch, Kent (d. 1704).

1. 'The Ancient and Modern State of the Hospital of Eastbridge in the city of Canterbury.' Printed from this manuscript, with some variations, in *Bibl. Topog. Brit.* i, 297–419 (pp. 10–207).

The volume has been subsequently used as a register of leases granted by the Master of Eastbridge Hospital, 1679–1730. The names of the lessees are indexed (pp. 209–399).

2. List of scholars entering the school at Eastbridge Hospital, 1754–8, and leaving, 1757–8 (p. 401).

3. Various collections by Battely:

Priory of St. Gregory, Canterbury (cf. *Bibl. Topog. Brit.* i, 420–4) (pp. 450–3).

Priory of St. Sepulchre, Canterbury (cf. *Bibl. Topog. Brit.* i, 425–8) (pp. 472–3).

Hospital of St. James by Canterbury (cf. *Bibl. Topog. Brit.* i, 428–34) (pp. 488–92).

Maynards Spittle (p. 499).

Hospital of St. Mary of the Poor Priests, Canterbury (cf. *Bibl. Topog. Brit.* i, 436–8) (pp. 502–3).

Hospital of St. Laurance, Canterbury (cf. *Bibl. Topog. Brit.* i, 438–41) (pp. 521–2).

Extract from charter of James I to Canterbury (p. 523).

'A clause drawn up by the Arch Bishop's Direction to be inserted in the Hospital Leases', 18 November 1718 (printed *Bibl. Topog. Brit.* i, 441) (p. 524).

Clause from the will of Matthew Browne, 12 December 1717 (printed *Bibl. Topog. Brit.* i, 442) (p. 525).

The Hospital of Harbledown and the Hospital of St. John the Baptist, Northgate, Canterbury (pp. 562–3).

Boundaries of Cockering lands, 1 May 1593 (p. 570).
Terrier of lands of Eastbridge Hospital, 1713 (p. 572).

572 pp.

1251. Not allotted.

1252. STAR CHAMBER

Collections of proceedings and procedures in the Star Chamber.

'Rules and Method of proceeding in all Causes in the Star Chamber', by Isaac Cotton. In the dedication to Sir Humphrey May, Chancellor of the Duchy of Lancaster, and Thomas May, his brother, Deputy Clerk to the Privy Council, Cotton describes himself as a clerk in the Star Chamber for thirty years. The treatise is dated 22 November 1610, but the copies in MSS. B.M. Stowe 418 and Lansdowne 639 are both dated 20 September 1622, and May was not appointed Chancellor of the Duchy until 1618 (ff. 1–58).

'A Relation of all the Passages and Proceedings in the star chamber and other Courts against the Marchants imprisoned for Tonnage and Poundage, Anno Domini 1629.' Proceedings against Richard Chambers of London, merchant, and others, in the Star Chamber, Exchequer, and elsewhere (ff. 62–131^{v}).

'An Information Exhibited by Sir John Bankes, Knight, his Majesty's Attorney Generall, in the high Court of Starr-chamber against John Bastwick, Dr. in Phisick, Henry Burton, Clarke, Rector of St. Mathewe's Church in Friday street, London, William Prynne, Prisoner in the Tower, and diuers others, for making, diuulgeing and dispersing of diuers scandalous Bookes and Libells against the whole Clergie of the Kingdome, and against the Gouernment of the Church of England', 12 March 1637 (ff. 134–48).

'A list of all those that are called into the Starchamber for staye in Towne, against the Proclamation, and for eatinge and dressinge of flesh on Fridayes', by William Noy, Attorney General, 2 February 1633 (ff. 149–52).

Proceedings in the Star Chamber against Oliver St. John [of Marlborough] for refusal to pay a benevolence, 1614 (ff. 154–161^{v}).

'The proceedinge in the Starchamber against Sir John Hollis and others for speeches used by them to Weston at the tyme of his execution at Tyburne about the death of Sir Thomas Overburie, 10 November 1615.' The proceedings are against Sir John Hollis, Sir John Wentworth and [Thomas] Lumsden (ff. 164–87).

Account of the jurisdiction of the Star Chamber with minutes of proceedings in the reign of Henry VII (ff. 187–201).

Belonged to Henry Powle (1630–92), Master of the Rolls. Old shelfmark A.19. List of contents (f. i).

v+205 ff.

1253. STAR CHAMBER

Report of Cases in the Star Chamber, Easter term 1 Charles I to Hilary term 3 Charles I, and also (ff. 185^{v}–7^{v}) a speech in the Star Chamber by Lord Keeper Coventry about the increase of sectaries.

In another hand are a chronological list of cases, giving the names of the parties and the nature of the cases (ff. iii–v), and some marginal notes and corrections to the manuscript.

Similar MSS. are B.M. Lansdowne MS. 620, ff. 1–116, and Bodleian Library MS. Rawl. A.127. See also J. S. Burn, *The Star Chamber*, 1870, 92–106.

Belonged to Henry Powle (1630–92), Master of the Rolls. Old shelfmark A.30.

v+189 ff.

1254. STATUTES OF DULWICH COLLEGE

Early 18th-century copy of the Statutes of Dulwich College, dated 14 November 1626. At page ii is an extract from the letters patent appointing the Archbishop of Canterbury Visitor.

Bound in vellum.

vi+92 pp.

1255. COLLATIONS FOR AN EDITION OF THE NEW TESTAMENT, 1804

Papers relating to an edition of the New Testament proposed by J. D. Carlyle (1759–1804), Professor of Arabic at Cambridge University. They consist principally of collations by various hands of Lambeth MSS. 1175, 1178, 1184, 1187–91, and 1196, and MS. C. 4 (subsequently returned with MS. 1184 and other manuscripts to the Patriarch of Jerusalem) with the edition of John Mill. For an account of Carlyle's intentions see H. J. Todd, *An account of the Greek manuscripts, chiefly biblical... deposited in the archiepiscopal library*. See also MSS. 1223–4.

Hints and observations, which Mr Carlyle takes the liberty of suggesting to the consideration of the gentlemen who have kindly promised their assistance in collating his Greek MSS. of the N.T. (Newcastle, n.d.) (ff. 1–4^{v}).

Forms of noting the various readings that may be discovered, and stating the doubts that may occur in the proposed collation (Newcastle, n.d.) (ff. 5–8).

Preliminary Observations, consisting of instructions for the collators, by the Revd. Jos[hua] Barnes, Berwick-upon-Tweed (ff. 9–15^{v}).

Collation of the Evangelists in MS. 1175 (MS. I.1), by the Revd. J[ohn] Farrer, Carlisle, 1804 (ff. 17–125).

Collation of Matthew and Mark in MS. 1178 (MS. I.4), by the Revd. John Forster, 1804 (ff. 126–39).

Collation of the Acts and Epistles in MS. 1184 (MS. I.10), by the Revd. W. Sanderson, Morpeth (ff. 150–208).

Collation of Lectionarium ex Evangeliis in MS. 1187 (MS. I.14), by the Revd. J[ohn] Farrer, 1804 (ff. 209–32).

Collation of the Evangelists in MSS. 1188–9 (MSS. I.15–16), by the Revd. Frederick Ekins, Morpeth (ff. 233^{v}–260).

Collation of the Acts of the Apostles in MS. 1190 (MS. I.17), by the Revd. Richard Bolton, 1804 (ff. 262–80).

Collation of the Acts and Epistles in MS. 1191 (MS. I.18), by the Revd. William Fleming, Hexham, 1804 (ff. 285^{v}–294).

Collation of the Evangelists in MS. C.4, by the Revd. George Bennet, 1804 (ff. 295–298^{v}).

Collation of the Acts and Epistles in MS. 1196 (MS. S.5), by the Revd. Jel[inger] Symons (ff. 300–35).

Collation of the Acts of the Apostles in MS. 1181 (MS. I.7), by the Revd. John Fenton (ff. 338–364^{v}).

Notes of contractions by William Haigh, 1804 (ff. 365^{v}–366^{v}).

List of omissions, additions, and transpositions (ff. 367–72).

Variant readings. Manuscript not stated (ff. 376^{v}–384^{v}).

List of the contents of MS. 1191 (MS. I.18) (ff. 385–387^{v}).

List of contents in the hand of Dr. Charles Burney [?] (ff. i^{v}–ii).

Given before 1812.

ii+398 ff.

1256. ARCHIEPISCOPAL ESTATES

Transcripts of deeds of exchange relating to archiepiscopal estates made between Henry VIII and Archbishop Cranmer, from the originals preserved in Lambeth Palace Library, made in 1777. The following documents are transcribed:

MS. 900 (C.M. XII), 13.
Indenture of exchange, 30 June 1538 (*C.L.P. For. & Dom.* xiii, pt. I, no. 1284) (pp. 1–15).

MS. 900 (C.M. XII), 23.
Letters patent of exchange, 31 July 1538 (*C.L.P. For. & Dom.* xiii, pt. I, no. 1519 (68)) (pp. 16–50).

MS. 900 (C.M. XII), 11.
Letters patent of exchange, 28 April 1540 (*C.L.P. For. & Dom.* xv, no. 613 (32)) (pp. 51–85).

MS. 900 (C.M. XII), 12.
Letters patent of exchange, 7 June 1542 (*C.L.P. For. & Dom.* xvii, no. 443 (15)) (pp. 86–137).

MS. 901 (C.M. XIII), 21.
Letters patent confirming exchanges, 31 August 1547 (See *C.P.R. 1 Edward VI*, 36–9) (pp. 139–53).

[1256 *cont.*]

Index of persons and places by A. C. Ducarel (pp. 157–67).

Bookplate of Archbishop Cornwallis.

xi+174 pp.

1257. Not allotted.

1258. BIBLIOTHECA BIBLICA

Copy of an unpublished supplement to *Bibliotheca biblica serenissimi Würtenbergensium ducis olim Lorckiana*, ed. J. G. C. Adler, 1787, containing a catalogue of Bibles and devotional works in the Württembergische Landesbibliothek at Stuttgart, [1816]. There are 3,131 entries published between the 15th century and 1815, and they are arranged by language and size. Two parts in one, written throughout in a continental hand. The divisions are as follows:

Polyglotta (ff. 1–4^v).
Graeca (ff. 4^v–22^v).
[Hebraica] (ff. 22^v–33^v).
Arabica (ff. 33^v–34^v).
Aethiopica (ff. 34^v–35).
Persica (f. 35).
Turcica (f. 35).
Coptica (f. 35^{r–v}).
Armena (ff. 35^v–36).
Georgica (f. 36).
Damulica (f. 36).
Malaica (f. 36^v).
Singalesica (f. 36^v).
Senica (f. 37).
Latina (ff. 37–86^v).
Lusitanica (ff. 86^v–87^v).
Hispanica (ff. 87^v–88).
Cantabrica (f. 88).
Italica (ff. 88^v–92).
Gallica (ff. 92–113^v).

Rhaetica (f. 114).
Germanica ante Lutherum, eoque vivo edita (ff. 114–42).
Germ[anica] omnium sectarum post Lutheri obitum (ff. 142–90).
Veteris teutonicae, francicae, Gothicae et Anglo-Saxonicae (ff. 191–5).
Anglica (ff. 195–212^v).
Hibernica (f. 213).
Wallicae S. Cambricae (f. 213).
Versionis in sermonem quo utuntur incola Man. Insulae (f. 213^v).
Ersa, seu Scotica aut Picta (f. 213^v).
Belgica et Batavica (ff. 213^v–223).

Danica (ff. 223–5).
Islandica (f. 225^{r-v}).
Groenlandica (f. 225^{v}). No entries.
Suecicae (ff. 225^{v}–226^{v}).
Finnica (f. 226^{v}). No entries.
Japponica (f. 226^{v}). No entries.
Slavonica in Russia usitata (ff. 226^{v}–227).
Vindica seu Croatica (f. 227^{v}).
Bohemicae editiones (f. 228).
Wendica (f. 228^{v}).
Lingua Valacha (ff. 228^{v}22–9).
Polonica (f. 229^{r-v}).
Lithuanica (f. 229^{v}). No entries.
Lettica (ff. 229^{v}–230).
Esthonica (f. 230).
Hungarica (f. 230^{r-v}).
Madagascariae (f. 231).
In usum Christ[ianorum] Equimaux (f. 231).
Lingua Mohawk (f. 231).

Given by Wyndham Knatchbull, subsequently Laudian Professor of Arabic in the University of Oxford, 1816.

i+232 ff.

1259. DESCRIPTIONS OF MANUSCRIPTS

Descriptions written before 1812 [by Charles Burney, 1757–1817] of two manuscripts of classical authors in or formerly deposited in Lambeth Palace Library.

MS. 1206 (Libanius, etc.). This account is the basis of that found in H. J. Todd, *Catalogue of the archiepiscopal manuscripts* . . . , 1812. The manuscript was deposited in the Library by J. D. Carlyle in 1806 and returned to the Patriarch of Jerusalem in 1817 (ff. 1–37).

MS. 1207 [Demosthenes]. See Todd, op. cit. (ff. 38–47).

Acquired *c.* 1817.

47 ff.

1260. RULES FOR NAVIGATION

A primer of instruction in navigation of merchant ships [by William Weston], 18th century. It contains rules for various aspects of navigation with numerous examples. The date 22 September 1729 occurs in one of the examples (f. 64). Many leaves have been removed from the back and three before f. 1.

Numbered '164' on the front cover.

i+69 ff.

1261. Not allotted.

1262. THE COLLECTS IN VERSE

'The Collects of the Church of England rendered into Verse', by Alexander Watford of Cambridge, 1842. The collects are set out with 'appropriate Psalm Tunes' chosen by Miss Calthrop of Isleham, daughter of the Revd. John Calthrop.

A printed letter addressed by Watford to Archbishop Howley, dated 30 June 1842, explains that he intended his version to become 'the opening Psalm of the Morning Service'. He estimates that each parish and chapel could be supplied with a 'Barrell'd Organ' set with twelve tunes for £30,500 to be raised by 'the Committee to be formed by the Archbishops and Bishops' (ff. i–ii).

A letter from Watford to Archbishop Howley, dated 23 July 1842, presenting the manuscript to the Library after Howley had declared its publication 'hopeless' (ff. iii–iv).

Bound in vellum with gold tooling by Messrs. Staunton and Sons.

Given by the author, 1842.

v+93 ff.

1263–98. Not allotted.

1299. LAMBETH PALACE CHAPEL

Inventories of the contents of Lambeth Palace Chapel.

'An Account of things belonging to the Chappel taken the 7th day of November 1699.' It includes a set of hangings at Croydon (ff. 1–3).

Another inventory, undated (f. 4).

ii+89 ff., mainly blank.

1300–1. GOEZE'S *ENLARGED DEFENCE*

'An Enlarged Defence of the Complutensian Greek New Testament. To which is annexed a Collection of the Principal Variations Between the Original Text and the Vulgate in that New Testament, with Critical Notes, by J. M. Goeze, Hamburgh, 1766. Translated from the Original German by William Alleyn Evanson, M.A., Lecturer of St. Luke's, Old Street, London', 1830–1. Dedicated to Thomas Burgess, Bishop of Salisbury.

MS. 1300 consists of Evanson's translation of Johann Melchior: *Ausfuhrlichere Vertheidigung des Complutischen Griechischen Neuen Testaments*, 1766.

vii+366 ff.

MS. 1301 contains the variant readings. ff. ii–iii are decorated with watercolours of Salisbury Cathedral.

v+378 ff.

1302–3. GOEZE'S *CONTINUATION OF THE ENLARGED DEFENCE*

'Continuation of the Enlarged Defence of the Complutensian Greek New Testament . . . By John Melchior Goeze, Hamburgh, 1769. Translated from the German by William Alleyn Evanson, M.A., Lecturer of St. Luke's, Old Street, London', 1830–1, consisting of a translation of *Fortsetzung der ausfuhrlicheren Vertheidigung*, 1769. Dedicated to Thomas Burgess, Bishop of Salisbury.

ii+183 and x+186 ff.

1304. LÜDERWALD ON I JOHN V. 7

'Historico-Critical Observations on the celebrated verse 1 John v. 7, by John Balthazar Lüderwald, Doctor of Divinity, Superintendent of the Grand Duchy of Brunswick and Pastor primarius of Vortsfelde. Brunswick, 1767. Translated from the original German by William Alleyn Evanson, M.A., Lecturer of St. Luke's, Old Street, London', 1832, consisting of a translation of *Historische und theologische anmerkungen über die stelle I Joh. v. 7*, 1767. Dedicated to Thomas Burgess, Bishop of Salisbury.

iii+185 ff.

1305. GOEZE'S *DEFENCE OF THE COMPLUTENSIAN BIBLE*

'Defence of the Complutensian Bible, particularly the New Testament, against the Accusations of Wetsten and Semler, by John Melchior Goeze, of Hamburgh . . . 1765. Translated from the Original German by the Revd. William Alleyn Evanson, M.A., Lecturer of St. Luke's, Old Street, London', 1829, consisting of a translation of *Vertheidigung der Complutischen Bibel . . ., 1765*. Dedicated [to Thomas Burgess], Bishop of Salisbury.

iv+255 pp.

1306–7. Not allotted.

1308. ORDINANCES FOR ECCLESIASTICAL COURTS

Ordinances and statutes of Archbishops Whitgift and Laud for the ecclesiastical courts of the Archbishops of Canterbury, copied from originals in the State Paper Office and certified by Sir Joseph Ayloffe, A. C. Ducarel, and Thomas Astle, 16 December 1767.

Latin.

Statuta sive Ordinationes Iohannis Whitgift, Cant[uariensis] Archiepiscopi, Croydon, 28 July 1587. *Concilia*, iv, 328–34 (pp. 1–36).

Statuta sive Ordinationes Wilielmi Laud, Cant[uariensis] Archiepiscopi, Lambeth, 29 March 1636. *C.S.P. Dom., 1635–6*, 336 (pp. 43–56).

xii+68 pp.

1309. UNIVERSITY OF GENEVA

'A concise account of the Public Establishments for Education at Geneva, Switzerland', [by Alexander John Gaspard] Marcet, M.D., physician of Guy's Hospital, 1814. Revised and augmented to January 1823 by the Revd. J. S. Pons of Sipson, Hounslow Heath.

The account covers elementary education and advanced studies at the University of Geneva. There are brief notes on the Professors of Divinity, whose names are indexed, at pp. 26–8.

Bookplate of Archbishop Howley.

iii+41 pp.

1310. LIST OF THE REGISTERS OF THE PREROGATIVE COURT OF CANTERBURY

A chronological list of the registers of wills proved in the Prerogative Court of Canterbury, made for Richard Argall, arm., Registrar, 1584, with additions to 1588.

The name of each register is stated and its date of commencement. The list begins with the March Register, 1401, but another hand has added the Rous Register, 1384. The margins contain the arms in colour of the Archbishops of Canterbury from Arundel to Whitgift.

A note on f. 5^{v} states that Argall died on 16 October 1588 and was succeeded by William Woodhall, arm.

Bound in vellum. Bookplate of John Towneley. Given by Richard Mant, subsequently Bishop of Down and Connor, 1818.

i+7 ff.

1311. Not allotted.

1312. CORONATION SERVICE OF GEORGE IV

A copy of the order of service for the coronation of George III and Queen Charlotte, 22 September 1761, altered in the hand of Archbishop Manners Sutton for the coronation of George IV, 19 July 1821. The order of service was printed from this manuscript.

viii+103 ff.

1313–48. Not allotted.

1349–50. PAPERS OF ARCHBISHOP SECKER

Sermons, notes, and some copies of letters in the hand of Archbishop Secker unless otherwise stated.

Given by Mrs. Cuyler Rose, wife of the Revd. Hugh James Rose, 1843.

1349. SECKER PAPERS

Abstract of Thomas Comber's *Scholastical history of the primitive and general use of liturgies in the Christian Church*, 1690. Made by Secker in 1749 (pp. 2–92).

Farewell sermon on the text Philippians 1, v. 27: Only let your conversation be as [it] becometh the gospel of Christ. Preached at Ryton, Co. Durham, where Secker was rector, 25 March 1733 (pp. 97–125).

Meditations on scriptural texts. That on Proverbs 3, v. 27 is noted as preached '12 times from 1740 to 1755' (p. 146). Endorsed on p. 150 by Secker 'To be burnt' (pp. 135–53).

Address delivered after a sermon on the text Romans 10, v. 10, at Wheatley, Oxon., 16 October 1757 (pp. 155–8).

Speech apparently delivered by Secker at the third reading in the House of Lords of a Bill for Disarming the Highlands (21 George II) [11 May 1748]. The speech, which is annotated perhaps for publication, proposed an amendment concerning the letters of orders of ministers of the Episcopal Church in Scotland registered before 1 September 1746. The text bears little resemblance to the report in *Parliamentary History*, xiv, 270–6. Bound in wrong order (pp. 159–66).

Copy of a letter from Secker [to Zachary Pearce], Bishop of Rochester, from Lambeth, 15 October 1763, dissuading him from resignation and complaining that the Crown neglected to consult the Clergy in the disposal of bishoprics (p. 167).

Copy of a letter from the same to the same, from Lambeth, 17 October 1763, discussing the method of resignation for Bishops and Archbishops, and urging Pearce not to resign (pp. 169–71).

Letter from Zachary [Pearce], Bishop of Rochester, to Secker, from Bromley, 17 October 1763, reporting a conversation with the Earl of Bath who stated that the Great Person [i.e. the King] was anxious to consult the Clergy in the appointment of Bishops. Gives an account of his translation from Bangor to Rochester (pp. 173–5).

Letter from Miss C[atherine] Talbot to the Revd. [Charles] Poyntz, from St. Paul's Deanery, 22 December 1757, urging him to wear the proper clerical costume when in London, and regretting its disuse (pp. 181–3).

vi+184 pp.

1350. SECKER PAPERS

Sermon on Ridicule on the text 2 Peter 3, v. 3: Knowing this first, that there shall come in the last days scoffers walking after their own lusts (ff. 2–7).

Draft charge or address to the clergy. Much corrected and not identified with any published charge (ff. 14–22).

Meditation or part of a sermon on the text Acts 4, v. 33: And with great power gave the Apostles witness of the Resurrection of the Lord Jesus (ff. 23–5).

[1350 *cont.***]**

Abstract of *An Enquiry into the rationale of christianity*. Printed but not published. A note by Secker says of this work that it was 'shown me by Dr. Jortin Jan. 1758. He knows the Author, who is a Xn sui generis, a Layman, & a serious & moral man.' The abstract is interspersed with observations in brackets by Secker (ff. 29–54).

Unfinished dissertation on Vows, חרם, Canaanites, Gibeonites (ff. 55–66).

ii+72 ff.

1351. EXTRACTS FROM ARCHIEPISCOPAL REGISTERS

Extracts by Andrew Coltee Ducarel, 'Curiae de Arc[ubus] Advocat[o]', from the registers of the Archbishops of Canterbury concerning Croydon, Surrey, and Doctors Commons. Entries relating to the first of these are marked with the letter 'C', and to the remainder with a cross. From the time of Grindal, references to legal officers are separately noted.

Bookplate of A. C. Ducarel. Old shelfmark 'B.32'. A note in the front states that the manuscript was bought at the auction of Ducarel's library, April 1786 [perhaps item 1455]. See also MS. 1358.

i+125 ff.

1352. Not allotted.

1353. COLLATIONS OF THE OLD TESTAMENT

Collations in an unidentified hand of Codex Alexandrinus, ff. 1–36, with the edition of 1816 by Henry Hervey Baber, 1817.

i+45 ff., mostly blank.

1354. STATUTES OF GUILDFORD HOSPITAL

The Statutes of the Hospital of the Blessed Trinity at Guildford, Surrey, 17 August 1629, transcribed by Charles Coker, junior, 1770. They are followed by details of the elections of Masters of the Hospital to 1769. There is an index and list of Masters at ff. 80v–81v. See also Lambeth MS. 727. The Statutes were printed by P. G. Palmer in 1927.

i+82 ff.

1355. HOSPITALS OF ST. JOHN THE BAPTIST, NORTHGATE, CANTERBURY, AND ST. NICHOLAS, HARBLEDOWN

Transcripts of statutes and other documents concerning the Hospitals of St. John the Baptist, Northgate, Canterbury, and St. Nicholas, Harbledown, 1711. They comprise the following items:

Statutes of Archbishop Parker, 15 September 1560, with additions made 20 August 1565 and 24 May 1574 (ff. 1v–11).

Decree and letter of Archbishop Whitgift forbidding the admission of children to the Hospitals, 20 May 1591, with a note of other orders concerning the same (ff. 12–13^{v}).

Decrees of Archbishop Abbot, 17 August 1618 (ff. 15–19).

Account of the deprivation of one Raworth, August [1630] (f. 19^{v}).

Commission from Archbishop Laud for appointing to places in the Hospitals, 28 February 1635, and orders concerning the distribution of firewood and the appropriation of money for repairs, 14 August 1635 (ff. 20–1).

Order of Archbishop Sheldon regulating the marriage of inmates, 19 February 1664 (f. 22^{r-v}).

Decrees of Archbishop Sancroft, 4 March 1687 (ff. 24–27^{v}).

Printed with the exception of items 4–5 in *Bibl. Topog. Brit.*, i, 214–25.

On the front cover 'No. 306'. Some pencil notes by S. W. Kershaw.

i+91 ff.

1356. STATUTES OF CANTERBURY CATHEDRAL

Copy of Statutes and Injunctions for the Cathedral and Metropolitical Church of Christ, Canterbury, containing the following items:

Statuta drawn up, but not confirmed, by Henry VIII, [8 April 1541]. *Latin*. *C.L.P. For. & Dom.* xvi, app. 4 (pp. 1–54).

Injunctions issued by Archbishop Parker at his metropolitical and ordinary visitation, 7 October 1573. *Latin*. Strype, *Parker*, ed. 1821, iii, 309–16 (pp. 56–70).

Statuta confirmed by Charles I, 1636. *Latin*. Laud, *Works*, v, pt. II, 506–44 (pp. 72–154).

Letter from Charles I to the Dean and Chapter of Canterbury, 3 January 1637. *Latin*. Printed, ib., 544–5 (pp. 155–8).

Letter from Archbishop Laud to the same, 26 January 1637. Printed, ib., vi, 484 (pp. 159–60).

See also MS. 1357.

iv+232 ff.

1357. STATUTES OF CANTERBURY CATHEDRAL

Copy of the Statutes confirmed by Charles I, 1636, with conspectus erratorum by Archbishop Laud. *Latin*. Printed, without the conspectus, Laud, *Works*, v, pt. II, 506–44 (pp. 1–152).

Letter from Charles I to the Dean and Chapter of Canterbury, 3 January 1637. *Latin*. Printed, ib., 544–5 (pp. 153–7).

Letter from Archbishop Laud to the same, 26 January 1637. Printed, ib., vi, 484 (pp. 158–60).

[1357 *cont.*]

Belonged to William Ayerst, 1724, and Richard Sutton, 1765, successively Canons of the third prebend at Canterbury. See also MS. 1356.

viii+164 pp.

1358. EXTRACTS FROM THE REGISTER OF ARCHBISHOP PECKHAM

Extracts by Andrew Coltee Ducarel from the Register of Archbishop Peckham, transcribed in the order in which the entries appear in the register, 1755.

Bookplate of A. C. Ducarel. Old shelfmark 'B.31'. A note in the front states that the manuscript was bought at the auction of Ducarel's library [April 1786, where probably item 1456]. See also MS. 1351.

v+325 ff.

1359. EXTRACTS FROM ARCHIEPISCOPAL REGISTERS

Extracts from registers of Archbishops of Canterbury, compiled after 1737. Extracts are taken from the Registers of Archbishops Sudbury (ff. 1–13^{v}), Courtenay (ff. 14–45^{v}), Arundel (ff. 46–99^{v}), Chichele (ff. 105–52), Stafford and Kemp (ff. 155–68^{v}), and Bourchier (ff. 169–78^{v}).

Bookplates of Osmund Beauvoir [1720–89], and the Rt. Hon. Henry Hobhouse. Old shelfmarks or numbers '99' and 'J.5'. Acquired after 1828.

v+183 ff.

1360. THEOLOGY

Three theological treatises. The author is not identified, but appears to have been well acquainted with the scientific developments of the time, including the work of John Wilkins and Robert Boyle. The treatises appear to have been composed in and after 1660.

'A sober view of Dr. Twisse's his Considerations, with a compleat Disquisition of Dr. Hammond's Letter to Dr. Sanderson, and a Prospect of all their Opinions Concerning God's Decrees.' Hammond's *A pacifick discourse of God's Grace and decrees*, here referred to, was published in 1660. There are marginal criticisms in another hand (ff. 1–120).

'Seeds of Eternity or the Nature of the Soul in which Everlasting Powers are Prepared' (ff. 134–44).

'The Kingdom of God.' This work is a harmony of the natural and spiritual worlds, and contains a long discussion of the physical properties of the world. A version of the first two chapters occurs at ff. 124–8 (ff. 148–366).

The author of the marginalia in the first item has written on f. i 'Why is this soe long detaind in a dark manuscript, that if printed would be a Light to the World and a Uniuersal Blessing.'

Bound in vellum.

iii+473 ff.

1361. LAMBETH PALACE AND LIABILITY FOR POOR RATES

'The Proceedings at Large in a Cause between His Grace Frederick, Lord Archbishop of Canterbury, Plaintiff, against John Suter, Defendant, which was Tryed in the Court of Common Pleas in Westminster Hall by a Special Jury, before The Right Honourable Sir William De Grey, Knight, Lord Chief Justice, upon a Feigned Issue agreed on by the parties, on Friday December the 6th 1776. Faithfully transcribed from the Short hand taken by me William Blanchard, No. 4 Dean Street, Fetter Lane.'

The trial concerned the liability of Lambeth Palace for payment of poor rates, and was decided in favour of the Archbishop. The proceedings are printed *in extenso* in Ducarel, *History and Antiquities of the Archiepiscopal Palace of Lambeth*, 1785, 89–132.

Given in 1888.

iv+114 ff.

1362. BIBLIA

Bound in two volumes. ff. iv+262+iii (vol. 1); ff. ii+284+iii (vol. 2). 13th century. Size 159×109 mm. Given to the church of Bredgar, Kent, in 1474, and still there in 1805 when it was rebound at the request of N. Nisbett, Rector of Tunstall. For a fuller description of the manuscript see N. R. Ker, *Medieval Manuscripts in British Libraries, i: London*, 1968.

1363. Not allotted.

1364. BIBLIA

ff. ii+601+iv. 13th century. Size 155×105 mm.

Written in France. Belonged to Jean Poylevet of Limoges in 1603.

See MS. 1362 for reference to a fuller description of this manuscript.

1365. PRIVATE DEVOTIONS

Private Devotions of John Gauden, later Bishop of Worcester, composed before 1660 and dedicated to 'my worthy Frend John Earle, Esquire'. The signature to the dedication is apparently autograph, but the remainder of the manuscript is not in Gauden's hand. The manuscript is discussed

[1365 *cont.*]

in Christopher Wordsworth, *King Charles the First, the author of Icon Basilike* . . ., 1828, 44 seq.

Signature of Benjamin Heywood Bright on p. xi.

Given by Benjamin Heywood Bright before 1828.

xvi+216 pp.

1366. GOSPELS (IN ENGLISH)

ff. ii+200+ii. 14th–15th century. Size 135×98 mm. Written in England. 'The Gift of Granville Sharp Esq. to ye Archbishop of Canterbury. 1815.'

See MS. 1362 for reference to a fuller description of this manuscript.

1367. PRAYERS

Anonymous prayers for use at Communion service, 18th century.

i+48 ff.

1368–9. Not allotted.

1370. GOSPELS OF MACDURNAN

See M. R. James, *Descriptive Catalogue of the Manuscripts in the Library of Lambeth Palace*, 1932, 843.

1371. MISCELLANEOUS PAPERS, 17TH CENTURY

A collection of treatises on legal and heraldic matters.

'A particular demonstration or recitall of Causes and Actions of Ecclesiasticall Conizance by reason of Canons, Constitutions Provinciall and Statutes of this land.' Undated and incomplete (ff. 1–13).

Collection of cases tried in the Star Chamber, Michaelmas and Hilary Terms 1612–13. A table of contents, referring to seventeen cases, is at f. 82 (ff. 26–82).

A treatise of nobility, perhaps by William Camden, Clarenceux King-of-Arms, probably occasioned by disputed claims to the barony of Abergavenny, 1598. An index (f. 111) to the many pedigrees quoted has been added (ff. 83–111).

Lists of knights made by the Earl of Essex at Rouen, 1591; Cadiz, [1596]; the Azores, [1597]; in Ireland, 1599, and by James I 'att his cominge into England', 1603 (ff. 113–14).

Belonged to Henry Powle (1630–92), Master of the Rolls. Bookplate of A. C. Ducarel and the date 1739. Old shelfmarks A.26 (crossed out) and C. (3 crossed out) 27 inside, and I.B.3 on the spine. Apparently item 1438 in the Ducarel sale, April 1786. Purchased from G. H. Last, bookseller, 1921.

v+116 ff.

1372. HISTORICAL AND DEVOTIONAL COLLECTIONS, 17TH CENTURY

A collection of historical and theological papers probably made by Thomas Brudenell, 1st Earl of Cardigan (1661). It contains the following items:

Contemporary copy of an address to both Houses of Parliament by Cardinal Pole, [28 November 1554], differing in some particulars from the version printed in Foxe, *Acts and Monuments*, bk. X (ff. 1–4^{v}).

Extract in English apparently from Luis de Granada, *A Memorial of a Christian Life*. *Beg.* It was a Custome amongst ye holly men; *Ends* whersoer there's true humillity there's alwaies muche Charitye (ff. 8–17^{v}).

Translation into English of Pedro de Ribadeneira, *De Tribulationibus*, bk. I, chaps. I–XII (incomplete) (ff. 20–48^{v}).

Accounts by John Fisher [or Percy], a Jesuit controversialist, of three conferences between himself and Francis White, Bishop of Ely (1631), and William Laud, Bishop of London, [1622]. The conferences were instigated by James I after Fisher's conversion of Mary, Countess of Buckingham, mother of the Duke of Buckingham, to Catholicism, and many copies of his account of the proceedings were issued by Fisher.

The items are as follows:

(*a*) 'A coppie of that short written paper which was the occasion of the conference betwixt D. White and me' (ff. 51–52^{v}).
(*b*) 'A relation of what passed in the first conference betwixt D. White and mee' (ff. 53–8).
(*c*) 'A relation of the seconde conference with Dotr Whyte at which was present his Mai[esty] . . .' (ff. 58^{v}–61^{v}).
(*d*) 'A briefe relatione of what passed in a thirde priuate conference betweene a Bp. and me . . .' (ff. 61^{v}–62^{v}).

With the exception of (*c*), the accounts were printed in *True relation of sundry Conferences . . . between certaine Protestant Doctours and a Jesuite called M. Fisher*, by A. C., 1626, and also in Laud's *Works*, ii, xix–xl (ff. 51–62^{v}).

Treatise entitled 'Christianae Fidelitatis Idea iuxta Primitivae Ecclesiae Prototypon.' *Latin* (ff. 63–70).

Life of John Fisher, Bishop of Rochester, entitled 'A Treatise conteyning the manner of life and death of ye most holly prelate and constant Martir of Christ, John Fisher, Bishopp of Rochester and Cardinall of ye holly church of Rome.'

This account was printed under the title *The life and death of that renowned John Fisher, Bishop of Rochester . . .*, by Thomas Bailey, 1655. The manuscript, of which this is a copy, was probably written about 1576, and has been attributed to John Young, President of Pembroke College, Cambridge, and to Thomas Watson, Bishop of Lincoln. A critical edition is in *Analecta Bollandiana*, x and xii, ed. F. Van Ortroy (ff. 72–115^{v}).

Bound in calf with shield of arms stamped on front and back. The arms are (1) Brudenell; (2) Entwistle; (3) Tayllard; (4) Reynes. The stamp

[1372 *cont.***]**

probably belonged to Thomas Brudenell, 1st Earl of Cardigan. The manuscript also belonged to Dr. Henry Smith.

Given by John William Horsley, Vicar of Detling, 1920.

i+117 ff.

1373. LETTERS AND PAPERS, 18TH CENTURY

Correspondence and papers of Benjamin Franklin, John Wesley, Archbishop Secker, David Wilkins, and others.

1. Letter from Benjamin Franklin to Granville Sharp, from Philadelphia, 30 May 1786, sending a copy of a proposed Book of Common Prayer, which he is doubtful will be accepted by the Convention (f. 1).

Letters to Thomas Secker, Bishop of Oxford and subsequently Archbishop of Canterbury, describing the last illness of Joseph Butler, Bishop of Durham, June 1752. There are three letters from [Martin Benson, Bishop of Gloucester] (ff. 3–9^{v}), and eight from Nathaniel Forster, chaplain to Bishop Butler (ff. 10–25). The correspondence is printed in full in Thomas Bartlett, *Memoirs of Bishop Butler*, 1839, 203–19 (ff. 3–25).

Remarks by Archbishop Secker on the interpretation of the codicils to his wills dated 8 April 1763 and 25 October 1765, placing his papers in Lambeth Palace Library (ff. 26–9).

Letter from E[lizabeth], wife of Morton Eden, later 1st Baron Henley, to Lady Bridget Tollemache, from Vienna, 3 May 1795, referring to a visit from the Queen to Lady Tollemache (f. 31). The letter was enclosed in a band endorsed in the hand of Archbishop Moore, referring to his son Robert (f. 33).

Letter from Archbishop Wake to [Israel Antoine] Aufrere, Minister at the Savoy Church, 20 March 1719, concerning a papist convert (f. 34).

Letter from John Wesley to [Henry] Rimius, from Reading, 24 October 1755, referring to the publication of Moravian hymns in England. Also a note by Rimius on the same subject. Printed *Letters of John Wesley*, ed. J. Telford, 1931, iii, 149 (f. 37).

2. Correspondence of David Wilkins, Lambeth Librarian, 1713–45. The correspondents are as follows:

J[ohn] Hudson, Principal of St. Mary Hall, Oxford, 30 May 1713, discussing various works of learning, the tax on paper, and forthcoming publications (f. 38).

[Jean Pierre] Rigord, French antiquary, from Paris, 1 September 1716, encouraging him in his Egyptian and Coptic studies. *French* (f. 40).

Arthur Bedford, from St. Paul's churchyard, 21 May 1724, seeking Wilkins's support in a dispute with the S.P.C.K. about the retention of accents in an edition of the New Testament in Arabic (f. 43).

[Matthew] Bagger, from London, 3 March 1725, about an index. *Latin* (f. 44).

Francis Hare, later Bishop of Chichester, 19 March 1726, about an edition of Prideaux's *Marmora Oxoniensia* intended by Wilkins. Supposes the Archbishop of York has stopped Wilkins's pension because 'you have spoken of him with too much freedom' (f. 46).

John Potter, Bishop of Oxford and subsequently Archbishop of Canterbury, from Cuddesdon, Oxon., 30 December 1725, mentioning his examination with [John] Mill of the inscriptions in *Marmora Oxoniensia* for a collection of inscriptions by Theodore John George Graevius. A new edition would be better printed in Oxford than London (f. 48).

Sir Thomas Hanmer, 4th Bt., from London, 11 February 1727, concerning property at Fressingfield, Suff. (f. 50).

John Hough, Bishop of Worcester, from Hartlebury, Worcs., 4 July 1726, informing him that the papers of his predecessor William Lloyd are in the hands of his widow who lives in Charterhouse yard (f. 52).

John Mather, President of Corpus Christi College, Oxford, and Vice-Chancellor, from Oxford, 8 July 1726, asking on behalf of the Delegates of the Press for further information about a new edition [of *Marmora Oxoniensia*] intended by Wilkins (f. 54).

A further letter about the same [from Oxford], 15 August 1726 (f. 56).

Archbishop Wake, 9 February 1727, stating that he has received two copies of a book by [Francis] Peck (f. 58).

Edmund Gibson, Bishop of London, 2 March 1727, about the appointment of a chaplain to 'the Factory' (f. 60).

David Wilkins to —, from Canterbury, 4 April 1727, stating that his wife will not let him leave her 'not even for one or two days' to visit Leeds Castle. Will visit 290 churches as Archdeacon of Suffolk (f. 62).

Matthew Bagger, from London, 23 May 1727, informing him that the Bishop of London has sent him as a missionary to Jamaica, and asking for certain books. *Latin* (f. 64).

Archbishop Wake, 31 October 1727, on matters of business. His gout better (f. 65).

Edward Chandler, Bishop of Coventry and Lichfield and subsequently Bishop of Durham, 2 November 1727, giving his opinion that 'your Saxon Orosius' would find few readers (f. 67).

Archbishop Wake, 2 December 1727, declaring his pleasure at the recovery of the Dean of Canterbury (f. 69).

Same, from Lambeth, 23 January 1728, hoping that the choice of a new Prolocutor will not occasion division (f. 71).

Same, 1 February 1728, about Wilkins's Coptic studies. [Daniel] Waterland wishes to see a manuscript of Wyclif in Lambeth Palace Library (f. 73).

Same, 16 March 1728. His recovery from illness (f. 75).

Edward Chandler, Bishop of Coventry and Lichfield and subsequently of Durham, 9 May 1728, thanking him for an invitation to Canterbury to himself and his wife, 'but as I never carry about with me a sister or wife,

[1373 *cont.***]**

when I visit my own Diocese, so to be sure I shall not incommode his Grace with my luggage when I travel into His' (f. 77).

Same, 6 June 1728. Thanks for hospitality (f. 79).

Archbishop Wake, 16 November 1728 (f. 80).

Same, 3 February 1729, giving advice about a petition to Parliament concerning [the enclosure of Aldham and Bayne Commons at] Hadleigh, Suff. (f. 82).

Robert Clavering, Bishop of Llandaff and subsequently of Peterborough, from Westminster, 8 February 1729, advising haste in presenting his petition to Parliament [about Hadleigh enclosure] (f. 84).

Edward Waddington, Bishop of Chichester, from Westminster, 11 February 1729, promising help in 'a work of Charity' (f. 86).

Archbishop Wake, 1 March 1729, stating that he has recommended all the Bishops to support Wilkins's Bill in Parliament [for Hadleigh enclosure] (f. 88).

Edward Waddington, Bishop of Chichester, from Eton, Bucks., 10 December 1729, about Wilkins's application in favour of Mr. Clubb (f. 90).

David Wilkins to Edward Chandler, Bishop of Durham, from Hadleigh, Suff., 6 November 1730, presenting a copy of his Coptic Pentateuch. *Latin draft* (f. 92).

Archbishop Wake, from Lambeth, 15 December 1730, hoping the success of his Coptic Pentateuch will encourage booksellers to publish his grammar and dictionary (f. 94).

Edward Chandler, Bishop of Durham, from Golden Square, 23 January 1731, thanking him for Coptic Pentateuch (f. 96).

Edward Waddington, Bishop of Chichester, from Chichester, 18 June 1731, sending a copy of the index of one of his registers, but doubting if any at Chichester can transcribe the originals (f. 98).

Same, from Chichester, 13 August 1731, about registers (f. 100).

Francis Hare, Bishop of St. Asaph and subsequently of Chichester, 23 October 1731, declining to appoint as domestic chaplain the nephew of his predecessor (f. 101).

Thomas Tanner, Bishop of St. Asaph, from Oxford, 28 April 1732, expressing his pleasure that Wake has entrusted publication of the Councils [*Concilia*] to Wilkins. Suggestions for the co-operation of the Irish clergy and promises of his own help (f. 103).

Francis Hare, Bishop of St. Asaph and subsequently of Chichester, 29 April 1732, informing him of the Bishop of Exeter's desire to assist 'your laborious undertaking' (f. 105).

Elias Sydall, Bishop of Gloucester, from St. James's Street, 6 May 1732, thanking him for assisting Mr. Ray (f. 107).

John Sterne, Bishop of Clogher, 26 January 1734, sending information from a manuscript and mentioning a new edition of Sir James Ware's *De Praesulibus Hiberniae* by [Walter] Harris (f. 109).

Archbishop Potter, 30 May 1738. Compliments (f. 111).

M[argaret] Wilkins to her brother Thomas, 6th Baron Fairfax of Cameron, from Hadleigh, Suff., 25 September 1739, with condolences on the death of 'our Dear sister'. Urges him to marry lest the title become extinct, and mentions other deaths in the family (f. 113).

John Wynne, Bishop of Bath and Wells, from Wells, 31 October 1739, doubting if the diocesan clergy can assist 'the work you have in hand', but recommending the libraries of Sir William Wyndham and Thomas Carew of Crocombe, and the collections of the late Dr. [Edmund] Archer (f. 115).

Margaret Hamilton to her godmother, Mrs. Wilkins, 21 December 1740, describing the distress caused by her father's bankruptcy, and asking for assistance (f. 116).

Thomas Hill, from Buxhall, Suff., 13 April 1741, concerning the disputed appointment of an overseer (f. 118).

Mrs. M. Clarke, from Hadleigh, Suff., 20 June 1741, concerning the renewal of the lease of a manor granted to her late uncle by the Dean and Chapter [of Canterbury] (f. 120).

Samuel Pegge, antiquary, from Godmersham, Kent, 23 June 1742, sending him a book, and asking for the loan of a volume of Wilkins's edition of Selden (f. 122).

Edward Watkinson, clerk, 7 June 1743, thanking him for favours (f. 124).

Samuel Norris, from Canterbury, 19 January 1744, concerning the Chapter dividend and various estate matters (f. 126).

Richard Widmore, from Westminster, 5 June 1744, on estate business (f. 127).

Thomas Wallace, from Whatfield, Suff., January 1745, concerning the insolence of a servant to Mrs. Ruffle of Whatfield Hall (f. 129).

Archbishop Wake, n.d., promising satisfaction on his return to Lambeth (f. 131).

David Wilkins to his sister-in-law, n.d., with apologies for not paying his respects (f. 133).

3. 'The Report of a Committee of the Board of Bishops to a General Meeting of the Bishops held at Lambeth Palace, February 25th 1799, respecting the Land Tax Assessed upon Church Property under Lease', with a paper of calculations referred to in the report. The committee approves the redemption of Land Tax on church property and makes proposals for its implementation. It is noted that the report was approved and recommended for transmission to Deans and Chapters. *Copy* (ff. 135–8).

Order of Prince George of Denmark, Lord High Admiral, that John Lock, Richard Gibbons, and James Hewet, employed 'in working in a Ferry boat at Lambeth', be not impressed in the Navy, 11 January 1704. On the dorse are physical descriptions of Lock, Gibbons, and Hewet. Signed and sealed.

Endorsed '78' and stamped '1547' (ff. 139–40).

140 ff.

1374–88. BURDETT-COUTTS PAPERS

Papers of Angela Georgina Burdett-Coutts (1814–1906), Baroness Burdett-Coutts of Highgate and Brookfield (1871). The papers principally concern the development of the colonial church and its legal status in relation to the Church of England. Baroness Burdett-Coutts endowed the sees of Capetown and Adelaide in 1847 as sees dependent on the Church of England (1384), but in consequence of the dispute between Robert Gray, Bishop of Capetown, and John William Colenso, Bishop of Natal, she feared that the colonial church might claim independence of the Church of England. Many of the papers are concerned with her petition to Queen Victoria on this matter, and an attempt to assert the dependence of the colonial church by legislative action in Parliament in 1865–6. In other volumes are papers relating to her interest in the colonial church elsewhere in Africa and Australia, and in Canada, the West Indies, India, Hong Kong, and Labuan and Sarawak (1385–6). A small quantity of papers concern her interest in education, particularly in the spread of the school grouping system (1387), and various charitable works in Carlisle, London, and Great Yarmouth (1388).

The papers were given to the Library by the Revd. W. H. G. Twining, Vicar of St. Stephen's, Rochester Row, 1923.

1374. BURDETT-COUTTS PAPERS

Ecclesiastical correspondence of Baroness Burdett-Coutts, 1864–73. The correspondents are as follows:

Charles Thomas Longley, Archbishop of Canterbury, 1865–8. Also a letter to him from Angela Georgina Burdett-Coutts, 12 July 1865. *Printed* (f. 17) (ff. 1–58).

William Thomson, Archbishop of York, 1865–8. Also a letter from John Postlethwaite, Bishop designate of New Westminster, British Columbia, 10 March 1866 (f. 69) (ff. 59–77).

Archibald Campbell Tait, Archbishop of Canterbury, 1865–73. Also a copy of a testimonial for the Revd. W. L. Collett (f. 91), and a letter from Sir George Grey to Tait, 5 May 1866 (f. 135) (ff. 78–169).

Samuel Wilberforce, Bishop of Oxford and (1869) Winchester, 1864–6, including a printed appeal for a mission to the Sandwich Islands, [1864] (f. 187) (ff. 170–217).

217 ff.

1375. BURDETT-COUTTS PAPERS

Correspondence of Baroness Burdett-Coutts mainly with Bishops, 1864–8. The correspondents are as follows.

Henry Phillpotts, Bishop of Exeter, 1864–7. Most of the letters are written in the hand of his daughter Sybella. The enclosures consist of letters from Reginald H. Barnes, Prebendary of Exeter, 4 December [1864] (f. 5), and from Phillpotts to John Abel Smith, M.P., 14 March 1866 (f. 18); copies of letters from Phillpotts to S. H. Walpole, 20 March 1866 (f. 22), and to the Bishop of Oxford, 22 and 26 March (ff. 41–2) (ff. 1–42).

Sybella Du Boulay, daughter of the preceding, 1864–7. The enclosures consist of letters from Connie and Jane Phillpotts, n.d. (ff. 64–6), and copies of letters from Samuel Wilberforce, Bishop of Oxford, to the Bishop of Exeter, 24 March 1866 (f. 92) and n.d. (f. 100) (ff. 43–162).

Letters from Bishops, mainly in reply to a copy circulated to them of a letter from Baroness Burdett-Coutts to the Bishop of Capetown, 1866–8. The names of the writers will be found in the index.

240 ff.

1376–7. BURDETT-COUTTS PAPERS

Correspondence of Baroness Burdett-Coutts with Sir Travers Twiss, Regius Professor of Civil Law at Oxford University, and legal adviser on ecclesiastical matters to the Baroness, 1865–8.

1376. BURDETT-COUTTS PAPERS

Correspondence, 1865–February 1866.

The enclosures consist of a letter from Archibald Campbell Tait, Bishop of London, 28 July 1865 (f. 26); letter from William James Farrer, solicitor, 26 February 1866 (f. 177), and a copy of a letter from Farrer of the same date [to *The Morning Post*] (f. 179).

180 ff.

1377. BURDETT-COUTTS PAPERS

Correspondence, March 1866–8.

The enclosures consist of a letter from William James Farrer, solicitor, 8 June 1866 (f. 82); newspaper cutting of a letter to *The Times* from 'A Hertfordshire Incumbent', 18 February [1866], concerning colonial churches and the royal supremacy (f. 110); *Fundamental provisions and regulations for the government of the United Church of England and Ireland within the diocese of Adelaide in South Australia*, 9 October 1855 (f. 111); memorandum on the financial state of the diocese of Adelaide, entitled *A self-supporting Diocese*, by Augustus Short, Bishop of Adelaide, 14 July 1866 (f. 115); letter from Aubrey George Spencer, Bishop of Jamaica, 14 November 1865 (f. 117); letter from William Hale Hale, Archdeacon of London and Master of the Charterhouse, 27 February 1867 (f. 125); letter from Edward George Earle Lytton Bulwer-Lytton, 1st Baron Lytton, 21 February 1867 (f. 131); letter from Marie Twiss, wife of Sir Travers Twiss, 2 March 1867 (f. 138).

212 ff.

1378. BURDETT-COUTTS PAPERS

Correspondence of Baroness Burdett-Coutts with William James Farrer, solicitor and legal adviser, 1859–73.

[1378 *cont.***]**

The enclosures consist of a copy of a letter from the Revd. Ernest Hawkins, secretary to the S.P.G., 11 February 1859 (f. 6); copy of a letter from the Revd. W. T. Bullock, secretary to the S.P.G., to Farrer, 24 November 1865 (f. 50); copy of a letter from John Abel Smith to George Hills, Bishop of British Columbia, 31 October 1865 (f. 51); letter from Edward Cardwell, Colonial Secretary, to Farrer, 21 December 1865 (f. 56); copy of a letter from the Revd. W. T. Bullock, secretary to the S.P.G., to Farrer, 13 January 1866 (f. 63); letter from the Revd. Ernest Hawkins, secretary to the Colonial Bishoprics Council, to Farrer, 5 March 1866 (f. 80), and a copy of a letter from the same to the same, 9 March 1866 (f. 84); copy of a letter from Farrer to the Revd. Ernest Hawkins, 10 March 1866 (f. 89); copy of a letter from the same [to the Revd. W. T. Bullock], secretary to the S.P.G., 30 July 1866 (f. 114); copy of a letter from Angela Georgina Burdett-Coutts to Edward George Geoffrey Smith Stanley, 14th Earl of Derby, 22 January 1868 (f. 141); copy of correspondence between E. M. Syfret, chairman of the committee of the Church of England Defence Association, and Thomas Earle Welby, Bishop of St. Helena, May–June 1873 (ff. 158–61); copy of a letter from Henry Barclay to Farrer, 13 June 1873 (f. 164).

166 ff.

1379. BURDETT-COUTTS PAPERS

Correspondence of Baroness Burdett-Coutts mainly with politicians, 1853–68. The correspondents are as follows:

John Barlow, Rector of Little Bowden, Northants., and secretary to the Royal Institution, and his wife Cecilia Anne Barlow, 1853–7 (ff. 1–60).

Ralph Barnes, Vicar of Ardington, Berks., and author of *Remarks on the judgement in the case of the Bishop of Natal*, 1865–6. Enclosures are a flysheet for the laying of the foundation stone of All Saints, Babbacombe, Devon, [1860] (f. 75), and letters from Charles John Ellicott, Bishop of Gloucester and Bristol, 1866 (f. 95), and Herman Merivale, Under-Secretary for India, 1866 (f. 97). Also included are two letters from Reginald H. Barnes, Prebendary of Exeter, 1866 (ff. 91–4) (ff. 61–98).

Edward Cardwell, later Viscount Cardwell of Ellerbeck, Colonial Secretary, 1865–6. Included is a letter from Cardwell to John Abel Smith, 1866 (f. 109) (ff. 99–127).

William Ewart Gladstone, subsequently Prime Minister, 1865–8 (ff. 128–62).

W. A. Newman, Dean of Capetown, 1857–8. Enclosed is a letter from Guy Gething, subsequently minister of Beaufort, diocese of Capetown, to Angela Georgina Burdett-Coutts, 1857 (f. 180) (ff. 163–87).

John Abel Smith, M.P., 1865–6 (ff. 188–241).

Edward George Geoffrey Smith Stanley, 14th Earl of Derby, Prime Minister, 1866–7 (ff. 242–54).

Spencer Horatio Walpole, Home Secretary, 1866 (ff. 255–82).

282 ff.

1380. BURDETT-COUTTS PAPERS

Miscellaneous correspondence of Baroness Burdett-Coutts, 1854, 1865–11 May 1866. The names of the writers will be found in the index.

177 ff.

1381. BURDETT-COUTTS PAPERS

Miscellaneous correspondence of Baroness Burdett-Coutts, 12 May 1866–8. The names of the writers will be found in the index.

248 ff.

1382. BURDETT-COUTTS PAPERS

Miscellaneous papers of Baroness Burdett-Coutts, mainly legal papers concerning the colonial church, 1865–9.

Case submitted by Angela Georgina Burdett-Coutts to Sir Travers Twiss, for securing her endowment of the colonial bishoprics of Adelaide, Capetown and British Columbia for the purposes originally intended, April 1865 (ff. 1–13).

Copy of the opinion of Twiss in the case submitted to him by Angela Georgina Burdett-Coutts, 23 June 1865 (ff. 14–19).

Case submitted by Angela Georgina Burdett-Coutts to Twiss concerning her endowment of colonial bishoprics, 19 February 1866 (ff. 20–4).

Further case submitted to the same with a copy of the opinion of Twiss, 26 March 1866 (ff. 25–8).

The Pall Mall Gazette, 21 May 1866. An account of the Colonial Bishoprics Bill is marked (ff. 29–36). Also part of the issue dated 28 May 1866 containing a further account of the Bill (f. 37) (ff. 29–37).

Copy of a petition of the bishop, clergy, and lay representatives of the diocese of Sydney to the Archbishop of Canterbury and the Upper House of Convocation, opposing the Colonial Bishoprics Bill, 14 December 1866 (ff. 38–9).

Blank printed forms for the conveyance and endowment of sites for schools under 5 & 8 Vict., [1869] (ff. 40–3).

43 ff.

1383. BURDETT-COUTTS PAPERS

Miscellaneous papers of Baroness Burdett-Coutts concerning colonial bishoprics, 1842–67.

[1383 *cont.***]**

Reprint of a circular letter recently sent to the headmasters of the chief Free Grammar Schools of England and Wales, by the Revd. Edward Coleridge, assistant master of Eton College, concerning recruitment from such schools of clergy for the colonies, 18 December 1842 (ff. 1–2).

Four new bishoprics in the Colonies, being the report of a general meeting of the Society for the Propagation of the Gospel appealing for funds to supply clergy in new dioceses in Australia and Africa, 19 March 1847 (ff. 3–4).

Memorial from 'members of the Church of England residing in Grahams Town' to Angela Georgina Burdett-Coutts, thanking her for endowing the diocese of Capetown, [1849] (ff. 5–6^{v}).

Colonial Bishoprics Fund. Abstract of receipts and payments for the year ending 31st December 1863, with net abstract . . . for twenty-three years, ending 31st December 1863, and a list of donations and subscriptions . . . 1855–63 (ff. 8–10).

Case of the Bishop of Natal. Judgement of the Lords of the Judicial Committee of the Privy Council upon the petition of the Lord Bishop of Natal, referred to the Judicial Committee by Her Majesty's Order in Council of the 18th June, 1864; delivered 20th March 1865. Endorsed, J. Hassard (ff. 12–18^{v}).

Remarks on the status of the Church of England in the colonies, consisting of seven principles deduced from the judgements of the Privy Council in the cases Long *v.* the Bishop of Capetown and the Bishop of Natal *v.* the Bishop of Capetown, [1865] (f. 19).

Copy of a petition from the bishop, clergy, and laity of the diocese of Victoria, Australia, to the Queen, criticizing the Colonial Bishoprics Bill, [1866] (ff. 20–3).

Letter from Miss Burdett Coutts to the Archbishop of Canterbury, relating the circumstances of her endowments of colonial bishoprics, and threatening to withdraw them unless legislation amended the conclusions of the Privy Council in the case of the Bishops of Capetown and Natal, 12 July 1865. *Two copies and two drafts.* F. T. Whitington, *Augustus Short*, 1887, 50–2 (ff. 24–34^{v}).

Extract from the *Tablet*, 11 November 1865, containing part of an address by Cardinal Manning, and extract from the *Guardian*, 1 November 1865, containing part of a letter from Robert Gray, Bishop of Capetown (ff. 36–7).

Letter from Miss Burdett Coutts to Earl Russell, K.G., stating her intention to withdraw her endowments of colonial bishoprics unless legislation amended their status as interpreted by the Privy Council in the case of the Bishops of Capetown and Natal, 28 December 1865. *Two copies* (ff. 38–41).

Church government in the Colonies, [by William Hale Hale, Archdeacon of London, 1867]. *Proof* (ff. 42^{v}–68).

Letter from Ashurst Turner Gilbert, Bishop of Chichester, president of the C.M.S., and the Revd. Henry Venn, honorary secretary of the same, to Edward Cardwell, Colonial Secretary, seeking that declarations, canons, and regulations adopted by colonial dioceses should be permissive only, 18 January 1866. *Printed. Two copies* (ff. 69–72).

Questions submitted by Angela Georgina Burdett-Coutts to Sir Travers Twiss, concerning ecclesiastical jurisdiction in British Columbia, with the opinion of Twiss, 30 January 1866 (ff. 73–4).

'Statement having reference to the rights of Founders of Endowments affected by the recent decision of the Privy Council, with special reference to the intention of Founders', by Messrs. Farrer, Ouvry, and Farrer (ff. 75–6). *Also two copies* (ff. 77–80^{v}).

Miss Burdett Coutts. Letter to Bishop of Capetown, declaring that the Bishop's intention to ordain a Bishop of Maritzburg is a breach of the conditions under which she endowed the see of Capetown, 27 February 1866. Another copy is MS. 1386 f. 193 (f. 81).

Draft of a letter by Angela Georgina Burdett-Coutts on the status of colonial bishoprics, with corrections in the hand of Sir Travers Twiss, [1866] (ff. 83–6).

Parliamentary papers. *Lords amendments to the Parliamentary Oaths Amendment Bill*, 23 April 1866 (f. 87); *Notices of Motions and Orders of the Day*, 23–4 April [1866] (ff. 88–89^{v}), and 30 April 1866 (ff. 90–1) (ff. 87–91).

Copy of questions submitted by Angela Georgina Burdett-Coutts to Sir Travers Twiss, concerning a proposed division of the diocese of British Columbia, with the opinion, 8 March 1866 (ff. 92–4).

The humble petition of Angela Georgina Burdett Coutts, of 1 Stratton Street, in the City of Westminster, and of 59 Strand, to the Queen, that any amendment of the law concerning colonial bishoprics may preserve the royal supremacy 'in the appointment of Bishops and the Chief Government of the Church', 2 May 1866. *Two copies* (ff. 96–98^{v}).

Parliamentary papers. Orders of the Day, 7 May [1866], and 17–18 May 1866. *Printed fragments* (ff. 100–101^{v}).

Paper of clauses proposed to be inserted in the Colonial Bishoprics Bill on behalf of Angela Georgina Burdett-Coutts, June 1866 (f. 102).

'Explanation for Clauses proposed to be added to the Colonial Bishoprics Bill' (f. 104).

Parliamentary paper. Notices of Motions and Orders of the Day, 5 June 1866. *Printed* (ff. 106–107^{v}).

Form of a motion to be moved during the reading of the Colonial Bishoprics Bill, 8 June 1866 (f. 108).

Parliamentary papers. *Bills Appointed, and Notices*, etc., 15 June 1866 (ff. 110–111^{v}); *Minutes of Proceedings* (House of Lords), 18 June 1866 (ff. 112–115^{v}), 29 June 1866 (f. 117), and 13 July 1866 (ff. 118–119^{v}) with

[1383 *cont.*]

the text of a motion moved by Lord St. Leonards (ff. 120–3); *Minutes of Proceedings* (House of Lords), 17 July 1866 (f. 124), and *Public Petitions,—Thirty-Second Report, 5–18 July, 1866* (ff. 125–136v) (ff. 110–136v).

A Bill [*with the amendments made by the Commons*] *intituled An Act to further amend the Acts relating to the Ecclesiastical Commissioners for England*, 4 August 1866 (ff. 137–142v).

Copy of opinion of Sir Travers Twiss and others concerning possible measures for securing Angela Georgina Burdett-Coutts's endowment of colonial bishoprics, 10 August 1866 (ff. 143–4).

Copy of a petition from the bishop, clergy, and laity of the diocese of Goulburn, New South Wales, to the Archbishop of Canterbury and the Upper House of Convocation, opposing legislation destroying 'the legal identity between the Church in this Colony and the Church in the United Kingdom', 5 March 1867 (ff. 145–6).

A Bill intituled An Act for enabling Her Majesty and Her Majesty's successors to erect three additional bishoprics, and for providing assistance to Bishops who require it for the more effectual performance of their duties, 27 June 1867 (ff. 147–9).

149 ff.

1384. BURDETT-COUTTS PAPERS

Papers concerning Baroness Burdett-Coutts's endowment of colonial bishoprics, 1846–7. The names of the writers will be found in the index.

Enclosed are printed pamphlets by the Revd. Edward Coleridge, viz. *A short account of the Church of England in Australia* . . . , [1841] (f. 15), *An appeal to the friends of the Church of England in behalf of their brethren in Australia*, 1837 (f. 19), and *A second appeal* . . . , 1841 (f. 20).

125 ff.

1385. BURDETT-COUTTS PAPERS

Correspondence of Baroness Burdett-Coutts about the colonial church in Australia, New Zealand, Labuan and Sarawak, America, India, and Hong Kong, 1846–80. The names of the writers will be found in the index.

AUSTRALIA, Diocese of Adelaide, 1847–67

The correspondence is principally with Augustus Short, Bishop of Adelaide. Included are a memorial to the Baroness from persons connected with the Province of South Australia thanking her for endowing the diocese of Adelaide, 3 July 1847 (f. 9); copy of a dispatch from Frederick Robe, Lieutenant-Governor of South Australia, and of a resolution of the Legislative Council, June 1848 (f. 36); *Ceremony of laying the first stone of the Collegiate School of St. Peter's, Adelaide . . . 24 May 1849* (f. 51); *Report of the Committee of the South Australian Church Society* . . . , 1851 (f. 65); *The Church Chronicle for the Diocese of Adelaide*, 12 July 1860 (f. 72);

A Self-Supporting Diocese, being an account by the Bishop of Adelaide of a scheme for the diocese, 14 July 1866 (f. 105).

ff. 1–114.

AUSTRALIA, Diocese of Brisbane, *c.* 1859–62

Included is a printed circular about immigration to Australia.

ff. 115–24.

AUSTRALIA, Diocese of Newcastle, 1858

The correspondence is principally with Elizabeth D. Blandy, sister of the Bishop of Newcastle.

ff. 125–34.

NEW ZEALAND, 1846–68

Included are an account by the Revd. Edward Coleridge of St. John's College, Bishop's Auckland, 1846. *Printed* (f. 137); *The Church of England Constitution in New Zealand . . . a letter to Sir William Martin . . .*, by S. Kempthorne, formerly member of the first Legislative Council, [1868] (f. 157).

ff. 135–63.

LABUAN AND SARAWAK, 1862–3

The correspondence is principally with John Sinclair, Archdeacon of Middlesex.

ff. 164–208.

CANADA, Diocese of British Columbia, 1866–80

Included are: *Columbia Mission. Appeal for the Diocese of New Westminster*, by John Postlethwaite, Bishop designate of New Westminster, *c.* 1866 (f. 209); *Papers relative to the proposed union of British Columbia and Vancouver Island* (Parliamentary Paper), 1866 (f. 211).

ff. 209–44.

CANADA, Diocese of Montreal, 1858

Correspondence with Francis Fulford, Bishop of Montreal, and Mary, his wife.

ff. 245–50.

CANADA, Diocese of Nova Scotia, 1865

Correspondence with John Sinclair, Archdeacon of Middlesex. Enclosed is a *Bill for the incorporation of the Diocesan Synod.*

ff. 251–6.

WEST INDIES, Diocese of Jamaica, 1826–68

Correspondence with Aubrey George Spencer, Bishop of Jamaica, and Reginald Courtenay, Bishop of Kingston, Co-adjutor Bishop of Jamaica. Included are a printed circular addressed by Archibald Campbell Tait, Bishop of London, to the Bishop of Jamaica, inquiring about the connection between the colonial church and the mother church, 13 October 1866 (f. 299); copy of verses 'To Psyche' by the Revd. C. Hare Townsend (f. 311), and of religious verses by the Bishop of Jamaica, 1 December 1867

[1385 *cont.***]**

(f. 315), and an extract from a charge by Spencer as Archdeacon to the clergy of Bermuda, 29 March 1826 (f. 324).

ff. 257–326.

INDIA, Diocese of Calcutta, 1865

Letter from George Edward Lynch Cotton, Bishop of Calcutta, 11 July 1865.

ff. 327–9.

HONG KONG, Diocese of Victoria, 1867–[8]

Enclosed is a copy of a letter from Charles Richard Alford, Bishop of Victoria, to Archbishop Longley, 6 December 1867.

ff. 330–42.

342 ff.

1386. BURDETT-COUTTS PAPERS

Correspondence of Baroness Burdett-Coutts about the colonial church in Africa, 1846–73. The names of the writers will be found in the index.

Diocese of Capetown, 1847–73

The principal correspondent is Robert Gray, Bishop of Capetown. There are also (ff. 223–47) papers concerning Guy Gething, a missionary sent to South Africa, 1858–9. Included also are a list of the clergy in the diocese of Capetown, [1848]. *Printed* (f. 39); an address to Miss Burdett-Coutts from Captain F. Rawstorne, civil commissioner and resident magistrate, and other residents of Colesberg, 11 November 1848 (f. 43); an address to the same from the clergy and laity of Graaff in the Eastern Province of the colony of the Cape of Good Hope, 20 November 1848 (f. 49); a printed letter from the Bishop of Capetown to members of the church in the diocese, 1 January 1850 (f. 67); *St. Augustine's College Tracts*, nos. 5 and 8 (ff. 233, 245).

ff. 1–247.

Diocese of Grahamstown, 1850–9

ff. 248–62.

Diocese of Mauritius, 1846–66

The principal correspondent is Vincent William Ryan, Bishop of Mauritius. Included are *Society for promoting female education in the East* (*Occasional Paper, no. XVII*), May 1863, and printed report of the Church of England Young Men's Society (f. 295).

ff. 263–99.

Diocese of Natal, 1848–72

The correspondence is partly concerned with the promotion of emigration to Natal. Also included are *Circular for emigrants to the Colony of Natal*, 1850 (f. 316); petition from the parish of Durban, Natal, to Convocation, concerning the Bishops of Capetown and Natal, 24 February 1866, and

an account of the objects of the Church of England Defence Association in Natal. *Printed* (f. 365); annual report of the Finance Board of the diocese of Natal, 3 October 1872. *Printed* (f. 369); accounts and report of the Church Clergy Fund of the diocese of Natal, 1872. *Printed* (f. 374).
ff. 300–77.

Diocese of St. Helena, 1850–1

Included is 'Application to Miss Burdett Coutts from the Ladies of St. Helena in behalf of the only country church in that Island', with plan and elevation of the church, 14 August 1850 (f. 380).
ff. 378–90.
390 ff.

1387. BURDETT-COUTTS PAPERS

Correspondence of Baroness Burdett-Coutts about education, 1858–76. The subjects discussed include training schools for teachers, Ragged Schools, the teaching of sewing, proposals for school grouping and ambulatory teachers, the humane treatment of animals.

Included are a memorandum on grouping schools in Devonshire for teaching purposes, *c.* 1865 (f. 55); newspaper cuttings concerning Miss Burdett-Coutts's scheme for grouping rural parishes for teaching purposes and providing ambulatory schoolmasters, 1865 (f. 59); reports made by examiners for the Baroness Burdett-Coutts prizes (f. 133); question paper for prize awarded by the Royal Society for the Prevention of Cruelty to Animals drawn up for pupils of the London School Board. *Printed* (f. 145); memorandum on 'Ragged or other Schools which may be placed under a Circulating Master', n.d. (f. 269), and a pamphlet entitled *The School Board and the Charity Organisation Society*, January 1876 (f. 271).

The names of the writers will be found in the index.

276 ff.

1388. BURDETT-COUTTS PAPERS

Correspondence of Baroness Burdett-Coutts about charitable and educational work in Carlisle, Chelsea, and Great Yarmouth, 1859–70. It comprises (*a*) ff. 1–90. Correspondence mainly with Samuel Waldegrave, Bishop of Carlisle, about the erection of St. Stephen's Church, Carlisle, 1862–3. Included are an appeal for funds by the Carlisle Diocesan Church and Parsonage Building and Benefice Augmentation Society, 1862. *Printed* (f. 7); plan of the site (f. 8^{v}); report accompanying plans by 'Church and State' [P. Bartlett, architect of Carlisle] (f. 10); comments on designs by John A. Cory, of Carlisle (f. 18); a printed appeal for funds, 1 July 1863 (f. 65). (*b*) ff. 91–150. Papers and correspondence about the Whitelands Training Institution for Schoolmistresses at Chelsea, 1866–70, including a report of the annual distribution of prizes, 1866 (f. 91); a list of second-year students awarded prizes in needlework, cutting out and general usefulness, and of first-year students awarded prizes for

[1388 *cont.***]**

needlework and as 'improvers', *c.* 1869 (f. 142); programmes for prize-givings, 1868 and 1870 (f. 143). (*c*) ff. 151–93. Papers about a benefaction to St. Andrew's, Great Yarmouth, to provide a church and reading room for wherrymen, 1859–61. Included are *The First Annual Report of the Norfolk Mission to the Wherrymen,* [1859] (f. 155); a printed appeal by wherry-men for a new church and reading room, [1859] (f. 176); class list for St. Augustine's College, Canterbury, for examinations in theology, classics, and mathematics, 1860 (f. 192).

The names of the writers will be found in the index.

193 ff.

The following printed pamphlets have been transferred to the printed-book shelves:

Documents relative to the erection and endowment of additional bishoprics in the Colonies, 1841–1855, with preface by the Revd. Ernest Hawkins, 1855.

Remarks on the judgement of the Judicial Committee in the case of the Bishop of Natal, by Ralph Barnes, 1866.

Extracts from the Journal of the Bishop of Mauritius, 1864.

Report of the proceedings of the inaugural meeting of the Carlisle Diocesan Church and Parsonage Building and Benefice Augmentation Society, 1862.

Rules of the Carlisle Diocesan Church and Parsonage Building and Benefice Augmentation Society, 1862.

Carlisle Diocesan Church and Parsonage Building and Benefice Augmentation Society. List of Officers and Subscribers, 1862.

The Burden of the Poor. A slight sketch of a poor district in the East End of London, by the Revd. Isaac Taylor, 1867.

1389–94. TWYSDEN PAPERS

Papers of Sir Roger Twysden, 2nd Bt. (1597–1672), of Roydon Hall, East Peckham, Kent. All the volumes have been rebound in white vellum, and contain the bookplate of Frederick Arthur Crisp, from whom they were purchased, 1933.

1389. TWYSDEN PAPERS

Memoranda by Sir Roger Twysden of business transacted by him as Justice of the Peace, May–October 1636. Precedents of 1591–2 concerning beacons are quoted.

16 pp., of which pp. 1–2 are vestigial.

1390. TWYSDEN PAPERS

'An Historicall Narrative of the two howses of Parliament and either of them, their committees and Agents violent proceeding against S^r^. Roger

Twysden, their imprisoning his person, sequestering his estate, cutting down his woods and Tymber, to his allmost undoing, and forcing him in the end to Composition for his own', by Sir Roger Twysden. Printed from this manuscript in *Archaeologia Cantiana*, i, 184–214, ii, 175–220, iii, 145–76, iv, 131–95.

Also arguments to prove that his case was not covered by the Order of Sequestrations (pp. 152–4), and 'Reasons why Sr Roger Twysden's case of intending to prefer a petition to the two howses can not bee construed to bee w^th^in the Ordenance of Sequestration, 1 April 1643' (pp. 155–60).

x+174 pp.

1391. TWYSDEN PAPERS

Correspondence between Sir Roger Twysden and Thomas Whetenhall, [of East Peckham], a papist, on theological matters, January–April 1659. There are two letters from Whetenhall and copies of two letters from Twysden.

10 ff.

LIEUTENANCY PAPERS, 1583–1668

Sir Roger Twysden intended to compile a history 'of the first raising of Lord Lieutenants and Deputy Lieutenants', and his collections for this work are preserved in Lambeth MSS. 1392–4, B.M. Add. MSS. 34147–78 and Maidstone U.48.

1392. TWYSDEN PAPERS

Entitled on the spine 'Sir Roger Twysden's Book of Musters etc. in Kent', 1583–95. The volume contains copies of documents concerning the military organization of Kent assembled by Sir Roger Twysden from the papers of his grandfather Roger Twysden. In many cases they have been annotated by Sir Roger Twysden after comparison with the originals. The papers are in the following order:

1583: f. 101^{r-v}
1584: ff. $102–108^{v}$, 115^{r-v}
1585: ff. 36^{r-v}, $92–93^{v}$, [99^{v}], 108^{v}–113
1587: ff. 4^{v}, 94–5, 113–15
1588: ff. $37–38^{v}$
1589: ff. 38^{v}–39, 42
1590: ff. $28–30^{v}$, $42^{v}–44^{v}$
1591: ff. 30^{v}–31, 59–64
1592: ff. 47–52, $64^{v}–79^{v}$
1593: ff. 80–6
1594: f. 87^{v}
1595: ff. $5–27^{v}$

This manuscript and MS. 1393 are calendared in full in *Kent Arch. Soc.* (*Kent Records*, x), ed. G. Scott Thomson, 66–112.

118 ff.

1393. TWYSDEN PAPERS

Entitled on the spine 'Levies of Men and Arms in Kent', 1595–7. The volume contains 17th-century copies of the originals. Some of the earlier documents are duplicates of documents copied in MS. 1392 [*q.v.*]. The volume probably represents the beginning of making fair copies of documents in his possession for Twysden's proposed history of the lieutenancy.

48 pp.

1394. TWYSDEN PAPERS

Entitled on the spine 'Sir Roger Twysden's Book Concerning the Lieutenancy of Kent', 1660–8.

The volume is divided into three sections: (*a*) copies of letters patent appointing Heneage Finch, 3rd Earl of Winchilsea, to be Lord Lieutenant of Kent, 10 July 1660 (p. 1); the appointment by the same of Sir Roger Twysden as Deputy Lieutenant, 16 July 1660 (p. 9); the renewal of his appointment by Thomas Wriothesley, 4th Earl of Southampton, Lord Lieutenant of Kent, 8 August 1662 (p. 13), and the Instructions issued to the Earl of Southampton, 17 July 1662, with a covering letter from the latter to Twysden (p. 16); an analysis by Sir Roger Twysden of the duties of the Deputy Lieutenant (pp. 25–9); (*b*) a narrative by Sir Roger Twysden in his own hand of his actions as Deputy Lieutenant, 1663–8 (pp. 47–53); (*c*) copies of letters and documents concerning the same, 1668 (pp. 55–60). The manuscript is printed in full in *Kent Arch. Soc.* (*Kent Records*, x), ed. G. Scott Thomson, 29–65.

vi+114 pp.

1395. NOTES ON THE PARISH AND CHURCH OF ALL HALLOWS, HOO, KENT

Collections from manuscript and printed sources for the history of the parish and church of All Hallows, Hoo, Kent, by Leland Lewis Duncan (1862–1923), with additions by Frederic John Hammond, Vicar of Allhallows, Hoo. The original manuscript is in the possession of the Kent Archaeological Society. *Typescript copy*. iii+62 ff.

Given by the Revd. F. J. Hammond, 1924.

1396. NOTEBOOK OF JOHN WORDSWORTH, BISHOP OF SALISBURY

'Notes on the history of Thomas Lankaster, Bishop of Kildare, Treasurer of the Cathedral Church of Salisbury, and Bishop of Marlborough, afterwards Archbishop of Armagh', by John Wordsworth, Bishop of Salisbury. The volume contains notes from manuscript and printed sources made by Wordsworth in 1890, with additions made at his request by William Reeves, Bishop of Down and Connor (ff. 19^{v}–31). The insertions include a letter to Wordsworth from the Revd. William Reynell, contributor of the Life of Lancaster in the *D.N.B.*, 7 October 1890 (f. 36), and a copy of Archbishop Lancaster's will, proved 12 June 1585 (f. 41).

Given by E. W. Watson, Regius Professor of Ecclesiastical History, Oxford, 1914.

55 ff.

1397. LAMBETH CONFERENCE, 1897

Papers of John Wordsworth, Bishop of Salisbury, concerning the Lambeth Conference, 1897. They comprise:

Printed papers concerning Conference arrangements.

Arrangements for the Devotional Day, 30 June (f. 1^{v}).

Order of Ceremonial for service at Westminster Abbey (f. 2), with hymns and anthem, 1 July (f. 3).

Arrangements for the visit of the Bishops to Canterbury, 2–3 July (f. 6).

Form of Service to be used at Ebb's Fleet, 2 July (f. 8), with directions for the procession (f. 10).

Account of *Richborough Castle*, by C. F. Routledge (f. 12).

Order of Service at St. Martin's church, Canterbury, 3 July (f. 14).

Order of Ceremonial at Canterbury cathedral for the reception of the Archbishops and Bishops attending the Conference, 3 July (f. 16).

List of guests at a luncheon at St. Augustine's College, Canterbury, 3 July (f. 18).

List of Bishops expected to attend the Conference (f. 20).

List of Bishops expected to attend the Conference, arranged, with some exceptions, in order of their dates of consecration (f. 22).

List of Bishops expected to attend the Conference, with their addresses in London and elsewhere (f. 24).

Arrangements for the conduct of business, 5 July (f. 26).

Instructions as to the reports of committees, 5 July (f. 27).

Agenda of the Conference, 8 June (f. 28).

Hymn and anthem sung at St. George's Chapel, Windsor, 13 July (f. 30).

Notes by Wordsworth on the sessions of the Conference, 5–10 July, as follows:

5 July Opening address (f. 31).
The Organization of the Anglican Communion (f. 31^{v}).

6 July The Relation of Religious Communities within the Church to the Episcopate (f. 36).
Critical Study of Holy Scripture (f. 40).

7 July Foreign Missions (f. 44).
Reformation Movements on the Continent of Europe and Elsewhere (f. 49).

[**1397** *cont.*]

8 July Church Unity (f. 52), including a printed account of the Moravian episcopate by William Stubbs, Bishop of Oxford, 1888 (f. 55).
International Arbitration (f. 59).

9 July The Office of the Church with Respect to Industrial Problems (f. 61).

10 July Duties of the Church to the Colonies (f. 65).

The debates on the Prayer Book and on Degrees in Divinity are not reported in detail.

Notes by Wordsworth on proceedings in committees appointed by the Conference, 9–21 July, with (f. 68) a list of the composition of all committees:

Committee I on the Organization of the Anglican Communion, with draft report of the committee, much corrected (ff. 71–74^{v}, 81–87^{v}).

Committee XII on 'questions of difficulty which may be admitted for its consideration by Bishops attending the Conference' (ff. 75–7).

Committee V on Reformation Movements on the Continent of Europe and elsewhere (ff. 78–80).

Notes by Wordsworth on sessions of the Conference to receive reports of committees, 22–31 July (ff. 89–125).

Wordsworth has added a list of the subjects of committees (f. 1), and a note of the sessions at which he spoke and committees on which he served (f. 30^{v}). Loose papers have been transferred to MS. 1401, ff. 1–19.

Probably given with other Wordsworth papers in 1911.

i+154 ff.

1398. THE ORNAMENTS OF THE CHURCH AND ITS MINISTERS, 1908

Papers of John Wordsworth, Bishop of Salisbury, concerning the report of a subcommittee of the Upper House of the Convocation of Canterbury on the ornaments of the church and its ministers, 1908 (number 416).

A speech made by John Wordsworth, D.D., Bishop of Salisbury, in the Upper House of the Convocation of Canterbury on presenting the Report No. 416, 5 February 1908 (ff. 1–8).

Also a newspaper cutting concerning the report (ff. 9–10).

Report of the sub-committee of the Upper House of the Convocation of Canterbury appointed to draw up a historical memorandum on the Ornaments of the Church and its Ministers, 1908. Interleaved copy annotated by Wordsworth, convener of the subcommittee, mainly consisting of additions to the appendix of effigies of Anglican bishops. Inserted are letters from Edward John Gough, Vicar of Newcastle upon Tyne, 23 August 1909 (f. 141), and Edward St. Arnaud Duke, Vice-Provost of

St. Mary's cathedral, Edinburgh, 30 August 1909 (f. 143). Loose papers have been transferred to MS. 1401, ff. 20–68 (ff. 18–145).

Given by Mary, widow of John Wordsworth, Bishop of Salisbury, 1911.

i+151 ff.

1399. CONFERENCE BETWEEN THE ANGLICAN AND SWEDISH CHURCHES, 1909

Papers of John Wordsworth, Bishop of Salisbury, concerning a conference at Uppsala between representatives of the Anglican and Swedish Churches, 1909. Wordsworth was a member of a commission appointed by the Archbishop of Canterbury in pursuance of resolution 74 of the Lambeth Conference, 1908, to correspond with the Swedish Church through the Archbishop of Uppsala on the possibility and conditions of an alliance between the Swedish and Anglican Churches. The commission's report to the Archbishop of Canterbury was printed under the title *The Church of England and the Church of Sweden*, 1911.

Letters and associated papers. They consist of a letter from Archbishop Davidson to the Bishop of Salisbury, 9 October 1909 (f. 1); newspaper cutting from the Swedish journal *Idun*, showing members of the conference, 3 October 1909 (f. 2); photographs of Uppsala cathedral (ff. 3–5); photograph of Gottfrid Billing (f. 6); copy of a letter from Archbishop Davidson to Johan August Ekman, Archbishop of Uppsala, 7 September 1909 (ff. 8–9).

Notes by Wordsworth on the Uppsala conference, 21–3 September 1909. Parts of this account are written over an erased account in pencil, also by Wordsworth. Inserted are letters from the Archbishop of Uppsala to Wordsworth, 29 December 1909 (ff. 52–3), and from Otto Ahnfelt, Bishop of Linköping, 3 November 1909 (ff. 54–5) (ff. 11–62).

Various printed papers. Cuttings from *The Living Church* of articles by G. Mott Williams, Bishop of Marquette, member of the Anglo-Swedish commission of the Lambeth Conference, concerning the form, intention, and continuance of Holy Orders in the Swedish Church, 1910 (ff. 63–79); *The Anglo-Swedish American*, September 1909 (ff. 82–5); *Salisbury Diocesan Gazette*, November 1909 (ff. 86–94); newspaper cutting from *The Guardian* of an article on the conference [by A. J. Mason], Master of Pembroke College, Cambridge, and member of the Anglo-Swedish commission of the Lambeth Conference, 20 October 1909 (ff. 95–8).

Loose papers have been transferred to MS. 1401, ff. 69–98.

Given by Mary, widow of John Wordsworth, Bishop of Salisbury, 1911.

iv+100 ff.

1400. LIST OF SWEDISH BOOKS

List by John Wordsworth, Bishop of Salisbury, of books in his library in Swedish and on Swedish subjects. Many of these books are now in Lambeth Palace Library (ff. 1–7).

Probably given with other Wordsworth papers in 1911.

i+28 ff.

1401. MISCELLANEOUS PAPERS OF JOHN WORDSWORTH, BISHOP OF SALISBURY, 1896–1911

Miscellaneous papers of John Wordsworth, Bishop of Salisbury, concerning the Lambeth Conference, 1897; a report to the Upper House of the Convocation of Canterbury on the ornaments of the church and its ministers, 1908; and negotiations between the Anglican and Swedish Churches, 1909.

LAMBETH CONFERENCE, 1897

The Organisation of the Anglican Communion, 1896, being the report of a committee of bishops under the chairmanship of Wordsworth appointed by the Conference (ff. 1–4v).

Notes by Brooke Foss Westcott, Bishop of Durham, in connection with committee III appointed to report on the critical study of Holy Scriptures. *Printed* (ff. 5–6v).

Proofs of *Report of the committee appointed to 'consider and report upon the subject of reformation movements on the Continent of Europe and elsewhere'*. The report is annotated by Wordsworth, who was a member of the committee though his name does not appear in the published list (ff. 7–10v).

Duplicated draft report of a committee appointed to consider 'Questions of Difficulty submitted for its consideration by Bishops attending the Conference' (ff. 11–12).

Letter from William Moore Richardson, Bishop of Zanzibar, to Wordsworth, 24 July [1897] (f. 13).

Notes by Wordsworth of resolutions and amendments in committees (ff. 15–19).

Transferred from MS. 1397.

THE ORNAMENTS OF THE CHURCH AND ITS MINISTERS, 1908

Papers of Wordsworth mainly concerning the publication of a report to the Upper House of the Convocation of Canterbury on the ornaments of the church and its ministers, 1908. They include the following:

Letters to Wordsworth from: Thomas Frederick Simmons, Prebendary of York, 25 February 1876 (f. 20), returning a letter from the Scandinavian scholar Gúdbrandr Vígfússon on the vestments of the Lutheran church, 10 February 1876 (f. 22); John Wickham Legg, liturgical scholar, 18 September 1907 (f. 24); Philip Frank Eliot, Dean of Windsor, 10 February 1908 (f. 26); John Henry Bernard, Dean of St. Patrick's, 23 March 1908 (f. 28); William Holden Hutton, Fellow of St. John's College, Oxford, 23 March 1908 (f. 30); Charles Fox Burney, Fellow and librarian of St. John's College, Oxford, 30 March 1908, enclosing a photograph of a crozier in the college library (f. 32); William Holden Hutton, 1 April 1908 (f. 34); William J. Cox, Vicar of Grace Church Chapel, Philadelphia, 30 May 1908 (f. 36); Fenwick Williams Vroom, Professor of Divinity at King's College, Nova Scotia, 22 June 1908 (f. 38); William Christopher Bell, Vicar of Norland, 22 September 1908 (f. 39); John Wickham Legg, 2 October 1908 (f. 41); William Moore Morgan, Prebendary and librarian of Armagh, 9 October 1908 (f. 46), and a postcard from the Bishop of Salisbury containing a description of the tomb of Thomas Legh Claughton, Bishop of St. Albans, 1892 (f. 50).

Also notes [by John Henry Bernard, Dean of St. Patrick's] of monuments in Irish cathedrals (ff. 51–5); memorandum of the will of John Burley, Rector of Milston, 1569 (f. 56); photographs of monuments (ff. 58–68).

Transferred from MS. 1398.

CONFERENCE BETWEEN THE ANGLICAN AND SWEDISH CHURCHES, 1909

Leaves from *Svensk Kyrkotidning*, 4 April 1910 (ff. 69–70).

The Church of England and the Church of Sweden, 1910. Proofs corrected by Wordsworth of a report to Archbishop Davidson of a commission appointed in pursuance of resolution 74 of the Lambeth Conference, 1908. The report differs in many points from that eventually published (ff. 71–94).

Editorials on 'The Church of England and the Church of Sweden' from *The Living Church*, 1 and 8 July 1911 (ff. 95–8).

Transferred from MS. 1399.

Given by Mary, widow of John Wordsworth, Bishop of Salisbury, 1911.

98 ff.

1402. THOMAS BILSON, BISHOP OF WINCHESTER (1547–1616)

'"Bishop Bilson and his Portrait", a paper read at Lambeth Palace on the occasion of the visit there of the Hampshire Field Club and Archaeological Society on the 12th May, 1914', by Alfred Bilson. The account includes sketches of the Bishop's arms in colour, a pedigree, and a photograph of the portrait in Lambeth Palace. The paper does not appear to have been read to the Society (*v. Papers and Proceedings*, vii. pt. II, xxi–iv).

21 ff.

1403. WATERCOLOURS BY ARCHBISHOP SUMNER

Thirteen water-colours by John Bird Sumner, Archbishop of Canterbury, of the grounds of Addington Park, Surrey. At f. 1 a distant prospect of the south front of the Archbishop's palace is shown.

Given by Arthur Christopher Benson, 1917.

iii+27 ff.

1404. REPORT ON ANTIQUITIES IN JERUSALEM, 1920

Report by Charles Robert Ashbee (1863–1942), Civic Adviser to the Pro-Jerusalem Society, on the extent of the damage caused by a blizzard to buildings of historic interest in Jerusalem, with numerous photographs, 13 March 1920. Ashbee, architect and friend of William Morris, was appointed civic adviser to the Pro-Jerusalem Society, founded in 1918 to preserve the amenities of Jerusalem.

12 ff.

1405. ST. MARY'S CHURCH, WINGHAM, KENT

Six photographs of the interior of St. Mary's Church, Wingham, Kent, mainly showing the Oxenden Chapel restored by Muriel Capel Cure, widow of Sir Edward Capel Cure, 1923.

Given by Lady Capel Cure, 1923.

ii+8 ff.

1406. ADDRESS TO ARCHBISHOP DAVIDSON, 1926

Illuminated address on vellum to Archbishop Davidson from members of the Church Assembly and others, presenting a portrait of him by Philip Alexius de Laszlo, 8 July 1926. The address is written and illuminated by Alfred Leonard Reeve, and the volume bound in leather by Douglas Bennett Cockerell. Contained in a wooden box.

v+19 ff.

1407–9. REVISION OF THE BOOK OF COMMON PRAYER, 1925–1927

Three proof copies of the *Book of Common Prayer* revised and amended by the Church Assembly, 1923, interleaved for the use of the House of Bishops of the Church Assembly meeting at Lambeth Palace, 1925–7. The book, known as the Quarto Book and printed in 1925, contains in tabular form the text approved by the Revised Prayer Book (Permissive Use) Measure (N.A.84) of the Church Assembly, with the amendments proposed by the House of Clergy (C.A.158) and the House of Laity (C.A.169) of the Church Assembly, 1923. The interleaves contain numerous notes and comments by William Temple, Bishop of Manchester and (1942) Archbishop of Canterbury (1407), Charles Leonard Thornton-Duesbury, Bishop of Sodor and Man (1408), and Frank Edward Brightman, Fellow of Magdalen College, Oxford (1409). A note pasted in MS. 1409 states that the volume belonged to Winfrid Oldfield Burrows, Bishop of Chichester, chairman of the committee of Bishops, but the annotations are mainly by Brightman.

ii+497 ff.

1410–14. COLLECTIONS CONCERNING GUILDFORD HOSPITAL

Collections concerning the Hospital of the Blessed Trinity, Guildford, [by Philip G. Palmer, Master of the Hospital], from the records of the Hospital, 1614–1861. The hospital was founded by George Abbot, Archbishop of Canterbury.

1410: 1614–55. 307 ff.
1411: 1655–91. 244 ff.
1412: 1691–1734. 334 ff.
1413: 1734–78. 270 ff.
1414: 1778–1861. 287 ff.

Given by Miss Emily Palmer, 1928.

1415. S. LANGTON

Commentaries of Stephen Langton on the Pentateuch and Joshua. ff. i+228+i. Size 310×225 mm. Belonged in the 17th century to the Cistercian abbey of Villars in Brabant.

See MS. 1362 for reference to a fuller description of this manuscript.

1416–55. DIARIES OF WILLIAM EWART GLADSTONE

Diaries of William Ewart Gladstone (1809–98), statesman. The diaries are kept in small pocket-books entered daily, 1825–96.

1416: 16 July 1825–21 October 1827. i+85 pp.
1417: 22 October 1827–22 October 1828. ii+44 pp.
1418: 23 October 1828–23 April 1830. i+31 ff.
1419: 24 April 1830–10 September 1831. i+47 ff.
1420: 11 September 1831–20 July 1833. i+75 ff.
1421: 21 July 1833–24 March 1834. ii+48 pp.
1422: 25 March 1834–30 September 1835. 53 ff.
1423: 1 October 1835–28 February 1838. i+88 ff.
1424: 1 March 1838–30 September 1839. i+113 pp.
1425: 1 October 1839–30 September 1841. i+75 ff.
1426: 1 October 1841–29 February 1844. i+149 pp.
1427: 1 March 1844–30 June 1846. i+149 pp.
1428: 1 July 1846–22 April 1848. i+147 pp.
1429: 23 April 1848–31 May 1850. i+149 pp.
1430: 1 June 1850–29 February 1852. i+135 pp.
1431: 1 March 1852–31 August 1853. i+137 pp.
1432: 1 September 1853–24 February 1855. i+70 ff.
1433: 25 February 1855–31 December 1856. i+138 pp.
1434: 1 January 1857–28 February 1859. i+161 pp.
1435: 1 March 1859–20 September 1860. i+129 pp.
1436: 21 September 1860–30 April 1862. i+129 pp.
1437: 1 May 1862–31 December 1863. i+66 ff.
1438: 1 January 1864–12 August 1865. i+129 pp.

[1416–55 *cont.*]

1439: 13 August 1865–30 April 1867. i+129 pp.
1440: 1 May 1867–31 December 1868. i+127 pp.
1441: 1 January 1869–20 September 1870. ii+141 pp.
1442: 21 September 1870–15 June 1872. i+71 ff.
1443: 16 June 1872–12 February 1874. i+145 pp.
1444: 13 February 1874–20 July 1875. i+141 pp.
1445: 21 July 1875–15 March 1877. i+140 pp.
1446: 16 March 1877–31 December 1878. ii+182 pp.
1447: 1 January 1879–23 July 1880. i+169 pp.
1448: 24 July 1880–9 April 1882. i+139 pp.
1449: 10 April 1882–31 December 1883. i+135 pp.
1450: 1 January 1884–7 September 1885. i+141 pp.
1451: 8 September 1885–11 June 1887. i+141 pp.
1452: 12 June 1887–6 May 1889. i+141 pp.
1453: 7 May 1889–28 February 1891. i+132 pp.
1454: 1 March 1891–30 June 1893. ii+178 pp.
1455: 1 July 1893–29 October 1896. i+179 pp.

Given by Henry Neville Gladstone, 1st Baron Gladstone of Hawarden, and Herbert John Gladstone, 1st Viscount Gladstone, 1928.

1456. WATER-COLOURS

Water-colours and a few engravings by George Samuel (d. 1823?), artist, of churches in Berkshire, Buckinghamshire, Essex, Kent, Hertfordshire, Middlesex, and Surrey. The places will be found in the index.

Given by Dr. George Williamson, 1915.

67 ff.

1457–62. DRAWINGS OF CHURCHES

Sketches and wash drawings of churches, probably made during the 1840s. In isolated cases the name of the architect and/or date of erection or restoration is appended. The drawings measure $7 \times 4\frac{1}{2}$ inches (1457–60), and 9×7 inches (1461–2). The places will be found in the index.

Given by Colonel A. C. Frere, 1930.

1457. Berkshire (ff. 1–46); Buckinghamshire (ff. 47–68); Cumberland (ff. 69–77); Derbyshire (f. 78).
78 ff.

1458. Durham.
62 ff.

1459. Hampshire (ff. 1–15); Isle of Wight (ff. 16–45); Lancashire (ff. 46–9); Lincolnshire (f. 50); Middlesex (f. 51); Northumberland (ff. 52–83); Oxfordshire (ff. 84–100); Staffordshire (f. 101); Surrey (ff. 102–3).
103 ff.

1460. Westmorland (ff. 1–16); Yorkshire (ff. 17–67).

67 ff.

1461. Cambridge (f. 1); Cumberland (f. 2); Durham (ff. 3–52); Huntingdonshire (f. 53); Lincolnshire (f. 54); Northumberland (ff. 55–8); Westmorland (ff. 59–61); Wiltshire (f. 62).

62 ff.

1462. Yorkshire.

55 ff.

1463–6. PAPERS OF CANON SAMUEL AUGUSTUS BARNETT

Papers of the Revd. Samuel Augustus Barnett (1844–1913), Vicar of St. Jude, Whitechapel, and (1906) Canon of Westminster, concerning the National Church Reform Union. The principal objects of the Union were resistance to Disestablishment, increase of lay participation in church government, reformation of patronage, and reapportionment of ecclesiastical revenues.

1463. BARNETT PAPERS

Leaflets and pamphlets of the National Church Reform Union, and (ff. 40–108) of the Society for the Liberation of Religion from State-Patronage and Control. Also included are (ff. 32–5) *Report of the Church Council* of St. Mary, Bryanston Square, 1871–2, and (ff. 109–20) offprints of newspaper articles and newspaper cuttings.

122 ff.

1464. BARNETT PAPERS

Subscribed copies of a memorial protesting against Disestablishment of the Church of England, and asserting that 'the endowments of the Church ought to remain sacred to religious uses; the people to have a voice in the election of its ministers, in the control of its funds, and in the arrangement of its services; and the basis of the Church to be so widened as to include the entire Christian thought and life of the nation', [1886].

130 ff.

1465. BARNETT PAPERS

Newspaper cuttings, mainly of articles and letters by Canon Barnett, 1885–96.

142 ff., of which ff. 15–142 are blank.

1466. BARNETT PAPERS

Miscellaneous letters and papers as follows:

Letters to Barnett from Edwin Abbott Abbott, scholar, 1878 (ff. 1–2v); Henry Montagu Butler, Master of Trinity College, Cambridge, 1913

[1466 *cont.*]

(ff. 6–9^{v}); William Henry Fremantle, Canon of Canterbury, and (1895) Dean of Ripon, 1886 (ff. 11–13^{v}); Philip Lyttelton Gell, secretary of the N.C.R.U., 1880 (ff. 14–17^{v}); Thomas Hughes, Q.C., member of the Council of the N.C.R.U., 1878 (ff. 20–21^{v}); Hon. Augustus Legge, Vicar of Sydenham, and (1891) Bishop of Lichfield, 1877 (ff. 22–3); Arnold Toynbee, social reformer, 1879 (ff. 24–9). Also letters from Barnett to his wife, 1882 (ff. 3–5^{v}).

Note on the memorial of 1886 [see MS. 1464] (ff. 30–3); address by Barnett entitled 'A modern monastery. A suggestion for a mission' (ff. 31–41); memorandum on a national church (ff. 42–3); addresses by Barnett on 'Common work as the basis of Christian union' (ff. 44–52), on the purpose of Toynbee Hall, 1889 (ff. 53–61), on 'the basis of unity is common worship' (ff. 63–8). Notes by Barnett for an address on church reform (ff. 69–83), and on an address or sermon on the causes of drift from religious observance, 1907 (ff. 85–92). Also memorandum by Barnett on 'Church Reform v. Disestablishment', 1912. *Typescript* (ff. 93–5); memorial signed by Barnett and others refusing assent to a proposed National Church, n.d. *Copy* (f. 97); extracts from letters by Barnett (ff. 99–109).

109 ff.

1467. CORRESPONDENCE OF THE REVD. EDWIN HATCH

Correspondence of the Revd. Edwin Hatch (1835–89), theologian and Reader in Ecclesiastical History, Oxford, 1865–89. Also letters of condolence on his death addressed to his wife (ff. 97–139^{v}); hymns by Hatch, some of which are printed in *Towards fields of light*, 1890 (ff. 140–53); an obituary notice of him from *Realencyclopädie für protestantische Theologie und Kirche* (f. 154). The names of the writers will be found in the index.

Also a letter from John Jewett Penstone to [Christopher] Wordsworth, Vicar of Stanford [-in-the-Vale], and later Bishop of Lincoln, n.d. (f. 155).

Given by Miss Ethel C. Hatch, 1951.

157 ff.

1468. MISCELLANEOUS PAPERS

Miscellaneous papers as follows:

Copy of an inventory of the goods of Archbishop Cranmer at Lambeth, Croydon, Bekesbourne, Canterbury, and Ford, 1553, with in many cases the names of persons to whom they were sold.

Given by Henry Gee, Professor of Church History, Durham, and (1917) Dean of Gloucester, 1913.

(ff. 1–23).

List of manuscripts belonging to John Raynolds, President of Corpus Christi College, Oxford, delivered by his executors to Archbishop Bancroft. Copied from Corpus Christi College MS. 352, p. 7.
(ff. 24–5).

Notes by J. B. Oldham on bindings in Lambeth Palace Library. *Typescript.*
(ff. 26–46).

Notes by R. Kaehler on the rectors of St. Margaret, Canterbury, with a list of the rectors, *c.* 1930.
(ff. 48–72^{v}).

Churchwardens' accounts for the parish of Loose, Kent. Extracts from and notes on by Waterman Gardner-Waterman, Vicar of Loose, 1929. *Printed.*
Given by the author, 1929.
(ff. 77–9).

Letter from Queen Victoria to Archbishop Howley for a collection for building churches in England and Wales, 1842. *Printed.*
Given by Charles George Kerslake, Rector of Pulham St. Mary, 1952.
(ff. 80–1).

Address by Anthony Wilson Thorold, Vicar of St. Pancras, and (1890) Bishop of Winchester, on 'The duty of the Evangelical Clergy in their ministrations', delivered to the Islington Clerical Conference, 1875.
(ff. 82–112).

'The Missionary Conference of Northern Rhodesia, 1922', by Frank H. Melland. *Typescript.*
(ff. 116–25).

Diocese of Masasi, Africa. Acts of the synod concerning initiatory rites, 21–3 November 1927. *Typescript.*
(ff. 126–53).

Invitation from the Lord Mayor of London to Archbishop Lang to a banquet at the Guildhall, 9 November 1931 (f. 154).

Old Catholics. Translations of accounts by Professor Andreas Rinkel, (1937) Archbishop of Utrecht, of meeting of the Anglican–Old Catholic Commission at Bonn, 2 July 1931 (ff. 155–67), and of the meeting of the Episcopal Synod of the Old Catholic Churches at Vienna, 7 September 1931 (ff. 168–73), with newspaper cuttings.
(ff. 155–80).

'Memorandum on the revision of the Communion Service', by Lord Hugh Cecil, (1941) 1st Baron Quickswood, author of *The Communion Service as it might be*, 1935. See MS. 1776. *Typescript.*
Given by the Earl of Selborne, 1963.
(ff. 181–7).

[1468 *cont.***]**

'List of works (excluding modern publications) in the library of the Cathedral Church of St. Paul, Dundee', with historical introduction. *Typescript.*

Given by the Revd. A. C. Don, 1964.

(ff. 188–207).

Papers of Mervyn George Haigh, chaplain to the Archbishop of Canterbury, and successively Bishop of Coventry and Winchester. They comprise: critique by Charles Gore, Bishop of Oxford, of *God the Invisible King*, by H. G. Wells, [1917] (ff. 208–14); letters to Haigh from Philip Thomas Byard ('Tubby') Clayton, Vicar of All Hallows, Barking-by-the-Tower, 1930. Printed F. R. Barry, *Mervyn Haigh*, 1964, 113 (f. 215); Archbishop Fisher, 1958 (f. 216); Herbert Hensley Henson, formerly Bishop of Durham, 1944. Printed op. cit., 92 (ff. 217–18); draft by Haigh and Frederick Dudley Vaughan Narborough, chaplain to the Archbishop of Canterbury, and (1946) Suffragan Bishop of Colchester, of Archbishop Davidson's reply, 22 October 1927, to the open letter of Bishop Barnes in *The Times* (ff. 219–20).

Given by Mrs. Monica Blackman, sister of Bishop Haigh, 1963.

(ff. 208–20).

Correspondence with Irvingites. A copy of a private correspondence by S. Royle Shore with members of the Irvingite Church with a view to union with the Church of England, 1921–31. The correspondents include Basil Seton and Henry Strange Hume, successively Bishops of the Irvingite church in Gordon Square, London, and the Bishops of London and Guildford. It includes correspondence with Claude Beaufort Moss, Vice-Principal of St. Boniface College, and Eric Osmund Cooper, Old Catholic priest, about Irvingite churches on the Continent (ff. 249–63), and with James Shafto Heath, Irvingite minister in Glasgow, about the Irvingite Church in Scotland (ff. 267–81).

Given by Canon J. A. Douglas, 1952.

(ff. 221–82).

282 ff.

1469. MISCELLANEOUS PAPERS

Miscellaneous papers, 1867–1964, as follows:

Translation of the Athanasian Creed. Papers of Edward William Watson, Regius Professor of Ecclesiastical History, Oxford, secretary of a committee appointed by Archbishop Davidson on 11 March 1909 following a resolution of the Lambeth Conference of 1908 that a new translation be made of the *Quicunque Vult*. In addition to Watson, the committee consisted of John Wordsworth, Bishop of Salisbury, chairman (succeeded by Archibald Robertson, former Bishop of Exeter); Alexander Francis Kirkpatrick, Dean of Ely; Walter Lock, Warden of Keble College, Oxford; Arthur James Mason, Master of Pembroke College, Cambridge;

Henry Barclay Swete, Regius Professor of Divinity, Cambridge; Cuthbert Hamilton Turner, Fellow of Magdalen College, Oxford. The papers comprise the correspondence of the committee (ff. 1–55); notes by C. H. Turner for the revised edition published in 1918 (ff. 57–8); text and translation prepared in 1904 (ff. 59–60); *Memorandum on the use and emendation of the Quicunque vult prepared for the Lambeth Conference of 1908 by the Bishop of Salisbury* (ff. 61–62ᵛ); corrected drafts of a report and translation for Archbishop Davidson, 22 May 1909 (ff. 65–76ᵛ), and 18 October 1909 (ff. 77–82ᵛ); offprint of article by C. H. Turner on 'A critical text of the Quicumque vult' (*Journ. Theol. Studies*, xi, 401–11) (ff. 84–9); the published edition entitled *The Athanasian Creed*, 1910, and the second revised edition of 1918, with corrected proofs (ff. 91–132).

Letter from Archbishop Longley to Edmund Hobhouse, Bishop of Nelson, New Zealand, 1867, inviting him to attend the so-called Fulford-Whitehouse meeting preparatory to the first Lambeth Conference (f. 133). Given by Miss Dorothy Hobhouse, 1964.

Correspondence of Archbishop Temple with the Marquess of Northampton, concerning the proposed provision of the Coronation Bible by the British and Foreign Bible Society, 1902 (ff. 134–148ᵛ).

Miscellaneous letters: Revd. W. A. Wigram, member of the Archbishop's Mission to the Assyrians, to Athelstan Riley, 1909–[19], on doctrinal matters (ff. 150–152ᵛ); William John Birkbeck to John Wordsworth, Bishop of Salisbury, 1910 (ff. 153–4); Halford John Mackinder, Director of the London School of Economics, to the Revd. A. C. Headlam, Principal of King's College, London, 1906 (ff. 155–7); Archbishop Davidson to the Archbishop [of York], 1926, about Prayer Book revision (ff. 158–9); Randall Thomas Davidson, Bishop of Winchester, to Miss Blanche Sitwell, n.d., on religious difficulties. *Extract*. Given by Miss Joan Wake, 1964 (f. 160); George Herbert Duckworth, secretary of the Royal Commission on Historical Monuments, to Archbishop Davidson, 1921 (f. 161); correspondence between the Revd. George Kennedy Allen Bell, chaplain to Archbishop Davidson, and (1928) Bishop of Chichester, and Yngve Brilioth, later Archbishop of Uppsala, 1923 (ff. 162–5).

Correspondence of the Revd. Alan Campbell Don, formerly chaplain to Archbishop Lang and Dean of Westminster, about Archbishop Lang, and particularly J. G. Lockhart's biography of him, 1946–57, with some newspaper cuttings (ff. 166–202).
Given by the Revd. A. C. Don, 1960.

Lawrence Edward Tanner, Librarian and Keeper of the Muniments of Westminster Abbey, to Mrs. Armitage Robinson, 1941, describing damage by war to the Abbey (ff. 203–204ᵛ).

Letters and papers of the Revd. Alan Campbell Don. Correspondence with the Bishop of Chichester about Don's Life of Archbishop Lang in the *D.N.B.*, 1950 (ff. 205–7); letters from Archbishop Fisher (f. 208), and Wilfrid Parker, former Bishop of Pretoria, (f. 209) about the deposit of papers of Archbishop Lang in Lambeth Palace Library, 1960; account by

[1469 *cont.*]

Don of the Lambeth Cross. *Typescript* (ff. 211–13); extracts from letters by an English clergyman in Edinburgh to the Revd. George Gaskin, Rector of St. Benet, Gracechurch Street, 1793, concerning the Episcopal Church of Scotland. Copied from original belonging to John Ogilvy of Inshewan, 1931 (ff. 214–19); sermon on Confirmation, 18th century (ff. 221–34); list of clergy of the Scottish Episcopal Church since 1689 (f. 236); *The Scottish Guardian*, 18 April 1947, containing the succession of Scottish Bishops to 1947 (ff. 237–244^{v}); cuttings of sermons by Don at consecration of Piers Holt Wilson, Bishop of Moray, Ross and Caithness, 1943 (f. 245), and at St. Ninian's Cathedral, Perth, 1948 (f. 246).

Privately issued postage stamp commemorating the visit of Archbishop Fisher to the Vatican, 1960 (f. 247).

Given by Canon Stanley Graham Brade-Birks, Vicar of Godmersham, 1961.

Letter from Judith Scott, secretary to the Council for the Care of Churches, to E. G. W. Bill, Lambeth Librarian, 1964, reporting the retrieval of the old pulpit of Lambeth Palace Chapel for Barnwood church (f. 250).

250 ff.

1470–1. TRANSCRIPT OF MALTESE MARRIAGE REGISTERS, 1801–92

Transcript by Edward Ambrose Hardy, Archdeacon of Malta, of registers of civil and military marriages solemnized by Anglican, Wesleyan, and Presbyterian ministers in Malta, 1801–92. The transcript appears to have been made in connection with evidence given by Hardy before the Privy Council in a *Case concerning the validity of certain mixed and unmixed marriages at Malta*, [1892], and includes all existing registers except a register of the Senior Military Chaplain, 1859–78. Anglican marriages were celebrated in the Governor's chapel until 1844. They were then celebrated in the collegiate church of St. Paul, Valletta, and from 1867 in Holy Trinity Church, Sliema, also. Where marriage was by licence, the licence was issued by the Chief Civil Commissioner until 1813, and then by the Governor until 1843. From that year until 1874 they were issued by the surrogate of the Bishop of Gibraltar, but when Bishop Sandford did not appoint a surrogate the duty reverted to the Governor.

Given by the Revd. A. J. Judson, nephew of Archdeacon Hardy, 1921.

1470. MALTESE MARRIAGE REGISTERS

Memoranda [by Archdeacon Hardy] on the places where marriages were solemnized (f. 1), and on the authority for the performance of marriages in Malta, 1801–19 (f. 1^{v}), and an account of the marriage registers with particular note of the registering of military marriages (ff. 2–3^{v}).

Transcript of marriage registers, 1801–66:

December 1801–November 1807. Register of the Revd. D. P. Cosserat, garrison chaplain (register IA) (ff. 4^{v}–10).

November 1805–October 1809. Register of the Revd. J. J. C. Miller, assistant garrison chaplain (register IB) (ff. 10^{v}–12).

February 1809–May 1813. Register of the Revd. F. Laing, chaplain to the Government (register IC) (ff. 11^{v}–15).

July 1813–August 1815. [Register of the Revd. J. J. C. Miller, acting chaplain to the Government] (register IC) (ff. 14^{v}–15).

November 1809–August 1815. Register of the Revd. J. J. C. Miller, assistant garrison chaplain (register ID) (ff. 15^{v}–18).

November 1812–November 1818. [Register of the Revd. J. J. H. Le Mesurier, chaplain to the forces] (military register I) (ff. 17^{v}–24).

February 1819–March 1832 (register of the collegiate church of St. Paul, Valletta, 2) (ff. 23^{v}–29).

April 1832–January 1850 (register of St. Paul's 3) (ff. 28^{v}–43).

January–September 1850 (register of St. Paul's 4) (ff. 42^{v}–43).

October 1850–October 1863 (register of St. Paul's 5) (ff. 42^{v}–59).

November 1863–March 1866 (register of St. Paul's 6) (ff. 58^{v}–64).

i+65 ff.

1471. MALTESE MARRIAGE REGISTERS

Transcripts of marriage registers, [1866]–92:

March [1866]–October 1879 (register of St. Paul's 6) (ff. 1^{v}–22).

November 1879–April 1892 (register of St. Paul's 7) (ff. 21^{v}–37).

June 1802–January 1879. List of omissions from registers (ff. 37^{v}–40).

September 1867–January 1892. Marriages solemnized at Holy Trinity church, Sliema (ff. 51^{v}–55).

June 1869–May 1892. Complete list of marriages solemnized by Wesleyan ministers in Malta (ff. 55^{v}–59^{v}).

May 1843–June 1892. Complete list of marriages solemnized by Presbyterian ministers in Malta (ff. 60^{v}–69).

January 1820–May 1859. List of marriages solemnized by the senior military chaplain in Malta (ff. 69^{v}–89).

i+95 ff.

1472–82. PAPERS OF F. A. WHITE CONCERNING PÈRE HYACINTHE

Papers of Frederick Anthony White, treasurer of the French Committee of the Anglo-Continental Society, concerning Père Hyacinthe, Rector of the Gallican Catholic Church in Paris, 1878–1903. Hyacinthe Loyson was ordained in 1851 and became a Carmelite, but, dissenting from the dogma

[1472–82 *cont.*]

of papal infallibility promulgated by the Vatican Council in 1870, he adhered to the Old Catholics. The Lambeth Conference of 1878 appointed a commission to communicate with Old Catholics desiring the help of the Church of England, and in the same year a conference at Farnham, held by the Bishop of Winchester, president of the Anglo-Continental Society, resolved to support Père Hyacinthe and to launch a fund for this purpose through the Anglo-Continental Society. At the Farnham Conference, Père Hyacinthe sought to be placed under the supervision of the Anglican episcopate, and the Archbishop of Canterbury selected the Primus of Scotland to exercise this function, subsequently delegated to the Bishop of Edinburgh. When the Bishop of Edinburgh resigned this task, it was assumed by Bishop Jenner until 1888, when the Gallican Catholic Church was placed under the authority of the Archbishop of Utrecht.

Given by F. A. White, 1931.

1472. WHITE PAPERS

MISCELLANEOUS PAPERS

Miscellaneous papers concerning negotiations between the Church of England and P. Hyacinthe Loyson, 1878–[89].

Account [by F. A. White] of a conversation with P. Hyacinthe, June 1878 (ff. 1–4).

Report to his Grace the Archbishop of Canterbury . . . on the present position of the Père Hyacinthe's movement in Paris, by F. A. White, November 1878. *Draft and printed proof* (ff. 5–22).

Report by F. A. White describing attempts to raise funds for the support of P. Hyacinthe, and listing points on which it is desired to consult Gladstone, 10 February 1878 (ff. 23–4).

Report by the same of an interview with Gladstone, 11 December 1878 (ff. 25–6).

Report [by the same] of discussions with [Félix] Carrier, a priest [of the Old Catholic Church of Switzerland], concerning the work of P. Hyacinthe, October 1878 (ff. 27–30).

Memorandum [by the same] on the financial needs of P. Hyacinthe's movement, n.d. (ff. 31–2).

Speech [by the same], apparently to a conference of English churchmen [*v.* ff. 38–41], reporting the progress of negotiations with P. Hyacinthe, [February 1879]. *Draft* (ff. 33–7).

Minutes of 'A private conference of English churchmen interested in the ministrations of Père Hyacinthe in Paris', 15 February 1879, signed by the Bishop of Winchester, chairman. Enclosed is a report on the conference issued to the press (ff. 38–41).

Summary of twelve points concerning the organization of the Gallican Catholic Church, discussed by P. Hyacinthe with Bishop Herzog, the Revd. R. J. Nevin and others, July 1879. *Duplicated* (f. 42).

Subscription to a common rule of four articles for the conduct of the work of Catholic Reform in France by P. Hyacinthe, Félix Carrier, and Paul Bichery, priests, 22 October 1879. *Duplicated copy. French* (f. 43).

Memorandum [by F. A. White] entitled 'Reform in the Church of France', containing an account of the early history of P. Hyacinthe and the establishment of a Gallican Catholic Church in Rue Rochechouart, Paris, and announcing a course of lectures to be given in London by P. Hyacinthe, [1880] (ff. 44–7).

M. Hyacinthe Loyson (Père Hyacinthe) in Paris. An appeal for funds to provide £1,000 a year for five years to build a church in Paris and pay additional clergy, issued by the French committee of the Anglo-Continental Society, [1880] (ff. 49–50^{v}). Also a proof copy (ff. 51–3).

Félix Carrier, priest [of the Old Catholic Church of Switzerland], *Emancipation de l'Eglise de France*, 1879 (ff. 54–58^{v}).

Catholic Reform and the Anglican Church..., by P. Hyacinthe, translated by Lady E. A. Durand, 1879. This pamphlet contains a statement of his aims by P. Hyacinthe, and his correspondence with the Archbishop of Canterbury, the Primus of Scotland, and Bishop Eduard Herzog in 1878 (ff. 59–72).

Newspaper cutting containing an account of a sermon by P. Hyacinthe in Paris on 'Dieu et la France', n.d. *French* (f. 73).

Memorandum from F. A. White to Archbishop Tait on 'the present [financial] crisis in the Gallican Church', n.d. *Copy* (ff. 76–77^{v}).

Letter from [Thomas] Yeatman, treasurer of the council of the Gallican Catholic Church in Paris, on the membership and finances of the Church, 3 March [1880]. *Copy* (ff. 78–82).

Special Appeal by the French Committee of the Anglo-Continental Society, [1880]. The appeal, which is for funds for a new church, also contains the names of this committee of the A.C.S. and a list of subscriptions received in 1879 and 1880 (ff. 83–88^{v}).

Compte-rendu de la réunion générale [de l'Eglise catholique-gallicane], 25 March 1880. *French. Endorsed*, Mr. Yeatman (ff. 89–90^{v}).

Report, perhaps by F. A. White, of a visit to Paris to investigate the affairs of the Gallican Catholic Church, [1880]. *Duplicated and incomplete* (ff. 91–2).

Appeal for funds by the New York Committee of the Anglo-Continental Society to build a new church in Paris, [1880]. *Printed* (ff. 93–4).

Gallican Church in Paris. An appeal for funds for a new church for P. Hyacinthe, [1880] (f. 95).

Greetings card from P. Hyacinthe to F. A. White (f. 100).

[1472 *cont.*]

Notes [by F. A. White] on the state and prospects of the Gallican Catholic Church, [1880] (ff. 101–7).

Notes [by the same] on the financial affairs of the said Church, [October 1880] (ff. 108–110v).

Reports by the secretary and treasurer of the French committee of the Anglo-Continental Society, 13 November 1879. *Copies* (ff. 111–13).

L'Evangéliste, 19 November 1880. A weekly religious journal, of which this issue contains a report of a sermon of P. Hyacinthe (ff. 115–118v).

Minutes of meetings of the joint committee on Ecclesiastical Relations and Religious Reform of the General Convention of the Protestant Episcopal Church in America, 1880 (ff. 120–9), with a resolution of the House of Bishops. *Copies* (ff. 130–2).

Papers concerning a course of lectures delivered in London by P. Hyacinthe, 1880 (ff. 134–5).

Report [by F. A. White] to Henry Cotterill, Bishop of Edinburgh, describing a visit to P. Hyacinthe in Paris, 3 December 1880. *Copy* (ff. 136–49).

Note [by the same] of a conversation with the Bishop of Edinburgh, 20 February 1881 (ff. 150–151v).

Letter from the same to the Bishop of Edinburgh, 1881, enclosing a translation of a letter from the Bishop to P. Hyacinthe. *Copies* (ff. 152–8).

Various notes and observations [by F. A. White], 1881 (ff. 159–68).

Reports and minutes of meetings of the French committee of the Anglo-Continental Society, May 1880–June 1881, as follows:

Report by F. A. White, treasurer, 27 May 1880 (ff. 169–74).

Report by the same, 6 December 1880. *Copy* (ff. 175–85).

Minutes of a meeting of the Bishop of Edinburgh, the Dean of Westminster, G. H. Wilkinson, Canon of Truro, and F. A. White, at the Deanery, Westminster, 10 March 1880, with agenda and notes, the latter including an appeal for funds for the Gallican Catholic Church. *Copy* (ff. 186–202).

Minutes of a meeting of the French committee of the Anglo-Continental Society at Lambeth, 16 March 1881 (ff. 203–7). Also a report of the treasurer. *Copies* (ff. 208–11).

Minutes of a meeting of the same at Lambeth, 1 June 1881, including notes on the meeting [by the Revd. R. T. Davidson]. *Copy* (f. 217); letter from the Bishop of Edinburgh to Archbishop Tait, May 1881 (ff. 218–219v); letter from the same to P. Hyacinthe, April 1881. *Copy* (ff. 220–221v); letter from the Revd. Frederick Meyrick to Archbishop Tait, May 1881 (f. 222), and notes on a report by [Jules] Gout, treasurer of the Gallican Catholic Church (f. 224) (ff. 212–25).

Financial reports and papers concerning the Gallican Catholic Church, 1879–81, as follows:

Various monthly accounts of the Gallican Catholic Church, 1879. *French* (ff. 226–38).

Summary of the accounts of the French committee of the Anglo-Continental Society, 1879–81. *Copy. French* (ff. 239–45). Also printed accounts of the committee, 1879 (ff. 247–8), and manuscript drafts (ff. 249v–252).

Financial notes [by F. A. White], 1879 (ff. 253–258v).

Accounts of the French committee of the Anglo-Continental Society, 1880 (ff. 259v–260).

'Heads of new [financial] arrangements between the Anglo-Continental Society's Committee and the Committee of the Gallican Church', [by F. A. White, 1881] (ff. 261–8).

Notes [by the Revd. F. Meyrick], n.d. (f. 269).

Account by Thomas Yeatman, treasurer of the Gallican Catholic Church in Paris, of a meeting to extinguish a debt on the church, n.d. (ff. 271–272v).

Receipts for printing by the Chiswick Press, 1880–1 (ff. 273–81).

Papers concerning a course of lectures delivered by P. Hyacinthe in London, 1880, as follows:

Notice of the lectures on 'Positive Christianity', May 1880. *Printed* (ff. 283–4).

Financial accounts of the lectures, [1880] (ff. 285v–286).

Text of the first lecture entitled 'Creation', 16 June 1880 (ff. 287–91).

Text of the second lecture entitled 'Original Sin', with newspaper cutting concerning the same, 18 June 1880 (ff. 292–6).

Text of the third lecture entitled 'Redemption', 23 June 1880 (ff. 297–300).

Text of the fourth lecture on 'Resurrection', 26 June 1880 (ff. 301–4).

Letter from T. A. Vaudry, priest of the Gallican Catholic Church, [to the Bishop of Edinburgh], November 1881. *Copy* (ff. 305–7).

Report of the subcommittee of American bishops on the Old Catholics in France, communicated to P. Hyacinthe, March 1882. *Copy* (ff. 308–310v).

Simple réponse à une calomnie, 1883. P. Hyacinthe's reply to statement by T. A. Vaudry, priest of the Gallican Catholic Church (ff. 311–313v).

Constitution religieuse of the Gallican Catholic Church, 1884. *French* (ff. 314–18).

The Gallican Catholic Church. Some account of its progress and of its present condition and prospects, ed. by Henry Lascelles Jenner, Presiding Bishop of the Gallican Catholic Church, [1885] (ff. 319–326v).

Verses by Mme Emilie Loyson, wife of P. Hyacinthe, on 'The Dead King', 1885. *Proof* (ff. 327–328v).

Fund for the support of M. Loyson (*Père Hyacinthe*), by W. H. Fremantle Canon of Canterbury, 1886 (ff. 329–32).

[1472 *cont.***]**

Report of the Catholic Gallican Church, 1887 (ff. 333–41).

La Crise de la République. Conférence faite à l'Eglise Catholique Gallicane de la Rue d'Arras par M. Hyacinthe Loyson, 1887. *French* (ff. 343–54).

Appeal by F. A. White for funds to relieve P. Hyacinthe, [1889]. *Duplicated* (ff. 355–6).

Newspaper cuttings, 1880–1, 1921 (ff. 357–62).

Correspondence relating to the dismissal of Charles Lecat from the treasurership of the council of the Gallican Catholic Church, 1881. *Copy* (ff. 363–97).

397 ff.

1473. WHITE PAPERS

Minutes of meetings of the French committee of the Anglo-Continental Society at Lambeth Palace, 1880–1 (ff. 1^{v}–13^{v}).

95 ff.

1474. WHITE PAPERS

Account of the P. Hyacinthe Fund of the French committee of the Anglo-Continental Society with Messrs. Herries Farquhar Chapman and Co., 1878–82.

20 ff.

1475. WHITE PAPERS

Letterbook of F. A. White containing carbon copies of his correspondence as treasurer of the French committee of the Anglo-Continental Society on the affairs of P. Hyacinthe, 1878–February 1881.

viii+251 ff.

1476. WHITE PAPERS

Letterbook of the same, similar to previous entry, March 1881–1885.

viii+258 ff.

1477. WHITE PAPERS

CORRESPONDENCE, 1878–1903

Correspondence of F. A. White with Archbishop Tait; Randall Thomas Davidson, chaplain, and (1903) Archbishop of Canterbury; Robert Eden, Bishop of Moray, Ross and Caithness, Primus of Scotland; R. J. Nevin, Rector of the American Church of St. Paul, Rome, and commissary of the Bishop of Edinburgh. The correspondents are as follows:

Archbishop Tait, 1879–81. Enclosed (ff. 13–16) is a letter from Tait to P. Hyacinthe, 1881. *Copy* (ff. 1–16).

Randall Thomas Davidson, chaplain to Archbishop Tait, 1879–82, 1887, 1902–3 (ff. 17–129).

Also included is an abstract of a letter from Davidson to the Bishop of Edinburgh, 1880 (f. 130).

Letters from the same [to the Bishop of Edinburgh], 1881 (f. 132), and to the Revd. W. H. Fremantle, 1880 (f. 133).

Two letters from Mrs. Davidson to White, 1880 (ff. 135–6).

Robert Eden, Bishop of Moray, Ross and Caithness, Primus of Scotland, 1879–80. The Bishop was appointed by Tait to exercise episcopal supervision over P. Hyacinthe. See also MS. 1478 (ff. 137–65).

Also included are letters from the same to the Revd. R. T. Davidson, 1878 (f. 166), and to P. Hyacinthe, 1878. *Printed* (f. 170).

R. J. Nevin, Rector of the American church of St. Paul, Rome, and commissary to the Bishop of Edinburgh, 1878–82 (ff. 172–256). Enclosed are:

Letter from Nevin, White, and P. Hyacinthe to [Cornelius] Roosevelt, benefactor of the Gallican Catholic Church, 1879. *Copy*. *French* (f. 190).

Letter from Nevin to Count [Gaston de Douville-Maillefeu], 1879. *Copy* (f. 208).

Letter from Frederick Dan Huntington, Bishop of Central New York, to Nevin, 1879. *Copy* (f. 211).

Letter from Nevin to [Thomas] Yeatman, treasurer of the Gallican Catholic Church, 1879. *Copy* (f. 212).

Letters from the same to P. Hyacinthe, 1880. *Copies* (ff. 237, 242).

Letters from the same to the Bishop of Edinburgh, 1881. *Copies* (ff. 257–9).

259 ff.

1478. WHITE PAPERS

CORRESPONDENCE WITH THE BISHOP OF EDINBURGH

Correspondence of F. A. White with Henry Cotterill, Bishop of Edinburgh, 1879–82. The Bishop succeeded the Primus of Scotland in the exercise of episcopal supervision over P. Hyacinthe.

Enclosed is correspondence between Cotterill and P. Hyacinthe, 1879–81. *Copies* (ff. 124, 279–86).

Abstract of a letter from Eduard Herzog, Bishop of the Old Catholics of Switzerland, to the Bishop of Edinburgh, 1883 (f. 275).

286 ff.

1479. WHITE PAPERS

CORRESPONDENCE WITH THE REVD. FREDERICK MEYRICK

Correspondence of F. A. White with Frederick Meyrick, Rector of Blickling and secretary to the French committee of the Anglo-Continental Society, 1878–86 (ff. 1–230).

[1479 *cont.***]**

Enclosures are:

Letter from the Revd. W. H. Fremantle to Meyrick, 1880 (f. 101).

Letter from the Bishop of Lincoln to the same, [1880] (f. 109).

Correspondence between Meyrick and P. Hyacinthe, 1880–1 (ff. 206–14).

Also included are:

Letter from R. Skinner, English chaplain in Berne, to White, with a memorandum on Skinner and a letter from the Revd. W. H. Grove to White, 1886 (ff. 231–6).

Letter from Meyrick to the Bishop of Edinburgh, 1881. *Copy* (f. 240).

Letters from the same to the Revd. W. H. Fremantle, 1880 (ff. 248–53).

Letter from the same to T. B. Lyman, Bishop of North Carolina, 1878 (f. 257).

Copies of a circular appeal for funds (ff. 237–9, 244–7, 254–6, 258–9).

261 ff.

1480. WHITE PAPERS

CORRESPONDENCE 1878–86

General correspondence of F. A. White concerning the affairs of P. Hyacinthe, 1878–86. The correspondents are as follows:

S. Beale, English resident in Paris, 1879 (f. 1).

Charles William Brudenell-Bruce, M.P., son of the first Marquess of Ailesbury, 1878 (f. 3).

Edward Harold Browne, Bishop of Winchester, 1879–80 (ff. 5–21). Also included are a letter from the same to the Revd. W. H. Fremantle, 1880 (f. 22), and an extract [by F. A. White] from a letter from the same to the Revd. F. Meyrick, 1878 (f. 24).

Archibald George Campbell, Rector of Knipton, 1880 (ff. 25–32).

Edward Cazalet, of Tonbridge, 1881 (ff. 33–42).

Henry Cotterill, Bishop of Edinburgh, 1881 (f. 43), and a synopsis of a letter from the same to Archbishop Tait, 1881 (ff. 45–7).

Arthur Cleveland Coxe, Bishop of Western New York, 1882 (f. 48).

William Croswell Doane, Bishop of Albany, 1878–81 (ff. 50–62).

Lady Durand, widow of Sir Henry Marion Durand, and secretary to a Ladies' Committee of the Anglo-Continental Society appointed to raise funds for the Gallican Catholic Church, 1879–81 (ff. 63–81).

Also included are:

Letters from the same to the Revd. W. H. Fremantle, 1880 (ff. 82–92).

Letter from the same to the Revd. F. Meyrick, 1880 (f. 93).

Letter from the same to the Revd. R. J. Nevin, 1879 (f. 96).

George Rodney Eden, chaplain to the Bishop of Durham, 1879 (f. 98).

Sir Walter Rockliffe Farquhar, 3rd Bt., member of the French committee of the Anglo-Continental Society, 1878–81 (ff. 99–112). Also included is a letter from the same to the Revd. W. H. Fremantle, 1880 (f. 113).

William Henry Fremantle, (1895) Dean of Ripon, member of the French committee of the Anglo-Continental Society, 1880–1, 1886 (ff. 115–42). Also included is a letter from the same to the Bishop of Edinburgh, 1880 (f. 143).

William Ewart Gladstone, statesman, 1879 (ff. 145–8).

Revd. Thomas Murray Gorman, 1879, 1885 (ff. 149–51).

Charles Green, Vicar of Beckenham, 1879 (f. 152).

Revd. Charles Reuben Hale, of Baltimore, 1881, and (1892) Bishop of Cairo, U.S.A. (f. 154).

Revd. Lewis Maydwell Hogg, a secretary of the French committee of the Anglo-Continental Society, 1879–81 (ff. 157–72).

Alexander James Beresford Beresford-Hope, politician and member of the French committee of the Anglo-Continental Society, 1878–9 (ff. 173–7). Also included is a letter from the same to the Revd. W. H. Fremantle, 1880 (f. 178).

Mrs. Alice Hunt, [1880] (ff. 180–5).

Arthur John Ingram, secretary to the Additional Curates Society, 1879 (f. 186).

John Jackson, Bishop of London, 1878 (f. 188).

Sir Walter Charles James, 2nd Bt., (1884) 1st Baron Northbourne, 1878 (f. 190). Also included is a letter from the same to the Revd. W. H. Fremantle, 1880 (f. 192).

Henry Lascelles Jenner, Vicar of Preston-next-Wingham, and Bishop of the Gallican Catholic Church, 1883–4 (ff. 194–201).

Samuel Wayland Kershaw, Lambeth Librarian, 1880 (f. 202).

Daniel Conner Lathbury, journalist, 1880 (f. 204).

Revd. Alfred Theophilus Lee, D.C.L., member of the French committee of the Anglo-Continental Society, 1878–9 (ff. 206–16).

John James Lias, Professor of Modern Literature, St. David's College, Lampeter, 1879 (f. 217).

Henry Parry Liddon, Canon of St. Paul's, 1878–80 (ff. 218–23). Also included is a letter from the same to the Revd. F. Meyrick, 1879 (f. 224).

John Maxwell Lyte, Curate of St. Peter's, Eaton Square, 1878–80 (ff. 226–30).

[1480 *cont.*]

William Dalrymple Maclagan, Bishop of Lichfield, and (1891) Archbishop of York, member of the French committee of the Anglo-Continental Society, 1878–80 (ff. 231–42).

Also included is a letter from the same to the Revd. W. H. Fremantle, 1880 (f. 243).

Letter to *The New York Times*, n.d. *Draft* (ff. 244–6).

John Oakley, Vicar of St. Saviour's, Hoxton, and (1883) Dean of Manchester, to George Howard Wilkinson, Canon of Truro, and (1893) Bishop of St. Andrew's, [1880] (ff. 247–51).

Henry Palmer, member of the French committee of the Anglo-Continental Society, 1880 (f. 252).

Also included is a letter from the same to Archbishop Tait, 1881 (ff. 253–4).

B[onamy] Price, economist, 1880 (ff. 255–61).

John Webb Probyn, political writer, 1882 (f. 262).

Cornelius Roosevelt, American financier and benefactor of the Gallican Catholic Church in Paris, 1878–81 (ff. 264–324). Enclosed (ff. 278–81) is a statement by Roosevelt describing the state of the movement in Paris, 1879.

Charles Waldegrave Sandford, Bishop of Gibraltar, 1880 (ff. 325–7).

A. M. E. Scarth, 1882 (ff. 328–31).

Arthur Penrhyn Stanley, Dean of Westminster, member of the French committee of the Anglo-Continental Society, 1880–1 (ff. 332–49).

Also included is a letter from the same to the Revd. W. H. Fremantle, n.d. (f. 350).

William Francis Cowper-Temple, 1st Baron Mount-Temple, member of the French committee of the Anglo-Continental Society, 1880–1 (ff. 352–62).

Also included is a letter from the same to the Revd. W. H. Fremantle, n.d. (f. 363).

Letters from the same to the Dean [of Westminster], 1878–[9] (ff. 365–8).

Arthur Steinkopff Thompson, former chaplain at the embassy in St. Petersburg, [1880] (f. 369).

Cornelius Vanderbilt, treasurer of the American committee to raise funds for the Gallican Catholic Church, 1881 (ff. 371–9).

Mrs. Elizabeth Watson, 1880 (ff. 381–6).

F. A. White to John Williams, Bishop of Connecticut, 1881. *Copy* (ff. 387–94).

Tyndale White, n.d. (f. 395).

George Howard Wilkinson, Canon of Truro, and (1893) Bishop of St. Andrew's, 1878–80 (ff. 397–436).

William Page Wood, 1st Baron Hatherley, to the Revd. W. H. Fremantle, 1880 (f. 437).

R. Woodward, [barrister], 1879 (f. 439).

Thomas Yeatman, treasurer of the council of the Gallican Catholic Church in Paris, 1880 (ff. 441–87).

Enclosed (f. 475) is a letter [to White] from Mme Emilie Loyson, 1880.

487 ff.

1481. WHITE PAPERS

CORRESPONDENCE WITH PÈRE HYACINTHE, 1878–89

Correspondence of F. A. White with P. Hyacinthe [Loyson], Rector of the Gallican Catholic Church in Paris, and his wife, 1878–89.

P. Hyacinthe, 1878–89 (ff. 1–268).

Also included are:

Synopsis of a letter from the same to the Bishop of Edinburgh, 1881 (f. 269).

Letter from the same to the Revd. R. J. Nevin, 1880. *Copy* (f. 272).

Mme Emilie Loyson, wife of P. Hyacinthe, 1878–83 (ff. 273–330).

Also included are:

Letters from the same to the Revd. R. T. Davidson, 1880 (ff. 331–6).

Letters from the same to the Revd. W. H. Fremantle, 1880 (ff. 337–40).

Letter and copy of letter to the Revd. F. Meyrick, 1878–81, enclosing (f. 345) a copy of a letter from the Bishop of Edinburgh to P. Hyacinthe, 1881 (ff. 341–6).

346 ff.

1482. WHITE PAPERS

FRENCH CORRESPONDENCE, 1878–86

French correspondence of F. A. White concerning the affairs of P. Hyacinthe, 1878–86. The correspondents are as follows:

E[ugène] Bersier, 1878–9 (ff. 1–8).

Paul Bichery, priest of the Gallican Catholic Church, 1880 (f. 9).

A. Boullien, priest, 1881 (ff. 11–14).

Félix Carrier, priest [of the Old Catholic Church of Switzerland], 1879–95 (ff. 15–45).

John de Chevrens, treasurer of the Gallican Catholic Church, 1881 (ff. 46–53).

M. Dieudonné, priest, 1879 (f. 54).

Comte [Gaston de] Douville[-Maillefeu], treasurer of the Gallican Catholic Church, 1879 (ff. 56–61).

[1482 *cont.*]

A. A. Dupont, priest, 1879–81 (ff. 62–101).

Also included is a letter from the same to Mme Emilie Loyson, 1879 (f. 102).

G. A. Escalger, priest, 1878 (ff. 104–12).

Also included is a letter from the same to the Revd. F. Meyrick, 1878 (f. 113).

Jules Gout, treasurer of the Gallican Catholic Church, 1881 (ff. 115–20).

Also included is a letter from the same to the Revd. F. Meyrick, 1881 (f. 121).

Eduard Herzog, Bishop of the Old Catholics of Switzerland, 1885.

Enclosed (f. 125) is a letter to him from the Revd. R. Skinner, English chaplain in Berne, 1885 (ff. 123–8).

— Kerckhoffs, [secretary to the council of the Gallican Catholic Church], 1881 (ff. 129–32).

Also included is a letter from the same to Lady Durand, 1880. *Copy* (f. 133).

M. Lartigau, priest of the Gallican Catholic Church, 1881–6 (ff. 136–66).

F. A. White to Abraham Lesneur, priest, 1882. *Copy* (f. 167).

[Joseph] Laurens, priest, 1879 (f. 169).

Charles Lecat, treasurer of the Gallican Catholic Church, 1880–3 (ff. 171–224).

C. Miel, minister of the French congregation in Philadelphia, [to P. Hyacinthe], 1879. *Copy* (f. 225).

E[mile] Mopinot, secretary to the council of the Gallican Catholic Church, to Mme Emilie Loyson, 1880. *Copy* (f. 228).

L. Sterliz, priest [of the Old Catholic Church of Switzerland], 1880 (f. 230).

T. A. Vaudry, priest of the Gallican Catholic Church, 1881 (ff. 234–42).

242 ff.

1483. ACCOUNTS OF ARCHBISHOP SECKER

Accounts of receipts and expenditure of Thomas Secker, Archbishop of Canterbury, 13 April 1758–5 July 1768.

Hol. (pp. 1–275).

Also (p. 277) the autograph signature of Helena, daughter of Queen Victoria and wife of Prince Christian of Schleswig-Holstein, and an account of a visit by her to Jesus Hospital, Bray, Berks., by the Revd. John Charles Gawthern, master and chaplain, 1910. Also (p. 281) an account by the same of a visit to Bray by William Stubbs, Bishop of Oxford.

Bound in green vellum.

Bookplate of Archbishop Secker.

Given by the Revd. John Charles Gawthern, 1936.

i+369 pp.

1484. LETTERS AND TRANSCRIPTS OF W. P. BLORE

Letters from W. P. Blore, librarian to the Dean and Chapter of Canterbury, to Irene Churchill, author of *Canterbury Administration*, 1933, concerning the medieval administration of the Archbishop of Canterbury, and including numerous transcripts mainly of records in the possession of the Dean and Chapter of Canterbury, 1935–9. The earlier part of the correspondence has been filed by Miss Churchill according to source and subject. Also included are Latin verses by Blore on the Dean of Canterbury's whooping-cough (f. 167).

200 ff.

1485. MONUMENTAL INSCRIPTIONS FROM LONDON CHURCHES

Copies of monumental inscriptions from churches in the city and suburbs of London, probably made in 1638. The following churches are included:

St. Paul's Cathedral (pp. 1–10)
Westminster Abbey (pp. 15–27)
Chelsea (pp. 29, 32)
Stepney (p. 29)
Stratford Bow (pp. 29–30)
Temple (p. 30)
Fulham (p. 30)
Putney (pp. 31–2)
St. Margaret, Westminster (pp. 32–3)
All Hallows, London Wall (pp. 33, 118–19)
St. Anne, Blackfriars (p. 33)
St. Christopher [-le-Stock] (pp. 33, 101)
St. Faith (pp. 33, 129–30)
St. Dionis, Backchurch (pp. 34, 101–2, 119)
St. Laurence, Jewry (pp. 34–5, 110)
St. Margaret, Lothbury (p. 34)
St. Mary, Abchurch (pp. 35, 103–4)
St. Martin, Orgar (p. 36)
St. Mary Magdalene, Old Fish Street (p. 36)
St. Michael, Cornhill (p. 36)
St. Michael, Crooked Lane (pp. 36–7)
St. Stephen, Coleman Street (pp. 37, 111–12)
St. Bartholomew-the-Great (pp. 37–8)
St. Swithin (pp. 38, 104–5, 120)
Bridewell (p. 39)

[1485 *cont.***]**

St. Dunstan-in-the-West (pp. 39, 140–3)
Holy Trinity, Minories (p. 39)
St. Saviour, Southwark (p. 39)
St. Martin-in-the-Fields (p. 40)
St. Giles-in-the-Fields (p. 41)
St. James, Clerkenwell (pp. 41, 145–7)
St. Mary, Whitechapel (p. 42)
Miscellaneous epitaphs of classical writers, statesmen, saints, etc. (pp. 65–97)
St. Olave, Hart Street (pp. 98, 117–18)
St. Andrew Undershaft (pp. 98–9)
St. Catherine Coleman (p. 99)
St. Helen, Bishopsgate (p. 99)
St. Martin, Outwich (p. 101)
All Hallows, Lombard Street (pp. 102, 120)
St. Edmund [the King], Lombard Street (pp. 102–3)
St. Clement, Eastcheap (p. 103)
St. Mary, Woolchurch (p. 105)
St. Stephen, Walbrook (p. 105)
All Hallows, Thames Street (p. 106)
St. Michael Paternoster [Royal] (p. 106)
St. Thomas the Apostle (pp. 107, 149)
St. Martin Vintry (pp. 107–8)
St. Mary, Aldermanbury (pp. 108, 113)
St. Mary-le-Bow (p. 108)
St. Mildred [Bread Street] (pp. 108–9)
'St. Syth' [St. Benet, Sherehog] (p. 109)
St. Pancras [Soper Lane] (pp. 109–10)
St. Olave, Upwell [Jewry] (pp. 110, 121)
St. Michael, Bassishaw (p. 113)
St. Mary Magdalene, Milk Street (pp. 113, 122)
St. Alban 'by love lane' [Wood Street] (pp. 114–15)
St. Giles, without Cripplegate (p. 116)
All Hallows, Barking (p. 118)
St. Peter-le-Poer (p. 119)
St. Anthony (p. 120)
St. [Mary] Zachary (p. 122)
St. Olave, Silver Street (p. 123)
St. Leonard, Foster Lane (p. 123)
St. Anne in the Willows [SS. Anne and Agnes] (p. 124)
St. Botolph, Aldersgate (pp. 124–8)
Christ Church [Newgate Street] (pp. 128–9)
St. Augustine (p. 129)
St. Martin, Ludgate (pp. 130–1)
All Hallows, Bread Street (p. 131)
St. Michael [? Mildred], Bread Street (p. 131)
St. Nicholas, Cole Abbey (p. 132)

St. Benet, Paul's Wharf (p. 132)
St. Andrew-by-the-Wardrobe (p. 133)
St. Mary Magdalene [Old Fish Street] (p. 133)
St. Gregory by St. Paul's (pp. 134–5)
St. Bartholomew's Hospital (pp. 135–6)
St. Bartholomew's Priory [Smithfield] (pp. 136–7)
St. Sepulchre [Holborn] (pp. 137–9)
St. Andrew, Holborn (pp. 139–40)
St. [Mary] Magdalene, Southwark (pp. 143–4)
St. Olave, Southwark (pp. 144–5)
St. Leonard, Shoreditch (p. 145)
St. Dunstan-in-the-East (p. 147)

On the front is written 'Nar[cissus] Luttrell: His Book, 1682'.

Purchased 1937.

iv+188 pp.

1486–7. TRANSCRIPT OF REGISTER Q OF THE DEAN AND CHAPTER OF CANTERBURY

Transcript of Register Q of the Dean and Chapter of Canterbury, being the register *sede vacante* after the death of Archbishop Peckham. The transcript is by W. P. Blore, librarian to the Dean and Chapter of Canterbury.

1486: i+127 ff.
1487: i+127 ff.

Given by W. P. Blore, 1937.

1488. PROBATE ACTS OF PECULIARS ETC., 16TH–19TH CENTURIES

Grants of probate or administration issued principally in peculiar or exempt jurisdictions. They are written on vellum, unless otherwise stated, and are in English during the Commonwealth and from 1733. All have lost their seals. The wills are not attached.

Deposited by Phillimore and Co. through the British Records Association (deposit 125), 1937. See also MS. 1837 f. 29.

1. Nicholas Drewe of Ogbourne St. Andrew, Wilts., 4 May 1590. Peculiar of the Dean and Chapter of Windsor.

2. Edward Fewtrell of Easthope, Salop, 20 August 1652. By the Keepers of the Liberties of England.

3. John Allin of Lammas, Norf., 8 August 1659. By the Keepers of the Liberties of England.

4. Thomas Rawson, 22 October 1667. Court Baron of Mansfield.

5. John Smith of Wells, Somerset, 17 June 1673. By the Bishop of Bath and Wells. *Paper*.

[1488 *cont.***]**

6. John Crell of Bocking, Essex, 5 June 1684. Deanery of Bocking, peculiar of Canterbury.

7. Richard Steton of Allchurch [Alvechurch], Worcs., 1 April 1685. Peculiar.

8. John Cowley of Banbury, Oxon., 2 September 1696. Peculiar of Banbury and Cropredy.

9. Henry Elton of East Woodhay, Hants, 7 November 1701. Peculiar.

10. Thomas Harbor of Hurstbourne Priors, Hants, 16 July 1702. Peculiar.

11. Humphrey Newberry of East Meon, Hants, 9 December 1702. Peculiar.

12. Thomas Beale of Bishop's Cleeve, Glos., 26 April 1703. Peculiar.

13. Francis Evans of the parish of St. Mary, Shrewsbury, gent., 7 May 1703. Peculiar.

14. Anne Faulkner of Temple Cowley, Oxon., 26 October 1704. Court Baron of Temple Cowley.

15. Mary Butcher of Newington Butts, London, 14 February 1705. Court of Arches.

16. Joseph Kent of Isleham, Cambs., yeoman, 17 May 1714. Peculiar.

17. William Fish of Sevenoaks, Kent, 28 April 1719. Court of Arches.

18. Richard Preston, senior, of Shalbourne, Wilts., 26 July 1720. Peculiar of Hungerford, Berks. *Paper*.

19. Richard Day of Mayfield, Sussex, 28 July 1721. Deanery of South Malling, peculiar.

20. William Adey of Ringwood, Hants, 15 October 1721. Peculiar.

21. Richard Embey of Bibury, Glos., 10 April 1722. Peculiar.

22. Flower Walters of Easton in Gordano, Somerset, 31 July 1724. Peculiar.

23. Richard Acton of Allchurch [Alvechurch], Worcs., 9 November 1724. Peculiar.

24. Thomas Smith of Buxted, Sussex, 10 May 1729. Deanery of South Malling, peculiar.

25. John West of Banbury, Oxon., 3 September 1729. Peculiar of Banbury and Cropredy.

26. Eli Hole of Henstridge, Somerset, 11 December 1730. Peculiar.

27. John Mace of Wantage, Berks., 27 June 1733. Peculiar. *Paper*.

28. John Wadelate of St. Faith, Hants, yeoman, 10 July 1736. Peculiar.

29. Anne Boosey of Writtle, Essex, widow, 31 May 1737. Peculiar of Writtle and Roxwell.

30. Edward Smith of Burroughclere alias Burghclere, Hants, yeoman, 24 February 1753. Peculiar.

31. John Higgins of Havant, Hants, 29 May 1758. Peculiar.

32. Mary Andrews of Thorn St. Margaret, Somerset, widow, 21 August 1769. Peculiar of prebend of Milverton, Wells.

33. Thomas Day of Spaldwick, Hunts., gent., 20 October 1775. Peculiar of Long Stow prebend of Lincoln. *Paper.*

34. Thomas Dunford of Evercreech, Somerset, carpenter, 10 November 1777. By the Dean of Wells.

35. Jane Jackson, wife of the Revd. Samuel Jackson, of Stisted, Essex, 27 April 1779. Deanery of Bocking, peculiar.

36. Richard Pearson, the elder, of Aylesbury, Bucks., victualler, 10 April 1795. Peculiar of Aylesbury prebend of Lincoln.

37. Richard Mitchell of Walford Farm, Wimborne Minster, Dorset, 4 July 1796. Peculiar.

38. Edward Gittos of parish of St. Mary Magdalene, Bridgnorth, Salop, tailor, 20 June 1807. Peculiar of Deanery of Bridgnorth.

39. John Cross, 9 October 1809. Peculiar of the lord of the 'Franchises and peculiar Jurisdiction of the Soken in the county of Essex'.

40. Thomas Bown of parish of St. Margaret, Leicester, warehouseman, 27 June 1823. Peculiar of St. Margaret's prebend of Lincoln.

1489. PAPERS OF ROBERT MYLNE, SURVEYOR TO ST. PAUL'S CATHEDRAL

Papers of Robert Mylne (1734–1811), Surveyor to St. Paul's Cathedral (1767), consisting of accounts, reports on the fabric, and letters, 1764–1801. The documents are badly damaged and many are accompanied by copies made by R. S. Mylne.

ACCOUNTS, 1764–1801

Account of Samuel Dowbiggen, carpenter, 1764–5. Endorsed, No. 10 (ff. 2–5). Also a copy by R. S. Mylne (ff. 6–12).

Account of legal expenses of the Archbishop of Canterbury, the Bishop of London, and the Lord Mayor of London, [Trustees of the Fabric], 1766–9. Endorsed, No. 9th (ff. 14–15).

Account of John Crang for repairs to the organ, 1768. Endorsed, No. 11th (f. 16). Also a copy by R. S. Mylne (f. 17).

Account of John Byfield for repairs to the organ, 1777. Endorsed, (1) by Mylne 'In consequence of an Examination by [Mes]srs Sneyler and Green, Organ builders'; (2) No. 11 (ff. 18–19). Also a copy by R. S. Mylne (f. 20).

Orders [by the Trustees of the Fabric] for the prevention of robberies, 1778 (f. 22). Also a copy by R. S. Mylne (ff. 23–4).

[1489 *cont.***]**

Estimate and account of John Willis for making twenty-four chairs for the Convocation Room, 1791 (ff. 25–7). Also a copy of the estimate by R. S. Mylne (f. 28).

'Abstracts of Accounts and notes on important matters connected with the Fabric of the Cathedral', [by R. S. Mylne], 1766–1801. The items include the purchase of 'the first designs' of Sir James Thornhill for the cupola, 1776 (f. 36); account of Aynsworth Thwaites for repairs to the clock, 1776 (f. 38); 'weight of Chain Bars Put to Southside of Cupola', 1781 (ff. 44–5) (ff. 29–52).

REPORTS ON THE FABRIC, 1781

Two reports by Robert Mylne to the Dean and Chapter of St. Paul's, describing extensive repairs undertaken to the south-west side of the cupola and the south transept, [20] March 1781 (ff. 54–7), and 15 November 1781 (ff. 58–61). *Drafts* (ff. 54–61).

LETTERS, ETC., 1778–98

Letters, etc. to Robert Mylne as follows:

Order by Archbishop Cornwallis, and Robert Lowth, Bishop of London, 4 November 1778, for payment of painter's account (f. 63).

George Pretyman, Bishop of Lincoln, 2 June 1790, approving works to the Deanery. The Archbishop has the Acts of Parliament relative to St. Paul's (f. 66).

Archbishop Moore, 20 July 1790. If Convocation meets at St. Paul's, it must not be put off because of the expense of taking down scaffolding. The organ can be dispensed with (f. 69).

George Pretyman, Bishop of Lincoln, 21 July 1790. The two Houses of Convocation go to St. Paul's on 11 August, and the cathedral must be ready to receive them (f. 72).

Christopher Wilson, Bishop of Bristol, 13 August 1791, approving payment of bills (f. 75).

Archbishop Moore, 12 August 1791, enclosing draft for £1,097. 5*s*. 9*d*. The vellum accounts are signed and will be sent from Scarborough (f. 78).

Beilby Porteus, Bishop of London, 30 August 1793, sending draft. Will send the account signed (f. 81).

Archbishop Moore, 6 July 1798, enclosing draft and promising to send vellum account from Lambeth (f. 84).

Engraved invitation to Robert Mylne to attend a service of thanksgiving at St. Paul's Cathedral 'for the many signal and important victories obtained by His Majesty's Navy in the course of the present War', 19 December 1797 (f. 86).

At f. i is a letter from R. S. Mylne to the Librarian, 1917.

Given by R. S. Mylne, 1917.

ii+86 ff.

1490. SERMONS AND PAPERS OF WILLIAM EDWARD COLLINS, BISHOP OF GIBRALTAR

Copies of sermons, charges, and addresses by William Edward Collins, Bishop of Gibraltar, 1895–1911. Many of the sermons are printed in *Hours of insight and other sermons*, 1912.

Also included are copies of reviews of books by him and obituary notices; photographs of Collins (f. 92^{v}), and of a chalice presented to him (f. 93).

Printed insertions are an offprint of 'A Letter from the Bishop to his People', *The Anglican Church Magazine*, [September 1910], and a memorial service held in Lambeth Palace Chapel, 1911.

Given by the Revd. Herbert Waddams, 1949.

95 ff.

1491. LETTERS AND PAPERS OF WILLIAM HODGE MILL

Letters and papers of William Hodge Mill (1792–1853), Regius Professor of Hebrew, Cambridge, and Rector of Brasted, Kent, 1846–53, principally concerning the Gorham controversy and anti-Tractarian and papal disturbances at Brasted. A list of contents is at ff. i–iv. The correspondents are as follows:

Walter Farquhar Hook, Vicar of Leeds, and (1869) Dean of Chichester, 19 May 1846, protesting at the proposed consecration of Bishop Gobat (f. 1).

Revd. John Brande Morris, 17 July 1846, concerning his secession to Rome (f. 3).

William Hodge Mill to the Revd. J. B. Morris, 12 August 1846, replying to the previous item. *Copy* (f. 5).

George Moberly, headmaster of Winchester, and (1869) Bishop of Salisbury, 12 February 1847, urging that Pusey cease to publish Roman Catholic devotional works (f. 9).

Henry Edward Manning, Archdeacon of Chichester, 12 October 1849, about opposition to the confirmation of Samuel Hinds as Bishop of Norwich (f. 11).

John Keble, Vicar of Hursley, 26 October 1849, about the same (f. 13).

Same, 28 October 1849, about the same (f. 15).

Same, 1 November 1849, about the same (f. 17).

Same, 4 November 1849, about the same (f. 19), enclosing a letter from Samuel Hinds, Bishop-elect of Norwich, to himself, 2 November 1849, defining his theological position. *Copy* (f. 20).

[1491 *cont.***]**

Revd. William Edward Heygate, 10 January [1850], about the Gorham judgement (f. 21).

Sir George Prevost, 2nd Bt., Perpetual Curate of Stinchcombe, 14 January 1850, offering to join in protest at the Gorham judgement (f. 23).

Henry William Wilberforce, Vicar of East Farleigh, 23 January 1850, on the dangers of the Gorham judgement and the possibility of Convocation addressing the Crown (f. 25).

Henry Edward Manning, Archdeacon of Chichester, 31 January 1850, commenting on proposal to erect new court to which ecclesiastical appeals be transferred from the Privy Council (f. 27).

Same, 8 March 1850, asking him to attend vestry meeting of St. Paul's, Knightsbridge (f. 29).

Charles James Blomfield, Bishop of London, to Alexander James Beresford Beresford-Hope, 11 March 1850, urging that the Gorham judgement has not altered doctrine, and that this can be done only by a Synod. *Copy* (f. 31).

Henry Edward Manning, Archdeacon of Chichester, 13 March 1850, enclosing paper for his signature. Gladstone's attitude (f. 33).

Edward Bouverie Pusey, Regius Professor of Hebrew, Oxford, [14 March 1850], about the same (f. 35).

Benjamin Webb, Curate of Brasted, 15 March 1850, urging Mill to preach at Oxford concerning the Gorham judgement (f. 37).

Robert Isaac Wilberforce, Archdeacon of the East Riding, n.d., on the doctrine of the eucharist. *Incomplete copy* (f. 40).

Benjamin Webb, Curate of Brasted, to the Revd. John Mason Neale, 27 March 1850, about the Bishop of Exeter. Mill and reservation of the sacrament (f. 43).

William Palmer, Fellow of Magdalen College, Oxford, 22 April 1850, on the consequences and dangers of the Gorham judgement (f. 45).

Richard Cavendish, brother of the 7th Duke of Devonshire, 22 April 1850, discussing a proposed reply to Archdeacon Hare on the Gorham controversy (f. 49).

Charles Hughes Terrot, Bishop of Edinburgh, 29 April [1850], about the effect of the Gorham controversy on the Scottish Episcopal Church (f. 55).

William Palmer, Fellow of Magdalen College, Oxford, 29 June 1850, announcing plans for a National Synod (f. 57).

Same, 4 July 1850, describing the plans in detail (f. 59).

Mill to the Revd. William Palmer, 11 July 1850, criticizing plans for a National Synod. *Draft* (f. 65).

Alexander James Beresford Beresford-Hope, 16 July 1850, about a meeting to address the Archbishop of Canterbury on the Gorham judgement (f. 67).

Henry Phillpotts, Bishop of Exeter, 6 September 1850, discussing the Gorham judgement (f. 69).

William Palmer, Fellow of Magdalen College, Oxford, to Dr. E. B. Pusey, 25 September 1850, protesting at the latter's actions. *Copy by Palmer* (f. 73).

Mill to the Revd. William Palmer, 27 September 1850, about the same. *Draft* (f. 75).

Alexander James Beresford Beresford-Hope, 27 September 1850, about Palmer's letter to Pusey (f. 79), enclosing a letter from himself to Pusey, 27 September 1850. *Copy* (f. 81).

William Palmer, Fellow of Magdalen College, Oxford, 6 October 1850, discussing the divergence in the views of Mill, and Pusey, Keble, and Hope (f. 82).

Henry Edward Manning, Archdeacon of Chichester, 15 October 1850, about opposition to the Gorham judgement (f. 84).

George Washington Doane, Bishop of New Jersey, to Mill, E. B. Pusey, Keble, and Hope, 22 October 1850, explaining the views of the American Bishops on a memorial from the London Union on Church Matters (f. 86).

Benjamin Webb, Curate of Brasted, 6 November 1850, describing anti-papal activities at Brasted (f. 88).

Same, 7 November 1850, about the same (f. 90).

Same, 13 November 1850, about the same (f. 92).

Same, 14 November 1850, about the same (f. 94).

Same, 16 November 1850, about the same (f. 98).

Same, 17 November 1850, about the same and choral services (f. 101).

Protest by Henry Harrison, incumbent, and the churchwardens of Kilndown, Kent, of which A. J. B. Beresford-Hope is one, at claim to jurisdiction by Cardinal Wiseman, 19 November 1850. *Printed* (f. 103).

Alexander James Beresford Beresford-Hope, 20 November 1850, discussing the communication of Bishop Doane's letter to the London Union on Church Matters (f. 104).

Declaration of the clergy and laity of Brasted against papal claims to jurisdiction in England, November 1850. *Draft* (f. 106).

Benjamin Webb, Curate of Brasted, 20 November 1850, about anti-papal activities at Brasted and opposition to the choir (f. 107).

Protest by parishioners of Brasted to the Revd. W. H. Mill, about papal aggression and Puseyism and against innovations in forms of worship, [1850] (f. 111).

[1491 *cont.***]**

Francis Henry Dickinson, 20 November 1850, urging moderation towards extremists (f. 117).

Henry Edward Manning, Archdeacon of Chichester, 23 November 1850, on the reasons for his resignation of the archdeaconry (f. 119).

Archbishop Sumner, 25 November [1850], accepting address from Brasted against papal aggression and approving its contents. *Copy* (f. 121).

Benjamin Webb, Curate of Brasted, 26 November 1850, enclosing previous item (f. 122).

Joshua Wilson Faulkner, churchwarden of Brasted, to the Revd. Benjamin Webb, 26 November 1850, about an address against innovations in forms of worship (f. 124).

Benjamin Webb, Curate of Brasted, 26 November 1850, about the same (f. 126), enclosing a letter from himself to J. W. Faulkner, 26 November 1850. *Copy* (f. 128).

Same, 27 November 1850, about counter petition at Brasted (f. 129).

Same, 29 November 1850, about the same (f. 131).

Mill to Archbishop Sumner, 29 November 1850, about disaffection at Brasted. *Copy* (f. 133).

Benjamin Webb, Curate of Brasted, 1 December 1850, about the same (f. 139).

Edward Bouverie Pusey, Regius Professor of Hebrew, Oxford, 6 December [1850], about a declaration acknowledging the royal supremacy (f. 141), enclosing the declaration. *Proof* (f. 143).

Notice of a lecture on Puseyism to be given at Brasted by the Revd. Robert Ainslir [? Ainslie, (1864) Canon of Lincoln], 15 January 1851. *Printed* (f. 145).

Resolutions of meetings in London on 27 February and 1 March 1851 to initiate a series of Anglican tracts to be known as 'Papers on Church and State'. *Printed* (f. 146).

Petition from inhabitants of Brasted to Archbishop Sumner, approving innovations in forms of worship, [1851]. *Copy* (f. 148).

Monition from Archbishop Sumner to James Patching and Charles Quin, churchwardens of Brasted, requiring removal of a lectern and faldstool, 15 September 1851. *Copy* (f. 150).

Monition from the same to the Revd. Benjamin Webb, requiring use of surplices and intoning to cease, 15 September 1851. *Signed and sealed* (f. 152).

William Hodge Mill to the churchwardens of Brasted, 24 September 1851, forbidding removal of lectern and faldstool. *Copy* (f. 153).

Same to Archbishop Sumner, 25 September 1851, giving his reasons for opposing the monition. *Copy* (f. 154).

Resolution concerning the Archbishop's monitions, 27 September 1851. *Copy* (f. 156).

William Hodge Mill to Archbishop Sumner, 29 September 1851, describing his conduct of services in obedience to monitions, and appealing for their revision. *Copy* (f. 158).

Archbishop Sumner, 18 October [1851], explaining his wishes for the services at Brasted. *Copy* (f. 162).

Same, 24 October 1851, about the same (f. 164).

Charles Fowler, secretary to the South Church Union, 6 November 1851, conveying support (f. 166).

William Hodge Mill to Charles Fowler, [1851], replying to previous item. *Draft* (f. 168).

Protest against the proselytizing practices of Bishop Gobat, 9 September 1853. *Printed* (f. 170).

List of signatures to the protest against the proselytism carried on by Bishop Gobat, [1853] (f. 171).

Benjamin Webb, Vicar of St. Andrew's, Well Street, London, to the Revd. John Mason Neale, 9 June 1865, concerning the 'fool's paradise' of *The Church Times* (f. 183).

Given by Thomas George Hill, Professor of Plant Physiology, University of London, 1945.

184 ff.

1492. PREPARATION FOR CONSECRATION

Meditations, exercises, and prayers for the use of a bishop-elect preparing for consecration, probably compiled by the Revd. R. Somerset Ward, honorary chaplain to the Archbishop of Canterbury.

Given by the author to William Temple, Archbishop of Canterbury, and deposited in the Library in 1945.

Typescript. v+44 ff.

1493. RITE OF THE ARCHDIOCESE OF BRAGA

'An Account of the Diocesan Use of the Archdiocese of Braga in Portugal', by Henry Frank Fulford Williams, Rector of Ideford. Thesis accepted for the degree of B.D. in the University of Cambridge, 1951.

Given by the author.

Typescript. iii+96 ff.

1494. ARCHBISHOP SHELDON

'Calendar of the Letter Book of Archbishop Sheldon, 1664–1670. MS. Add. C. 308 (S.C. 28473) in the Bodleian Library, Oxford', by E. A. O. Whiteman, Fellow of Lady Margaret Hall, Oxford. Inserted is an

[1494 *cont.***]**

off-print of 'Two letter books of Archbishops Sheldon and Sancroft' by Dr. Whiteman in *Bodleian Library Record*, iv, no. 4.

Given by the author, 1953.

Typescript. ii+33 ff.

1495. RELIEF OF THE VAUDOIS

Account book of sums collected from parishes within deaneries throughout the dioceses of Bath and Wells and Bristol for the relief of the Vaudois Protestants, by authority of briefs issued under the Great Seal, [1704]. The names of incumbents and churchwardens are stated. Sums collected from Dissenters at Bath, Shepton Mallet, and Bristol are included (f. 44^{v}).

Given by the British Records Association (deposit 295), 1940.

iv+46 ff.

1496. THE KING'S RIGHT OF INDULGENCE

'The King's Right of Indulgence In Spirituall Matters, With the Equity Thereof, Asserted by One of his Faithfull Subjects', 1665, [by Arthur Annesley, 1st Earl of Anglesey]. The treatise was published in 1688.

ix+179 ff.

1497. THEOLOGY

'Pious Meditations on the Lord's Prayer', by Cornelius Middleguest, 1687.

[Given by Arnold Keppel of Datchet, 1953.]

vii+146 ff.

1498. TREATISE ON SACRED POETRY

Author's draft, very much worked over, of Lib. 1, chapters 1–8, of a learned treatise entitled 'The Discovery of Sacred Poesie', written in the first quarter of the 17th century. The author, who is not identified, quotes extensively from Hebrew and from classical writers.

The manuscript is bound in a fragment of a grant by John Beveridge, Precentor of Lincoln (1621–32), to John Ovebye [Overbury], of Hinckley, Leics., of the rectory of Kibworth Beauchamp, Leics.

88 ff.

1499. CARDINAL POLE'S LEGATION

'Negotiati delle Legationi del Cardinale Reginaldo Polo mandato da Papa Giulio III in Inghilterra per la reduttione di quel regno all'obedienza della Sede Apostolica et in Francia per trattar la pace tra' Henrico II e Carlo V Imperatore, l'anno MDLIII.'

Italian and Latin. 17th century. Bound in vellum.

Old press marks 343 [Bibl. Mattei] and the number 7660 pasted on the spine. Belonged to W. E. Collins, Bishop of Gibraltar. Given by Lord Northbourne, [1911].

x+236 ff.

1500. STATUTA CATHEDRALIS DUNELMENSIS

'Statuta et Ordinationes Ecclesiae Cathedralis Christi et Beatae Mariae Virginis Dunelm[ensis]', 20 March 1555. A copy written in the second half of the 17th century. The statutes of Durham Cathedral are printed in Surtees Society, cxliii, 72–191.

On the front cover is written in ink 'No. 317'.

iv+118 ff.

1501–31. EELES COLLECTION

Collection of Francis Carolus Eeles.

Given, 1954.

1501. EELES COLLECTION

ANTIPHONALE, ETC.

ff. i+432+ii. Early 16th century. Size 190×135 mm. Written for the use of Augustinian canons in the Netherlands.

See MS. 1362 for reference to a fuller description of this manuscript.

1502. EELES COLLECTION

PONTIFICALE.

ff. i+132+i. 14th century. Size 315×240 mm.

See MS. 1362 for reference to a fuller description of this manuscript.

1503. EELES COLLECTION

ORDINARIUM CISTERCIENSE

ff. i+107+i. 15th century. Size 195×140 mm. Written in France.

See MS. 1362 for reference to a fuller description of this manuscript.

1504. EELES COLLECTION

PSALMI PENTITENTIALES, LATINE ET ITALICE

ff. xix+34+xxiv. 15th century. Size 167×110 mm. Written in Italy.

See MS. 1362 for reference to a fuller description of this manuscript.

1505. EELES COLLECTION

'ORDINARIUS DE OFFICIO SEPULTURE', ETC.

ff. i+86+i. 15th–16th centuries. Size 125×90 mm. Written in Germany for the use of Dominican nuns.

See MS. 1362 for reference to a fuller description of this manuscript.

1506. EELES COLLECTION

KALENDARIUM

ff. i+6+i. 1531. Size 240×172 mm.

See MS. 1362 for reference to a fuller description of this manuscript.

1507. EELES COLLECTION

OFFICIA LITURGICA

Psalms, collects, hymns, etc. ff. ii+278+iii. Late 15th century. Size 128×95 mm. Written in western Germany for Augustinian use. Phillipps MS. 673.

See MS. 1362 for reference to a fuller description of this manuscript.

1508. EELES COLLECTION

HORAE (partly in Italian)

ff. ii+140+ii. Early 16th century. Size 160×115 mm. Written in Italy, perhaps for use in Genoa.

See MS. 1362 for reference to a fuller description of this manuscript.

1509. EELES COLLECTION

PONTIFICALE

ff. xi+122+ix. 1522–8. Size 136×97 mm. Written in England for the use of Thomas Bale, O.S.A., Bishop of Lydda and Suffragan to Cuthbert Tunstall, Bishop of London, from 1522 to 1528.

See MS. 1362 for reference to a fuller description of this manuscript.

1510. EELES COLLECTION

FRAGMENTS

Guardbook of manuscript and printed fragments from bindings. They include the following:

No. 4. 14th–15th centuries. The lower part of a leaf. Written space *c.* 150 mm. wide. Two fragments of a Sarum Missal containing part of the service for the Vigil of Pentecost, as in the printed edition (ed. F. H. Dickinson) colls. 420–3.

No. 6. Parts of two sheets of a printed almanac, including the title-page Imprint 'By James Paterson Mathematician. Printed at Holy-rood-house for the year 1688'.

Nos. 8–9. Two leaves (fol. xiiii and fol. xx) from *Gesta Romanorum*, (Strassburg: Printer of the 1483 Jordanus de Quedlinburg [Georg Husmer?], 6 August 1489). *B.M.C.* i. 139; Hain* 7746; Proctor 621.

No. 12. 13th century. A bifolium of Hours of B.V.M. Written space 135×80 mm. 19 lines to the page. Germany.

Nos. 14–15. Two leaves (I^8 and I^9) from Robertus Caracciolus de Licio, *Sermones quadragesimales, etc.* (Cologne: Ulrich Zel, 17 January 1473). *B.M.C.* i. 181; Hain* 4429; G. K. W. 6067; Proctor 880; Pellechet 3247; Polain 983.

Nos. 20–1. 14th century. A leaf of a Processional (St. Laurence, 10 August; Assumption of B.V.M., 15 August) written in England. Cut in two and used as pastedowns of an octavo book. Written space 170×125 mm. 10 long lines and music. Notes in the upper margin of the recto of no. 20 and the lower margin of the recto of no. 21 were copied on no. 23 by W. H. St. John Hope in July 1905.

No. 31. 15th century. One leaf of a missal.

No. 43. 15th century. A leaf of a breviary with part of the office of 11,000 virgins. Written space 145×110 mm. 2 cols. 23 lines. Germany.

Nos. 44–5. 13th century. Two fragments of one leaf in a small neat Italian hand of Justinian, *Institutiones*, end of bk. 1 and beginning of bk. 2.

Nos. 47–8. Flyleaves from printed books containing verses and scribbling in sixteenth-century hands. On one is written 'Thes buck pertins to ye Maistres of Grahame.'

No. 50. A paper flyleaf inscribed 'Thes buek pertins to ye maistres off Grahame. Ane man without marcy sall mess / Ande he sall heif mercy yat marcyfull is.' There are further scribbled verses in other hands.

Nos. 51–2. Early 14th century. Two adjacent leaves of a noted missal, containing settings of Sanctus and Agnus Dei (cf. *Sarum Missal*, ed. W. Legg, 1916, 7–8). Written space 230×155 mm. 2 cols. 13 lines and music. England.

Nos. 54–5. 14th century. Two leaves of Sarum Customary found in Glasgow containing portions relating to the preparation of the sacred elements and the reading of the Gospel in the final service as in pp. 71–5, 90, 100, 103–4 of W. H. Frere, *Use of Sarum*, vol. i. Formerly the cover of a book.

1511. EELES COLLECTION

ANTIPHONALE

ff. i+77+i. 14th century. Size 430×310 mm. Written in Italy, for use in the diocese of Perugia.

See MS. 1362 for reference to a fuller description of this manuscript.

1512. EELES COLLECTION

BREVIARIUM CISTERCIENSE

ff. ii+203+ii. Early 15th century. Size 153 × 112 mm. Written in France for Cistercian use in the diocese of Rodez and perhaps for use at Bonnecombe.

See MS. 1362 for reference to a fuller description of this manuscript.

1513. EELES COLLECTION

PONTIFICALE

ff. 124+i. Late 15th century. Size 232 × 152 mm. Written in France, probably for the use of Jacques Hémeré, Bishop of Bethlehem 1492–8.

See MS. 1362 for reference to a fuller description of this manuscript.

1514. EELES COLLECTION

PONTIFICALE

ff. ii+112+ii. Late 12th century. Size 230 × 170 mm. Written in Spain for use in the diocese of Gerona.

See MS. 1362 for reference to a fuller description of this manuscript.

1515. EELES COLLECTION

STATUTES OF ST. PAUL'S CATHEDRAL

Copy made about the middle of the 18th century of the 'Statuta Minora Ecclesiae Sancti Pauli' (Sparrow Simpson MS. B) in the possession of the Dean and Chapter of St. Paul's (shelfmark W.D.20). The foliation of the original manuscript is entered in the margin. The text has been corrected by Thomas Secker, Dean of St. Paul's (1750) and subsequently Archbishop of Canterbury (1758), and in places compared with the appendix to Dugdale's *History of St. Paul's Cathedral*, ed. 1716.

The manuscript was bought at the sale of F. H. Dickinson's library at Sotheby's in 1886 by W. Sparrow Simpson, and was previously seen by him when compiling *Registrum statutorum et consuetudinum Ecclesiae Cathedralis Sancti Pauli Londinensis*, 1873.

Letter from F. H. Dickinson to Sparrow Simpson, 1886 (p. v).

The contents are as follows:

Capitula libri sequentis (p. xiv).

List of Archbishops of Canterbury (p. xxii).

List of Bishops of London to Henry Compton (p. xxiv).

[Statuta et consuetudines] (Sparrow Simpson, op. cit., 1–111) (pp. 1–121).

Redditus spectantes ad Elemosinariam Sancti Pauli Londinensis, tum ad sustentacionem puerorum, tum ad elemosinam faciendam (pp. 121–2).

Taxacio bonorum spiritualium et temporalium Decani et Capituli . . . (pp. 123–7).

Hic incipiunt pitancie Ecclesiae Sancti Pauli . . . (pp. 127–36).

De terminis statutis ad solvendas firmas . . . (pp. 136–8).

Taxacio maneriorum spectancium ad ecclesiam Sancti Pauli (pp. 138–9).

Taxacio pensionum ecclesiarum in civitate et suburbiis quas decanus et capitulum sancti Pauli annuatim percipiunt (pp. 139–40).

Taxacio ecclesiarum pertinentium ad ceram (p. 140).

Taxacio pensionis ecclesiarum pertinentium ad missam beatae Virginis . . . (pp. 140–1).

Maneria pertinencia ad pitancias et ad Cantarias (p. 141).

Taxacio pensionum ecclesiarum pertinentium ad Cantarias in Ecclesiam sancti Pauli (p. 141).

Taxacio ecclesiarum et Pensionum pertinentium ad veterem Fabricam (p. 142).

Summa taxacionis . . . (p. 142).

Recepta Camerarii ecclesiae sancti Pauli Londinensis tam de redditibus (pp. 143–5).

Stipendia ministrorum dictae Ecclesiae (pp. 145–6).

Redditus pertinentes ad victualia et pitancias Capellanorum, Vicariorum, puerorum, pauperum et aliorum ministrorum ecclesiae Sancti Pauli . . . (pp. 146–8).

Extract from statutes of Cardinal Wolsey. *Latin* (p. 148).

[Carta Edwardi Regis III], 25 June 1339. (Sparrow Simpson, op. cit., 112–22) (pp. 149–58).

[Bulla Innocentii Pape tercii], 30 March 1216. (Sparrow Simpson, op. cit., 122–3) (pp. 158–60).

[De allocacionibus factis pro libertatibus Ecclesiae Sancti Pauli.] (Sparrow Simpson, op. cit., 124) (p. 160).

De allocatione libertatum per Justiciarios Regis Edwardi I.] (Sparrow Simpson, op. cit., 124–5) (p. 161).

Constitutiones et Statuta et declaraciones consuetudinum antiquarum et approbatarum tempore Magistri Radulphi de Disceto Decani sancti Pauli. (Sparrow Simpson, op. cit., 125–34) (pp. 161–70).

Statuta edita per Radulphum de Baldok, Decanum et Capitulum Ecclesiae Londinensis, Anno gracie MCCLXXXXVIII, pro capellanis perpetuis habitum gestantibus in eadem, et aliis Ministris ecclesiae predictae. (Sparrow Simpson, op. cit., 134–8) (pp. 171–6).

[Contencio inter Capellanos et Vicarios, quorum Major Status.] (Sparrow Simpson, op. cit., 138–40) (pp. 176–9).

[De Servientibus.] (Sparrow Simpson, op. cit., 140–1) (pp. 179–80).

Vetus Rentale prebendae ecclesiae sancti Pauli in Holborn (p. 181).

[1515 *cont.*]

Novum Rentale ejusdem prebendae tempore magistri Henrici de Idesworth (p. 182).

[Memorandum de dono Alardi, Decani.] (Sparrow Simpson, op. cit., 141–2) (pp. 182–3).

[Literae Patentes Ricardi II, Regis, De Unione, Annexione et Incorporacione Cantariarum], 17 May 1391. (Sparrow Simpson, op. cit., 142–5) (pp. 183–6).

Fragment of an epitome of Cardinal Wolsey's Statutes. (Sparrow Simpson, op. cit., 263–4) (p. 187).

[Literae Roberti Braybrooke, Episcopi, de Unione, Annexione, et Incorporacione Cantariarum], 28 June 1391. (Sparrow Simpson, op. cit., 145–8) (pp. 187–92).

[Litere Roberti Braybrooke, Episcopi], 26 June 1391. (Sparrow Simpson, op. cit., 148–51) (pp. 192–6).

[Injuncciones Roberti de Braybrook.] (Sparrow Simpson, op. cit., 151–4) (pp. 192–201).

[Litere Roberti Braybrooke, Episcopi], 24 October 1401. (Sparrow Simpson, op. cit., 163–6) (pp. 201–6).

[Visitacio Roberti Gilbert Episcopi], 20 October 1438. (Sparrow Simpson, op. cit., 169–71) (pp. 206–10).

xxv+214 pp.

1516. EELES COLLECTION

MANUAL OF PRAYERS

'A Manual for the Sacrament Containeing the Duties before, at and after it.' An Anglican manual of prayers and meditations composed for the laity, probably in the late 17th century.

Inscribed 'P. H. B. to A. H. B. June 1878'. Bookplate of F. C. Eeles.

i+55 ff.

1517. EELES COLLECTION

LIST OF LITURGICAL BOOKS

A rough list of liturgical books printed between the 15th and 19th centuries, compiled by F. C. Eeles.

33 ff.

1518. EELES COLLECTION

LIVERPOOL CATHEDRAL LIBRARY

Catalogues of books and manuscripts in or intended for Liverpool Cathedral Library, and of some books and manuscripts belonging to Sir Frederick M. Radcliffe.

'List of some of the MSS. and early printed books bought by Sir Frederick M. Radcliffe with a view to presentation to the Library of Liverpool Cathedral', 4 January 1940 (ff. 1–27).

An inscription (f. i) by Eeles states that the manuscripts were 'largely chosen and purchased by Dr. F. C. Eeles (a lay-canon of the Cathedral) on behalf of the donor Sir Frederick Radcliffe between 1933 and 1946 (approximately). Many of the printed books were bought under the same partnership.'

'Books [and one manuscript] in possession of Sir Frederick Radcliffe from the Library of Canon Christopher Wordsworth [Canon of Salisbury, d. 1938], purchased by him' (ff. 28–30).

Catalogue of printed books on liturgy in the library of Liverpool Cathedral (ff. 31–140).

Typescript copy. i+140 ff.

1519. EELES COLLECTION

DIRECTIONS FOR HEARING HIGH MASS

'Directions for Hearing High Mass on Sundays and Holy Days Thro' the Year.' The manuscript contains a version in English of a Paris missal with instructions and explanations for the use of the laity, and was written no later than 1720. It appears to be written in an English [or Scottish] hand, and may perhaps have been composed for an English or Scottish expatriate in France.

Some additional devotional material has been added at a later date 'For the use of Sister Elizabeth Frances Wall'.

Bookplate of F. C. Eeles.

vii+653 pp.

1520. EELES COLLECTION

SCOTTISH ECCLESIASTICAL AFFAIRS

Collection of extracts from printed books, sermons, and other documents, made in about 1682 by a Scottish clergyman. Comments in another hand in the margins. The manuscript contains the following items:

'Some Scripture testimonies annent Church communion and Separation' (pp. 1–7).

'Some Sentences or Testimonies out of the Harmonie of Confessiones, 1 March 1566', with extracts from other Confessions (pp. 7–10).

'The sayings of some particular Authores more Ancient and Moderne to this same purpose' (pp. 10–37).

'Ane Cope of a letter Written to a friend upon the First of June [16]82 to be communicat to others who called for advyce annent hearing of Conformists' (pp. 37–119).

[1520 *cont.*]

'Some remarkes excerpted out of doctor Owen's Treatise called evangelicall love, peace and unitie, And his book against Stillingfleet etc' (pp. 119–25).

'Some notes of 2 Sermons upon Rev. 18 cap. 4 v. in the 2[d] of [which] Church separation and communion is in generall shortlie considered, and more particularlie our separation from Rome is justified. Preached Anno [16]80' (pp. 125a–140).

'Some Testimonies excerpted out of severall Authores annent [the] Church of Rome's corruptiones and Separation from her' (pp. 141–6).

'Ane briefe and sober examination of some reasones or considerationes against hearing conforme Ministers' (pp. 147–63).

'Some fewe remarkes on the Sermon of a conformist annent Separation who runes upon the other extreame' (pp. 163–78).

'Some notes of Ane Sermon upon Rev. 19. 13 . . . Anno [16]80' (pp. 179–86).

'Some Notes of ane Sermon upon Rev. 9. v. 21 . . . Preached Anno [16]80' (pp. 187–97).

Sermon on Rev. 21: v. 7. Preached [16]80 (pp. 198–223).

Inscribed on the inside cover 'ex dono Francisci Caroli Eeles, mcmxxxi'.

Bound in vellum.

iv+226 pp.

1521. EELES COLLECTION

PRAYERS

A collection of private prayers, 18th century.

On the spine the number 210.

iii+175 pp.

1522. EELES COLLECTION

SCOTTISH PRAYER BOOK

'A Book of Common Prayer For Morning and Evening, With a Litany and an Office for the Holy Eucharist according to the Primitive Model. To which proper Rubricks are added for Direction and some few Notes at the foot of the Page. By D. T. R[attray].'

The Communion Office is entitled 'An Office for The Sacrifice of the Holy Eucharist, being the Antient Liturgy of the Church of Jerusalem'.

This manuscript contains the Scottish order of service as printed under the title *A Form of Morning and Evening Prayer, daily throughout the Year. Together with an Office For celebrating the Christian sacrifice*, 1748. It comprises the Communion Office included in *The Ancient Liturgy of the*

Church of Jerusalem by Thomas Rattray, nonjuring Bishop of Dunkeld, posthumously published in 1744, together with an order for Morning and Evening Prayer and a Litany based on Greek models.

Stamp and bookplate of Bibliotheca almae Ecclesiae Brechinensis.

ii+78 ff.

1523. EELES COLLECTION

FORM OF ADMITTING A PENITENT

'Form of admitting a Penitent for Fornication to the Peace of the Church', drawn up [and annoted by Alexander Jolly, Bishop of Moray].

An inscription (f. 1) in the hand of Alexander Penrose Forbes, Bishop of Brechin, records the presentation of the manuscript to him by 'the Revd Mr [Charles] Pressly of Fraserburgh for many years the Bishop's assistant'.

The letter N is written in ink (f. i). The end papers are similar to MS. 1524 which comes from Bibliotheca almae Ecclesiae Brechinensis.

vi+29 ff.

1524. EELES COLLECTION

SCOTTISH ECCLESIASTICAL AFFAIRS

Various items concerning Scottish ecclesiastical affairs, principally in the diocese of Brechin, 19th century. They are as follows:

Act of consecration of the Episcopalian chapel in Dundee, by George Gleig, Bishop of Brechin, Primus, 12 July 18 [n.y.]. *Copy* (ff. 1–5).

Account by George Hickes, nonjuror Bishop of Thetford, of measures taken for the consecration of nonjuror Bishops in 1693. This is a copy of *Records of the New Consecrations*, pp. 1–3, published by Richard Rawlinson after 1731. It is printed in J. H. Overton, *The Nonjurors*, 1902, 84–8. The present manuscript is a 19th-century copy (ff. 6–15).

Account of the Muchalls schism, dated 27 March 1861 (f. 16).

Letter from the Revd. Patrick Cheyne to John Dowden, (1886) Bishop of Edinburgh, 25 November 1874, describing the history of the Scottish Communion Office. *Extract* (ff. 16^{v}–17^{v}).

Account by the Revd. John Moir of church affairs in Lochlee, Forfar, and Brechin in the time of his grandfather, the Revd. Peter Jolly, and his father [David Moir, Bishop of Brechin], in a letter to the Bishop of Brechin, 9 December 1863. *Copy* (ff. 18–36).

The letter N is written in ink (f. i). Stamp of Bibliotheca almae Ecclesiae Brechinensis.

i+61 ff.

1525. EELES COLLECTION

SCOTTISH PRAYER BOOK

'An Order for Morning and Evening Prayer Daily throughout the Year, together with The Litany and An Office for The Sacrifice of The Holy Eucharist, being the ancient Liturgy of The Church of Jerusalem', 1741.

The order of service contained in this manuscript was first printed in 1748 under the title *A Form of Morning and Evening Prayer, daily throughout the Year. Together with an Office For celebrating the Christian Sacrifice.* The Communion Office is that drawn up by Thomas Rattray, nonjuring Bishop of Dunkeld, and included in *The Ancient Liturgy of the Church of Jerusalem*, 1744.

Inscribed (f. i) 'Reedfoord, August 7th MDCCXLI'.

[Formerly in Brechin Diocesan Library.]

iv+52 pp.

1526. EELES COLLECTION

SCOTTISH ECCLESIASTICAL AFFAIRS

'An Examination of the alledged Persecution of the Episcopall Clergie in the Diocese of Aberdeen', [1718].

A pamphlet, prepared for the printer but apparently not published, in defence of the proceedings of Presbyterian church courts against episcopalian clergy in the diocese of Aberdeen after the suppression of the Jacobite rebellion of 1715.

Bookplate of F. C. Eeles.

ii+39 ff.

1527. EELES COLLECTION

SCOTTISH COMMUNION OFFICE

'An Office for The Sacrifice of the Holy Eucharist, being the Antient Liturgy of the Church of Jerusalem.' A 19th-century copy of part of the contents of MS. 1522.

iv+77 ff.

1528. EELES COLLECTION

COLLECTION OF NONJURORS' OFFICES

A copy [by the Revd. James Walker Harper, (1909) Canon of Perth] of a collection of Nonjurors' Offices appended to a copy of the Book of Common Prayer of the Church of England, [1726], in Perth Cathedral Library. It contains the following items:

A Communion Office, taken partly from primitive liturgies, and partly from the first English Reformed Common-Prayer-Book, 1718. Included are the

Preface (ff. 5v–8v), the Order of Confirmation (ff. 47–48v), the Order for the Visitation of the Sick (ff. 49–51), and the Communion of the Sick (ff. 54v–55v).

Devotions for the altar . . . Taken from Mr. Johnson's unbloody sacrifice, n.d. (ff. 9–24).

Private prayers. No title, author, or date (ff. 24v–26v).

Advice to such as go into foreign parts . . ., n.d. (ff. 27–36).

Private devotions before, at and after the Christian Sacrifice . . ., 1718 (ff. 36v–46v).

Instructions for gentlemen or others going into foreign parts . . ., n.d. (ff. 52–4).

Prayers composed by the Honble ARCH[IBAL]D C[AMP]B[EL]L, later Bp. [of Aberdeen] of the Church of Scotland, n.d. *Incomplete* (ff. 56–62). A tracing of the title-page of this work (f. 75).

Belonged to the Revd. James Walker Harper, *c.* 1905. Bookplate of F. C. Eeles.

ii+75 ff.

1529. EELES COLLECTION

COMMUNION OFFICE

'An Office for the solemn ministration of the Eucharist Sacrifice, with full rubrics and private devotions for priests both before and after celebrating . . . compiled from several liturgies', 1833. The Office appears to have been composed for private use by the Revd. [W. C. A.] Maclaurin, Scottish Episcopalian minister at Elgin, and the sources used include the Book of Common Prayer, the Roman and Eastern liturgies, and the hymns of Isaac Watts.

Bookplate of F. C. Eeles.

iv+165 ff.

1530–1. EELES COLLECTION

TREATISE ON THE HOLY COMMUNION

A copy written in the late 19th century of a treatise by the Revd. Al[exander] Lunan entitled *The Office of the Holy Communion*, published in Edinburgh, 1711.

Belonged to E. M. Lomas.

ii+69 and 56 ff.

1532. EELES COLLECTION

PROCEEDINGS OF THE PRESBYTERY OF KINCARDINE O'NEIL

Notebook containing extracts from a register of the proceedings of the presbytery of Kincardine O'Neil, Aberdeen, 1700–1.

32 ff.

1533–5. EELES COLLECTION

BIBLIOGRAPHY OF SCOTTISH ECCLESIASTICAL HISTORY

A bibliography of printed books relating to Scottish ecclesiastical history, arranged by date of publication, 1601–1854. Many of the entries are taken from booksellers' catalogues and from Brechin Diocesan Library. Written in notebooks supplied by Walker and Co., booksellers and stationers, Aberdeen.

1533: 1601–1700. 173 pp.
1534: 1701–99. ii+210 pp.
1535: 1800–54. ii+202 pp.

1536. EELES COLLECTION

CORRESPONDENCE OF JOHN FALCONER

A copy of letters addressed principally to John Falconer, Scottish non-juring Bishop, by Thomas Rattray, (1731) Bishop of Dunkeld, Archibald Campbell, Bishop of Aberdeen, and others, on ecclesiastical and liturgical subjects, 1703–39. Included (pp. 118–60) are letters on the schism of the English Nonjurors over Usages, 'all taken from copies in Bp. [John] Alexander's [of Dunkeld] hand-writing'. The names of the writers will be found in the index.

iii+181 ff.

1537. EELES COLLECTION

LETTER-BOOK OF THOMAS STEPHEN

Letter-book of Thomas Stephen, 1836–63. Stephen was editor of *The Episcopal Magazine* and of *The Church Warder*, and wrote extensively on liturgical questions and Scottish ecclesiastical history. He was medical librarian at King's College, London, 1838–58. He frequently advocated a tax on steam power in several letters to Chancellors of the Exchequer. See also MS. 1538. The names of the correspondents will be found in the index.

i+140 ff.

1538. EELES COLLECTION

NOTEBOOK OF THOMAS STEPHEN

Notebook of Thomas Stephen, 1836–65 [see also MS. 1537], containing autobiographical notes, extracts from books read, and copies of letters. The end of the manuscript has been used reversed as a letter-book, 1864–5. The names of the writers will be found in the index.

ii+141 ff.

1539. EELES COLLECTION

BISHOP KEITH'S ORDINAL

Transcript made in 1856 by the Revd. G. Sutherland, of T[rinity] C[ollege], G[lenalmond], of liturgical writings of Robert Keith, Bishop of Caithness, Orkney, and the Isles, Primus, in the Episcopal Chest at Edinburgh. In 1743 the Scottish bishops in synod requested Keith to adapt the Ordinal of 1620 in order to promote the use of the Scottish liturgy in place of the English Prayer Book, and the manuscripts copied by Sutherland appear to contain the results of Keith's work. The manuscript contains the following items:

Copy collated by Keith of *The forme and maner of ordaining ministers, and of consecrating Archbishops and Bishops, used in the Church of Scotland*, 1620 (ff. 1–16).

Copy of an Ordinal drawn up by Bishop Keith, [1743] (ff. 17–38).

Form of baptism for children used by Bishop Keith (ff. 39–40).

Order of confirmation by Thomas Rattray, Bishop of Dunkeld (ff. 42–5).

Extract from letter from William Dunbar, Bishop of Aberdeen, to Bishop Keith, 29 March 1739 (ff. 46–7).

See also MS. 1545, ff. 132–58, 160–213.

iii+49 ff.

1540. EELES COLLECTION

NOTES ON SCOTTISH ECCLESIASTICAL HISTORY

Copy [by the Revd. Patrick Cheyne] of manuscript and printed material relating to Scottish ecclesiastical history in the 18th century, taken principally from papers of John Falconer, nonjuring Bishop, and John Alexander, Bishop of Dunkeld.

Extracts from letters to Bishop Falconer from Thomas Rattray, (1731) Bishop of Dunkeld, 1718–22 (pp. 9–22); from Archibald Campbell, Bishop of Aberdeen, 1712–22 (pp. 23–34), and correspondence concerning disputes of English Nonjurors concerning the Usages, 1717–57 (pp. 35–60). Some of this material is also in MS. 1536.

Extracts from letters to Bishop Alexander from Andrew Gerard, Bishop of Aberdeen, 1728–58 (pp. 68–97).

Letter from the Revd. William Smith to Arthur Petrie, Bishop of Moray, 1779, about English Nonjurors (pp. 98–100).

Miscellaneous notes (pp. 151–77).

This and the following manuscript probably belonged to James Nicolson, Dean of Brechin (see J. Dowden, *Scottish Communion Office 1764*, 1922, v).

vi+178 pp.

1541. EELES COLLECTION

NOTES ON SCOTTISH ECCLESIASTICAL HISTORY

Notes and copies of letters relating to Scottish ecclesiastical history in the 18th and early 19th centuries [by the Revd. Patrick Cheyne], and extracts in another hand from the correspondence of William Skinner, Bishop of Aberdeen, Primus, 1838–53.

A. NOTES [BY THE REVD. PATRICK CHEYNE]

On ecclesiastical affairs in Aberdeen, 1715–16 (pp. 3–6).

Sale of books of John Alexander, Bishop of Dunkeld (p. 6).

Synod of Aberdeen, 1717 (p. 7).

Appointment of bishops, 1776 (pp. 7–12).

Consecration as coadjutor of Aberdeen of John Skinner, (1786) Bishop of Aberdeen, 1782 (pp. 13–17).

George Garden, minister at Aberdeen (p. 18).

Account of church services, 1807 (pp. 18–21).

Note on Roger Aitken, minister at Lunenburg, Nova Scotia, 1813–14 (pp. 22–3).

Note on George Innes, Bishop of Brechin (pp. 23–4).

Notes on the Scottish liturgy, 18th century (pp. 24–31).

Correspondence of Scottish bishops and others concerning the consecration of Samuel Seabury, Bishop of Connecticut, 1783–5. The names of the writers will be found in the index (pp. 33–57).

Royal Reservation (pp. 58–9).

Divinity Studies (p. 60).

Letter from Andrew Gerard, Bishop of Aberdeen, to John Alexander, Bishop of Dunkeld, 1738–61 (pp. 61–87).

Communion Office and Prayer Book (pp. 88–90).

Repeal of Penal Laws, 1792 (pp. 91–2).

B. CORRESPONDENCE OF WILLIAM SKINNER, BISHOP OF ABERDEEN, PRIMUS, 1838–53

Extracts from Bishop Skinner's correspondence as follows:

Skinner to James Walker, Bishop of Edinburgh, 1838, on administration of Communion before general synod according to the Scottish Office (pp. 95–8).

Michael Russell, Bishop of Glasgow and Galloway, to Skinner, 1839, about discussions with the Archbishop of Canterbury for a Bill to extend communion with Scottish and American Churches (pp. 98–101).

Charles Hughes Terrot, Bishop of Edinburgh, to the same, 1842, suggesting Scottish archiepiscopate. *Two letters* (pp. 102–4).

Henry Phillpotts, Bishop of Exeter, to the same, 1842, on a charge to the clergy by the former (pp. 105–6).

W. E. Gladstone to the same, 1853, on legal disabilities (pp. 107–9).

Patrick Cheyne, incumbent of St. John's, Aberdeen, to the same, 1843, on the Scottish form of Confirmation (pp. 109–15).

Michael Russell, Bishop of Glasgow and Galloway, to the same, 1843, on the same subject (pp. 115–17).

Patrick Torry, Bishop of St. Andrews, Dunkeld, and Dunblane, to the same, [1843], stating his practice with regard to Confirmation (pp. 118–20).

Circular letter from Skinner, 1843, concerning the form of Confirmation (pp. 120–3).

William Forbes, [of Medwyn], to the same, 1844, suggesting a Scottish archiepiscopate (pp. 123–8).

W. E. Gladstone to the same, 1850, on the Gorham Case (pp. 129–32).

Alexander James Beresford Beresford-Hope to the same, 1850 (p. 132), enclosing letter from Charles James Blomfield, Bishop of London, 1850, concerning the Gorham Case (pp. 133–8).

The same to the same, 1850, on the same subject (pp. 139–41).

Thomas George Spink Suther, minister at Edinburgh and (1857) Bishop of Aberdeen, to Charles Hughes Terrot, Bishop of Edinburgh, 1850, about the Gorham Case (pp. 142–53).

Charles Wordsworth, (1852) Bishop of St. Andrews, Dunkeld, and Dunblane, to Skinner, n.d., on the admission of laymen to synods. *Two letters* (pp. 153–7).

Michael Russell, Bishop of Glasgow and Galloway, to the same, 1844, on the use of the English and Scottish Communion Offices (pp. 158–60).

Patrick Torry, Bishop of St. Andrews, Dunkeld, and Dunblane, to the same, 1844, on the same subject (pp. 161–7).

Michael Russell, Bishop of Glasgow and Galloway, to the same, 1844 (pp. 172–3), enclosing letter from Archbishop Howley to himself, 1844, about schismatical priests of the English Episcopal sect (pp. 168–72).

ii+182 pp.

1542. EELES COLLECTION

CORRESPONDENCE OF JOHN SKINNER, BISHOP OF ABERDEEN, ETC.

Copy of correspondence of John Skinner, Bishop of Aberdeen and Primus, 1804–6, and of other papers, made in 1878 from a copy of the originals by William Joss in 1815.

Correspondence of Bishop Skinner concerning the union of English and Scottish Episcopalians. Some of the material is used in John Skinner, *Annals of Scottish Episcopacy*, 1818. The names of the writers will be found in the index (ff. 1–20^{v}).

Extracts from a diary, 1729–54, and copy of baptismal register, 1729–69, of the Revd. Alexander Lunan. Lunan was presbyter of the Scottish Episcopal Church at Blairdaff, Aberdeen, and from 1744 at North Water

[1542 *cont.*]

Bridge, Forfar. This is a copy of a copy of the original made by William Joss, whose mother was Lunan's niece, in 1840 (ff. 21–45v).

Baptismal register of the Revd. Alexander Jamieson for Maykirk in Luthermuir, Kincardine, 1770–80 (ff. 46–7).

List of persons confirmed in the chapel at Luthermuir by George Innes, Bishop of Brechin, 1778; by Arthur Petrie, Bishop of Moray, 1782, and by John Skinner, Bishop of Aberdeen, 1787 (f. 47v).

Inventories of clothes and furniture, 1751–2. In another hand (ff. 48–50v).

Two letters from Walter Denham to [James] Nicolson, Dean of Dundee [Brechin], 1879 (ff. 73–5).

Belonged to James Nicolson, Dean of Brechin.

75 ff.

1543. EELES COLLECTION

MISCELLANEOUS LETTERS AND PAPERS

Guardbook containing miscellaneous letters and papers on Scottish ecclesiastical affairs, 18th–19th centuries, and papers of F. C. Eeles, 1909–18.

A. Scottish Ecclesiastical Affairs

Charles James Blomfield, Bishop of London, to Patrick Torry, Bishop of Dunkeld and (1844) St. Andrews, Dunkeld, and Dunblane, 1841, regretting his inability to appoint Torry's son to a chaplaincy in India (f. 1).

Archibald Campbell, Bishop of Aberdeen, to John Falconer, Scottish nonjuring Bishop, 1713, concerning a book by the former and mentioning attempts to dissolve the Union of England and Scotland (f. 2).

Stephen Hyde Cassan, Vicar of Bruton, Wilts., to —, 1826, enclosing prospectus (f. 4).

Alexander Penrose Forbes, Bishop of Brechin, to Mrs. — Ridgway, n.d., arranging visit (ff. 5–6).

Same to same, n.d., accepting invitation (f. 7).

Walter Kerr Hamilton, Bishop of Salisbury, to Edward Harston, Vicar of Sherborne, 1857, about schools at Sherborne and restoration of the Lady Chapel (ff. 9–10).

William Harper, [Scottish episcopalian minister at Elgin], to —, 1729, referring to destitution at Orkney (f. 11).

[George] Innes, [later Bishop of Brechin], to an unnamed Bishop, 1778, concerning charges against [Roger] Aitken, [a candidate for Holy Orders]. *Copy. V.* f. 69 (ff. 13–14v).

James Edward Stuart, the Old Pretender, to an unnamed Scottish Bishop, 19 May 1740, concerning a dispute between the College of Bishops and the clergy of Edinburgh over the appointment of a Bishop of Edinburgh

(f. 16), and also the terms of an arrangement between the College of Bishops and the Old Pretender for the appointment of bishops after the Concordat of 1731 (f. 15). *Copies* (ff. 15–16).

Declaration of Alexander Jolly, (1798) Bishop of Moray, at his consecration as coadjutor of Moray and Ross, 1796 (f. 17).

Alexander Jolly, Bishop of Moray, to [Roger] Aitken, [minister of St. John's Chapel, Aberdeen], 1800, with condolences. *Draft* (f. 18).

Same to —, 1812, with condolences. *Copy* (f. 20).

Same to —, 1824, about consecration of chapel at Forfar, Angus. *Copy* (f. 21).

'Copy of the Right Honourable [Simon Fraser, 11th] Lord L[ova]t's letter in answer to the Right Honourable [Duncan Forbes] Lord Pr[esiden]t [of the Court of Session], 29 Oct. 1745.' *Copy*. Printed *Culloden Papers*, ed. H. R. Duff, 1815, 238 (f. 22).

Michael Henry Thornhill Luscombe, missionary bishop on the Continent, to David Low, Bishop of Ross and Argyll, 1827, describing his activities in France. *Copy* (ff. 23–6).

Returns of income made by clergymen in the West Indies to Henry Hamilton, Governor of Bermuda, 1790. The clergymen are Alexander Richardson, James Barker, and John Moore. *Copy* (ff. 27–8).

Michael Russell, (1837) Bishop of Glasgow and Galloway, to the Revd. William Browning, 1832, about the actions of George Gleig, Bishop of Brechin and Primus (ff. 29–30).

Same to same, 1835, about liturgical publications (ff. 31–2).

John Skinner, Bishop of Aberdeen, Primus, to Patrick Torry, Bishop of Dunkeld and (1844) St. Andrews, Dunkeld, and Dunblane, 1814, concerning a proposed address to the Crown (ff. 33–4).

John Skinner of Forfar, son of Bishop John Skinner, to the same, 1822, on local affairs (ff. 35–6).

Circular from the same [sent to the Bishops and Clergy of the Scottish Episcopal Church], 1824, proposing a synod of clergy and laity. Addressed to the Revd. Robert Spark at Laurencekirk, Kincardine. Partly printed in J. M. Neale, *Life of Patrick Torry*, 1856, 112–14 (ff. 37–8).

William Skinner, Bishop of Aberdeen, Primus, to Patrick Torry, Bishop of Dunkeld and (1844) St. Andrews, Dunkeld, and Dunblane, 1837, about the election of a Primus (ff. 39–40).

Same to same, 1851, about Bishop Low's threat to resign if [Robert] Eden consecrated [Bishop of Moray and Ross] (f. 41).

G[eorge] Smith, English nonjuring Bishop, to David Fife, minister at Dundee, 1744, about divisions between Scottish and English Nonjurors. *Copy* (ff. 43–4).

Charles Hughes Terrot, (1841) Bishop of Edinburgh, to John William Donaldson, philologist, [1835], congratulating him on Fellowship at Trinity College, Cambridge (f. 45).

[1542 *cont.*]

P[atrick] T[orry, Bishop of St. Andrews, Dunkeld, and Dunblane], to [William Skinner, Bishop of Aberdeen, Primus], 1849, declining to act as pro-Primus owing to ill health. *Draft* (f. 47).

Note on back of cover addressed to the Revd. Patrick Cheyne (f. 48).

Newspaper cutting concerning John Skinner, Dean of Aberdeen, d. 1807 (f. 49).

Arthur Ranken, synod clerk of the diocese of Aberdeen, and (1880) Dean of Aberdeen and Orkney, to Patrick Cheyne, minister of St. John's Chapel, Aberdeen, 1855, enclosing extract from minutes of the Synod of Aberdeen, 1789, about Auchindoir, Aberdeen (ff. 50–3).

Extract by the same from minutes of Synods at Aberdeen, 1813–19, mainly concerning St. John's Chapel, Aberdeen (ff. 54–5).

Notes about the election of Bishops, etc. (ff. 57–61).

Note on the collections of Patrick Cheyne, minister of St. John's Chapel, Aberdeen. [Perhaps Lambeth MSS. 1540–1] (f. 62).

Private address perhaps delivered to the clergy, with corrections [in the hand of Alexander Jolly, Bishop of Moray], 1835 (ff. 63–67^{v}).

Declaration by the Revd. Andrew Wood and Alexander Dickson, beadle, to the Revd. William Harper concerning the behaviour of Roger Aitken, a candidate for Holy Orders, 'taken in the presence of the Clergy of Edinburgh at the earnest Desire of the Revd. Mr. James Brown in Montrose', 1775. *V.* ff. 13–14^{v} (ff. 69–72^{v}).

Group of letters originally sewn together and endorsed in the hand of Alexander Penrose Forbes, Bishop of Brechin, 'chiefly on the Admission of the Laity into Church synods, and on a move on the part of some Danish Clergy towards receiving valid Ordination, 1852'. The writers are as follows:

William Ewart Gladstone, statesman, to Forbes, 1848 (ff. 75–76^{v}).

Alexander James Beresford Beresford-Hope to the same, 1852 (ff. 77–79^{v}).

Same to same, 1852 (ff. 81–84^{v}).

Same to same, 1852 (ff. 85–86^{v}), enclosing a copy of a letter from Nugent Wade, Rector of St. Anne's, Soho, to Hope, 1852 (ff. 87–88^{v}), and a translation by Wade of a letter to himself from Ludvig Daniel Hass, [Danish] pastor, [1852] (ff. 89–90).

Alexander James Beresford Beresford-Hope to the same, 1852 (ff. 91–4).

William Skinner, Bishop of Aberdeen, Primus, to the same, 1852 (ff. 95–96^{v}).

Robert Isaac Wilberforce, Archdeacon of the East Riding, to the same, [1852] (ff. 97–100).

Gilbert Rorison, incumbent of Peterhead, to the same, [1852] (ff. 101–107^{v}).

Letters to James Nicolson, Dean of Brechin, 1882–4. The correspondents are:

James Brown Craven, Rector of Kirkwall, historian, 1884, referring to Nicolson's possession of manuscripts of the Revd. Patrick Cheyne (f. 108).

John Dowden, (1886) Bishop of Edinburgh, 1882, thanking him for two manuscripts of the Revd. Patrick Cheyne (ff. 110–11).

William Forbes, of Medwyn, 1883, about family letters. *Three letters* (ff. 113–119ᵛ).

William Walker, incumbent of Monymusk, Aberdeen, (1896) Dean of Aberdeen and Orkney, 1884, seeking information for biography of John Skinner, Bishop of Aberdeen (ff. 120–1).

Richard William Jelf, Principal of King's College, London, to Thomas Stephen, medical librarian at the college, 1859, on the latter's retirement (ff. 122–123ᵛ).

[Thomas Stephen] to —, 1862, on the Scottish liturgy (ff. 124–126ᵛ).

Newspaper cuttings about works of Thomas Stephen, 1849–53 (ff. 127–30).

Revd. G[ ] Gordon, of Elgin, to Thomas Stephen, 1862, replying to letter (ff. 131–2).

B. Papers of F. C. Eeles

Papers concerning the revision of the Scottish liturgy, 1909–18. Included are the following items:

Scottish Communion Office. Suggestions with regard to the Invocation, February 1909, containing suggested versions by Bishops and other clergy at a conference of Bishops and Presbyters on liturgical revision (ff. 133–41).

Minutes of discussions on the Invocation between Bishops and certain presbyters, [1909]. *Typescript copy* (ff. 142–6).

John Skinner Wilson, Dean of Edinburgh, to Eeles, 1910, on the Invocation (ff. 147–148ᵛ).

A table of proper Psalms for Sundays and Holy Days throughout the Year, n.d. (f. 149).

Order of psalms for two months in use at daily service in St. Patrick's Cathedral, Armagh. *Printed* (f. 150).

'Notes on Provost Deane's Suggested Scheme of Psalms', by A[rthur] J[ames] M[ason, Master of Pembroke College, Cambridge], n.d. (ff. 151–3).

Table of psalms proposed for Sundays and weekdays. Proof corrected by Eeles (ff. 154–6).

Suggested scheme for the Sunday use of Psalter, n.d. Two copies of which one is annotated by Eeles (ff. 157ᵛ–160).

Analyses by Eeles of versions of the Psalter (ff. 162–88), with his recommendations (f. 189).

[1542 *cont.*]

Henry Riley Gunny to John Skinner Wilson, Dean of Edinburgh, 1910, commenting on revised proof of Scottish Communion Office (ff. 190–3).

E. G. P. Wyatt, liturgical scholar, to Eeles, 1910, on Scottish liturgical revision (ff. 194–195^{v}).

Proposals of the committee of the conference of Bishops and Presbyters on the Scottish Communion Office for an amended Consecration Prayer, 1910. In the hand of J. S. Wilson, Dean of Edinburgh (ff. 196–7), with suggestions on the Invocation by Eeles (ff. 200–1).

Terms of an agreement between the Cambridge University Press and the publication committee of the Scottish Episcopal Church concerning copyright, [1912]. *Printed* (f. 202).

Form of an agreement between the Cambridge University Press and the publication committee of the Scottish Episcopal Church for the publication of the Scottish liturgy and Schedule of Deviations sanctioned by the Provincial Synod of the same on 7 December 1911, 1912. *Printed* (ff. 203–204^{v}).

Provisional report of an executive committee of the Scottish Episcopal Church recommending the nomination of a Central Publications Committee, [1912]. *Printed* (ff. 205–6).

Provisional report of a committee of the Representative Church Council on the composition of Diocesan Boards, [1912]. *Printed* (f. 207).

Suggestions for discussions at a conference on the Lectionary and Psalter, drawn up by Walter John Forbes Robberds, Bishop of Brechin and Primus, and others, 1912, with pencil annotations. *Typescript* (ff. 208–10).

Minutes of a conference at Edinburgh on the revision of the Lectionary and method of reciting the Psalter, 1912. *Typescript copy* (ff. 211–16).

Report of the Publication Committee of the Episcopal Church in Scotland, 1913 (f. 217).

John Skinner Wilson, Dean of Edinburgh, to Eeles, 1913, concerning cost of publishing the Prayer Book. *Typescript* (ff. 218–19), enclosing, Report of the publication committee of the Scottish Episcopal Church, [1913]. *Typescript copy* (ff. 220–4).

Minutes of a conference at Edinburgh on the revision of the Lectionary and Psalter, 1914. *Typescript copy* (ff. 225–9).

Letters to Eeles about a Scottish hymnal, 1914. Also included are a note [by Eeles] on Scottish pre-Reformation hymns and a table of office hymns in the Aberdeen Breviary which are not in the Sarum Breviary (ff. 247–9); circular of The Scottish Gaelic Song Society (f. 250); appendix by Athelstan Riley of Scottish hymns for addition to the *English Hymnal*. *Typescript* (ff. 255–87).

Minutes of conference at Edinburgh on the revision of the Lectionary and Psalter, 1915. *Typescript copy* (ff. 288–90). Also 'adjusted' minutes of the same. *Typescript copy* (ff. 291–3).

John Skinner Wilson, Dean of Edinburgh, to Eeles, 1918, about sales of Scottish Prayer Book. *Typescript* (ff. 294–5).

H. J. Witherspoon to Eeles, n.d., about ordination by presbyters (ff. 296–300).

J. Cromarty Smith to —, n.d., on Presbyterian Orders. *Draft* (ff. 301–5).

Draft letter to a newspaper from 'An Official of one of the Scottish Dioceses' on Presbyterian Orders. In the hand of Eeles (ff. 306–14).

Proposals by James Cooper, professor at Glasgow, for establishing a theological magazine in Scotland, including minutes of a meeting in Edinburgh, 1910 (ff. 315–324v).

A bibliography of the Scottish liturgy, 1915, by Eliza H. Dowden and F. C. Eeles (ff. 326–332).

Miscellaneous notes, mainly on Scottish seals (ff. 333–7).

Comparative extracts from [The Order of the Divine Offices of the British Orthodox Church, 1734, i.e. Nonjurors], and from a prayer book belonging to William Cartwright, English nonjuring Bishop (ff. 338–45), and a list of books belonging to Cartwright (f. 346).

List of some liturgical books in Perth Cathedral Library and in the possession of Canon James Walker Harper (ff. 347–8), and some lists by Eeles of editions of liturgical books (ff. 349–55).

Application from the managing committee of the *Scottish exhibition of national history, art, and industry, Glasgow, 1911*, for the loan of items. *Printed* (ff. 356–7). Also extracts from the catalogue, some of them by Eeles (ff. 358–69).

369 ff.

1544. EELES COLLECTION

BAPTISMAL REGISTER FOR ABERDEEN

Transcript of the baptismal register of the Episcopal Church in Old Aberdeen, 1730–52.

Also a list of communicants on Whit Sunday 1735 (ff. 1–3), and a list of intending communicants at Easter 1751.

Typescript. i+58 ff.

1545. EELES COLLECTION

PAPERS ABOUT THE LITURGY, INCLUDING CORONATION SERVICES

Guardbook of papers of F. C. Eeles concerning the Scottish liturgy and Coronation Services.

A. Papers about Coronations

John Edwin Watts Ditchfield, Vicar of St. James-the-Less, Bethnal Green, to Archbishop Frederick Temple, [1902], about intoxicants at the King's Dinners (ff. 1–2).

[1545 *cont.*]

Same to Arthur Foley Winnington-Ingram, Bishop of London, 1902, on the same subject (ff. 3–4ᵛ).

Fragment of a prayer [in the hand of Francis Paget, Bishop of Oxford] (f. 5).

Sir Henry Farnham Burke, Somerset Herald and subsequently Norroy King of Arms, to Archbishop Davidson, 1911, suggesting alterations to the Coronation Service of George V (ff. 7–8).

Eight photographs of the interior of Westminster Abbey prepared for the Coronation of Edward VIII (ff. 10–17).

Albert Augustus David, Bishop of Liverpool, to Eeles, 1937, concerning the Coronation of George VI. *Typescript, not signed personally* (f. 18).

Order for special services to be used on the day of the coronation of . . . Edward VII, 1902, by Arthur Gascoigne Douglas, Bishop of Aberdeen and Orkney. *Proof* (ff. 19–28).

Newspaper cutting about the Stone of Scone from *The Scotsman*, 1951 (ff. 29–30).

Correspondence between Eeles and A. R. Mowbray and Co., publishers, 1952, about his book, *The coronation service* (ff. 31–4).

Eeles to Laurence Tanner, keeper of the muniments and library at Westminster Abbey, 1952, about a book by the latter. *Typescript copy* (f. 35).

Laurence Tanner to Eeles, 1952, about the Coronation. *Typescript* (f. 36).

Eeles to William D. Maxwell, minister of Whitekirk, 1952, about the possibility of a Scottish Coronation. *Typescript copy* (f. 37).

Revd. Francis Noel Davey, Director of the S.P.C.K. Correspondence with Eeles about Coronation Services, 1952. *Typescript* (ff. 38–41).

Frank Streatfield, Vicar of Colden Common, to Eeles, 1953, criticizing the latter's book *The coronation service*. *Typescript* (f. 42).

M. Croome to the same, 1953, on the same subject. *Typescript* (ff. 43–4).

Eeles to the Revd. Frank Streatfield, [1953], about the Coronation Service. Endorsed, not sent (f. 45).

Frank Streatfield, Vicar of Colden Common, to Eeles, 1953, on the same subject (f. 46), enclosing a pamphlet by himself entitled *The hallowing of our queen* (ff. 47–53).

B. Miscellaneous Liturgical Papers of F. C. Eeles

Transcript of a copy made in 1757 by Robert Forbes, (1762) Bishop of Ross, of a further copy by James Gadderar, Bishop of Aberdeen, of Forms of Absolution of Archbishop Laud and George Hickes, nonjuror Bishop of Thetford. *Typescript* (ff. 55–7).

Transcript of letters of orders of Patrick Rose, later Dean of Brechin, 1768 (f. 58), and of John Strachan, 1744 (f. 59); also of deeds appointing

Strachan coadjutor to the Bishop of Brechin, 1787, and Bishop of Brechin, 1788 (f. 60). *Typescripts* (ff. 58–60).

Transcript of act of consecration of the episcopalian chapel in Dundee by George Gleig, Bishop of Brechin, Primus, 12 July 18[ ]. See also MS. 1544, ff. 1–5. *Typescript* (f. 61).

Epitaph for Thomas Rattray, Bishop of Dunkeld, Primus (f. 62).

Parish magazine of St. Mark the Evangelist, Marylebone Road, February 1905, containing a letter by a newly appointed incumbent in north-east Scotland in the latter half of the 18th century, taken from a manuscript in Brechin Diocesan Library. *Printed* (ff. 63–4).

List of the contents of a book containing liturgical collections in the possession of Robert Forbes, (1762) Bishop of Caithness. Also included are the following items:

(*a*) Letter from Thomas Deacon, English nonjuror Bishop, to clergy in London, 1744 (ff. 71–3).
(*b*) 'Prayers used before the Restauration' (ff. 74–7).
(*c*) Annotations by Archbishop Sancroft in a copy of the Prayer Book apparently for the revision of 1662 (ff. 78–87).

Copies (ff. 65–87).

Certificates of some marriages and baptisms performed in parishes in Aberdeenshire, 1695, 1704, 1742. *Copies* (ff. 89–90).

Notes on printed books and manuscripts in Brechin Diocesan Library: Book of Common Prayer, 1701, presented by Queen Anne to chapel at Montrose (ff. 91–92^{v}); fragmentary Prayer Book, 1637 (f. 93); account and collection book of Brechin Qualified Chapel, 1799 (f. 94); 'Communion Office for the use of the Church of Scotland . . .', Aberdeen, 1786 (f. 95); 'A Companion for the Altar', New York, 1816 (f. 96); 'The Churchman's Profession . . .', New York, 1821 (f. 96^{v}); 'Familiar Instructions for . . . Public Worship', New York, n.d. (f. 97); 'A Companion for the Book of Common Prayer', New York, [1827] (f. 98); contents of Lambeth MSS. 1522 and 1525 (ff. 99–100). Brechin Diocesan Library was deposited in Dundee University Library in 1962.

Prayers by Peter Jolly, incumbent of Lochlee, Forfar, 1783–1839. *Copy* (ff. 101–2). Also a letter from William Presslie to [?Richard Mant, Bishop of Down, Connor, and Dromore], about liturgical discrepancies in Scotland, mentioning an annotated prayer book of William Abernethy Drummond, Bishop of Edinburgh. *Copy* (f. 102^{v}).

'A Form of Prayer . . . in the Chapels of the Scotch Episcopal Church . . . for a Public Fast and Humiliation . . .', Aberdeen, 1796. *Copy* (ff. 103–16).

'A Form of Prayer . . . in the Chapels of the Scotch Episcopal Church . . . for a Public Fast and Humiliation . . .', Aberdeen, 1800. *Copy* (ff. 117–30).

Scottish Ordinal. *The forme and maner of ordaining ministers and of consecrating of Archbishops and Bishops, used in the Church of Scotland, Edinburgh, 1620*. Printed from a transcription by Robert Forbes, (1762) Bishop

[1545 *cont.*]

of Ross, of a copy of the Ordinal of 1620 by Robert Keith, Bishop of Caithness, Orkney, and the Isles, Primus, collated by Forbes with a copy of the original edition. See also MS. 1539. *Two copies* (ff. 132–58).

Proposed edition of Scottish liturgies of the 18th century, containing 'The Order of Confirmation or Chrism', by Thomas Rattray, Bishop of Dunkeld (ff. 160–5); 'The Form and Manner of Ordaining Bishops, Priests and Deacons', by Rattray (ff. 166–87); 'An Ordinal . . . for the Use of the Church of Scotland', by Robert Keith, Primus, 1743 (ff. 188–213). *Proofs*. Found in an envelope endorsed by Eeles, 'never published' (ff. 160–213).

213 ff.

1546. EELES COLLECTION

LITURGICAL NOTES

Notebook of [F. C. Eeles] containing extracts and notes from Scottish liturgical works in Scottish libraries and elsewhere. They include the following:

'The Communion-Office for the use of the Church of Scotland . . .', Edinburgh, 1781. Copy in the Theological Library at Edinburgh (pp. 7–10).

'The Communion Office for the use of the Church of Scotland . . .', Leith, 1762. Copy in the Theological Library at Edinburgh (pp. 11–24).

'The Book of Common Prayer . . . according to the use of the Church of Ireland', Dublin, 1716. This copy in the Scottish Episcopal Church Library belonged to and was annotated by William Abernethy Drummond, Bishop of Edinburgh, by whom it was bequeathed to Alexander Jolly, Bishop of Moray (pp. 26–7, 43–63).

List of editions in Aberdeen Diocesan Library of 'A Collection of Hymns and Anthems for the use of the Episcopal Church of Scotland', Aberdeen, 1779 (pp. 30–3).

List of editions in Aberdeen Diocesan Library of 'The Communion Office for the use of the Church of Scotland', Edinburgh, 1722 (pp. 34–41).

Collection of Offices in Brechin Diocesan Library belonging to Patrick Torry, Bishop of St. Andrews, Dunkeld, and Dunblane (pp. 64–6).

'The Communion-Office for the use of the Church of Scotland . . .', Bristol, 1767 (p. 67).

'A Dictionary of the Church . . .', by the Revd. William Staunton, New York, 1839 (pp. 68–70).

'Buchan', by the Revd. J. B. Pratt, Aberdeen, 1858 (p. 71).

'Remarks on the necessity of conforming to Order, with respect to Clerical Vestments . . .', by an undergraduate of Balliol College, Oxford [John Noble Shipton, Rector of Othery], Bristol, 1820 (p. 73).

Extracts from *The Borough* and *The parish register* by George Crabbe (pp. 72–6).

'A View of the History, Doctrine . . . of the Episcopal Church in Scotland . . .', by the Revd. Robert Adam, Edinburgh, 1809 (p. 77).

List of editions of a Form of admitting penitents by John Alexander, Bishop of Dunkeld (p. 77).

Notes on seals (p. 79).

Notes on the Russian and Armenian liturgies (pp. 80–3).

'Scottish Communion Tokens other than those of the Established Church', by the Revd. Robert Dick, Edinburgh, 1902 (pp. 101–3).

Notes on hymns and anthems (pp. 104–5).

'The Communion Office for the use of the Church of Scotland', Edinburgh, 1722. Copy in Perth Cathedral Library (pp. 107–9).

Photograph of communion plate at Montrose (p. 233).

234 pp.

1547. EELES COLLECTION

PRAYERS OF INTERCESSION

'Prayers of Intercession for their use who mourn in secret for the Publick Calamities of this nation.' The prayers appear to have been composed for use in private gatherings of members of the Church of England during the Commonwealth [1650–60].

44 pp.

1548. EELES COLLECTION

INSTITUTIONES THEOLOGICAE

'Institutiones Theologicae . . . in usum juuentutis Roxoland in seminario Kolomnensi, curis asuspiciis et mandato illustrissimi D.D. Theodosii Episcopi Kolomnensis et Kaschiviensis . . .', 1779.

Written in Latin for a seminary of the Russian Orthodox Church at Kolomna, Russia.

Bound in leather.

ii+229 ff.

1549. EELES COLLECTION

REGULATIONS FOR NUNNERY OF VAL DE GIF

A copy written in French in the 18th century of regulations for the administration of the Benedictine nunnery of Val de Gif, diocese of Paris, 1682. It contains:

'Reglemens pour les Officiers de L'Abbaye Royale de nostre Dame du val de Gif, dressez en l'année mil six cent quatre vingt deux par Madame Anne Victoire de Clermont, Abbesse de laditte Abbaye, & approuuez par

[1549 *cont.***]**

Messire Gardeau, curé de St Estienne du Mont & visiteur de ce Monastere en sa visite du — de la mesme année' (ff. 3–41).

In another hand, 'Reglemens Generaux faits dans les Chapitres pour le bon ordre du Monastere' (ff. 42–53v).

Printed *Revue d'Histoire Ecclesiastique*, lviii, 816–45.

Purchased by William Barclay David Donald Turnbull, Scottish antiquary, from [Thomas] Rodd, bookseller, 1835. Bookseller's label of Boyveau et Chevillet, Paris. In pencil is written 'MS 73' and also the number 207. Number 245 in an unidentified English bookseller's catalogue [? Thomas Rodd]. Bookplate of F. C. Eeles.

i+56 ff.

1550. EELES COLLECTION

RUSSIAN CHURCH

Translations into English of documents relating to the Russian Orthodox Church in the 19th century by Richard White Blackmore, chaplain to the Russia Company (1819–47) and then Rector of Donhead St. Mary, Wilts.

1. 'The Oustaff or the Code of Laws of the Russian Spiritual Consistories together with other documents relating to the Church in Russia. Printed by the order of the Most Holy Governing Synod', 1841. The chapters are as follows:

General propositions (ff. 1–2).
On the preservation and diffusion of the Orthodox faith (ff. 3–14).
On the Divine Service (ff. 15–16).
On the good ordering and building of churches (ff. 16–27).
On the incorporation and dissolution of churches (ff. 27–8).
On the clergy (ff. 29–37).
On parishes (ff. 38–40).
On the management of the houses of the bishops (ff. 40–6).
On the management of monasteries (ff. 46–50).
On the management of churches (ff. 50–4).
On the buildings belonging to the courts of the Spiritual Jurisdiction (f. 54).
On the buildings belonging to the Diocesan Jurisdiction (ff. 54–6).
On the jurisdiction of the Diocesan Judicature (ff. 56–9).
On the order of conducting trials (ff. 59–66).
On measures of deprivation and correction (ff. 66–9).
The application of measures of deprivation and correction to the different degrees of misdemeanours and offences (ff. 69–76).
On disputes between persons of the spiritual calling (ff. 76–7).
On complaints against spiritual persons for injuries sustained (ff. 77–8).
On illegal marriages (ff. 78–81).
On the breaking off and dissolving marriages (f. 81).

On the dissolution of marriages (ff. 82–3).
On divorce (ff. 83–8).
On the certification of the legality of marriages (ff. 89–92).
On the imposition of ecclesiastical penance (f. 92).
On the composition of the Consistory (ff. 93–5).
On the external organization and the times of attendance at the court of the Consistory (f. 96).
On the manner of conducting business in the Consistory (f. 97).
On the introduction of affairs (ff. 97–100).
On the presentation of affairs (ff. 100–1).
On the hearing and deciding affairs (ff. 101–6).
On the putting affairs into execution (ff. 107–11).
On the receipts, keeping and expenditure of money (ff. 111–14).
On keeping and preserving papers relating to proceedings and on the archive (ff. 114–17).
On the order of the communications (ff. 118–19).

List of contents (ff. 120–125^{v}).

Oath to be taken by priests at ordination. Appendix 3 [to the Code of Laws] (ff. 127–30).

2. Article 'On the Orthodoxy of the Russian Church', from a periodical entitled *Christian Reading*, published at the Spiritual Academy, St. Petersburg, 1843 (ff. 134–208).

3. 'The Short Catechism of the Russian Church', approved by the Most Holy Synod for the use of schools, published by the Synodal Press, St. Petersburg, 1843. An earlier edition of this work was published by Blackmore in 1845 (ff. 213–30).

4. Appendix to the Short Catechism adapted to military service. Published by the Synodal Press, St. Petersburg, 1843 (ff. 231–6).

5. Appendix to the Longer Catechism of the Russian Church adapted for the use of military schools (ff. 237–40).

6. Letters of orders of a deacon and a priest of the Russian Church, 1819 (ff. 242–53). A faint copy of a letter from Blackmore to William Palmer, Fellow of Magdalen College, Oxford, from Kronstadt, 1843 (f. 241).

7. 'The instructions of the Bishop to a newly appointed priest extracted from the Canons of the Holy Apostles and Holy Fathers, given to him at his Ordination for his private perusal' (ff. 255–65), and 'General Instructions from the Bishop to a Priest' (ff. 265–93). Printed by the Synodal Press, St. Petersburg, 1815 (ff. 255–93).

8. 'Analysis of Baron Rosencampf's History of the Russian Church' (ff. 294–324).

On the flyleaf is inscribed 'R. W. Blackmore, Donhead St. Mary 1857'. Bookplate of F. C. Eeles.

ii+326 ff.

1551. EELES COLLECTION

LITURGY OF THE FIRST THREE CHRISTIAN CENTURIES

'The Liturgy of the First Three Christian Centuries', being a translation into English of Ferdinand Probst: *Liturgie der drei ersten christlichen Jahrhunderte*, 1870, parts II and III.

Bookplate of F. C. Eeles.

Typescript. v+268 ff.

C.M. XIV. EELES COLLECTION

Nos. 7–12. A small group of documents given by F. C. Eeles.

7. Rental of the lordship of Atherstone (Warws.), 11 May [1 Edward VI] 1547. 8 mm.

8. Mandate of Pope Paul V to the Vicar General in Spirituals of the Bishop of Pistoia (Italy) ordering him to decide the matter of the patronage of, and presentation to, the church of St. Michael Carmignano (dioc. Pistoia).
1 September 1609. Leaden bulls on hemp cords.
Notarial instrument of the sentence recorded on the dorse: in a later hand and dated 24 October 1609.

9. Licence given by Archbishop Abbot on 27 January 1613 to Nicholas Howlett, S.T.B., to hold the rectories of Reepham and Winterton (Norf.) together, confirmed by the attached letters patent of James I dated 28 January 1613.
Great seal attached.

10. Copy of the will of William Tagborne of Croydon, Surrey (dated 21 November 1617), proved before John Hayward, LL.D., in the court of the archbishop's peculiar of Shoreham and Croydon on 21 January 1618.
Tag for seal. Nicholas Weston Registrar.

11. Exemplification of an action before the King's justices at Haverfordwest for the recovery of houses and lands in Prendergast, Llandewi Velfrey, and other places.

14 September [15 Car. I] 1639.
Seal of the justices in the counties of Caernarvon, Cardigan, and Pembroke.

12. Marriage licence issued by the Vicar-General of the Archbishop of Canterbury (Randall Davidson), for the marriage of Leonard Edgar Whitaker of the parish of Diss (Norf.) and Edith Olave Cox of the parish of St. Mary, Primrose Hill (London).
25 April 1903. Paper seal.

1552–8. BEAUVOIR PAPERS

Papers of the Revd. William Beauvoir (1669–1725). Beauvoir was a native of Guernsey, and served as a naval and military chaplain from 1695 to 1714. In that year, through the interest of Gilbert Burnet, Bishop of Salisbury, he was appointed chaplain to the Earl of Stair and accompanied him on his embassy to France (1715–20). During this period he acted as intermediary between Archbishop Wake and Louis Ellies Du Pin, doctor at the Sorbonne, in negotiations designed to achieve union between the Anglican and Gallican Churches. He was collated to the rectory of Bocking, Essex, in 1719.

All the volumes contain the bookplate of Osmund Beauvoir. They were purchased for the Library in 1956.

1552. BEAUVOIR PAPERS

CORRESPONDENCE BETWEEN ARCHBISHOP WAKE AND THE REVD. WILLIAM BEAUVOIR, ETC.

A. Correspondence between William Wake, Archbishop of Canterbury, and William Beauvoir, Chaplain to the Earl of Stair, British Ambassador to France, 1717–21

The correspondence relates mainly to a scheme for union between the Church of England and the Gallican Church.

Wake [to Beauvoir], 25 September 1717. Regret at the death of [M.] Ravechet [Syndic of the Sorbonne]. Ecclesiastical preferments (f. 1).

Same to the same, 28 November 1717. Difficulties of subscribing to books published in France. Inquires about *Thesaurus Anecdotorum*. Printed. J. L. Mosheim, *Ecclesiastical History*, trans. and ed. A. Maclaine, 1768, app. III, no. I (f. 3).

[Beauvoir] to Wake, 11 December 1717. Du Pin and other doctors of the Sorbonne believe union with the Church of England most effectual means of uniting all western churches. Proceedings against Jesuits at Rennes. *Copy*. Extr. Maclaine, op. cit., app. III, no. II (f. 5).

Wake to Beauvoir, 2 January 1718. Thanks for French tracts. Praises writings of Du Pin (f. 6).

Same to the same, 18 January 1718. Hopes of preferment for Beauvoir; purchase of books; growing divisions in the royal family (f. 8).

Same to the same, 14 February 1718. Describes basis for unity of Anglican and Gallican Churches, and hopes Du Pin will draw up scheme.

Printed. J. H. Lupton, *Archbishop Wake and the project of Union . . . between the Gallican and Anglican Churches*, 1896, 49–51 (f. 10).

Same to the same, 22 March 1718. Has written to Du Pin. Possibility of war with Spain (f. 12).

[1552 *cont.***]**

Same to the same, 15 April 1718. Preferment for Beauvoir. Doubts whether Regent will break with Rome. Distinguishes between essential and non-essential doctrine (f. 14).

Same to the same, 10 May 1718. Sends letters to Du Pin and Piers [de Girardin]. His activity for Beauvoir's preferment (f. 16).

Same to the same, 27 May 1718. Introduces J. F. Scholtz, German student of divinity, who bears letters for Du Pin and Girardin, and sends former Wilkins's Coptic New Testament (f. 18).

Same to the same, 5 July 1718. Correspondence with Du Pin. Possible vacancy of living of Burstow, held by John Flamsteed, Astronomer Royal, suitable for Beauvoir (f. 20).

[Beauvoir to Wake], 16 July [1718]. Du Pin has made draft of a plan of union. Thanks for offer of Burstow. *Draft on back of letter to Beauvoir* (ff. 22–23^{v}).

Wake to Beauvoir, 11 August 1718. Doubts whether Regent strong enough to break with Rome, and until then 'the rest is meer speculation'. Approves of Du Pin's scheme for consecration of Bishops. Inquiries about books. Catalogue completed of printed books in his own and Lambeth Palace libraries; manuscripts will now be catalogued (ff. 24–5).

Same to the same, 30 August 1718. Introduces Sir Thomas Lowther and the Revd. [Thomas] Payne. Has little hope of union, and cannot continue private negotiations. Cannot accept Commonitorium unless Gallicans alter doctrine.
Extr. Maclaine, op. cit., app. III, no. III (ff. 26–7).

Same to the same, 8 October 1718. Has written to Du Pin and Girardin to urge break with Rome. Action by State essential.
Extr. Maclaine, op. cit., app. III, no. IV (ff. 28–9).

Same to the same, 6 November 1718. Preferment for Beauvoir; purchase of books. Reception of his previous letter to Du Pin and Girardin of which copies have been circulated. Will provide information about Anglican Orders. Books for Du Pin.
Extr. Maclaine, op. cit., app. III, no. VII (ff. 30–1).

Same to the same, 18 November 1718. Successful outcome of dispute with Spain. Describes principles of union between Anglican and Gallican Churches. *Copy*.

Lupton, op. cit., 76–8 (ff. 32–33^{v}).

Same to the same, 2 December 1718. Purchase of books from France. Compares Anglican and Gallican relationship with Pope. Urges Beauvoir to cultivate leading Gallicans. Noailles should know Archbishop of Canterbury more powerful than when legatus natus.
Extr. Maclaine, op. cit., app. III, no. IX (f. 34).

Same to [the same], 23 January 1719. Illness of his family. Sends letter for Du Pin. Concerning agent of Protestant church of Transylvania and

[Daniel Ernst] Jablonski, Bishop 'of the Bohemian Unity'. Sends books on Anglican Orders for Du Pin. Manner of overtures to the Gallican Church. The papal authority.

Extr. Maclaine, op. cit., app. III, no. X (ff. 36–37v).

Same to the same, 5 February 1719. Interception of his letters. Union requires consent of State and rejection of papal power.

Extr. Maclaine, op. cit., app. III, no. XI (f. 38).

Same to the same, 24 February 1719. Opposition to Noailles and the Sorbonne. No reformation possible without State. Is engaged in two or three other transactions with foreign Protestants. Outlines plans for union with Gallicans.

Extr. Maclaine, op. cit., app. III, no. XII (ff. 40–1).

Same to [Beauvoir], 16 March 1719. Preferment for Beauvoir. Carelessness of French booksellers. Revival of persecution of Protestants. Sends letter for Jablonski. Will not defend his correspondence with Du Pin if published. Sunderland promises Beauvoir first crown living available.

Extr. Maclaine, op. cit., app. III, no. XIII (ff. 42–3).

Piers de Girardin, doctor at the Sorbonne, to Wake, [30 April 1718]. On his zeal to promote unity of Anglican and Gallican Churches. *Latin copy.*

Lupton, op. cit., 56–7 (ff. 44–5).

Address [by Piers de Girardin] to the Sorbonne, 17 March 1718. Urges distinction between essentials and non-essentials; papal decisions not held as articles of faith, and Gallican Church not under papal subjection. *Latin copy.*

Lupton, op. cit., 52–5 (ff. 46–47v).

Wake [to Beauvoir], 29 April 1719. Purchase of books. Concern at Du Pin's illness. Fears Girardin faint-hearted. Can do no more without support of Regent. Has seen M. de Valogne.

Extr. Maclaine, op. cit., app. III, no. XIV (f. 48).

Louis Ellies Du Pin, doctor at the Sorbonne, to Wake, 30 April 1719. Thanks for book on Anglican Orders. Hopeful of unity despite divided opinions. Papal bull 'Unigenitus'.

Enclosed is a copy of an address to the Sorbonne by Du Pin, 1 April 1719. *Latin copies* (f. 50).

Wake [to Beauvoir], 29 May 1719. Encloses letter to Du Pin. Regrets intended publication of this correspondence. His high regard for Du Pin (f. 51).

Enclosing:

Wake to Du Pin, 1 May 1719. Condoling on state of his health, and looking to the unity of the Gallican and Anglican Churches. *Latin copy.*

Lupton, op. cit., 94–5 (ff. 52–3).

Wake to Beauvoir, 2 June 1719. Grief at death of Du Pin, and commission to buy print of him. Wonders if their correspondence will still be printed.

[1552 *cont.*]

Dutch ambassador's chaplain. Has obtained Marsh Gibbon for him, and believes [Robert] Clavering will exchange Bocking for it (f. 54).

Same to [the same], 15 June 1719. Introduces [John] Walker, Fellow of Trinity College, Cambridge. Has recommended exchange of Marsh Gibbon for Bocking. Picture of Du Pin. Hopes correspondence with Du Pin will not be published, and that negotiations will be resumed with successor (ff. 56^{v}–57).

Same to the same, 27 June 1719. Goes to Bath. Inquiries about books (f. 58).

'Relation de ce qui s'est passé entre Monsieur Du Pin et Mr. L'archeveque de Cantorbery au sujet des Lettres qu'ils se sont mutuellement escrites', copied by Beauvoir from the original by Du Pin, 24 July 1719. *French.*

Lupton, op. cit., 98–9 (ff. 60–1).

Wake to Beauvoir, 27 August 1719. Takes the waters at Bath for his health (f. 62).

Same to the same, 18 January 1720. About the purchase of French books (f. 64).

Same to the same, 9 February 1720. Books. Decline of enthusiasm in the Sorbonne for project of union; the Court will do nothing. Is willing to continue correspondence in private. South Sea Bubble.

Extr. Maclaine, op. cit., app. III, no. XVI (ff. 66–7).

Same to the same, 3 March 1720. Commissions for books. The next Pope will repair breach with Gallicans. Desires correspondence to continue (f. 68).

Same to the same, 31 March 1720. His fears for the Appellants. Princess of Wales to use influence for Girardin. Books. If Mr. Chaillet officiates in the English Chapel he should be ordained.

Extr. Maclaine, op. cit., app. III, no. XVII (ff. 70–1).

Same to the same, 19 April 1720. Princess of Wales writes to Madame on behalf of Girardin, who despairs: Noailles ensnared; Archbishop of Cambrai desires cardinalate; Regent fears Spanish party and Jesuits. Fears persecution of French Protestants. Commissions for books.

Extr. Maclaine, op. cit., app. III, no. XVIII (ff. 72–3).

Same to the same, 3 January 1721. Will not interfere in election at Merton College (f. 74).

Extract from *An essay on generosity*, by Henry Mills, master of Whitgift's Hospital, 1732 (ff. 77–79^{v}).

Bull 'Pastoralis officii' of Pope Clement XI, 28 August 1718. *Latin copy* (ff. 86–93).

B. Papers of William Beauvoir relating to his residence in Paris as chaplain to the Earl of Stair, and chiefly concerning the admission of converts to the Church of England, 1715–20.

Account of services conducted by Beauvoir in the Earl of Stair's chapel in Paris. Endorsed, 'Mr. Russel's memorial to the Bishop of Bangor &c' (ff. 95–7).

Lists, petitions, and some acts of abjuration of Roman Catholicism of persons wishing to be admitted to the Church of England, 1714–20. They include (ff. 111–14) letters of minor orders, 1700 and 1703, and act of abjuration of Jean Richelet, Benedictine monk, 1718; (ff. 107–108^{v}) list of some baptisms and marriages performed, 1718 and 1720; (ff. 128–136^{v}) translation into French of the Thirty Nine Articles, with numerous signatures (ff. 95–137).

Account of delays in bringing to trial [French Protestants] held by *lettres de cachet*. Endorsed, 'Lettre de Mr. Bachelier touchant les prisonniers de Meaux'. *French* (ff. 138–139^{v}).

Extract from register of baptisms of the parish of St. Peter Port, Guernsey, for William Beauvoir, 1669 (f. 140).

Certificate of the marriage of William Beauvoir and Elizabeth Brown, 6 April 1714 (f. 141).

Account of naval and military chaplaincies held by William Beauvoir, his chaplaincy to the Earl of Stair, and the destitution of his widow (f. 143).

Letter [from Osmund Beauvoir to Baron Le Fort], 9 September 1754, concerning his father's papers etc. *Draft and translation into French* (ff. 145–7).

Extracts from the Wake–Beauvoir correspondence, 1717–21 (*v.* ff. 1–79^{v}), with a few annotations by Norman Sykes, Dean of Winchester. *Typescript* (ff. 148–240).

240 ff.

1553. BEAUVOIR PAPERS

'COMMONITORIUM'

'Commonitorium de Modis ineundae pacis inter Ecclesias Anglicanam et Gallicanam', by Louis Ellies Du Pin, doctor at the Sorbonne, [1718], a discussion of the basis for union between the Anglican and Gallican Churches.

Endorsed 'For Sr Beauvoir'.

Latin. Hol.

i+9 ff.

1554. BEAUVOIR PAPERS

MISCELLANEOUS CORRESPONDENCE OF THE REVD. WILLIAM BEAUVOIR

Miscellaneous correspondence and papers of the Revd. William Beauvoir, 1703–23, as follows:

Charles Delafaye [to Beauvoir], 1717, enclosing letter for the Duchess of Cleveland from the Duke of Marlborough. News of the Court (f. 1).

Basil Kennett to the same at Gibraltar, 1712. [Nath(an)] Taubman is his successor as chaplain to the English Factory at Leghorn. [Daniel] Lombard, Fellow of St. John's College, Oxford, is chaplain to the envoy at Genoa (ff. 3–4).

Letter of protection from the Earl of Stair, requesting free passage in France for Beauvoir, 1715. *Signed and sealed* (f. 5).

Instructions from the Earl of Stair to Beauvoir, ordering him to inquire at Bordeaux and other ports about ships acquired by the Pretender, and to dispatch wine, 1715 (ff. 7–8).

Thomas Crawfurd, servant to the Earl of Stair, to Beauvoir, 1715–16, concerning the Jacobite rebellion. *Four letters* (ff. 9–15).

Beauvoir to Anthony Hammond, poet and pamphleteer, 1716. About purchase of wine and books. Seeks his patronage (ff. 17–18).

Same [to the same], 1716. About ecclesiastical preferments and his own career. Purchase of books for Lord Caernarvon (ff. 19–20).

Same [to the Earl of Stair, 1716], reporting a conversation with the Intendant of Bordeaux and his own expulsion from the city. *Draft* (ff. 21–22^{v}).

Same [to Anthony Hammond], 1716. About the purchase of wine at Bordeaux and his own difficulties there (f. 23).

[— Wilson] to Beauvoir, 1716. Informs Beauvoir of a plot to assassinate him (f. 25).

Edmund Gibson, Bishop of London, to the same, 1723. About ordination of a kinsman (f. 27).

Joseph Wilcocks, (1731) Bishop of Rochester, to the same, 1718. Archbishop Wake's interest on his behalf (f. 29).

John Evans, Bishop of Meath, to the same, [1716]. Personal matters (f. 31).

Timothy Godwin, Bishop of Kilmore and Ardagh, to the same, 1718. Advice on ecclesiastical preferment. Small amount of patronage in his own gift (ff. 33–34^{v}).

Same [to the same], 1718. Gifts and purchases of books (ff. 35–6).

J[ohn] Robethon, secretary to George I, to the same, 1718. Personal matters. *French* (f. 37).

Same to the same, 1719 [? N.S.]. Seeking intercession of Earl of Stair to ensure proper burial of relative of minister in Hanover who died a Protestant at Vendôme. *French* (f. 39).

Henri de Massue de Ruvigny, 1st Earl of Galway, to the same, 1719. Introducing one Beuf to the Earl of Stair. *French. Signed* 'Gallway' (f. 41).

Piers de Girardin, doctor at the Sorbonne, to the same, n.d. About visit to the Abbé d'Arriaudin. *French* (f. 43).

[Piers de Girardin to the same], 1717. Describes Louis XV and a sermon preached in the Sorbonne on [M.] Ravechet, [Syndic of the Sorbonne]. *French* (ff. 45–46v).

Account of debates in the Sorbonne, 1718. *French* (f. 47).

Piers de Girardin to Beauvoir, n.y. Visits the Bishop of Waterford. *French* (f. 48).

Same to the same, 1720. The Regent leaves many benefices vacant apart from some filled by favourites. Suggests method by which the Princess of Wales may obtain a benefice for him from the Regent. Comments on the ecclesiastical settlement in France. *French* (ff. 49–50).

Louis Ellies Du Pin, doctor at the Sorbonne, [to the same, 1718]. *French* (f. 51).

The same [to the same], 1719. New Year wishes. *French* (f. 54).

The same to [Archbishop Wake, 1717]. Sending gift of a book. *French* (f. 56).

— Falaiseau, Prussian diplomat, to Beauvoir, 1720. Invitation. *French* (ff. 58–9).

Same to the same, 1720. Bidding him farewell. *French* (ff. 60–1).

[Balthazar] Gibert, Professor of Rhetoric at the Collège Mazarin, [to the same], 1720. Sends gift. *French* (f. 62).

Amy Lullin, doctor at the Sorbonne, to the same, [1720]. Bidding him farewell. *French* (f. 64).

C. Serjault, Almoner to the King, to the same, n.d. Seeks assistance for a friend obliged to leave France for an affair of honour. *French* (ff. 66–7).

— Quinot, Abbé, to the same, [1720]. Invitation. *Latin* (f. 68).

Bernard de Montfaucon to the same, 1720. Asking for information about a lighthouse built by the Romans off the coast of Britain. *French* (f. 70).

Same to the same, n.d. About a copy of inscriptions at Smyrna sent to Masson. *French* (f. 72).

Pastors of the Evangelical Churches of Piedmont to the same and to other chaplains of the English and Dutch ambassadors in Paris, 1720. Seek support in applying to Protestant merchants in Paris for aid to Protestants in Piedmont. *French* (ff. 74–5).

David Wilkins, Lambeth Librarian, [to Beauvoir], 1718. Introducing the Revd. [Thomas] Payne, chaplain to the Factory at Constantinople. Transcript of manuscript of Chrysostom for Montfaucon (ff. 76–7).

[1554 *cont.***]**

Same to the same, 1718. Possibility of crown living for Beauvoir. Wake offers living in Lancashire in his gift meanwhile (ff. 78^{v}–79).

Same [to the same], 1719. Asking for translation of passages in 'Wm. the Conqueror's Norman Laws'. Offers to exchange books with Montfaucon (f. 80).

Same to the same, 1719. Archbishop active to obtain crown living of Marsh [Gibbon] for Beauvoir. Books for Wake (ff. 82^{v}–83).

Same to the same, 1719. Introduces [John] Walker, of Trinity College, Cambridge, visiting libraries in Paris on behalf of Dr. Bentley (f. 84).

Same to the same, 1720. About disputed nomination of churchwardens at Hadleigh, Suffolk, and about appointment of surrogates. Wake unwilling to buy Canterbury missal but will offer it to Lord Harley. Bishop of St. Asaph to assist with confirmations at Wake's visitation (ff. 86^{v}–87).

Same to the same, 1720. Has been appointed Canon of Canterbury (ff. 88^{v}–89).

Sir Hans Sloane to Mrs. Beauvoir, 1724. Condolences on husband's death (f. 90).

Same to the same, 1724. About sale of some prints (f. 92).

Same to the same, 1724. On the same subject (f. 94).

Account of a storm at sea [by Beauvoir], aboard H.M.S. *Association*, 26 November 1703 (f. 98).

Account [by Beauvoir] of the capture of Port Mahon by James Stanhope, (1718) Earl Stanhope, and of operations by Sir Edward Whitaker in the Mediterranean, 1708 (ff. 101–25).

Account [by the same] of mutiny at Gibraltar, 20 May 1710 (ff. 126–8), and resolutions of a council of war there of the same date (f. 130).

'Paraphrase sur l'Oraison Dominicale', being a rendering of the Lord's Prayer into verse. *French* (f. 131).

[Beauvoir to the Earl of Stair], 1720, informing him of the arrest of persons attending the Earl's chapel. *Draft* (f. 133).

v+136 ff.

1555. BEAUVOIR PAPERS

Letters from Beauvoir to his wife, 1715. The earlier letters are addressed to his wife by her maiden name, Elizabeth Brown.

French and *English*.

xi+181 ff.

1556. BEAUVOIR PAPERS

Letters from the same to the same, 1716–February 1717.

French and *English*.

iii+164 ff.

1557. BEAUVOIR PAPERS

Letters from the same to the same, August 1717–August 1718. *French* and *English* (ff. 1–175).

Certificates of Beauvoir's service as naval and military chaplain, 1695–1711, from Admiral Sir Edward Whitaker (f. 179); Vice-Admiral Sir Thomas Hardy (ff. 181–3); Admiral Sir Stafford Fairborne (f. 185); Captain William [?] Ken (f. 187); Lieut. Thomas Teddeman and George Dumaresq, Captain in Major-General Seymour's regiment of marines (concerning destruction of French fleet at Vigo) (ff. 189–90); Captain Stephen Martin (f. 192); Vice-Admiral Sir Thomas Hardy (f. 193); Captain R. Arris (f. 195); Admiral Sir Edward Whitaker (f. 197); Admiral Sir Stafford Fairborne (f. 201); Major-General Roger Elliott, Governor of Gibraltar (f. 202).

Beauvoir to [John] Robethon, secretary to George I, [1719]. Describes his career and seeks nomination to crown benefice. *French. Draft* (ff. 203–204^{v}).

Certificates of Beauvoir's subscription and declaration of conformity to the liturgy by law established, 1719. Signature and seal of Archbishop Wake (ff. 205–6).

Memorial inscription for Beauvoir. *Latin* (f. 207).

v+209 ff.

1558. BEAUVOIR PAPERS

Letters from Beauvoir to his wife, September 1718–22.

French and *English*.

v+215 ff.

1559. LETTERS OF FRANCIS LEE

Copies in his own hand of letters by Francis Lee (1661–1719), M.D., member of the Philadelphian sect, mostly undated.

Bookplate of John Haddon Hindley (1765–1827). Belonged to John Lee (1783–1866) of Hartwell House, Bucks.

Given by the British Records Association (deposit 242), [1950].

24 ff.

1560. PAPERS OF JOHN LEE, CIVILIAN

Papers of John Lee (1783–1866), Fellow of the College of Advocates, relating principally to the dissolution of Doctors' Commons. They consist of the following:

Summary of an appeal to the Visitor of Christ Church, Oxford, by [Thomas] Lamprey, removed by the Dean from his chaplaincy for marriage, 1737 (ff. 1–2^{v}).

[1560 *cont.***]**

Order of the Privy Council that Masters of Requests and eight of the eleven Masters of Chancery be appointed henceforth from civilians, 1633. *Copy* (f. 3).

Another copy (f. 5).

Notes and copies of documents by Lee relating to Doctors' Commons:

(*a*) Notes on disputes between the College of Advocates and the Dean and Chapter of St. Paul's concerning the site of the College, 18th century (f. 7).

(*b*) George Harris, D.C.L., Fellow of the College of Advocates, to the Dean of Arches, the Judge of the Admiralty and the members of the College of Advocates, 1781, offering £500 towards purchase of Mountjoy House (f. 8).

(*c*) William Battine, Fellow of the College of Advocates, to Sir William Wynne, President of the same, 1807, on the usual day of business of the College. *Extract* (f. 10).

Resolutions concerning the days of meeting of the College of Advocates, [1823] (f. 12).

Agenda of meeting of the College of Advocates, with annotations by Lee, 1823 (ff. 14–15).

Memorandum by Lee and John Haggard, Fellows of the College of Advocates, concerning noxious smells emanating from premises adjoining the College, 1826. *Copy* (f. 16).

Note of some cases of prosecution for nuisance, 1826 (f. 18).

Resolution of a meeting of the College of Advocates concerning the inspection of certain deeds, etc., 1829. *Draft* (f. 19).

Agenda of a meeting of the College of Advocates, 1830. *Draft* (f. 20).

Memorandum by Lee on portraits in the Court and Hall of the College of Advocates, n.d. (f. 22).

Memorandum by the same on the occupants of certain houses belonging to the College of Advocates, n.d. (f. 24).

Memorandum by the same recommending the division of the offices of Official Principal of the Diocese of Canterbury and Dean of the Peculiars now combined in the latter (f. 26).

Petition of George Boulton, lawyer's clerk, [1832] (f. 29).

Petition of merchants, shipowners, underwriters, and members of Lloyds to Queen Victoria, against the removal of the Admiralty Court to Westminster, [1858]. Endorsed by Lee (f. 31).

Petition of members of the Bar and surrogates of Doctors' Commons to the House of Commons, for compensation for loss of fees owing to the transfer of testamentary jurisdiction of the judicial committee of the Privy Council and the Prerogative Court of Canterbury to Chancery proposed by the Testamentary Jurisdiction Bill, 1854. *Copy of draft* (ff. 34–7).

Petition of the College of Advocates to the House of Lords for the protection of their interests in the Testamentary Jurisdiction Bill, [1858]. *Copy* (ff. 38–50).

Minutes of a meeting of the College of Advocates, mainly concerning the sale of corporate property, 18 March 1858 (ff. 51–2).

Minutes of the same, recommending sale of corporate property to the Government, 11 November 1858 (ff. 53–4).

Minutes of the same, concerning the disposal of corporate property, 22 December 1859 (f. 55).

Account of legal expenses incurred [by the Revd. James Pycroft], relating to the dissolution of Doctors' Commons in the Parliamentary Sessions, 1858–9 (ff. 57–59v).

Report in *The Times* of session of the Court of Admiralty, 13 January 1860. *Copy* (f. 61).

[Revd. James] Pycroft to Lee, 1860, concerning action in Parliament to prevent the dissolution of Doctors' Commons (ff. 63–64v).

Lee to the Librarian of the College of Advocates, 1860, protesting at proposed sale of the college library (f. 65).

Frederick Thomas Pratt, D.C.L., Fellow of the College of Advocates, to Lee, 1861, informing him of the proceeds of the sale of the library (f. 67).

Same to the same, 1865, asking for copies of documents (f. 69).

Henry Watts, under-treasurer of the College of Advocates, to the same, 1865, informing him of failure to sell corporate property to the Metropolitan Board of Works (ff. 71–2).

Same to the same, 1865, about the completion of the sale (f. 73).

Inventory of the tenants' fixtures, fittings, and furniture in the Court, dining-room, and library of the College of Advocates, 1865 (ff. 75–6).

Assent of the Fellows of the College of Advocates to sale of stock belonging to the corporation, 1865. *Copy* (f. 77).

Lee to the Trustees of the corporate property of the College of Advocates, 1865, protesting at the sale of the library, and proposing the establishment of legal prizes. *Copy* (ff. 79–80).

Frederick Thomas Pratt, D.C.L., Fellow of the College of Advocates, to Lee, 1865, about division of sale money (ff. 81–2).

Messrs. Dawes and Sons to the same, 1865, sending share of sale money for London and Northamptonshire properties and closing the account of the Trustees (f. 83).

Lee to Messrs. Dawes and Sons, 1865, objecting to distribution of sale money. *Draft* (f. 85).

[1560 *cont.*]

Frederick Thomas Pratt, D.C.L., Fellow of the College of Advocates, to Lee, 1865, answering objections to distribution of sale money, and proposing society to assist needy members of legal profession (ff. 87–9).

Given by the British Records Association (deposit 242), 1955.

90 ff.

1561. LAMBETH PALACE AND ADDINGTON MANSION BUILDING ACCOUNTS

'An account of sums received and expended by Christopher Hodgson, esq., nominee appointed by the Most Reverend William, Lord Archbishop of Canterbury, the Most Reverend Edward, Lord Archbishop of York, and the Right Reverend Charles James, Lord Bishop of London, under an Act of Parliament passed in the tenth year of the reign of His Majesty King George the 4th, intituled "An Act for assisting the repairing, altering and improving Lambeth Palace belonging to the see of Canterbury, and the taking down and rebuilding some parts thereof, and the making additions to and altering and improving the Mansion House at Addington belonging to the same see" ', 1829–33.

A duplicate of the account deposited in the Office of the Vicar-General by Act of Parliament, 14 September 1833. Contains:

Accounts for Lambeth Palace, 1829–33 (pp. 1–40).
Accounts for Addington Mansion, 1829–31 (pp. 41–58).
Audited statement of both accounts, 1833 (pp. 59–61).

Given by the Church Commissioners, 1955.

v+95 pp.

1562. PAPERS OF JOSHUA WATSON

Papers of Joshua Watson (1771–1855), philanthropist, treasurer of the National Society, and active member of the pre-Tractarian high-church party. They comprise:

Letter [from Caroline Harriet Abraham, wife of Charles John Abraham, Bishop of Wellington, New Zealand], 1851. Describes teaching of natives in New Zealand. *Extr.* (ff. 1–2).

Charles Parr Burney, Archdeacon of St. Albans, to Watson, 1828. Thanks for assistance to distressed clergyman (ff. 3–4).

Same to the same, 1838. Congratulations on marriage of daughter. 'Queen's, the Royal Institution and Clergy Children' (ff. 5–6).

Reginald Heber, Bishop of Calcutta, [to the same], 1825. Describes plans for missionary school for the Garrows, a hill tribe in Assam.
Printed. A. B. Webster, *Joshua Watson*, 1954, 159–63 (ff. 7–12^{v}).

William Howley, Bishop of London, and (1828) Archbishop of Canterbury, to the same, 1826. About [Joseph] Wolff and the spread of Christianity in the East (ff. 13–14).

Same to the same, 1833. On behalf of a committee of the S.P.C.K., requests him to sit for his portrait to be preserved in his family (ff. 15–16^v).

John Inglis, Bishop of Nova Scotia, to the same, 1831. Describes voyage to Halifax; comparison of missionary work in India and Nova Scotia; colonial policy of Viscount Goderich; schemes for church reform.

Extr. Webster, op. cit., 167–8 (ff. 17–23).

John Henry Newman, Fellow of Oriel College, Oxford, to the same, 1835. Thanks for subscription to chapel at Littlemore, Oxon. (f. 24).

Sir James Alan Park, Justice of Common Pleas, to the same, 1810. Proposes commutation of sentence of death on a forger to one of transportation (ff. 26–7).

Edward Bouverie Pusey, Regius Professor of Hebrew at Oxford, to the same, [1830]. Referring to dispute with H. J. Rose on religion in Germany (f. 28).

Same to the same, [1832]. Discussing pending election of a professor of Sanscrit at Oxford and urging claims of W. H. Mill (ff. 30–31^v).

Sir John Richardson, Justice of Common Pleas, [to the same], 1839. About a family bereavement (f. 32).

John Medows Rodwell, Rector of St. Ethelburga's, Bishopsgate, London, [to the same], 1843. Describes the activities of the Bishop of New Zealand and strife in the southern island with the native population (ff. 34–35^v).

Extract [by John Medows Rodwell] from a letter by Mrs. [Mary] Martin, [wife of William Martin, Chief Justice of New Zealand], 1845, describing the work of the Bishop of New Zealand and disputes with Wesleyans (ff. 36–39^v).

George Augustus Selwyn, Bishop of New Zealand, to Watson, 1846. Describes the progress of his diocese, and particularly the growth of the College at Bishop Auckland.

Extr. Webster, op. cit., 170 (ff. 40–41^v).

Extract from letter by [Sarah] Selwyn, wife of the Bishop of New Zealand, 1844. Describes pacification of natives by the Bishop.

Webster, op. cit., 169 (f. 42).

William Stevens, Treasurer of Queen Anne's Bounty, [to John James Watson, (1825) Canon of St. Paul's], 1802. Personal matters, mentioning Joshua Watson (f. 43).

Thomas Sikes, Vicar of Guilsborough, to the same, 1824. Describes visits from [John Henry] Hobart, [Bishop of New York, Charles Atmore] Ogilvie and [John Jebb] Bishop of Limerick (ff. 44–5).

John Matthias Turner, Bishop of Calcutta, [to Watson], 1829. Deplores the inadequacy of the Church of England in South Africa (ff. 46–47^v).

[1562 *cont.*]

William Tyrrell, Bishop of Newcastle, New South Wales, to the same, 1852. An account of the state of the Church in Australia.

Extr. Webster, op. cit., 167–8 (ff. 49–57).

John Watson, father of Joshua, to his nephew, 1816. An account of his own life (ff. 58–59^{v}).

Joshua Watson [to Henry Card, Vicar of Great Malvern, 1819]. About [insertion of his arms in window of Great Malvern church] (f. 61).

Same [to Reginald Heber, Bishop of Calcutta], n.d. Discussing a pension for Heber.

Webster, op. cit., 164 (ff. 62–63^{v}).

Same to [Anna] Rose, [widow of the Revd. Hugh James Rose, 1841]. Visit of [George Washington] Doane, Bishop [of New Jersey], to preach consecration sermon at Leeds parish church. Believes J. H. N[ewman] has given up editorship of *British Quarterly* [? *British Critic*] (ff. 64–65^{v}).

Same to the same, n.d. Personal matters (ff. 66–67^{v}).

Same to the same, n.d. Louisiana bonds (ff. 68–71^{v}).

Same to James Endell Tyler, (1845) Canon of St. Paul's, [1831]. Giving reasons against publication by S.P.C.K. of a work by Isaac Watts (ff. 72–4).

Same [to John James Watson, Canon of St. Paul's], 1834. Personal matters. *Incomplete* (ff. 75–76^{v}).

Same to his niece, [1844]. Family affairs (ff. 77–78^{v}).

Same to [—, 1848]. Mentions St. Augustine's College, Canterbury (ff. 79–80^{v}).

Fragment of letter from the same, 1848 (f. 81).

M[ary] S[ykes] W[atson, daughter of Joshua], to Mary Watson, 1838. Personal matters (ff. 82–83^{v}).

William Wilberforce, philanthropist, to Watson, 1820. About a meeting of S.P.G. for the relief of the Vaudois (ff. 84–6).

Same to the same, 1823. About a donation from him to the National Society (ff. 87–8).

Christopher Wordsworth, Master of Trinity College, Cambridge, to the same, 1838. About the 'Birmingham scheme', and personal matters (f. 89).

Same to [Mary Sykes] Watson, 1832. Arrangements for a visit. Account of dispute between the Archbishop of Dublin and Robert Daly (ff. 91–92^{v}).

Same to the same, [1836]. Mainly local affairs at Buxted (ff. 93–4).

Same to the same, 1838. Personal matters, mainly his health (ff. 95–96^{v}).

Christopher Wordsworth, headmaster of Harrow, (1868) Bishop of Lincoln, to Watson, 1837. Personal matters. A visit from Keble (ff. 97–8).

Same to the same, 1838. Alteration in his duties as headmaster. A mathematics master appointed (ff. 99–100).

William Wordsworth, poet, to the same, 1833. Inquiries about his health. The importance of the Archbishop at the present time. His eyes inflamed. *Copy* (ff. 101–3).

PAPERS ABOUT ELY CHAPEL, HOLBORN

Ely Chapel in Holborn, the former chapel of the Bishop of Ely's London House, was bought by Watson and presented to the National Society for use as a church for the Central Schools.

Miscellaneous accounts, 1813–29 (ff. 104–6, 110–15, 118).

Oliver Hatch [to Watson], 1819. About the accommodation in the chapel (f. 107).

Same to the same, [1819]. About the purchase of the chapel (f. 108).

Watson to Archbishop Howley, 1829. Proposes surrender of the chapel to the National Society, and gives extracts from conveyance, 1820. *Copy* (ff. 116–117^{v}).

Notes on terms of lease of the chapel, n.d. *Torn* (ff. 119–120^{v}).

Extract from *The Saturday Magazine*, 16 October 1838, containing an account of the chapel, with engraving (ff. 121–122^{v}).

Extract from the same about Ely Palace, with engraving, 17 November 1838. *Printed* (ff. 123–124^{v}).

Historical notes on Ely chapel (f. 125).

M. B. Blackwall to H. Stretton, 1841. About sale of the freehold of the chapel (f. 126).

Given by A. B. Webster, 1954.

127 ff.

1563. ILLUMINATIONS OF THE NATIVITY

Scenes of the Nativity, illuminated and written by A. Trevor and his wife, parents of the donor, 19th century.

Given by Mrs. M. E. D. Wathen, 1957.

i+13 ff.

1564–84. SHANGHAI REGISTERS

Registers of marriages, baptisms, confirmations, and burials at Shanghai, China, according to the rites of the Church of England, 1849–1951.

A. Holy Trinity Cathedral, Shanghai

[Holy Trinity Church until 1875]

1564: Register of marriages, 1 April 1852–9 July 1859. 43 ff., including many blank.

[1564–84 *cont.***]**

1565: Register of marriages, 9 July 1859–22 March 1888. Also included are a few marriages solemnized at the Church of Our Saviour, the Seaman's Church, and at private residences.

Endorsed, No. IB.

198 pp.

1566: Register of marriages, 2 April 1888–10 December 1900.

Endorsed, No. 2.

200 pp.

1567: Register of marriages, 14 December 1900–31 January 1910.

Endorsed, III.

198 pp.

1568: Register of marriages, 5 February 1910–15 February 1921.

Endorsed, IV.

226 pp.

1569: Register of marriages, 26 February 1921–11 November 1925.

Endorsed, No. V.

154 pp.

1570: Register of marriages, 16 November 1925–24 August 1931.

Endorsed, Vol. VI.

147 pp.

1571: Register of marriages, 7 September 1931–2 June 1937.

Endorsed, Vol. VII.

150 pp.

1572: Register of marriages at Holy Trinity Cathedral, Shanghai, 3 June 1937–27 March 1943 and 29 September 1945–7 April 1947.

Also an appendix of ten marriages solemnized 26 February 1944–5 October 1946, of which three (pp. 130–2) were performed in Civilian Assembly Centres—internment camps operated by the Japanese occupying authorities—and one (p. 139) at St. Paul's Church, Nanking.

Endorsed, Vol. VIII.

150 pp.

1573: Register of marriages, 12 April 1947–2 April 1951.

Endorsed, Vol. IX.

156 pp., including many blank.

1574: Register of baptisms, 14 October 1849–17 October 1859.

Endorsed, No. 1.

85 ff.

1575: Register of baptisms, 24 October 1859–14 May 1885.

Endorsed, No. 2.

292 pp.

1576: Register of baptisms, 14 May 1885–3 October 1900.
Endorsed, No. 3.
289 pp.

1577: Register of baptisms, 14 October 1900–11 February 1915.
Endorsed, No. 4.
404 pp.

1577A: Register of baptisms, 21 February 1915–31 March 1943 and 18 November 1945–12 August 1951.
Also on separate sheets baptisms performed at Civilian Assembly Centres, 16 April 1943–24 August 1945; confirmations, 9 December 1943; marriages, 31 March and 14 April 1945 (pp. 373–93).
Endorsed, No. 5.
426 pp.

1578–9: Chronological index of marriages and baptisms, 1849–1940.
A–I. *Typescript*. 164 ff.
J–Z. *Typescript*. 201 ff.

1580: Register of confirmations, 1904–51.
102 ff.

B. St. Andrew's Church, Shanghai

1581: Register of marriages, 1907–29.
101 ff., including many blank.

1582: Register of Baptisms, 1907–37.
401 ff., including many blank.

C. Registers of Burials

1583: Register of burials in the Old Cemetery, Shantung Road, Shanghai, 1859–68 (pp. 1–48); the New Cemetery, 1868–98 (pp. 49–305), and the New Cemetery at Bubbling Well Road, 1898–9 (pp. 305–7).
394 pp., including many blank.

1584: Register of burials in the Seaman's Cemetery, Pootung, 1859–80, with a note of some further burials, 1885–6 (p. 216).
389 pp., including many blank.

Given by the Foreign Office, 1954.

1585. LAMBETH PALACE LIBRARY CATALOGUE

Draft index by David Wilkins, Lambeth Librarian, of his catalogue of MSS. 1–878 in Lambeth Palace Library, 1720 [Library Records F.40]. The latter part of the book bound in wrong order. It is written on part of a commonplace book of theology in the hand of Archbishop Tenison.

Phillipps MS. 10697. The old shelfmark $\frac{\text{R}}{14290}$.

Given by the Minet Library, London, 1955.

378 pp.

1586–9. PAPERS OF SIR LEWIS TONNA DIBDIN

Papers of Sir Lewis Tonna Dibdin, Kt. (1852–1938). Dibdin held the offices of Chancellor of the Diocese of Rochester (1886–1903), of Exeter (1888–1903), and of Durham (1891–1903); counsel to the Attorney-General in charity matters (1895–1903); Dean of the Arches, Auditor of the Chancery Court of York, Master of the Faculties (1903–34); Vicar-General of the Province of Canterbury (1925–34); First Church Estates Commissioner (1905–31). He was also a member of the Royal Commission on Church Discipline, 1904–6, and on Divorce, 1909–12.

The papers were given to the Library by L. G. Dibdin, 1958.

1586. DIBDIN PAPERS

MISCELLANEOUS PAPERS

Miscellaneous papers of Sir Lewis Dibdin, 1711–1933. They comprise:

Confirmation by Abra[ham] Kemp of valuation of a site for parsonage house at Bow, London, 1711. *Copy* (f. 1).

Account by Dibdin of the lying-in-state of the Emperor Napoleon III at Chislehurst, Kent, 1873 (ff. 2–10).

Case concerning lay organization in the Diocese of Rochester submitted for the opinion of Sir J. Fitzjames Stephen and Henry Richmond Droop, 1878. *Printed* (ff. 11–14).

Letter from Dibdin to *The Times*, 3 December 1881, concerning the Manchester Synod. *Draft* (ff. 15–17).

Sketch of plan for amending rights of patronage of benefice in Church of England, [by Revd. Humphrey Senhouse Pinder, 1875]. Postage date stamp '1886' (f. 18).

Notes on marriage procedure and fees for the [guidance] *of the clergy of the Diocese of Rochester*, by Dibdin, 1887. *Corrected proof* (ff. 19–28).

Notes by Dibdin of evidence in an application by the Rector and Churchwardens of St. Margaret's Lee for a faculty to introduce a second Holy Table and erect chancel gates, heard in the Consistory Court of Rochester, 1887.

See also MS. 1588 f. 34 (ff. 29–31).

Arthur Day to Dibdin, 1891, concerning a sequestration (f. 32).

Arthur Burch, Registrar of the Diocese of Exeter, to the same, 1891, concerning a sequestration at Colebrooke, Devon (f. 34).

Notes by Dibdin of cases concerning sequestration, [1891] (ff. 35–106).

Election address by Dibdin for elections to the House of Laymen in the Diocese of London, 1893. *Printed* (f. 107).

Memorandum by Dibdin for an unnamed Bishop on sequestration, recommending legislative changes, 1893. *Copy* (ff. 110–17).

Election address by Dibdin for elections to the House of Laymen in the Diocese of London, 1896. *Printed* (f. 118).

Arthur Burch, Registrar of the Diocese of Exeter, to Dibdin, 1896, enclosing a map of the diocese showing surrogates and places where surrogates might be appointed (ff. 119–120v).

Enclosing:

An ecclesiastical map of the diocese of Exeter . . . compiled under the direction of the Revd. H. Bramley, 1895 (f. 121).

William Robert Moore, lawyer, to the same, 1896, concerning surrogates (f. 122).

Enclosing:

'List of vacancies in Surrogates, Diocese of Rochester' (f. 124).

Arthur Burch, Registrar of the Diocese of Exeter, to the same, 1896, concerning meeting of standing committee of Diocesan Conference (f. 126).

The Chancellor's charge at the visitation of the churchwardens of the Diocese of Durham, 1900. Shortened version printed *Durham Diocesan Gazette*, vol. xiv, no. 3 (ff. 128–59).

Memorandum by Dibdin on church ornaments, [1902]. Endorsed, 'For Mr. Balfour' (ff. 160–72).

Letter from Dibdin to an unnamed Bishop, [1904], concerning Minor Orders and the duties of laymen. *Typescript copy* (ff. 173–83).

Notes on the Reformatio Legum and its relation to the law and practice of the Church of England as to divorce. Corrected proof of Dibdin's evidence to the Royal Commission on Divorce and Matrimonial Causes, 1912, iii, 42–58 (ff. 184–98).

Latin text and English translation in parallel columns of the section *De Adulteriis et Divortiis* in *Reformatio Legum Ecclesiasticarum* by Archbishop Cranmer. *Duplicated* (ff. 199–217).

Evidence by Dibdin to the Select Committee of the House of Lords on the Church in Wales, 1914. *Printed* (ff. 218–225v).

Description by Dibdin of a visit to Lambeth Palace on 2 August 1914 (ff. 226–31).

A. R. Powys, secretary to the Society for the Protection of Ancient Monuments, to E. V. Oliver, secretary to the Ancient Monuments Committee, 1914, protesting at misrepresentation of the Society's views. *Typescript copy* (ff. 233–5).

Report of Ancient Monuments (Churches) Committee to the Archbishops of Canterbury and York. The committee was appointed by the Archbishops and consisted of Dibdin, Sir Alfred Kempe, and Sir Charles Chadwyck-Healey, 1914. *Printed* (ff. 236–243v).

Memorandum [by Dibdin] on the 'Report of Ancient Churches Committee', [1914]. *Typescript copy* (ff. 244–8).

Memorandum [by the same] for Welsh Bishops on the formation of a Provincial Convocation subsequent to the disestablishment of the Welsh Church, [1915]. *Corrected typescript copy* (ff. 249–54).

[1586 *cont.***]**

Description by the same of a visit to London on 11 November 1918 (Armistice Day). *Typescript* (ff. 256–9).

John Sankey, (1932) 1st Viscount Sankey, to Dibdin, 1920, thanking him for memorandum on Welsh Church Tribunals (f. 260).

Memorandum by Dibdin on ecclesiastical courts in Wales, 1919. *Typescript copy* (ff. 261–75).

Judgement [by Dibdin, Dean of the Arches] in case concerning Lord Bathurst's right to pews in Cirencester parish church, [1922]. *Typescript copy* (ff. 276–86).

'Sale of Livings', being an article by Dibdin for *Church Councillor's Gazette*, 1922. *Typescript* (ff. 287–92).

Note by Dibdin on the career of Sir Alfred Kempe, Chancellor of the Diocese of London, 1922. Endorsed, 'written for a notice in the *Proceedings of the Royal Society*'. *Typescript* (ff. 293–4).

Judgement by Dibdin, Dean of the Arches, in case of Marson *v.* Unmack, concerning offertories and collections at West Horsley, Surrey, [1923] (ff. 295–311). Also correspondence between Dibdin and the Bishop of Winchester concerning the same case, 1923 (ff. 312–15).

Dibdin to Archbishop Davidson, 1925, concerning criticisms of Church Assembly by Arthur Benson. *Typescript copy* (ff. 316–17).

Judgement by Dibdin, Dean of the Arches, in case of the rector and churchwardens of St. Nicholas Acons *v.* London County Council, concerning Disused Burial Grounds Act, 1884, 1928 (ff. 318–21). Also a newspaper cutting concerning the same (f. 322).

Memorandum by Dibdin on 'Mr. [J. V.] Bullard's Memorandum "On the bearing of the Canon Law upon the present situation" ', [1928], concerning the powers of Convocation in Prayer Book Revision. *Typescript copy* (ff. 324–5).

Enclosing:

Memorandum by the same on 'Report of a Committee of the Lower House of York Convocation "On the Canon Law" 1926. No. 374'. *Typescript copy* (ff. 326–30).

Speech by Dibdin in the House of Laity on Reservation during debate on the Prayer Book Measure, 9 February 1928. *Typescript copy* (ff. 331–9).

Memorandum on the relations of Church and State, apparently prepared by Dibdin for the Archbishops' Commission on the Relations between Church and State, appointed 5 February 1930. *Typescript copy* (ff. 340–52).

Memorandum and proposals by Dibdin for alterations to the Prayer Book, [1933], prepared for the Archbishops' Commission on the Relations between Church and State (C.C.S. 94). *Duplicated* (ff. 353–62).

Memorandum by Dibdin on 'Lawful Authority', 1933, prepared for the Archbishops' Commission on the Relations between Church and State (C.C.S. 109). *Duplicated* (ff. 363–70).

370 ff.

1587. DIBDIN PAPERS

LECTURES AND ADDRESSES

Lectures and addresses by Sir Lewis Dibdin, 1882–1923. They comprise:

Address to conference of the Union of Lay and Clerical Associations on the need for unity among evangelicals, 1882 (ff. 1–29).

Address to candidates for ordination in the Diocese of Rochester, 1887, concerning relations with the laity (ff. 29–46).

Address on Church and State. An expanded draft of a paper read at the Church Congress at Hull, 1890 (ff. 47–64).

Ticket for course of lectures on English Church History delivered at Christ Church, Hampstead, by Dibdin and the vicar, [1890]. *Printed* (f. 65).

Lecture on Disestablishment and Disendowment delivered at Christ Church, Hampstead, n.d. *Copy* (ff. 66–147).

Lecture on Establishment, probably delivered at Christ Church, Hampstead, n.d. (ff. 148–89).

Notes for lecture on Disestablishment and Disendowment, n.d. (ff. 190–5).

Lecture on the State of Church Laws and Courts and Convocations, n.d. (ff. 196–239).

Lecture on the Royal Supremacy, n.d. (ff. 240–66).

Address to the Rochester Diocesan Society on the housing of the poor, 189[ ] (ff. 267–86).

Draft of an article on the Proposed Overthrow of the Church in Wales, contributed to *The Nineteenth Century* (1894), xxxvi, 100–10 (ff. 287–339).

Lecture on Church Law delivered at Durham, 189[ ] (ff. 340–63).

Lecture on the Hundred of Elthorne, Middx., n.d. It is written on the back of sheets of Dibdin's article on Archbishop Benson in *Quarterly Review* (1897), clxxxvi, 293–322 (ff. 364–95).

Lecture on charities, [189] (ff. 396–455).

Lecture on the Court of Arches delivered to undergraduates of St. John's College, Cambridge, 1921, with (f. 456) letter of invitation from the Master, Sir Robert Forsyth Scott (ff. 456–68).

Sermon on the Central Fund of the Church of England, written by Dibdin for the Revd. Thomas Garbutt Wilton, Vicar of Dormans Land, Surrey, 1923. *Typescript copy* (ff. 469–75).

475 ff.

1588. DIBDIN PAPERS

SCRAPBOOK

Scrapbook of newspaper cuttings of letters, articles, speeches, and judgements, etc. by Sir Lewis Dibdin. They comprise:

Speech concerning the constitution of ecclesiastical courts, 1881 (f. 1).

'The Present Aspect of the Ritual Struggle'. *The Churchman*, December 1881 (ff. 2–7).

Report on resolutions of a joint committee of both Houses of Convocation concerning ecclesiastical courts, [1882] (ff. 8–10).

Review of George Trevor, 'On the Ecclesiastical Courts' (*The Churchman*, April 1882) (ff. 10–12); a second review of the same book (*The Churchman*, July 1882) (ff. 13–16^{v}).

Address on church discipline and church courts. *Report of the Church Congress* (*Derby*), 1882, 129–33 (ff. 17–19). Also a statement on the Royal Supremacy. Ibid., 224 (f. 20).

To the Evangelical Clergy of the Church of England, [1882]. *Proof* (ff. 21–2).

'A Bishop's Power to Refuse Institution'. *The Record*, 26 January 1883. (f. 23^{r-v}).

The Great Statute of Appeals. Reprinted from *The Record*, 17 March 1883 (ff. 24–25^{v}).

Address on ecclesiastical courts. *Report of the Church Congress* (*Reading*), 1883, 506–9 (ff. 26–8).

On 'Bricks'. *Boys and Girls Companion*, January 1884, 8–10 (ff. 29–30).

Letter to the Bishop of Rochester, concerning the fabric of churches. *Rochester Diocesan Chronicle*, 1 February 1887 (f. 31^{r-v}). Also a statement as to a diocesan inventory of church property. Ibid., 1 June 1887 (ff. 32^{v}–33^{v}).

Judgement in the Consistory Court of Rochester in application by the rector and churchwardens of St. Margaret's Lee for a faculty to erect chancel gates, etc. *The Record*, 21 October 1887. See also MS. 1586 ff. 29–31 (f. 34^{r-v}).

Article on 'Endowment and Establishment'. *Hook's Church Dictionary* 14th edn., 1887. *Corrected proof* (ff. 35^{v}–36).

Review of Mrs. Humphrey Ward, *Robert Elsmere*. *The Record*, 11 May 1888. *Corrected proof* (ff. 37^{v}–38).

Paper on the Dean of Peterborough's proposals concerning the Ornaments Rubric. *The Record*, 8 November 1889 (f. 39^{r-v}).

Review of Gilbert Child, *Church and State under the Tudors*. *The Record*, 5 September 1890 (ff. 40^{v}–41).

Judgement in the Consistory Court of Rochester in application for faculty to erect tower and peal of bells at St. Peter's, Brockley. *Proof* (f. 42).

Address on 'Church and State'. *Report of the Church Congress* (*Hull*), 1890, 63–7. *Corrected proof* (ff. 43–4).

Article on 'The Discipline Bill and Canon Law'. *The Record*, 26 February 1892 (f. 45^{r-v}).

Article on 'The Discipline Bill "Benefit of Clergy"'. *The Record*, 11 March 1892 (ff. 46^{v}–47^{v}).

Article on 'The Discipline Bill'. *The Record*, 1 April 1892 (ff. 48^{v}–49^{v}).

Letter to *The Times* on the qualification of churchwardens, 5 April 1892 (f. 50); another letter on the same subject, 16 April 1892 (f. 51).

Statement on preaching. *Report of the Church Congress* (*Folkestone*), 1892, 608 (f. 52).

Statement by Dibdin on the court of final appeal in ecclesiastical causes, 1899. *Corrected proof* (ff. 53–6).

Article on 'Simony' contributed to *The Contemporary Review*, February 1893 (ff. 57–64).

Address on the Parish Councils Bill. *Report of the Church Congress* (*Birmingham*), 1893, 221–5 (ff. 65–7).

Report of debate on the Parish Councils Bill in Canterbury Diocesan Conference. *The Guardian*, 19 July 1893 (f. 68^{r-v}).

Opinion on *Admission into Statutory Livings*, 1893. *Corrected proof* (ff. 69–73).

Exposition of clause 13 ('the charity clause') of the Parish Councils Bill, [1893]. *Corrected proof* (ff. 74–7).

Opinion on the *Appointment, Tenure and Retirement of the Beneficed Clergy*, delivered [to St. Albans Diocesan Conference, 1896]. See below ff. 95–8 (ff. 78–85).

Speech at Canterbury Diocesan Conference on the Local Government Act. *The Guardian*, 18 July 1894 (f. 86^{v}).

Address on 'Church Reform and Discipline'. *Report of the Church Congress* (*Exeter*), 1894, 448–52. *Corrected proof* (ff. 88–90).

Obituary notice on Anthony Wilson Thorold, Bishop of Winchester, [1895]. *Proof* (ff. 91–2).

Charge on the Benefices Bill delivered to churchwardens at Durham visitation. *The Record*, 29 May 1896 (f. 93^{r-v}).

Letter to *The Times* on the Benefices Bill, 15 June 1896 (f. 94).

Address on the *Appointment, Tenure and Retirement of the Beneficed Clergy*, delivered [to St. Albans Diocesan Conference, 1896]. *Corrected proof*. See above ff. 78–85 (ff. 95–8).

Letter to *The Times* on the Benefices Bill, 23 June 1898 (f. 99).

Address on 'Mutual Relations of Clergy and Laity'. *Report of the Church Congress* (*Bradford*), 1898, 63–6. *Proof* (ff. 100–1).

[1588 *cont.*]

Review of W. Sanday, *The Catholic Movement and the Archbishops' Decision* (*Church Quarterly Review*, 1899, 233–9) (ff. 102–5).

Letter to *The Fortnightly Review*, November 1899, on 'The Lambeth Decision'. *Proof* (f. 106).

Letter to the same, March 1900, on the same subject. *Proof* (ff. 107–8).

Correspondence between Dibdin and the Archbishop of Canterbury on the granting of marriage licences. *The Times*, 31 May 1903 (ff. 109–11).

Judgement by Dibdin, Dean of the Arches, in case of the London County Council *v.* Dundas and others, concerning faculties for Holy Trinity Church, Stepney. *The Times*, 6 August 1903 (ff. 112–15).

Reports of an address to the Authors' Club on the records of the Court of Arches. *The Standard*, 13 January 1914 (ff. 116–20); *The Church Times*, 16 January 1914 (f. 121^{r-v}); *The Guardian*, 16 January 1914 (ff. 122^{r-v}).

Letter to *The Times* on Parliament and Convocation, 21 July 1914 (f. 123).

Letter to *The Guardian* on the Clergy and the War, 24 February 1916 (f. 124).

Paper on *Lord Wolmer's Parochial Church Councils* (*Powers*) *Bill*, [1921]. *Corrected proof* (ff. 125–9).

Article on 'Reconstruction of Financial Resources'. *The Record*, 23 October 1919 (f. 130^{r-v}).

Presidential address to the Poor Clergy Relief Corporation. *The Record*, 29 July 1920 (f. 131).

Address to the same. *The Record*, 28 July 1921 (f. 132^{r-v}).

Correspondence with the Bishop of Gloucester about upkeep of bishops' palaces. *The Times*, 10–13 March 1923 (ff. 133–5).

Letter to *The Times* on reform of ecclesiastical courts, 4 July 1923 (ff. 136–7).

Judgement by Dibdin, Dean of the Arches, on appeal by the vicar and churchwardens of Riby, Lincs., against decision of the Chancellor of Lincoln. *The Daily Telegraph*, 24 March 1926 (f. 138).

Statement on *The Benefices* (*Ecclesiastical Duties*) *Measure*. Reprinted from *The Guardian*, 8 October 1926 (f. 139).

Letter to *The Times* on defeasance clause in a faculty, 15 December 1927 (f. 140).

Letter to the same on 'reservation', 20 April 1928 (f. 141).

Statement at parochial meeting at Dormans Land, Surrey, on the Prayer Book Measure. *The Church Times*, 27 April 1928 (f. 142).

142 ff.

1589. DIBDIN PAPERS

LIST OF PAPERS OF SIR LEWIS DIBDIN

A list of papers belonging to Sir Lewis Dibdin covering the years 1872 to 1933. They are numbered in chronological order, and the numbers have in many cases been written on the originals in green crayon. Some of the items are noted as destroyed in 1957.

i+45 ff.

1590–1679. PAPERS OF CLAUDE JENKINS

Papers of Claude Jenkins (1877–1959), Regius Professor of Ecclesiastical History, Oxford, and sometime Lambeth Librarian. The papers are divided into the following sections:

(1) Miscellaneous manuscripts acquired by Jenkins (1590–1615).
(2) Papers of *The Church Quarterly Review*, 1901–29 (1616–29).
(3) Personal papers (1630–42).
(4) Indexes and transcripts by Jenkins (1643–79).

1590–2. JENKINS PAPERS

Three Formularies or precedent books of ecclesiastical law compiled by Registrars of the dioceses of Chichester, Hereford, Ely, and Lincoln, with later additions by the Vicar-General of the Archbishop of Canterbury and the Master of the Faculties, 17th–18th centuries. The compilation was probably started by Robert King, Master of Trinity Hall, Cambridge, and Vicar-General to Bishop Wren from 1661 [*v.* MS. 1591 f. 34]. The compiler used documents dating from the episcopates of Antony Watson, Bishop of Chichester, Launcelot Andrewes, successively Bishop of Chichester, Ely, and Winchester, Matthew Wren, successively Bishop of Hereford, Norwich, and Ely, Benjamin Laney, successively Bishop of Lincoln and Ely, and Peter Gunning, successively Bishop of Chichester and Ely. The bulk of the documents relate to the dioceses of Chichester and Ely. Sometime after King's death the volumes appear to have passed to the Registrar of the diocese of Lincoln, and probably passed to Canterbury on the translation of Thomas Tenison from that see to the Primacy. Thereafter the books were discontinued until the time of Archbishop Cornwallis when they were filled up.

1590

Formulary of many types of ecclesiastical deeds, using material principally of the diocese of Chichester from the beginning of the 17th century and of the diocese of Ely for the early years of the episcopate of Matthew Wren.

At f. 2^v is a list of fees payable at the confirmation and consecration of Thomas Tenison, Bishop of Lincoln.

At f. 1 the inscription 'Book of Forms 2d', in the hand of Tenison, and on the front cover the number '2'.

Inside the front cover is written a price in very faint pencil, now illegible.

158 ff.

1591

Formulary similar to the last. It is divided into two parts:

1. Forms of deeds relating principally to the episcopate of Matthew Wren, Bishop of Ely, with some deeds of an earlier date and a few dating from the episcopates of Benjamin Laney and Peter Gunning, Bishops of Ely (ff. 1–49^v).

2. Forms of deeds issued by the Vicar-General of the Archbishop of Canterbury and by the Master of the Faculties, with index, temp. Archbishop Cornwallis (ff. 50–135^v).

Inside the front cover the inscription 'First Book of Forms' in the hand of Archbishop Tenison, and on the front cover the number '1'. Also inside the front cover in pencil the price '£4 10', and the [?] bookseller's mark '13/259'.

136 ff.

1592

Formulary similar to the last, and also divided into two parts:

1. Forms of deeds for the episcopates of Benjamin Laney, Bishop of Lincoln (ff. 4–39^v), and of Thomas Tenison, Bishop of Lincoln, subsequently Archbishop of Canterbury (ff. 40–2).

2. Forms of deeds issued by the Vicar-General of the Archbishop of Canterbury and by the Master of the Faculties, with index, temp. Archbishop Cornwallis. Written in the same hand as MS. 1591 ff. 50–135^v (ff. 2–3, 42^v–90).

Inscribed on the front cover the number '3'.

90 ff.

1593. JENKINS PAPERS

DIARY

Diary of Kyrle Ernle Money, Canon of Hereford, 1806–45.

On the inside of the front cover a certificate that the manuscript was referred to in an affidavit of Ellinor Wilmot sworn before J. Walker Carsley, commissioner, 2 April 1876.

Price 12*s*. 6*d*.

168 ff.

1594. JENKINS PAPERS

BOOK OF RECIPES

Book of culinary recipes written in several hands from both ends of the volume, with indexes, *c*. 1813–62.

The inscription, Matilda Jones, 1 January 1813 (f. 1).

179 ff., of which ff. 56–91, 97–140 blank.

1595. JENKINS PAPERS

SURVEY OF TIMBER, ETC.

Survey of timber in Blackland Wood, [Wilts.], with notes of sales of timber, 1816–17.

30 ff., of which ff. 8–30 blank.

1596. JENKINS PAPERS

DIARY

Diary of George Onslow Deane, entered in *Marshall's New British Gentleman's Pocket Book*, recording his activities in and near Little Burstead, Essex, 1 January–12 June 1846. Deane matriculated at Christ Church, Oxford, on 4 June 1846.

Inside the front cover the price 3*s*. 6*d*.

109 ff., of which ff. 55–109 blank.

1597. JENKINS PAPERS

JOURNAL AND PAPERS OF ALEXANDER EWING, BISHOP OF ARGYLL AND THE ISLES

Journal and papers of Alexander Ewing, Bishop of Argyll and the Isles, comprising:

Historical account of the Scottish Episcopal Church and the diocese of Argyll and the Isles by Alexander Ewing, addressed *To the members of the Episcopal Church of Argyll and the Isles*, February 1848. *Printed sheets* (ff. 1^v–4^v).

Statement and appeal relative to the Diocese of Argyll and the Isles in the West of Scotland, 1852, containing an appeal for funds. *Printed sheets* (ff. 4^v–7^v).

Papers preparatory to Ewing's departure for the Continent, 1855, viz. medical certificate as to his state of health (f. 8); licence of absence for a year granted by the Primus and College of Bishops of the Scottish Episcopal Church (f. 9); a letter from Archbishop Sumner to Ewing (f. 11); letter commendatory from Charles James Blomfield, Bishop of London, authorizing Ewing to minister to and confirm members of the Church of England (f. 13).

Journal by Ewing on a tour of the Continent to Vevey, Switzerland, by way of Paris and Berne, 1855 (ff. 15–41).

Notes and writings, partly in the hand of Ewing, about the death of his wife, 1856, with copies by her of verses (ff. 103^v–117^v).

On flyleaf the price 8*s*. 6*d*.

118 ff., of which ff. 41^v–103 blank.

1598. JENKINS PAPERS

ACCOUNTS, ETC.

Domestic and personal accounts of [Sir Thomas Trevor, 1st Bt., of Enfield, Middlesex, son of Sir Thomas Trevor, Baron of the Exchequer], 1632–56 (ff. i, 1–61^{v}, 181–7).

The volume also contains medical recipes, late 17th century (ff. 62^{v}–76^{v}, 174–176^{v}, 180^{r-v}); miscellaneous accounts, mostly legal, of Walter Howell, 1714–38 (ff. 77–97^{v}, 159^{v}–173^{v}); sermon preached before William III and Queen Mary (ff. 177–178^{v}); method of surveying an estate for sale (f. 179^{v}).

i+187 ff., of which ff. 98–159 blank.

1599. JENKINS PAPERS

CATALOGUE OF SHARSTED LIBRARY, ETC.

Catalogue of a library of printed books at Sharsted, Kent, compiled after 1861. The letter 'A' is missing (ff. 2–54). The remainder of the volume contains five sermons by the Revd. Claude Jenkins (ff. 54^{v}–61, 67–73, 82–97).

Stamped on the front cover 'Sharsted Library'.

101 ff.

1600. JENKINS PAPERS

JOURNAL

Journal of a tour of Scotland and Northern England in the form of ten letters unsigned and without addressee, 25 August–21 October 1846.

39 ff.

1601. JENKINS PAPERS

FARMING ACCOUNTS

Farming accounts for an estate at Sharsted, Kent, 1851–2. List of contents (f. 1).

i+179 ff.

1602–3. JENKINS PAPERS

JOURNAL OF A TOUR OF EGYPT AND PALESTINE

Journal of a tour of Egypt, Palestine, and the Lebanon, returning through Greece, Constantinople, and Vienna, by Randall Thomas Davidson, subsequently Archbishop of Canterbury, Craufurd Tait, George Courthope, Claude Hankey, and George Horner, 9 December 1872–18 June 1873.

64 and 90 ff.

1604. JENKINS PAPERS

CORRESPONDENCE OF THE REVD. CECIL WRAY

Correspondence of the Revd. Cecil Wray, perpetual curate of St. Martin in the Field, Liverpool, 1826–78. The names of the writers will be found in the index.

620 ff.

1605–8. JENKINS PAPERS

DIARIES OF LUCY TAIT

Diaries and memoranda books of Lucy Tait, eldest daughter of Archbishop Tait, 1891–7, 1918–28.

1605: December 1891–December 1893. i+130 ff.
1606: February 1894–January 1897. i+178 ff.
1607: November 1918–December 1922 and February–April 1928. ii+202 ff.
1608: March 1923–November 1927. 200 ff.

1609. JENKINS PAPERS

SILHOUETTES

Volume containing 165 silhouettes of politicians and other persons, with index, late 19th century.

64 ff.

1610. JENKINS PAPERS

DIARY

Diary of A. Faunce De Laune, of Sharsted Court, Sittingbourne, Kent, describing a journey from Tokyo to England, via Vancouver, Chicago, and New York, 1892.

i+153 ff.

1611. JENKINS PAPERS

HAMPSHIRE INCUMBENTS

Alphabetical list compiled by [Dr. S. Anderson, of Elstree, Herts.] of Hampshire incumbents, 1250–1910.

Typescript with manuscript additions.

591 ff.

1612–13. JENKINS PAPERS

DALTON'S *COLLEGIATE CHURCH OF OTTERY ST. MARY*

Author's grangerized copy of John Neale Dalton, *Collegiate Church of Ottery St. Mary*, 1917, with reviews, newspaper cuttings, and (in MS.

[1612–13 *cont.*]

1612 only) numerous photographs. Loose letters from 1612 have been removed to 1680, ff. 1–20.

1612 contains pp. vi–xxiv, 1–80.
1613 contains pp. xi–xxiv, 81–309.

1614. JENKINS PAPERS

KENTISH WILLS

'Abstracts of Wills relating to the County of Kent contained in the Archiepiscopal Registers at Lambeth, edited by Leland L. Duncan' (1862–1923). The volume is number V in a series, and contains abstracts arranged topographically as follows:

Hunton	Thomas Clynton, Kt., 1415 (f. 404).
Hythe	Alice Fulcombe, of Hythe, widow, 1589 (ff. 406–7). Thomas Taylour, of the same, yeoman, 1589 (ff. 408–9).
Ickham	William Heghtredbury, 1373 (ff. 410–12).
Ivychurch	Robert de Charwelton, clerk, 1368 (ff. 413–16).
Kenardington	Edmund de Passele, [Kt.], 1327 (ff. 417–18).
Lamberhurst	Katherine Wallere, widow, 1424 (f. 419). Richard Walsyngham, 1389. [no abstract] (f. 419).
Lee	Thomas Ryculff, of Holy Trinity the Less, London, 1452 (ff. 420–1). John Gylberd, junior, of Lee, 1389 (f. 422).
Leeds	Guy de Mone, Bishop of St. David's, 1407 (ff. 423–5).
Leigh	Richard Bourbage, Vicar of the same, 1435 (f. 426). John James, of Leigh, 1560 (ff. 426–8).
Lesnes	Thomas Young, clerk, 1377 (ff. 432–5). Robert Launde, Kt., citizen of London, 1383 (ff. 435–8).
Leveland	Richard Lord Ponynges (Poynings), 1387 (ff. 440–3).
Lewisham	Elizabeth Crowe, of Lewisham, widow, 1589 (ff. 444–5). John Batte, of Lewisham, 1552 [admin.] (f. 445).
Linstead	Thomas Knotte, of Linstead, 1560 (f. 446).
Longfield	Richard Cordon als Broun, Archdeacon of Rochester, 1452 (ff. 447–51).
Lullingstone	John Pecche, citizen of London, 1380 (ff. 452–3). John Bernes, of Lullingstone, 1389 [admin.] (f. 453).
Lydd	John Mottisfont, Vicar of Lydd, 1420 (ff. 455–6). Thomas Godefray, of Old Romney, 1430 (ff. 457–8). William Love, Rector of Sybbysdenne (Sibson, Leics.), 1437 (ff. 458–9). Mildred Sebrond, of Lydd, widow, 1589 (ff. 459–60).
Lyminge	Walter Cachepol, Rector of Lyminge, 1369 (f. 462). William de Preone, Rector of the same, 1404 (ff. 463–5).

Maidstone	John Stoyl, of Maidstone, 1368 (ff. 467–9).
	William Vaus, of the same, 1368 (ff. 469–74).
	John Wytclyf, Rector of the same, 1383 (f. 475).
	Robert Sybbethorp, Rector of the same, 1390 (ff. 476–8).
	John Goolde, clerk, 1406 (ff. 479–80).
	John Wootton, Master of the College of All Saints, 1417 [no abstract] (f. 480).
	Thomas Feld, Dean of Hereford, 1419 (ff. 481–4).
	Richard Wydenyle, senior, 1441 (ff. 484–5).
	John Pyccarde, of Maidstone, 1454 (f. 485).
Malling	Simon Chagne, of Malling, 1389 [no abstract] (f. 486).
Marden	Stephen Browne, of Marden, 1560 [admin.] (f. 486).
Margate	Frauncis Leuindall, of the Isle of Thanet, tailor, 1589 (ff. 487–9).
Milton	Thomas Beele, 1453 (ff. 491–3).
Minster in Sheppey	John Northwode, Kt., 1379 (f. 494).
	William Cheyne, esquire, 1441 (ff. 495–6).
Minster in Thanet	Thomas de Sancto Nicholas, Kt., 1375 (ff. 497–8).
Monkton in Thanet	Stephen Edmond, of Monkton in Thanet, 1425 (ff. 500–1).
	John de Wynewyk, Treasurer of York, 1360 (f. 501).
Newenden	Luke Outon, of Newenden, 1589 (f. 502).
Nonington	Richard Norman, of Nonington, husbandman, 1589 (f. 503).
Northbourne	John Westhorp, 1408 (ff. 504–6).
Northfleet	Peter de Lacy, 1375 (f. 507).
	Anne Sprackman, of Northfleet, 1615 (ff. 507–10).
Orpington	Nicholas [Isteley], Rector of Orpington, 1371 (ff. 512–15).
	John Wodehull, Rector of the same, 1383 (f. 516).

112 ff.

1615. JENKINS PAPERS

1. CHRIST CHURCH CATHEDRAL, OXFORD

Drawing in colour of stained-glass window in the Lucy Chapel, Christ Church Cathedral, Oxford, depicting St. Cuthbert holding the head of St. Oswald.

This window is reproduced in colour in S. A. Warner, *Oxford Cathedral*, 1924, facing p. 100, and the drawing may have been made for this purpose.

Size $27\frac{1}{2}+43$ inches.

[1615 *cont.*]

2. *THE CHURCH QUARTERLY REVIEW* PAPERS, 1901–29 (1616–29)

Papers of the editors of *The Church Quarterly Review*, 1901–29. Arthur Cayley Headlam, Principal of King's College, London, and (1923) Bishop of Gloucester, was editor of the journal 1901–21, and Jenkins was sub-editor, 1903–18, and then joint editor, 1921–7.

1616–20. JENKINS PAPERS

Editorial correspondence, 1901–29. The correspondence is arranged alphabetically by years, and the names of the writers will be found in the index.

1616: Correspondence, 1901–4. 304 ff.
1617: Ditto, 1905–6. 387 ff.
1618: Ditto, 1907–9. 357 ff.
1619: Ditto, 1910–14. 319 ff.
1620: Ditto, 1915–29 and n.d. 265 ff.

1621. JENKINS PAPERS

MINUTES

Minutes of meetings of the Directors of *The Church Quarterly Review*, 1907–21 (ff. 1–66).

Minutes of statutory general meetings of shareholders in The Church Quarterly Review Limited, 1907–22 (ff. 118^{v}–136^{v}).

iii+137 ff.

1622. JENKINS PAPERS

REGISTER OF REVIEWS

Register of books reviewed in *The Church Quarterly Review*, with the names of the reviewers, 1902–8.

115 ff.

1623. JENKINS PAPERS

ACCOUNTS

Accounts of The Church Quarterly Review Ltd., 1907–29.

xiv+127 ff.

1624. JENKINS PAPERS

REGISTER OF SUBSCRIBERS

Alphabetical register of subscribers to *The Church Quarterly Review*.

59 ff.

1625. JENKINS PAPERS

BANK BOOK

Bank book of The Church Quarterly Review Ltd. in account with Messrs. Hoare, 1907–26.

68 ff.

1626. JENKINS PAPERS

CERTIFICATES OF SHARES

Counterfoils of certificates of shares (numbers 1–25) in The Church Quarterly Review Ltd., 1907–8.

25 ff.

1627. JENKINS PAPERS

CERTIFICATES OF SHARES

Counterfoils of certificates of shares (numbers 26–33) in The Church Quarterly Review Ltd., and two completed but undetached certificates (numbers 34–5), 1908–12.

25 ff.

1628. JENKINS PAPERS

MISCELLANEOUS PAPERS

Miscellaneous papers concerning *The Church Quarterly Review*:

Memorandum and Articles of Association of The Church Quarterly Review, Limited, 1907 (ff. 1–20^{v}).

Memorandum and Articles of Association of The Church Quarterly Review, Limited, 22 June 1907 (ff. 21–40^{v}).

Annual balance sheets and accounts of The Church Quarterly Review, Ltd., 1906, 1908–19, 1921–5 (ff. 41–106).

106 ff.

1629. JENKINS PAPERS

MISCELLANEOUS PAPERS

Miscellaneous papers concerning *The Church Quarterly Review*:

Letter from Messrs. William B. Keen & Co., chartered accountants, to Headlam, 1906 (ff. 1–3).

Proposals to form a limited company to own *The Church Quarterly Review*, [1907]. *Duplicated* (f. 4).

Memorandum of agreement between Headlam, trustee for The Church Quarterly Review Ltd., and Messrs. Spottiswoode & Co., Ltd., publishers, 1907 (ff. 5–6).

Certificate of incorporation of The Church Quarterly Review Ltd., 1907 (f. 7).

Report of the Directors of The Church Quarterly Review Ltd. in compliance with the Companies Act, 1900, 1907. *Draft* (ff. 8–9^{v}).

[1629 *cont.*]

Advertising account of The Church Quarterly Review Ltd., 1907–8 (f. 10).

Report of The Church Quarterly Review Ltd., 1 April 1907–31 March 1908. *Draft* (ff. 11–16).

Account of sales of *The Church Quarterly Review*, 1907–9 (ff. 17–25).

Letter from Jenkins, secretary of The Church Quarterly Review Ltd., to Messrs. Spottiswoode & Co., Ltd., 1909 (f. 26).

Three letters from Messrs. Macmillan & Co., Ltd., to Headlam, 1909 (ff. 28–34).

Agenda for meeting of the Directors of The Church Quarterly Review Ltd., 1911. *Draft* (f. 35).

Memorandum [by Headlam] for meeting of the Directors of The Church Quarterly Review Ltd., [1911]. *Draft* (ff. 37–41).

Letter from Headlam to Jenkins, 1917 (ff. 42–3).

43 ff.

1630. JENKINS PAPERS

Personal letters and papers of Claude Jenkins at Oxford and as Professor of Ecclesiastical History, King's College, London, 1898–1935. The names of the writers will be found in the index.

ff. 1–86. Correspondence as an undergraduate of New College, Oxford, and subsequently, 1898–1904.

ff. 87–244. Correspondence and papers as Professor of Ecclesiastical History, King's College, London, 1918–35. Included are drafts of his application for the professorship, with (ff. 100–1) a list of his publications, and also (ff. 102–9) testimonials on his behalf. Other papers are *Regulations for admission of professors and readers to higher degrees*, and *Regulations on university titles* (ff. 120–123ᵛ); list of names and addresses of members of King's College (ff. 124–5); *Memorandum by the Theological Board on the Central Entrance Examination* (ff. 126–7); *Report on the needs of the King's College Hostel for theological students . . .*, 1910 (ff. 128–31); examination papers (ff. 132–4); examiners' mark lists: undated (ff. 135–57), 1930 (ff. 158–75), 1932 (ff. 176–97), 1934 (ff. 198–216), 1935 (ff. 217–44).

244 ff.

1631. Not allotted.

1632. JENKINS PAPERS

KING'S COLLEGE, LONDON

Register of attendance at lectures given by Claude Jenkins, Professor of Ecclesiastical History, King's College, London, on palaeography, Roman History, Early Church History, and English Church History, 1928–9.

33 ff.

1633. JENKINS PAPERS

Personal papers of Claude Jenkins, Canon of Canterbury.

ff. 1–24. Papers about alterations to the canonical lodgings, 1891–1929. They include thirteen rough plans of rooms in the lodgings of the first stall (ff. 2–14); deed authorizing Earl Stanhope and Sir John Mowbray, 1st Bt., Church Estates Commissioners, to raise £1,500 by mortgage for rebuilding the lodgings, 1891. Endorsed with cancellation stamp of Queen Anne's Bounty, 1922 (ff. 15^{v}–16^{v}); deed authorizing James Duncan, Canon of Canterbury, to rebuild lodgings, 1891 (ff. 17–18^{v}); deed of mortgage between Duncan and Queen Anne's Bounty for raising £1,500, 1891 (ff. 19–20); valuation of fixtures and fittings belonging to Mrs. B. Robinson purchased by Jenkins, 1929 (ff. 21–2); receipt for notarial fee on installation, 1929 (f. 24).

ff. 25–54. Papers about memorial to Archbishop Becket in Canterbury Cathedral, 1930–5. They include: *Suggested memorial to Archbishop Becket in Canterbury Cathedral.* Proof from *Kent Herald* (f. 25); memorandum by the Dean and Chapter of Canterbury objecting to proposed design. *Typescript* (f. 26); draft memorandum by Edward Hoare Hardcastle, Archdeacon of Canterbury, of objections to the memorial, 1930 (ff. 28–30), and final version of same. *Typescript copies* (ff. 31–3); memorandum by the same of an interview with Archbishop Lang about proposals for Becket commemoration, 1930. *Typescript copy* (ff. 34–5); 'memorandum by Dr. Jenkins on an interview with Mr. Croom and Prebendary [Henry Falconar Barclay] Mackay on 7 April 1930' (ff. 37–41); statement by the Dean and Chapter of objections to proposed memorial, with draft. *Typescript* (ff. 45–6); extracts by Jenkins from minutes of special meetings of the Dean and Chapter, 1930–1 (ff. 47–8); memorandum by Archdeacon Hardcastle on the history of proposals for Becket memorial, 1931 (ff. 50–2); notes on the same, mainly by Jenkins (f. 53).

ff. 55–90. Correspondence with the Dean and Chapter, 1924–44. The names of the writers will be found in the index.

ff. 91–220. Papers about new statutes for Canterbury Cathedral, 1912–56. They include: memorandum of conference between the Dean and Chapter and Archbishop Lang about new statutes. *Typescript copy* (ff. 97–8); minutes of an informal meeting between the Cathedral Commissioners and the Consenting Body (the Dean and Chapter), 1932. *Duplicated* (ff. 99–104); statement and memorandum by James Maurice Wilson, Canon of Worcester, on the respective authority of the Dean and Chapter of Worcester, 1912. *Typescript copy* (ff. 105–18); statutes of Rochester Cathedral. *Printed draft* (ff. 119–28); draft by Jenkins of new statutes for Canterbury Cathedral (ff. 130–216).

220 ff.

1634. JENKINS PAPERS

GENERAL CORRESPONDENCE

General correspondence of Claude Jenkins, 1902–58. The names of the writers will be found in the index.

311 ff.

1635–6. JENKINS PAPERS

Sermons preached by Jenkins at St. Martin-in-the-Fields, London, 1904–15.

1635: 1904–9. 247 ff.
1636: 1910–15. 205 ff.

1637. JENKINS PAPERS

Sermons preached by Jenkins, 1908–31:

St. Paul's Covent Garden, London, 1908 (ff. 1–7).
Gloucester, 1923 (ff. 9–15).
Gray's Inn, 1924 (ff. 16–28).
Royal Holloway College and King's College, London, 1926 (ff. 29–38).
Royal Holloway College, 1927 (ff. 39–52).
Gray's Inn, 1927, including (ff. 53–54^{v}) Order of Service (ff. 53–63).
Gloucester, 1928 (ff. 65–76).
N.p., [1929] (ff. 77–81).
Canterbury, 1929, including (ff. 82–3) Order of Service (ff. 82–105).
N.p., 1929 (ff. 106–13).
Canterbury, 1929, including (ff. 114–115^{v}) Order of Service (ff. 114–19).
Do., 1930, including (f. 121) Order of Service (ff. 121–68).
Do., 1931 (ff. 170–234).

234 ff.

1638. JENKINS PAPERS

Sermons preached by Jenkins, 1932–[57] and undated:

Canterbury, 1932 (ff. 2–62).
Westminster Abbey, 1933, including (ff. 64–67^{v}) Order of Service for members of London University (ff. 64–81).
Canterbury, 1933 (ff. 83–137).
[Do.], 1933 (ff. 139–50).
N.P., 1933 (ff. 151–6).
[Canterbury], 1933 (ff. 158–63).
[Do.], 1934 (ff. 164–91).
Royal Holloway College, 1936 (ff. 192–9).
New College, Oxford, 1937 (ff. 201–6).
Christ Church, Oxford, 1940 (ff. 208–19).

Do., 1950 (ff. 220–34).
Do., [1957] (ff. 236–45).
N.p. and n.d. (ff. 246–311^{v}).

311 ff.

1639. JENKINS PAPERS

LECTURES

A course of lectures by Jenkins on Lyndwood's *Provinciale*, using the expanded text in the Oxford edition of 1679.

200 ff.

1640. JENKINS PAPERS

LECTURE

Lecture by Jenkins on Tractarianism.

39 ff.

1641. JENKINS PAPERS

MISCELLANEOUS PAPERS

Miscellaneous papers of Claude Jenkins, 1901–52:

Paper on the Doctrine of the Atonement read by Jenkins to the Fortnightly Society, New College, Oxford, 1901 (ff. 1–4).

Verses. Begin, 'The dear Archdeacon in the Chair . . .' (ff. 5–6).

Paper on the Calendar by Jenkins (ff. 7–13).

Paper on booksellers' catalogues and book-collecting by Jenkins (ff. 14–17).

Obituary of H. R. L. Sheppard, Dean of Canterbury, written by Jenkins for *The Times*, and revised 1932. *Typescript* (ff. 19–29).

'Note on the Present Position of Canon Law', by Ernest Fraser Jacob, Professor of Medieval History, Manchester, and Percy George Ward, Vicar of Harston, for the Canon Law Commission, 1944. *Typescript copy* (ff. 31–2).

Memorandum on the Declaration of Assent, prepared by Mr. Justice Vaisey for the Canon Law Commission, 1945. *Duplicated* (ff. 33–40).

Memorandum on the revision of the Coronation Service, by Edward Craddock Ratcliff, Ely Professor of Divinity, Cambridge, 1952. A copy in the hand of Jenkins (ff. 41–59).

Memorandum of some 'practical considerations' concerning the Coronation of Elizabeth II by Jenkins, 1952 (ff. 61–6).

Lecture by Jenkins to mark the centenary of the Oxford Movement, 1933 (ff. 67–97).

Lecture on Diocesan Registers and the Canterbury and York Society, delivered by Jenkins at the Jubilee Annual Meeting of the Society, 1954 (ff. 98–117).

[1641 *cont.***]**

Will made by Jenkins, and signed and witnessed but not proved, 1944 (f. 118).

Protest against an edition of the Revised Version of the Bible without the marginal notes of the Revisers. *Printed* (ff. 119–20).

List of meetings of the University Graduates' Club, 1901–2. *Printed* (f. 121).

St. Martin-in-the-Fields Monthly Messenger, July 1912 (ff. 122–129^{v}).

Partly used Ration Book issued to Jenkins during the First World War, 1914–18 (ff. 130–139^{v}).

Programme of the St. Martin's Party for Listeners-in [to broadcast religious services], held at the Royal Albert Hall, 1924, with satirical sketches of the staff at St. Martin's, including Jenkins (ff. 140–4).

Interim report of the Archbishops' Committee on the Supply of Candidates for Holy Orders, 1924. *Printed* (ff. 145–7).

Prospectus announcing publication of *The British Museum Quarterly*, 1926 (ff. 148–149^{v}).

Leaflet issued by the Ministry of Information, 1940. *Printed* (f. 150).

Seating plan for the choir of Canterbury Cathedral at the enthronement of Archbishop Temple, with tickets and leaflet of instructions, 1942. *Printed* (ff. 151^{v}–156).

Mark papers for the preliminary examination of candidates for Holy Orders, King's College, London, with remarks on the candidates by Jenkins and a copy of the examination paper in Church History, 1906 (ff. 157^{v}–178).

179 ff.

1642. JENKINS PAPERS

PAPERS OF ADVISORY COMMITTEE ON LITURGICAL REVISION

Papers of an advisory committee on liturgical revision appointed by Archbishop Davidson according to a resolution of the Upper House of the Convocation of Canterbury, 6 July 1911. The committee met under the chairmanship of Archibald Robertson, Bishop of Exeter, 1912–15; Jenkins was secretary. Correspondence with Jenkins is at ff. 1–36, and with the Bishop of Exeter at ff. 37–73. The names of the writers will be found in the index. Also included are minutes of the meetings of the committee and other papers as follows:

A copy of the resolution of the Upper House of the Convocation of Canterbury appointing the committee, 1911 (f. 74); agenda of the first meeting, 22 October 1912. *Printed* (ff. 75–6); minutes of the second meeting, 28–9 January 1913. *Proof* (ff. 77–85); minutes of the third meeting, 1 April 1913. *Proof* (ff. 86–95); minutes of the fourth meeting, 30 June 1913. *Proof* (ff. 96–103); minutes of the fifth meeting, 28 July 1913. *Proof* (ff. 104–7); rough minutes of meeting, 20–1 October 1913, with (ff. 128–35) copy and proofs of recommendations, October [1913] (ff. 108–35); rough minutes of the sixth meeting, 26–7 January 1914, and (ff. 156–66) proofs (ff. 136–66); minutes of the seventh meeting, 19 October 1915. *Proof* (ff. 167–91); report of the committee 'on matters referred to them in connection with reports nos. 427 and 463', 1913. *Proof* (ff. 192–7); note of recommendations of the committee for submission to the Upper House of Canterbury Convocation, 26–7 January 1914. *Proof* (ff. 198–201); letter from the Bishop of Exeter to the members of the committee, 1915. *Proof* (ff. 202–3); memorandum by Walter Howard Frere, member of the Community of the Resurrection, Mirfield, and (1923) Bishop of Truro, on alternative forms of service. *Proof*. See also ff. 50–62 (ff. 204–9); *Resolution of the joint committee on the royal letters of business as amended and accepted by the Upper House on Feb. 10, 11, and April 28, 29, 30, 1915*. Convocation of Canterbury no. 487B (ff. 210–39); report of the committee on the resolutions of the Joint Committee of the Upper House of Canterbury Convocation [487B]. *Proof* (ff. 240–59); report from Jenkins to Archbishop Davidson on the work of the committee on revision of the liturgy, also setting out in parallel columns (*a*) the Report of the Joint Committee, 487B; (*b*) the report of the advisory committee thereon; (*c*) original proposals regarding the report considered by the committee, 1916 (ff. 260–316).

316 ff.

1643–55. JENKINS PAPERS

INDEX OF PAROCHIAL CLERGY

Index of parochial clergy in England and Wales mainly during the Interregnum, compiled by Jenkins principally from records in Lambeth Palace Library, the British Museum, the Public Record Office, and diocesan registries, *c.* 1620–63.

1643: Abbas Combe–Ayton. 89 ff.
1644: Babcary–Bishampton. 96 ff.
1645: Bishopsbourne–Brixworth. 89 ff.
1646: Broad Chalk–Cirencester. 150 ff.
1647: Clacton–Cynon; Elm–Fylingdales. 187 ff.
1648: Gaddesden–Harptree. 97 ff.
1649: Harrietsham–Horsey. 93 ff.
1650: Kirkby–Llanddeusant. 94 ff.
1651: Llansaintfraed–Llansannan. 93 ff.
1652: London–Presteigne. 190 ff.
1653: Preston–Sloley. 192 ff.
1654: Totham–Werrington. 97 ff.
1655: Woodmancote–Zennor. 48 ff.

1656–64. JENKINS PAPERS

INTRUDED CLERGY

Notebooks containing an index of names compiled by Jenkins to the Triers' Admission Books, 1654–9 (Lambeth MSS. 996–9). The manuscript referred to as '1656' is now Lambeth MS. 996A.

1656: Abbot–Berry. 98 ff.
1657: Cabecke–Crossman. 98 ff.
1658: Crowe–Eyton. 98 ff.
1659: Facombe–Gwydenham. 98 ff.
1660: Habergham–Johnson. 98 ff.
1661: Johnston–Mott. 94 ff.
1662: Mountague–Raynolds. 94 ff.
1663: Read–Stillingfleet. 94 ff.
1664: Stocke–Weaver. 94 ff.

1665–8. JENKINS PAPERS

CALENDAR OF PARLIAMENTARY SURVEYS

Calendar by Jenkins of vols. i–xvi of the Parliamentary Surveys in Lambeth Palace Library (MSS. 902–17), noting principally valuations of livings and names of incumbents, written on the back of examination papers of students at King's College, London.

1665: Parliamentary Surveys I–V. (MSS. 902–6). xi+167 ff.
1666: Parliamentary Surveys VI–IX. (MSS. 907–10). iii+168 ff.
1667: Parliamentary Surveys X–XIII. (MSS. 911–14). ii+167 ff.
1668: Parliamentary Surveys XIV–XVI. (MSS. 915–17). ii+167 ff.

1669–72. JENKINS PAPERS

Notebooks containing an index of places mentioned in the Minute Books of the Committee for Plundered Ministers, 1645–53, compiled by Jenkins from B.M. Add. MSS. 15669–71, Bodleian Library MSS. Bodley 322–9 and Sion College Arc. L. $\frac{40}{11}\ \frac{2a}{17}$.

1669: Abbotston–Floore. i+163 ff.
1670: Fobbing–Loxton. i+163 ff.
1671: Ludborough–Stanmore. i+162 ff.
1672: Stansted–Ystrad Meurig. 164 ff.

1673–4. JENKINS PAPERS

List of contents by Jenkins of the Composition Books for First Fruits in the Public Record Office, 1624–60, written on the back of examination papers of students at King's College, London.

1673: 1624–38. (C.B. 17, 19). ii+160 ff.
1674: 1639–60. (C.B. 20–2). ii+179 ff.

1675–7. JENKINS PAPERS

List of contents by Jenkins of the Minute Books of the Committee for Plundered Ministers, 1645–7. (B.M. Add. MSS. 15669–71.)

1675: 1645. (Add. MS. 15669). viii+197 ff.
1676: 1646. (Add. MS. 15670). ii+156 ff.
1677: 1647. (Add. MS. 15671). iii+146 ff.

1678. JENKINS PAPERS

LIBRARY OF LORD BURLEIGH

Transcript by Jenkins of the priced catalogue in the British Museum of the sale of the manuscripts belonging to William Cecil, 1st Baron Burleigh, 21 November 1687. [B.M. shelfmark 821.i.8 (1).]

37 ff., of which ff. 15–37 are blank.

1679. JENKINS PAPERS

CATALOGUE OF LAMBETH PALACE LIBRARY

Transcript [by Jenkins] of a catalogue of Lambeth Palace Library formerly in the possession of Archbishop Sancroft [Bodleian Library MS. Tanner 268 ff. 137–70]. The modern shelfmarks of many manuscripts have been identified by Jenkins.

i+92 ff.

1680. GUARDBOOK

Miscellaneous letters and papers:

ff. 1–20. Letters to John Neale Dalton, Canon of Windsor, concerning his *Collegiate Church of Ottery St. Mary*, 1916, transferred from MS. 1612.

ff. 21–60. Letters and papers of William Stubbs, Bishop of Oxford, removed from a copy of A. C. Ducarel, *History of Lambeth Palace*, 1785, as follows: letters from Charles Lutwidge Dodgson (Lewis Carroll), Student of Christ Church, Oxford, 1895, enclosing (f. 23) photograph of Archbishop Longley taken by Dodgson in 1864 (ff. 21–3); John Evans, secretary to the S.P.C.K., and (1869) Canon of St. Paul's, 1865 (ff. 24–25^{v}); Robert Charles Jenkins, Rector of Lyminge, 1866 (ff. 26–9); Henry Longley, barrister, son of Archbishop Longley, 1872 (ff. 30–1); Thomas Walter Perry, secretary to the English Church Union, 1866 (ff. 32–33^{v}); George Walter Prothero, historian, n.d. (ff. 34–35^{v}); C[harles] A[bbot] Stevens, [Vicar of All Saints, Blackheath], 1865 (ff. 36–37^{v}); Stubbs to [the Bishop of London, 1866]. *Copy* (ff. 38–39^{v}); report on Lambeth Palace Library by Stubbs written for [Archbishop Longley] (ff. 40–42^{v}); photographs of Kettel Hall, Oxford (ff. 44–5), and of the interior of Knaresborough church (f. 46); drawings on blotting paper, probably by Henry George Liddell, Dean of Christ Church, Oxford (*v.* H. L. Thompson, *Life of Liddell*, 1899, between pp. 194 and 195) (ff. 47–54); miscellaneous printed items: personal arms of Stubbs (f. 55); ticket for

[1680 *cont.***]**

the enthronement of Archbishop Longley, 1862 (f. 56); *Proposed Latin Version of the Book of Common Prayer*, 1864 (ff. 57–58^v); regulations for readers in Lambeth Palace Library, 1869 (f. 59).

Given by L. M. Stubbs, 1942.

ff. 61–62^v. Letter from Archbishop Longley to his sister Catherine, 1867, discussing the first Lambeth Conference.

Given by Mrs. W. Radcliffe, 1951.

ff. 63–4. Letter from William Froude to Robert Hurrell Froude, Archdeacon of Totnes, 1839, concerning the undergraduate career of the historian James Anthony Froude.

Purchased, 1958.

ff. 65–113. Letters from John Keble, Vicar of Hursley, including letters about the Oxford Movement, Tract XC, and the Belfast Miracles. There are six letters to Charles Marriott, Fellow of Oriel College, Oxford, 1845–54 (ff. 65–75^v), and nine letters to John Frewen Moor, Vicar of Ampfield, of which Keble was patron, author of *The birth-place, home, churches . . . connected with the author of 'The Christian Year'*, 1854–64 (ff. 76–104). Also miscellaneous receipts of Keble and his executors, 1864–7 (ff. 105–13).

Purchased, 1960.

ff. 114–19. Letters to Nicholas Vansittart, 1st Baron Bexley, from the Earl of Shaftesbury, 1842 (f. 114), and St. Andrew St. John, of Lynn, mentioning Coke of Norfolk, 1821 (f. 116).

Letter from John Sargent, Rector of Grafham, to John Thornton, treasurer of the Church Missionary Society and British and Foreign Bible Society, reporting the death of Henry Martyn, Hindustani scholar, [1813] (ff. 118–19).

Given by Lady Thornton, 1962.

ff. 120–30. Letters from William Wilberforce, philanthropist, to John Jebb, Bishop of Limerick, 1815–30 (ff. 120–9). Also verses 'On a portrait of Mr. Wilberforce sent to a Lady by Mr. Stephen' (f. 130).

ff. 131–154^v. Letters to John Jebb, Prebendary of Hereford. The correspondents are: John Keble, Vicar of Hursley, 1847–62, mainly about the Hampden case, and including (ff. 132–4) draft of a letter from Jebb to Keble about the 39 Articles, 1841 (ff. 132–45); Henry Edward Manning, Archdeacon of Chichester, 1840, about Charles Marriott (ff. 146–147^v); John Henry Newman, Fellow of Oriel College, Oxford, 1836, about an article for the *British Critic*, Pusey, the need for 'a bolder as well as a higher line', and suffragan bishops (ff. 148–9); Robert Wilberforce, Archdeacon of the East Riding, 1843, about a visit from W. F. Hook, his own writings, the Irish Convocation, endowment of additional bishoprics and church reorganization (ff. 150–154^v).

Given by Miss E. M. Jebb, 1961.

ff. 155–78. Letters from Samuel Bentley, printer, to John Bowyer Nichols, printer and antiquary, 1827–34 and n.d. (ff. 155–74), and a letter to John Gough Nichols, son of the latter, n.d. (f. 175).

Also a letter from Richard Bentley, brother of Samuel, to William Upcott, antiquary and autograph collector, n.d. (f. 177).

Purchased, 1962.

ff. 179–99. Letters from Arthur Penrhyn Stanley, Dean of Westminster, to an unnamed Bishop, 1858 (f. 179); to Professor [? R. Payne Smith], 1868, concerning the Ritual Commission (ff. 181–182v); to an unnamed correspondent, 1873, defending his omission to use the Authorized Version (ff. 183–184v); to Hugh Colin Smith, of the Bank of England, 1877, recommending Alfred Burtt, who has arranged the archives at Westminster Abbey, for a post in the Bank (ff. 185–6); to Sir [? James] Paget [1st Bt., surgeon], 1879 (ff. 187–8); to Dr. [James Harrison] Rigg, Methodist, 1879 (f. 189); to an unnamed correspondent, 1879 (f. 190); to Sir George Grove, 1879 (ff. 192–3); to an unnamed correspondent, n.d. (f. 194).

Letter from Lady Augusta Stanley, wife of the preceding, to Robert J. Simpson and Henry Carr, 1879 (ff. 196–7), and to [Robert J.] Simpson, n.d. (ff. 198–199v).

Purchased, 1962.

ff. 200–38. Letters to Arthur Penrhyn Stanley, Dean of Westminster, mostly invitations and acknowledgements, 1862–79. The names of the writers will be found in the index.

Purchased, 1962.

ff. 239–248v. Letters to James Atlay, Bishop of Hereford, 1864–82. The correspondents are: Archbishop Longley, 1864 (ff. 239–40); Archbishop Tait, 1878 (ff. 241–2); Randall Thomas Davidson, chaplain to Archbishop Tait, and (1903) Archbishop of Canterbury, 1882, about Tait's death, and enclosing (f. 245) a letter from Tait (ff. 243–248v).

Given by Miss Agnes Atlay, 1938.

ff. 249–50. Letter from Thomas Robinson, Archdeacon of Madras, to the Bishop of London, 1828, sending a copy of his charge to the clergy of the archdeaconry of Madras.

ff. 251–61. Correspondence between Archbishop Davidson, and Sir Almeric William FitzRoy, Clerk of the Privy Council, 1910–21, concerning the funeral of Edward VII, a Peace Proclamation and Thanksgiving Service, the dissolution of Convocation.

Given by Miss Winifred A. Myers, 1962.

261 ff.

1681. POEMS (in French)

A roll containing seven French poems printed from this manuscript by A. Wallensköld, 'Le ms. Londres, Bibl. de Lambeth Palace, Misc. rolls

[1681 *cont.***]**

1435', *Mémoires de la Société Néophilogique de Helsingfors*, vi (1917), 1–40. The first poem is imperfect at the beginning and the last is imperfect at the end. Size *c.* 1540×115 mm. Early 14th century. Written in France (?). In Dorset in the late 14th century. Formerly Misc. Rolls 1435.

See MS. 1362 for reference to a fuller description of this manuscript.

1682–93. MINUTES OF PAROCHIAL MISSION WOMEN'S ASSOCIATION

Minutes of the Parochial Mission Women's Association, 1862–1923. Each volume has a separate index of places. Minute book for January 1883–December 1886 missing.

Bookplates of Church House Library.

1682: November 1862–March 1869. i+352 pp.
1683: April 1869–June 1872. iii+373 pp.
1684: July 1872–June 1874. iii+365 pp.
1685: June 1874–March 1876. xxi+355 pp.
1686: April 1876–November 1879. i+513 pp.
1687: December 1879–December 1882. 512 pp.
1688: January 1887–July 1890. i+409 pp.
1689: July 1890–October 1894. iii+431 pp.
1690: October 1894–December 1898. i+400 pp.
1691: December 1898–January 1904. i+403 pp.
1692: February 1904–April 1909. i+404 pp.
1693: May 1909–December 1916. i+402 pp.

1694–1700. PAPERS OF THE WYE BOOK CLUB

Papers of the Wye Book Club, Kent, 1755–1886. The purpose of the Club was to purchase books by subscription for circulation among members.

Given by the Misses Young, of Spring Grove, Wye, through the Revd. E. J. Selwyn, 1889.

1694. WYE BOOK CLUB PAPERS

Rules of the Club, 1755 (ff. 1–3).

Accounts of quarterly subscriptions, fines for absence from meetings, and of books borrowed, 1755–64 (ff. 5–25).

At the back of the book is an account of books purchased, 1756–66 (ff. 26–37^{v}).

Letter from the Revd. E. J. Selwyn, Rector of Pluckley, 1889 (f. i).

iii+39 ff.

1695. WYE BOOK CLUB PAPERS

Account of books purchased, 1764–76. Prices are stated, and until 1767 the names of members selecting books for purchase.

58 ff.

1696. WYE BOOK CLUB PAPERS

Account of books purchased, 1776–1807. Prices are stated, and annual lists of members are given from 1785.

65 ff.

1697. WYE BOOK CLUB PAPERS

Minutes of meetings, 1812–60.

Account of books purchased and circulated, 1808–20 (ff. 2–11, 15–19, 22–47).

Revised rules of the Club, 1811 (ff. 12–14).

i+74 ff.

1698. WYE BOOK CLUB PAPERS

Minutes of meetings, 1861–73.

28 ff.

1699. WYE BOOK CLUB PAPERS

Account of books borrowed and of fines for absence from meetings, 1764–84.

64 ff.

1700. WYE BOOK CLUB PAPERS

Miscellaneous papers.

Annual statements of account, 1836–62 (ff. 1–27).

Annual statements of the wine account, 1835, 1837–62 (ff. 28–54).

Wine account book, 1869–86 (ff. 55–66^{v}).

Receipts for annual dinners of the Club at the King's Head Inn, Wye, 1836–69 (ff. 77–110).

Petty cash account, 1863–72 (ff. 112–15).

Miscellaneous receipts for subscriptions and purchase of books, etc. (ff. 135–49).

List of subscriptions for the presentation of a coffee pot to the Revd. R. D. Wilmot, secretary of the Club, 1854 (ff. 150–1).

Rules and regulations of the Club, 1862. *Printed* (f. 152).

Memorandum by Charles Jenyns, chairman, about annual dinners of the Club, 1884 (f. 153).

Memorandum by the same on the disposal of the records of the Club, 1884 (f. 155).

155 ff.

1701. TITHE ASSESSMENTS AFTER THE GREAT FIRE OF LONDON

Assessments of certain London parishes for a rate in lieu of tithes, made according to the provisions of 22 and 23 Chas. II cap. 15 for settling the maintenance of clergy in parishes burnt in the Great Fire.

The assessments are for the following parishes:

No. 1. All Hallows, Lombard Street, 29 September 1672. Parchment roll. *2 mm.*

No. 2. Ditto, 15 September 1681. (Re-assessment). Parchment roll. *1 m.*

No. 3. St. Martin's Vintry and St. Michael Royal, [1672]. Parchment roll. *5 mm.*

No. 4. St. Mary Aldermary and St. Thomas the Apostle, 23 September 1674. Parchment roll. *3 mm.*

No. 5. St. Mary-le-Bow, St. Pancras, Soper Lane, and All Hallows, Honey Lane, with Order of the Court of Aldermen of the City of London, 13 February 1673. Parchment roll. *3 mm.*

No. 6. St. Dionis, Backchurch, 9 September 1674. Parchment.

No. 7. Ditto, 29 August 1681. (Re-assessment). Parchment.

No. 8. St. Vedast and St. Michael-le-Querne, 21 July 1671. Parchment.

No. 9. Ditto, 19 September 1674. Parchment.

1702. INDEX TO PARLIAMENTARY SURVEYS

'An Alphabetical Index [of places] to the Surveys of Church Lands in the Manuscript Library at Lambeth [MSS. 902–22]', by Andrew Coltee Ducarel, 1760. A copy of the index by Ducarel now kept in the Reading Room, and like it containing the preface and list of addenda.

At p. i a note by Ducarel of a suit in the Exchequer (Travis *v.* Oxton and others), 1775, successfully establishing the legal validity of the Surveys as evidence. On p. vi a note by S. W. Kershaw, Lambeth Librarian.

xxvii+382 pp.

1703. ABSTRACT OF ANCIENT DEEDS

'Abstract of some Chartae Antiquae in the Augmentation Office, Digested & Examined by Dr. [Andrew Coltee] Ducarel, A.D. 1764 & 1765.'

The deeds are arranged by counties and referenced by letter of the alphabet and running number as follows:

Bedfordshire–Kent	D.
Lancaster–Rutland	E.
Salop–Southampton, Suffolk–Warwick	F.
Stafford, Westmorland–Yorkshire	G.

'Chartae Antiquae or Notes of English Antiquities in unknown or uncertain places, Remaining in the Augmentation Office and Taken by

Dr. Ducarel, A.D. 1765 & 1766, with a Compleat Index.' The deeds in this section are all numbered C. (pp. 189–220).

Bookplate of Ducarel. Old shelfmark 'C.7'.

xii+222 pp.

1704. INDEX OF ANCIENT DEEDS

'An Index of Ancient Deeds, Charters and Other Instruments Remaining in the Augmentation Office, A.D. 1765', [by Andrew Coltee Ducarel]. The volume contains an index locorum (ff. 2–64), and index virorum (ff. 68–135^{v}). Deeds described in MS. 1703 are included in both indexes.

On f. i a note by Ducarel that 'this index was taken from the Deeds themselves by Dr. Ducarel in 1764 & 1765'.

Bookplate of Ducarel. Old shelfmark 'C.8'. Note in the hand of S. W. Kershaw, Lambeth Librarian, inside front cover.

iii+137 ff.

1705. CATALOGUE OF LIBRARY

Catalogue of the library of Andrew Coltee Ducarel, 1783.

Bookplate of Ducarel. Note (f. i) by H. J. T[odd], 'I bought this for 5s'.

ii+284 ff.

1706. CATALOGUE OF MONASTIC COLLECTION

Catalogue of books and pamphlets concerning monastic orders and buildings in England and Wales, [compiled by Samuel Weyland Kershaw, Lambeth Librarian], 1884. The catalogue is arranged alphabetically by counties. Titles in the library at Lambeth and those desired for it are distinguished.

At ff. i–ii^{v} a list of *Pamphlets and papers on the monastic remains of England and Wales*.

ii+147 ff.

1707–8. ARCHBISHOP TENISON'S LIBRARY IN ST. MARTIN-IN-THE-FIELDS

Thomas Tenison, Vicar of St. Martin-in-the-Fields, London, and (1694) Archbishop of Canterbury, founded a public library in the parish in 1684. The books were sold by auction at Sotheby's in 1861–2, but some appear to have been removed to Lambeth on Tenison's elevation to the Primacy.

1707. TENISON LIBRARY

Catalogue entitled in Tenison's hand, 'Catalogue of my Books in my Closet in St. Martin's Library'. The catalogue was written in about 1693,

[1707 *cont.*]

and additions have been made subsequently of books published before this date. A few of the entries are by Tenison who has also indicated books 'wanting' and books 'removed to Lambhith'.

ii+77 ff.

1708. TENISON LIBRARY

'The Catalogue of Archbishop Tenison's Library in St. Martin's Lane.' The catalogue was written in about 1693 and is in the same hand as MS. 1707. Additional entries in various hands have been made up to 1715.

iii+551 ff.

1709. NOTES ON THE CONDITION OF THE EASTERN CHURCHES

Report by Arthur Cayley Headlam, (1923) Bishop of Gloucester, to Archbishop Benson, on ecclesiastical conditions in Asia Minor, Egypt, and Greece, 1890.

At f. i a letter from Headlam to Archbishop Benson, 1891.

Typescript. iii+64 ff.

1710–12. REGISTERS OF SERVICES

Registers of services held in the church of St. Mary, Bourdon Street, London, 1921–32.

1710: 1921–4. ii+72 ff.
1711: 1927–9. ii+67 ff.
1712: 1930–2. ii+69 ff.

1713. ADDRESS ON THE CHURCH IN SOUTH AFRICA

Address on the Church in South Africa, delivered by Edwin James Palmer, (1908) Bishop of Bombay, to the Junior Clergy Missionary Association Conference at Hereford, November 1907.

A note (p. 4) by Palmer reads, 'I refused to have it [the address] printed just as it was delivered because some of the illustrations were given in confidence. The blue marks indicate my alterations for printing.'

x+122 pp.

1714. REGISTRUM SACRUM ANGLICANUM

Manuscript of *Registrum sacrum anglicanum*, 1858, by William Stubbs, (1889) Bishop of Oxford, with additions for the second edition, 1897.

iii+317 pp.

1715. REGISTER OF LAMBETH DEGREES

Register of Lambeth Degrees, 1539–1948, compiled by William Stubbs, (1889) Bishop of Oxford, and continued from 1883 by A. J. Clements, secretary to the Archbishop of Canterbury.

The following items are inserted:

The Lambeth Degrees, by Cecil Wall. (Reprinted from the *British Medical Journal*, 1935, 854) (pp. i–v).

Regulations for the award of Lambeth Degrees. *Temp.* Archbishop Davidson. *Printed* (pp. vii-ix).

Regulations for the same, n.d. *Printed* (pp. xi–xii).

Form of conferring degrees by the Archbishop of Canterbury. Temp. Archbishop Fisher (pp. xiii–xvi).

Notes on Lambeth Degrees. (*Notes and Queries*, 2nd series, xii, 529, and 3rd series, i, 133–4, 238) (pp. 7–11).

Notes on the same. (*Gentleman's Magazine*, 1864, 130, 504–5, 633–8, 770–4) (pp. 13–27).

Letters from W. H. McMenemey, D.M., F.R.C.P., to Irene Churchill, assistant Lambeth Librarian, concerning R. P. Grindrod, with photograph of Grindrod, 1952 (pp. 114–18).

Newspaper cutting from *The Church Times*, 27 December 1957 (pp. 120–1).

Given by Ernest Edward Holmes, Canon of St. Paul's, [1930].

xxvi+121 pp.

1716–1716B. ANTI-SEMITISM IN POLAND, LITHUANIA, AND ROUMANIA

Scrapbooks concerning the persecution of Jews in Poland, Lithuania, and Roumania, 1936–7, compiled by the Comité pour la Défense des Droits des Israélites en Europe Centrale et Orientale.

Given by the committee to Archbishop Lang, 1937.

1716. ANTI-SEMITISM

Scrapbook (volume I1). The contents, which are duplicated unless otherwise stated, are as follows:

Reports of the Jewish Telegraphic Agency for Poland and Lithuania, February–April 1937 (ff. 1–25).

Reports of the same for Roumania, January 1936–April 1937 (ff. 26–66).

L'Attitude de l'Eglise Orthodoxe envers la Bible, 1937. *French* (f. 67).

La Situation en Roumanie au mois de mars 1937. *French* (ff. 68–70).

La Situation des minorités et particulièrement des Israélites, date erased. *French* (ff. 70–4).

[**1716** *cont.*]

Report of measures taken by the Roumanian government, 1937. *French* (ff. 75–6).

Mémorandum sur la situation économique des Israélites en Pologne, adressé au nom du Comité par MM. Justin Godart et Boris Gourevitch à Monsieur le Ministre des Affaires Etrangères, le 6 Avril 1934, suivi d'une lettre de réponse du 18 Avril 1934. *French* (ff. 78–82).

Memorandum from the Central Council of Jews in Roumania to the President of the Council of Ministers, protesting at legislation discriminating against Jews, 11 March 1937. *French* (ff. 83–95).

W. Filderman: *Le problème du travail national et la crise du Barreau en Roumanie*, 1937 (ff. 96–127^{v}).

Madeleine Coulon: *De graves événements dans le Barreau roumain*, 1937 (ff. 130–46).

Three memoranda from the Central Council of Jews in Roumania to ministers of the Roumanian government, protesting against the persecution of minorities, 14–15 April 1937. *French. Typescript copies* (ff. 148–61).

i+172 ff.

1716A. ANTI-SEMITISM

Scrapbook (volume I), containing duplicated reports from the Jewish Telegraphic Agency concerning the persecution of Jews in Poland and Lithuania, January 1936–February 1937.

i+148 ff.

1716B. ANTI-SEMITISM

Scrapbook (volume III), containing duplicated reports from the Jewish Telegraphic Agency concerning the persecution of Jews in Poland, Lithuania, and Roumania, April–May 1937.

i+30 ff.

1717. ST. MICHAEL, CROOKED LANE, LONDON

Book of certificates of consent by the Rector and Churchwardens of the Parish of St. Michael, Crooked Lane, London to the transfer of remains from the churchyard to other places of burial, with 152 receipts for remains so transferred, 1831–2. Index of names.

ii+180 ff.

1718. SUBSIDY BOOK

Auditor's book for the collection of four subsidies granted in 15 Charles II. The volume contains the following sections:

Names of auditors appointed to receive the accounts of the collectors of the first and second subsidies, with the counties for which they are accountable (f. 1^{r-v}).

Names of commissioners and collectors for the first and second subsidies, arranged by counties, 1663 (ff. 2–52^{v}).

Ditto for the third and fourth subsidies, 1664 (ff. 53–103).

Bound in vellum. Bookplate of A. Waugh.

ii+115 ff.

1719. MISCELLANEOUS LETTERS AND PAPERS, 18TH CENTURY

Miscellaneous letters and papers, including correspondence of Archbishops Tillotson, Herring, and Secker.

1. Letters and papers of and about Archbishop Secker:

A[bigail] Frost, daughter of Secker's nephew Thomas Frost, to [Ann] Frost, her sister, after 1760. Concerns a gold box given to Secker at the Christening of George III (f. 1).

Ann Frost to [Thomas] Frost, her father and Secker's nephew, 1764. Personal matters; Secker's health (ff. 2–3).

John Frost, Rector of Bishop's Court, to his brother [Thomas Frost] and sister, 1760. A visit to Lambeth (f. 4).

Beilby Porteus, trustee under Secker's will, and (1787) Bishop of London, to Abigail Frost, 1772. About the performance of trusts created by Secker's will (ff. 5–6).

The same to Mrs. Frost, 1779. On the same subject (f. 7^{r-v}).

The same to the same, 1779. On the same subject (ff. 9–10).

Secker to his [sister], 17[19]. Congratulations on the birth of a son, and advice about her health (f. 11^{r-v}).

Secker [to Thomas Frost], his nephew, 1751. About his financial arrangements for the latter's brother (ff. 13–14).

The same to his brother, [1739]. Remarks about Methodists, including George Whitefield. *Fragment* (f. 15^{r-v}).

The same to Mrs. Frost, his sister, wife of Thomas Frost, 1748. About the death of his wife (f. 16).

George Stinton, trustee under Secker's will, and Canon of Peterborough, to [Miss Frost], 1779. About his trusteeship (f. 18).

Catherine Talbot to Thomas Frost, 1768. On leaving Lambeth (ff. 19–20).

The same to the same, 1768. About a mortgage; the marriage of Lord Hillsborough; the disposal of effects at Lambeth (ff. 21–2).

The same to the same, 1768. The sale of furniture at Lambeth (f. 23^{r-v}).

The same to [the same], 1769. Dispute about dilapidations at Lambeth. The sum of £2,600 paid to Archbishop Cornwallis for dilapidations and furniture. The greenhouse and its contents (ff. 25–7).

Funeral expenses of Secker, 1768 (ff. 28–29^{v}).

[1719 *cont.***]**

Porteus and Stinton, trustees under Secker's will, acknowledge the receipt of £5,000 stock, 1768. *Signed and sealed* (ff. 30–1).

Inventory of Secker's plate, and account of its disposal, 1768 (ff. 32–33^{v}).

Catherine Talbot to Mrs. Benson, 1761. About the coronation of George III. *Typescript copy* (ff. 39–43).

List of documents presented to Lambeth Palace Library by the Revd. J. C. Gawthern, 1924. *Typescript* (f. 44).

List of letters and papers, including those listed on f. 44, belonging to the same. *Typescript* (ff. 46–51).

Given by the Revd. John Charles Gawthern, 1924.

2. Six letters in shorthand by Archbishop Secker, 1743–57. The addressees named are [Benjamin] Holloway, Rector of Bladon, 1753 (f. 59), and William Toovey, 1757 (f. 60) (ff. 53–60).

Also two other letters in shorthand from an unnamed writer, 1782 and 1787 (ff. 61–2).

Given by [the Bishop of Oxford], 1917.

3. Letter from Thomas Herring, Archbishop of Canterbury, to [the Archbishop of York], 1750. News of the Court and the Board of Regency. Possibility of war with France—the West Indies. The Bishops of Durham and Bristol. Appointments in Oxford. Relief of Protestants. His lack of money (ff. 63–6).

Purchased, 1960.

4. Letter from George Berkeley, Bishop of Cloyne, to — Clarke, Vice-Provost of Trinity College, Dublin, 1746. Defers a visit to Ireland (f. 67).

5. Letter from John Tillotson, Dean of Canterbury and (1691) Archbishop of Canterbury, to Nicholas Hunt, 1688. Condolences on his health. *Signed*. Printed Birch, *Life of Tillotson*, 1752, 135–9 (f. 69^{r-v}).

Given by the Countess of Cottenham, 1954.

6. Receipts and accounts for repairs to the Scottish Episcopal Qualified Chapel at Brechin, 1739–1806. Also (ff. 98–9) a letter from Alexander James Beresford Beresford-Hope to the Dean [of Brechin], n.d. (ff. 71–99).

Given by F. C. Eeles, 1955.

7. Description of a manuscript, now Lambeth MS. 943, thought to have been lost, headed 'Codices MSS Whartoniani'. Endorsed by Archbishop Secker, 'An account of the supposed loss of some MS by Mr. [Henry] Hall, [chaplain to Archbishop Herring, and Fellow of King's College, Cambridge], several of which are found' (ff. 100–5).

105 ff.

1720. BENJAMIN KENNICOTT ON THE BOOK OF HABAKKUK

Translation by Benjamin Kennicott, Canon of Christ Church, Oxford, of the Book of Habakkuk from Hebrew into English, with textual and historical notes, [1747–58]. At ff. i–ii criticisms by Thomas Secker, Bishop of Oxford, and subsequently (1758) Archbishop of Canterbury.

iii+15 ff.

1721. BENJAMIN KENNICOTT ON THE BOOK OF JOB

Notes for a commentary on the Book of Job by Benjamin Kennicott, Canon of Christ Church, Oxford, consisting of an interleaved printed edition of the text in English in the Authorized Version and in Hebrew set out in hemistichs in parallel columns from chapter III to the end. At ff. i–iii^{v} are introductory remarks by Kennicott.

Given by Shute Barrington, Bishop of Durham.

iii+85 ff.

1722. VALUATIONS OF WADDESDON RECTORY, BUCKS.

Valuations of Waddesdon Rectory, Bucks., by the Revd. Benjamin Skinner, Rector of the second Portion, 1771–7, including also a copy of a valuation of the same, 1756 (ff. 40^{v}–46^{v}), and a valuation of the parish of Kibworth, Leics. (ff. 7–9^{v}).

48 ff.

1723. PHOTOGRAPHS OF ITALY AND EGYPT

Photographs of buildings and works of art chiefly in Italy and Egypt, *c.* 1880. See also MS. 1972.

iii+54 ff.

1724. THE ARCHBISHOP OF CANTERBURY'S OPTION

Treatise by P[aul] Jodrell, barrister, of Lincoln's Inn, entitled 'A Letter to Dr. Topham, Master of the Faculties, on the Subject of the Arch Bishop of Canterbury's Right of Option, wherein the Objections thereto contain'd in a Tract entitled The Case of what is commonly called the Arch Bishop's Option are particularly consider'd', 1750. For the Archbishop's Option see Gibson, *Codex Juris Ecclesiastici*, ed. 1761, 115 (pp. 1–97).

iv+162 pp.

1725. LETTERS FROM AND ABOUT J. R. GREEN

Letters from and about John Richard Green, historian, 1854–79: (1) letters from Green mainly to relatives, 1854–79 (ff. 1–134^{v}); (2) letters about Green's education addressed to his uncle, [N.] Castle, of Oxford, 1854–5 (ff. 135–169^{v}). Also included is a pamphlet entitled *The girl of the period*, 1868 (ff. 170–175^{v}). The names of the writers will be found in the index.

Given by R. A. James, 1957.

176 ff.

1726. LAMBETH PALACE AND PARISH

Miscellaneous papers, as follows:

Letter from Lavinia, wife of George John Spencer, 2nd Earl Spencer, to Edward Blore, 1828, concerning the reconstruction of Lambeth Palace (ff. 1–2). Another letter from the same to the same, n.d. (ff. 3–4).

Vouchers and accounts of Christopher Hodgson, nominee of the Archbishops of Canterbury and York, and of the Bishop of London, for alterations and improvements to Lambeth Palace and Addington Mansion, 1829–31 (ff. 5–27).

List of stained glass removed from Lambeth Palace by Archbishop Moore in 1803, included in 'A Catalogue of the Highly Valuable and Interesting Collection of the late E. B. Vigurs, Esq., . . . which will be sold by Auction . . . on Tuesday, September the 25th, 1849.' *Typescript copy* (ff. 28–30).

'Report on Lambeth Palace Chapel by W. Burgess, architect, Nov. 9. 1876', with plans and drawings (ff. 31–63).

Account of the restoration of Lambeth Palace, 1945–55, by Rosamund, wife of Archbishop Lord Fisher of Lambeth. *Typescript* (ff. 64–78).

Inventory of furniture removed from Lambeth Palace to the Great Hall, 1948, during restoration of war damage. *Typescript* (ff. 79–98).

Specifications of alterations and decorations to no. 6, Lambeth Palace Cottages, by Messrs. Seely and Paget, architects, 1952, with (f. 112) plan. *Typescript* (ff. 99–112).

Order of the Privy Council directing the Commissioners of the Admiralty to grant protection to seven named bargemen of the Archbishop of Canterbury employed on the ferry between Lambeth and Westminster, 27 February 1696. *Seal* (f. 113).

Order of the Commissioners of the Admiralty to all commanders and officers of His Majesty's Ships and to all pressmasters not to impress five named bargemen employed on the ferry at Lambeth, 10 March 1701. On the dorse descriptions of the bargemen (f. 114).

Letter from Sir Stanford Edwin Downing, Secretary to the Ecclesiastical Commissioners, to Mrs. Dorothy Gardiner, author of *The Story of Lambeth Palace*, 1930, concerning bargehouses at Lambeth, with (ff. 119–27) notes from leases in the possession of the Commissioners (ff. 116–28).

Given by T. G. Gardiner, Canon of Canterbury, 1935.

'Measurement of the proposed Alteration to the Foot Path leading to Carlisle Lane', Lambeth, 18th century (f. 129).

Minute of a meeting of the trustees of Archbishop Tenison's Charity School for Girls in Lambeth, 6 April 1754, concerning a fine. *Copy* (f. 131).

List of subscriptions to Archbishop Tenison's Charity School, Lambeth, 1759. Endorsement in the hand of Archbishop Secker (f. 132).

Account of the annual sum allowed by Archbishop Herring to 'Fitzwalters, the Gardener at Lambeth', partly in the hand of Archbishop Secker, and endorsed by him 'Lambeth Garden. Fitzwalter's proposal' (f. 133).

Letter from John Sealy, treasurer of Lambeth Sunday School, to Archbishop Moore, 1796, enclosing (ff. 136–137^{v}) leaflet concerning establishment of a Sunday School in the parish of St. Mary, Lambeth. *Printed* (ff. 134–137^{v}).

Form of Service for the dedication of new altar steps in Lambeth Palace Chapel, 22 March 1905. On the front a photograph of the west entrance to the Chapel. *Printed* (ff. 140–141^{v}).

Given by A. J. Clements, 1963.

Programme of a Coronation Party at Lambeth Palace, 8 July 1911. *Printed* (f. 142).

Given by A. J. Clements, 1963.

Form of Service for the marriage in Lambeth Palace Chapel of W[illiam] A[ntony] A[cton], banker, to J[oan] C[inetta] P[earson], 29 June 1932. *Printed* (ff. 143–6).

Given by A. J. Clements, 1963.

146 ff.

1727. MISCELLANEOUS LETTERS AND PAPERS

Guardbook containing miscellaneous letters and papers, 1589–1904.

Letters to Thomas Stewart Townsend, Bishop of Meath, from Lord John George Beresford, Archbishop of Armagh, Samuel Hinds, successively chaplain to Archbishop Whately and Bishop of Norwich, and others, 1836–52, about Irish church affairs, including relations with the Roman Catholic Church. The names of the writers will be found in the index (ff. 1–43).

Given by Miss Agnes Wyatt, 1961.

Miscellaneous letters. Letter from Edward Harold Browne, Bishop of Winchester, to the Revd. James Baker, chaplain of Winchester College, 1875, declining to inhibit a clergyman from preaching (f. 44); letter from Archbishop Sumner to — Kirkby, n.d., approving arrangements for a visit 'except the Surplices, which I have always confined to the clergy of the parish' (f. 46); Archibald Campbell Tait, Bishop of London and

[1727 *cont.*]

(1868) Archbishop of Canterbury, to the Revd. Septimus Cox Holmes Hansard, Curate of St. Mary, Marylebone, London, 1853 (ff. 48–9) (ff. 44–9).

Given by Miss Agnes Wyatt, 1961.

Papers of Edmund Hobhouse, Bishop of Nelson, New Zealand. They comprise: photograph of Bishop Hobhouse (f. 50); letters from Hobhouse to his father, 1853, describing a journey to Canada and the east coast of the United States. *Typescript copies of originals in possession of S.P.G.* (ff. 51–62); letter from Sir Robert Joseph Phillimore, 1st Bt., to Bishop Hobhouse, 1861, concerning Ecclesiastical Discipline Bills. *Copy* (f. 63); remarks on the same by Sir William Martin, formerly Chief Justice of New Zealand, 1862 (ff. 64–5); correspondence of Bishop Hobhouse with Baron Blachford, 1882, concerning the colonial episcopate (ff. 66–68^{v}); letter from Viscount Cranborne to —, 1900, about church to be built at Mafeking (ff. 69–70^{v}); obituary of Bishop Hobhouse, reprinted from *The Guardian*, 27 April and 4 May 1904 (ff. 71–6) (ff. 50–76).

Given by Miss Dorothy Hobhouse, 1960.

Minutes of a subcommittee of committee 6 of the Lambeth Conference, 1897, concerning Holy Orders of other Churches. The minutes are signed G. Mott Williams, Bishop of Marquette (ff. 77–85).

Miscellaneous papers. Inventory of the possessions of the Revd. — Starismore, Vicar of Calthorpe, [Norf.], and an account of his death, 1 January 1747 (f. 86); letter from J. C. Cooper [?], of Worlington Hall, to Thomas Greene, M.P. for Lancaster, 1828, concerning a Bill to commute tithes (f. 87); Archbishop Howley to Christopher Hodgson, 1844, about public dinners at Lambeth (f. 89); Henry Hart Milman, Dean of St. Paul's, to [George] Scharf, [subsequently (1882) Director of the National Portrait Gallery], 1860, about the library at St. Paul's (f. 90); William Remington, officiating minister of St. Michael, Lichfield, to George Gaskin, secretary of the S.P.C.K., [1799], listing books, including children's books, which he seeks to borrow (f. 92). Endorsed with the number '1459' (ff. 86–93).

Purchased, 1958.

Letter from Charles Inglis, Bishop of Nova Scotia, to Messrs. Goodall and Turner, 1809, on financial matters (f. 94).

Given by the Army and Navy Club, London, 1962.

Letter from Charles James Blomfield, Bishop of London, to Mrs. [Maria Frances] D'Oyly, [wife of George D'Oyly, Rector of Lambeth], 1838, declining to confirm her daughter (ff. 95–96^{v}).

Given by the Revd. Giles Hunt, 1962.

Letter from William Ewart Gladstone to Edward White Benson, Bishop of Truro, 1881, asking him to serve on Royal Commission on ecclesiastical courts (f. 97).

Letter from Harold Ernest Bilbrough, Bishop of Dover and (1927) Newcastle upon Tyne, to [Lucy] Tait, 1921 (ff. 98–9).

Letter from Archbishop Whitgift to Nathaniel Bacon, son of Sir Nicholas Bacon, 1589, asking him to arbitrate in a dispute between Symon Pecock, clerk, and Laurence Webster. *Signed* (f. 100).

Archbishop Secker to — Garden, Scottish Presbyterian, 1767, declining to give preferment to [Norman] Sievwright (f. 102).

Given by Miss Marion Walker, n.d.

Letter from Robert Banks Jenkinson, 2nd Earl of Liverpool, Prime Minister, to Archbishop Manners Sutton, 1813, concerning the Bishop of Gloucester's refusal of some office. *Photocopy* (ff. 103–4).

Given by the National Register of Archives, 1961.

Letters from Bishops, mostly addressed to John Jackson, Bishop of London, mostly interesting only as autographs, 1847–1903. The names of the writers will be found in the index (ff. 105–84).

Given by T. S. Blakeney, 1959.

184 ff.

1728. PHOTOGRAPHS

Guardbook containing photographs of Archbishops of Canterbury and of Bishops, including photographs of portraits, and of Lambeth Conferences, etc.

1. Photograph of a portrait of Archbishop Parker at Lambeth Palace (f. 1); seventeen photographs of portraits and engravings of Archbishop Whitgift. The photographs are numbered on the back and a key (f. 2) identifies the originals (ff. 2–17); photograph of a portrait of Etheldreda, wife of Archbishop Wake (f. 18); photograph of a portrait of Archbishop Herring by Allan Ramsay, in the Herring family until 1963 (f. 19); two sketches of Archbishop Frederick Temple by Miss Goodwin, daughter of Harvey Goodwin, Bishop of Carlisle (f. 20); signed photograph of Archbishop Davidson [by A. A. Campbell-Swinton]. Given by Mrs. Jane Jackson, 1962 (f. 21); signed photograph of Archbishop Lang, 1928 (f. 22); signed photograph of W. J. F. Robberds, Bishop of Brechin Primus of Scotland, 1931 (f. 23).

2. Photographs of portraits of Bishops. Photograph of a portrait of Gilbert Burnet, Bishop of Salisbury, by John Riley (f. 24); photograph of a portrait of John Hough, Bishop of Worcester (f. 25); photograph of a portrait of Richard Terrick, Bishop of London, by Benjamin West, in the possession of the Earl of Harrowby. Given by the Earl of Harrowby, 1961 (f. 26).

3. Photograph of the Bishops attending the Lambeth Conference, 1867. Given by Dr. A. C. Don, 1959 (f. 27); photograph of the Bishops attending the Lambeth Conference, 1888, with key (ff. 28–9).

4. Miscellaneous photographs. Coloured photograph of clergy at Westminster Abbey on Jubilee Day, 21 June 1887, with a key on the back (f. 30); two photographs of Bishops at a meeting at Lambeth Palace to discuss Prayer Book revision, 1926–8. Given by A. J. Clements, 1961

[**1728** *cont.*]

(ff. 31–2); photograph of the entry in the register of John Fisher, Bishop of Rochester, of his installation and enthronization, 1505. Signed on back: Irene J. Churchill (f. 33); photograph of the crypt at Wells, *c.* 1900 (f. 34); photographs of Glastonbury Abbey, 1908 (ff. 35–45^{v}).

45 ff.

1729. MISCELLANEOUS PAPERS

Guardbook containing miscellaneous papers.

Calendar of rolls of the Dean and Chapter of Canterbury concerning ecclesiastical suits, mostly on appeal during vacancies of the see of Canterbury in the second half of the 13th century, by Charles Eveleigh Woodruff, honorary librarian to the Dean and Chapter, 1927. Matrimonial causes are omitted from the 227 causes listed. *Typescript* (ff. 1–38).

Transcript of E.S. Roll 20 of the Dean and Chapter of Canterbury 'in causa matrimoniali inter M. Giffard actricem per Johannem de Haverelle etc. et Johannem de Draytune reum per Thomam Wismam procuratorem etc.' *Typescript* (ff. 39–86).

Notes on a contemporary copy of Archbishop Laud's statutes for Canterbury Cathedral, 1637, by Miss E. L. Weekes. *Typescript copy* (ff. 87–91).

List by C. E. Welch of the contents of a formulary for the Archdeaconry of Lewes, compiled in the 16th and 17th centuries, deposited in the diocesan record office at Chichester. *Typescript copy* (ff. 92–109).

Given by Chichester County Archivist, 1952.

Transcript by the Revd. Henry Frank Fulford Williams of a charge by Richard Corbet, Bishop of Norwich, to the diocesan clergy, 1634. *Typescript* (ff. 110–17).

Given by the Revd. H. F. Fulford Williams, 1960.

Notes by Michael Woodward, Warden of New College, Oxford, of a 'progress' of the college estate at Kemnall in the parish of Chislehurst, Kent, 1659–75, with a terrier of the manor of Kemminghold in the same parish, *c.* 1622, transcribed and edited by R. L. Rickard, assistant librarian of New College. *Typescript* (ff. 118–46).

Given by R. L. Rickard, 1950.

Correspondence between John Herne and his brother Robert concerning the striking of a gold medal from coins given by Archbishop Laud on the scaffold to their grandfather John Herne, of Lincoln's Inn, counsel to Laud at his trial, 1703. Copied by Miss H. E. Peek from copies belonging to Mrs. Oxenham of Drewsteignton, Devon. *Typescript* (ff. 147–56).

Given by Miss H. E. Peek, 1949.

Catalogue by M. J. Sommerlad of letters and papers of Edmund Gibson, Bishop of London, and his descendants, deposited in the Bodleian Library, Oxford, by Major-General C. J. G. Dalton, 1960. *Photocopy* (ff. 157–83).

Given by M. J. Sommerlad, 1960.

Transcript of Archbishop Secker's autobiography in Lambeth Palace Library, by the Revd. Claude Jenkins, Lambeth Librarian (ff. 184–247).

Given by the Revd. Claude Jenkins, 1959.

Notes by John Wordsworth, Bishop of Salisbury, on the formulation of the *Responsio Archiepiscoporum Angliae ad litteras apostolicas Leonis Papae XIII*, 1897, copied from the endleaves of a volume belonging to Andrew Wordsworth of Childe Okeford, 1959. *Typescript* (ff. 248–9).

Papers about a round dining table formerly belonging to New Inn presented by Thory Gage Gardiner, Rector of Lambeth, to the see of Canterbury 1909, with historical notes about New Inn (ff. 250–4).

List of the vicars of Bapchild, Kent, 1291–1918, compiled by the Revd. Hugh Fraser Lord, Vicar of Bapchild (ff. 255–62).

Account of the Chancellorship of York Minster by the Revd. George Austen, Chancellor of York Minster, 1922. *Typescript* (ff. 267–93).

Account of the Nanteos Cup, or Grail, by the Revd. Lionel Smithett Lewis, Vicar of Glastonbury, with correspondence on the same subject with Archbishop Fisher, 1951 (ff. 294–308).

308 ff.

1730. ACCOUNTS OF ARCHBISHOP ABBOT

Domestic accounts of George Abbot, Archbishop of Canterbury, at Lambeth and Croydon, 1614–22.

Included are a list of horses, 1622 (f. 1); inventories of silver, 1617 and 1621 (f. 6); list of his servants, 1614 (f. 7^{r-v}); list of chaplains, 1614–23 (f. 8^{r-v}).

Given by — Knyvett, 18[ ].

170 ff.

1731. SCHOOLS IN THE DIOCESE OF OXFORD

'An account of the Charity Schools and Day Schools and Sunday Schools in the Diocese of Oxford, 1808.'

The survey is arranged by parishes, and states how schools are supported, subjects taught, number of pupils, whether a Sunday School, and if so how many attend, population, whether schools for Dissenters.

18 ff.

1732. SCHOOLS IN THE DIOCESE OF SALISBURY

'A Return of all the Schools of every description in the Diocese of Salisbury', by John Fisher, Bishop of Salisbury, 1808.

The survey is arranged by county and parish, and tabulates information about Endowed, Charity, and Sunday Schools.

67 ff.

1733. PALATINATE

'A short historical Review of the Grievances and Hardships of the Reformed Church in the Palatinate', late 18th century.

Endorsed 'No. 262'.

i+19 ff.

1734. CANADA

Anonymous treatise entitled, 'Observations on a Constitution and Government proper to be granted and enforced in the Province of Quebec', *c.* 1791.

Inscribed 'No. 321' and the letter 'A' on a label; endorsed 'Views, etc. No. 2'.

ii+93 pp., of which pp. 47–93 are blank.

1735. AUGMENTATION OF LIVINGS

'Plan of a Bill for imposing a Tax upon Non residence to be applied to the augmentation of small livings', addressed to the Archbishop of Canterbury, early 19th century.

Endorsed 'No. 319'.

iv+112 pp., of which pp. 56–112 are blank.

1736. FAMILY OF SKINNER

Genealogical notes in several hands on the families of Birkhened and Skinner, tracing their connection with John Moore, Archbishop of Canterbury, 17th–18th centuries.

i+25 ff.

1737. WATER-COLOURS

Satirical and humorous water-colours by W. Millett of clerical subjects, namely pews, churchwardens, behaviour in church, plurality, the social privileges of the clergy, 1885.

Bookplate of Archbishop Davidson.

33 ff.

1738. THE CHURCH IN SOUTH AFRICA

Newspaper cuttings concerning the excommunication of Frederick Henry Williams, Dean of Grahamstown, for refusal to accept the authority of a Provincial Synod held at Capetown, by Nathaniel James Merriman, Bishop of Grahamstown, 1879.

Given by Archbishop Tait.

72 pp.

1739. CAMBRIDGE UNIVERSITY LECTURES

'A course of lectures delivered at Cambridge by William Farish [Jacksonian Professor of Natural Experimental Philosophy] on the Arts and Manufactures, more particularly those relating to Chemistry.'

Inside the front cover is written the name C[harles] Jenyns, St. John's College, 1819.

Given by the Revd. E. J. Selwyn, 1889.

i+89 ff.

1740. CAMBRIDGE UNIVERSITY LECTURES

Lectures on Political Economy by George Pryme, subsequently (1828) Professor of Political Economy at Cambridge, 1818. The lectures have been collected by W. H. and C[harles] J[enyns].

Probably given by the Revd. E. J. Selwyn.

i+88 ff.

1741–3. EDMUND GIBSON PAPERS

Letters and papers of Edmund Gibson, Bishop of London (1669–1748).

Purchased, 1960.

1741. EDMUND GIBSON PAPERS

Letters to Edmund Gibson, Bishop of London, 1699–1737. The correspondents are as follows:

G[eorge] H[ickes], Nonjuror, 10 January 1699, concerning Gibson's edition of the Anglo-Saxon chronicle (f. 1).

John Strype, historian, 26 October 1717, commenting on the style of suffragans, and requesting information about the Society of Antiquaries for his edition of Stowe (ff. 2–3).

George Smalridge, Bishop of Bristol, 6 November 1715, quoting from an ordination address by him (f. 4).

The same to the Bishop of N[orwich], 7 November 1715, concerning his subscription to a declaration by the Archbishop of Canterbury and the Bishops (f. 6).

John Strype, 3 September 1717, on the appointment of suffragans (f. 8).

Edward Saul, Rector of Harlaxton, 22 October 1720, concerning Bishop Sanderson's abbreviation of confirmation service at Grantham after the Restoration; Sir Thomas Clarges has rebuilt Bitchfield chancel; South Sea stock (ff. 10–11).

Thomas Tanner, Chancellor of Norwich, and (1732) Bishop of St. Asaph, 10 October 1722, sending a treatise by Sir Henry Spelman on deeds, much damaged by rats; has many papers on commissions for examining fees of temporal and ecclesiastical courts, 1623; account of

[1741 *cont.***]**

election of proctor for Convocation by Dean and Chapter of Norwich (ff. 12–13).

The same, 15 October 1722, mentioning Spelman's treatise; the rights of Deans in the election of proctors (f. 14).

Note by Gibson on collation by commission granted after vacancy in a living (ff. 16–19).

Thomas Tanner, 25 January 1723, defending practice in diocese of Norwich of collation by commission granted after vacancy in a living (ff. 20–23^{v}).

John Taylour, 16 April 1723, about papers of Bishop Kidder (ff. 24–5).

Thomas Tanner, 31 August 1723, about an Act to ascertain boundaries of Swaffham, 18 & 19 Chas. II; asks opinion on the privilege of Members of Parliament in ecclesiastical courts (f. 26).

Edward Gee, Dean of Lincoln, 6 May 1724, about improvement in the printing of Bibles and Prayer Books; asks to be excused, because of his health, summons as lector theologiae to visitation of St. Paul's (f. 28).

John Ecton, of Queen Anne's Bounty, 13 February 1725, about dues to the Bishop of London (f. 30).

Humphrey Henchman, civilian, 22 December 1725, concerning regulations by the Archbishop of Canterbury for granting marriage licences, and describing his own practice in diocese of London (ff. 32–3).

The same, 22 December 1725, quoting a letter from Archbishop Tenison to Sir Thomas Cook, Vicar-General, concerning the grant of marriage licences (ff. 34–5).

Anonymous, 6 June 1723, reporting rumours that popish priests perform Anglican rites and are admitted to Anglican Orders (f. 36).

Extract from a letter by a clergyman in Wiltshire, 9 May 1724, about regulations to reduce the price of Bibles and Prayer Books (f. 38).

Philip Yorke, Attorney General, and (1754) 1st Earl of Hardwicke, to Charles Townshend, 2nd Viscount Townshend, Secretary of State, 22 September 1726, advising that a conventicle kept [by John 'Orator'] Henley with an inner door barred does not infringe the Toleration Act (ff. 40–2).

'Copy of a Letter sent from Winchester by a Romish Priest to Mrs S-n in the year 1727' (ff. 44–9).

Anonymous, n.d., complaining of the manner in which some clergy pray for the King (ff. 50–51^{v}).

'XXV Sunday after Trinity anno 1727. An Enquiry concerning the Proper Lessons to be used for this Sunday' (ff. 52–5).

Thomas Curteis, Vicar of Wrotham, 12 April 1729, advocating changes in the liturgy for the benefit of moderate Dissenters (f. 57), and enclosing 'emendanda quaedam in liturgia publica siquando superioribus visum fuerit' (ff. 58–61).

Francis Fox, Vicar of St. Mary, Reading, 30 April 1730, enclosing item by John Proast, Archdeacon of Berkshire, against Tindal (f. 62).

The same, 12 May 1730, about the Deists (f. 63).

Daniel Waterland, Master of Magdalene College, Cambridge, 30 August 1730, on the introduction of the Athanasian creed into the public services of European Churches (ff. 65–6).

The same, 4 September 1730, on the use of the Athanasian creed in the Reformed Churches (ff. 67–8).

'A summary view of the particular evidences concerning the reception of the Athanasian creed into the *public services*', by Waterland (f. 69).

Daniel Waterland, 3 January 1731, on 'moral and positive duties' (ff. 70–1).

The same, 10 January 1731, on the same subject; a sermon by Bishop Sherlock (ff. 72–3).

The same, 10 December 1730, on his controversy with Dr. Arthur Sykes; account of a defence of the doctrine of grace in the sacraments by himself; the creeds; disputes with the Deists, including Thomas Chubb (ff. 74–5).

The same, 21 January 1731, on moral and positive duties; disputes with the Deists; a charge (ff. 76–7).

The same, 29 December 1730, on disputes with the Deists; moral and positive duties; theological studies in Cambridge University (ff. 78–9).

The same, 22 November 1730, criticizing writings by Bishop Burnet; Mr. Gerdes, 'the Lutheran minister at Bishop-gate'; the use of the Athanasian creed in the Reformed Churches; comments on treatise by Chubb, and disputes with the Deists; Conybeare; the Bishop of Bangor (ff. 80–1).

Statement by pastor Nolterius, chaplain to the King of Prussia, about the use of the Athanasian creed in Prussia. *Latin* (f. 82), and a statement on the same subject by Rollo 'minister at Berlin and superintendent'. *Latin* (f. 83).

Daniel Waterland, 29 July 1731, on the interpretation of Scripture; the doctrine of the Trinity; an omission in the printing of the Prayer Book (ff. 84–5).

Richard Biscoe, Rector of St. Martin Outwich, London, 13 December 1733, commenting on proposals by Gibson for church reform (ff. 86–93).

Daniel Waterland, [1735], apparently concerning his election as prolocutor to the Lower House of Convocation (f. 94).

The same, 15 September 1734, apparently about his nomination to the see of Bristol by Gibson, opposed by the Queen (f. 96).

The same, 16 September 1734, on the same subject (f. 98).

[1741 *cont.***]**

The same, 29 January 1735, wishing to be excused the office of prolocutor (ff. 100–1).

Titus Wendey, Vicar of Stebbing, 7 March 1733, complaining that Dissenters distress the clergy by charging them poor rates (f. 102).

Thomas Tanner, [1727], urging restoration of clause concerning adultery by clergy to Act of Indemnity (f. 104).

Anonymous, 16 March 1734, on discipline and the enforcement of the duties of churchwardens (ff. 106–107^{v}).

John Lewis, Vicar of St. John the Baptist, Margate, 2 August 1734, about Calamy's loss of Bishop Williams's diary of liturgical commission, 1689, which came from Tillotson's papers; Laud's liturgical alterations for Scottish Prayer Book in Norwich city library; Coverdale's translation of the psalms (ff. 108–109^{v}).

The same, 20 July 1734, stating that a volume possessed by Gibson is the original abstract of the liturgical alterations made in 1689; Calamy had only a copy of Williams's minutes of the proceedings, and another copy belonged to Burnet; has himself written an account of the liturgy (f. 110).

Charles Wheatly, Vicar of Furneux Pelham, 14 August 1734, repeating account by Lewis [*q.v.*] of the manuscripts of the liturgical revision, 1689; the original amendments possessed by Gibson are those owned by Tenison in 1709; will submit his Review of the Rational Illustration . . . to Gibson; account of the writing of the *Rational Illustration* . . . (ff. 112–13).

Benjamin Bulkeley, Rector of Withicombe, 7 January 1735, about converts to popery in Devonshire; list of books (f. 115).

Edward Maynard, Canon of Lichfield, 21 April 1735, offering Gibson the loan of his collection of pamphlets acquired from Tillotson's library in 1694, which he has presented to Magdalen College, Oxford (f. 116).

[Francis Hare, Bishop of Chichester], 29 July 1735, containing severe criticisms of a book by the Bishop of Winchester. *Torn* (ff. 118–19).

Anonymous, 11 March 1736, urging repeal of Act of 21 Henry VIII cap. 13, which hinders him taking a lease, and describing controversies with Presbyterian neighbour (ff. 120–1).

Anonymous, n.d., about the date of Easter (f. 122).

Thomas Marshall, Vicar of St. John the Baptist, Peterborough, 18 October 1736, mentioning a printer's error in a prayer book by Baskett (ff. 123–4).

Peter Hay, 20 November 1736, ecclesiastical and other news from Danzig (ff. 125–126^{v}).

John Lewis, 6 December 1736, about the recovery of tithes (ff. 127–128^{v}).

Philip Morant, Vicar of Broomfield, historian of Essex, 4 June 1737, about Quakers (f. 129).

Anonymous, n.d., protesting at playing cards on Sundays (ff. 132–133^{v}).

William Newton, Vicar of West Hythe, 1 September 1737, giving account of disturbance during divine service at Gillingham, Kent (ff. 134–5).

Miles Man, of the Town Clerk's Office, Guildhall, 3 February 1737, stating that at the last election of Common Councillors for the City of London three or four Roman Catholics took the oath of supremacy and allegiance as well as the abjuration (f. 136).

Certificate by the churchwardens of All Hallows the Great and the Less, London, of distribution of £10 to the poor under the will of Edward Waddington, Bishop of Chichester, 25 December 1737 (f. 137).

Old shelfmarks '17.D.2' and 'No. 9'. Bookplate has been removed. See also MS. 2168.

ii+140 ff.

1742. EDMUND GIBSON PAPERS

Miscellaneous letters and papers, as follows:

Notes by Gibson on ordination etc. *Latin* (f. 1).

'An answer to some queries concerning the history of the resurrection of Jesus as it is with some variety related by the Evangelists' (ff. 2–5^{v}).

'The Differences in the Chiefe points of Religion Between the Roman Catholiques and us of the Church of England, Together with the agreements which wee for our parts profess and are ready to Embrace if they for theirs were as ready to accord with us in the same.' Written in the same hand as f. 170.

Endorsed, 'Bp. Cosin's Differences between Papists and Protestants' (ff. 7–10).

Navy. 'And impartial account of the present state of Discipline, Administration of Justice and of Religion in his Majesty's Navy, by one of the Chaplains who has been such many years.' The author is Brian Hunt, at one time (1723–6) a missionary to South Carolina (ff. 11–14^{v}).

Also notes by Gibson on Hunt's statement and on the state of religion in the Swedish, Danish, and Dutch navies (ff. 15–16^{v}).

Further statement by Hunt on the state of religion in the English navy in the reign of Charles II, subsequently, and in foreign Protestant navies (ff. 17^{v}–18).

Commonwealth. List of augmentation books and other records of the Trustees for the Maintenance of Preaching Ministers, 1650–9, written in the second half of the 17th century.

Endorsed by Gibson, 'Catalogue of MSS. in the Secretary's Chamber'. The manuscripts in this list appear to be those now at Lambeth (ff. 19–20).

List of livings in the gift of the Archbishop of Canterbury (ff. 21–3).

List by Gibson of livings in the Deanery of Canterbury, stating value in the King's Book and real value and the names of incumbents, late 17th century (f. 25).

[1742 *cont.***]**

Charterhouse. Petition from Andrew Tooke and John Gough, teachers at the Charterhouse, to the Governors of the same, complaining of the conduct of the Master and manciple (ff. 27–9).

Summary of the revenue of the Archbishop of Canterbury on the several rent days, November 1694–November 1695 (ff. 31–2).

Notes from Act Books of the Court of Delegates, 1538–45, 1601–9, 1619–39 (ff. 33–34ᵛ).

List by Gibson of some contents of the registers of the Privy Council, 1660–84 (ff. 35–42ᵛ).

Ireland. 'An Abstract of the number of Protestant and Popish familys as returned to the Hearth Money office, anno 1732' (ff. 43–8).

Ireland. 'A List of the Nobility and Gentry who are Generally Esteem'd to have one Hundred pounds a year and upwards in the Province of Ulster, as Divided into Churchmen, Dissenters and Papists', with remarks on the same, *c.* 1730 (ff. 49–56).

List of Lambeth degrees given by the Archbishop of Canterbury, 1660–1716 (ff. 57–8).

'Some general heads for the more Speedy, Safe and Provident manner of Managing Briefs for Fires, Repairs or Rebuilding Churches &c' (ff. 59–60).

Spelman. 'A Brief Account of some Original MSS (prepared most of them for the Press & happily preserved) wrote by the Learned Sir Henry Spelman, The Revd. Mr. Jeremy Stephens . . . the Reverend Mr. Ephraim Udall and others, in defense of the English Monarchy, Hierarchy, Academys, Spirituall Courts, Inferior Clergy, with Tythes due to them . . . Proper to be placed in the Bodleian Library', by Philip Stubbs, Archdeacon of St. Albans, [1723]. See *Bodleian Library S.C. 27681* (ff. 61–2).

Letter to Gibson asking him to vote for the election of Nathan Hickman to a Radcliffe Travelling Fellowship of Oxford University, [1731] (f. 63).

Statement of suit of the Crown *v.* Peirce 'in a Quare impedit for the Advowson of Bedale' [Yorks.], with opinion of Sir Francis Pemberton, [1692–7] (ff. 65–6).

Verses entitled 'The Golden Age Retriev'd'.
Begin: Sicilian Muse begin a Loftie flight.
End: Honest George Churchill may supply the Place (ff. 67–68ᵛ).

Oath of homage of John Potter, Bishop-elect of Oxford, [1715]. *Copy* (f. 69).

Prospectus of *A parochial account of the Diocese of Chichester* (f. 71).

Statement of case concerning right of nomination to a chapel of ease at Hammersmith on appeal to the House of Lords, [1711]. *Printed* (f. 72).

Reasons humbly offer'd against the Bill for ascertaining the Tythe of Hops, [1736] (f. 73).

Proposals (by way of subscription) for a new and most correct sett of maps for England and Wales, by William Whiston, 1715. Endorsed, 'For the Revd. Mr. Haslewood' (ff. 74–5).

Statement by John Lowther, 1st Viscount Lonsdale, of the objects and course of studies of a school founded by him, [1696]. *Copy* (ff. 76–8).

Opinion by William Salkeld, sergeant-at-law, on questions arising from the Copyright Act of 8 Anne cap. 21, 1713 (f. 79).

Commission from Queen Mary to the Bishops of Winchester, Durham, London, St. Asaph, Chichester, and Llandaff, to declare void the sees of Lincoln, Worcester, and Hereford, 15 March [1554]. *Copy*. See *C.P.R. Phil. and Mary, I*, 175 (f. 81).

Verses in the hand of Thomas Tanner, Bishop of St. Asaph. Crum 507.

(*a*) 'To Dr. Crosthwait (a heavy man)', signed J. W.
Begin: Since at Tavern I ca'nt meet you.
End: The Feet confinement is of Sense.

(*b*) 'On the Parliament's sitting on St. Cecilia's day.'
Begin: Let the States meeting such as Cecilia's prove.
End: This consort *Walls* Kingdoms, he *Wall'd* but a Town

(f. 82).

Verses addressed 'A C-rl-tt Amico suo G. P-rc-v-ll Hiberno Salutem'.
Begin: Hora dum nondum sonuit secunda.
End: Crus tibi mittunt.
Endorsed, Charlett. Percival.
Latin (f. 83).

Extract from the charter of the East India Company requiring the Archbishop of Canterbury or Bishop of London to approve ministers sent to the East Indies, 1730 (f. 84).

'The valuation of all the Dignities and Prebends in the Cathedral Church of the Holy Trinity in Chichester', *c.* 1700 (ff. 86–7).

Notes by Gibson on legal cases concerning obligation of spiritual peers to answer 'upon Oath and not upon Honour' (f. 88).

Two deeds of appointment by the Lord High Admiral of William Owen to naval chaplaincy on H.M.S. *Dragon*, 1706 and 1709 (ff. 90–1).

Memorandum by William Hanmer, deputy remembrancer of First Fruits and Tenths, concerning 'The case of the Bishops with relation to First Fruits, but more particularly such of their Lordships who have been Translated before the respective days of payment specified in their bonds', with annotations by Gibson, *c.* 1714. See also f. 95 (ff. 92–3).

Judgement in the hand of Philip Yorke, Attorney-General, in suit the King *v.* the inhabitants of Lambeth, concerning liability of tithes to Poor Rates, 8 George I (f. 94).

[1742 *cont.*]

Case for legal opinion concerning the liability of Bishops to payment of First Fruits, *c.* 1714. See also ff. 92–3 (f. 95).

The Case of the patrons of the Churches in Scotland, considered with regard to the Bill now depending in the Honourable House of Commons, 1712. The Bill is 10 Anne cap. 21 (ff. 97–8).

The Daily Courant, 7 February 1734 (f. 99).

An exact list of those who voted for bringing in the Excise-Bill, and *An exact list of those who voted against bringing in the Excise-Bill*, [1733] (ff. 100–1).

Greek alphabet 'ex codicibus MSS', by the Revd. [John] Lewis, [Vicar of St. John the Baptist, Margate, 1734]. See MS. 1741, f. 109[v] (ff. 102[v]–103).

The British Journal, 15 June 1723 (ff. 104–5).

Licence for Sir John Baker of Sissinghurst, Kent, 2nd Bt., to celebrate divine service in his domestic chapel, 1637. From the register of Archbishop Laud. *Latin copy* (f. 106).

Notes by Gibson of objections by Dissenters to the Book of Common Prayer, n.d. (f. 108).

Notes by the same on Burnet's *History of his Own Times* (ff. 110–111[v]).

List by the same of pamphlets, 1623–96. Endorsed, 'Extract out of Mr. Field's Pamphlets' (ff. 112–113[v]).

Notes by the same on White Kennett's *Historical register and chronicle of English affairs* (ff. 114–17).

'Articuli venerabilis Domini Ricardi de Scrope Archiepiscopi Eboracum contra Henricum quartum intrusorem Regni Angliae', 1399. A copy of B.M. MS. Cotton Vesp. E.IV, 94 (ff. 118–127[v]).

Extract from manuscript of Hardyng's Chronicle [? B.M. MS. Lansdowne 204] relating to Sir Henry Percy (Hotspur), in the same hand as the previous item (ff. 128–9).

Reasons for the repeal of that part of the statutes of Colleges in the Universities of Cambridge and Oxford, which require the taking of Orders under a penalty (ff. 130–1).

Proposals for printing an historical account of typography, [by John Bagford, 1707]. *Printed* (ff. 132–133[v]).

Preface to the reports of Sir Creswell Levinz, [1722] (ff. 134–135[v]).

A preface to the life and reign of King Edward the Sixth, by John Strype (f. 136).

Extracts by Gibson from letters from Jan de Laet to Sir Henry Spelman concerning Anglo-Saxon studies, 1640–1, and a copy by the same of 'Leges Aethelberti Regis, latine versae a clarissimo viro J. de Laet', and 'Judiciorum Decreta quae Hlotharius et Eadricus Cantuariorum Reges statuerunt,' annotated by de Laet. See Hickes, *Thesaurus*, 1703, pt. IV, 88–93.

Latin (ff. 137v–149).

Engravings of seals and of the ruins of Walsingham Priory, 1720, 'sumptibus Societatis Antiquariae Lond.' (ff. 150–1).

Warrant for Launcelot Blackburn, Bishop-elect of Exeter, to hold Shobrooke rectory in commendam, 11 February 1717. *Copy* (f. 152).

Letter from Patrick Cockburn, Vicar of Long Horsley, [to Gibson], 24 October 1737, about the burial of an English soldier at Edinburgh. Enclosing:

Memorandum by Cockburn on the right of the episcopal clergy in Scotland to use the office for the dead (ff. 154–157v).

Correspondence between George II and Federick, Prince of Wales, concerning the birth of Princess Augusta, [1737]. *Printed* (ff. 158–9).

Calligraphic specimens by Moses Marcus, teacher of languages, in Hebrew and other languages (f. 160).

Annals of Colchester, 219–1244, from 'a Manuscript of Colchester Taken out of the Records of the said Town' (f. 161).

Accounts of Archbishop Sheldon, by R[alph] S[heldon].

(*a*) 'Moneys Allowed by Gilbert, Lord Archbishop of Canterbury, (when Bishop of London and since) to Tenants and Purchasers' (ff. 162–4).

(*b*) Account of money given by the same 'to publique and Charitable uses', Mich. 1660–4 March 1668 (ff. 165–6).

Directions to the clergy for drawing up terriers preparatory to episcopal visitation, 1738. *Printed* (f. 167).

Papers apparently arguing against Comprehension, n.d. Endorsed, E. Spear and C. Mottram (ff. 168–169v).

Account of a feat of memory by one Mehaux. Written in the same hand as ff. 7–10 (f. 170).

Some considerations on the unhappy state of the people, in those many parishes in England, where there are no resident ministers . . . (ff. 171–172v).

Memorandum on the Celtic language, entitled 'That the Preservation of the Celtic Languages is of considerable Consequence in the Illustration of History and contributes to the Honour of a Learned Nation' (f. 173).

Account of a case in the Court of Arches concerning Philip Havers, claimant to the rectory of Mount Bures, 1678 (f. 174).

'Directions for the Bishops in case they shall be assessed towards the raising of horse and Armes otherwise then is provided by the Act for settling of the Militia', *c*. 1663 (f. 176).

Letter from William Beaum[ont] to an unnamed Bishop, n.d., disclaiming right to Rede rectory (f. 178).

'The Forme of Consecrating Churches, Chapells and Church Yards . . . or places of Buriall', 17th century (ff. 179–83).

[1742 *cont.*]

Correspondence between Thomas Pelham-Holles, 1st Duke of Newcastle, Secretary of State, and Gibson, 1729, concerning a dispute in the Chapter of Lincoln about payments due to Edward Gee, Dean of Lincoln, to whom a dispensation for non-residence has been granted. Enclosures include a copy of the opinion of Philip Yorke, Attorney-General (ff. 199–200), and of correspondence between the Duke of Newcastle and the Bishop of Lincoln (ff. 187–189^{v}, 197, 201–5), and notes of the grant of dispensations (ff. 212–23) (ff. 185–223).

Old shelfmarks '17 13.13' and 'No. 12'. See also MS. 2168.

223 ff.

1743. EDMUND GIBSON PAPERS

COLLECTIONS

'Collections [by Gibson] out of our Histories and Records since the Reformation, relating to the Differences and Transactions between the Church of England on one hand and the Puritans and Dissenters on the other.' The collections are divided into three parts: (1) objections to the government, worship, and discipline of the Church of England; (2) attempts at reformation and improvement; (3) concessions and proposals made for Comprehension.

The records used include the Journals of Convocation, 1555–1717 (pp. 95–110); copy of Bishop Stillingfleet's proposals for reforming the Church (pp. 111–18); copy of Archbishop Tillotson's proposals for reform (Birch, *Life*, 182–4) (pp. 151–3); draft of 'An Act for Uniting Protestant Subjects. From Mr. Humfrey's, October [16]96' (pp. 155–8).

Old shelfmarks '17.D.4' and 'No. 20'. See also MS. 2168.

158 pp.

1744–5. PHOTOGRAPHS OF CATHEDRALS

Two volumes of photographs of cathedrals and of Archbishops and Bishops, *c.* 1873–4. The names of persons and places will be found in the index.

Given by Jocelyn Perkins, Canon of Westminster, 1958.

1+32 ff. and 29 ff.

1746. BOOK OF ESTHER

Hebrew scroll containing the complete text of the Book of Esther, probably 16th century. It is written on nine sheets of vellum stitched together and decorated with rounded arches and flowers. The first section is written in a hand superior to that of the rest of the scroll, which is somewhat coarse.

Size: $7\frac{1}{2} \times 168$ inches.

Given by Mrs. Mary Tufnell Barrett, 1961.

1747. LETTERS TO BISHOP GOBAT, ET AL.

Letters in Amharic to Samuel Gobat, Bishop in Jerusalem, and others, with translations into English, 19th century. The letters to Gobat are from Sahle Dengel, Emperor of Ethiopia (d. 1855) (f. 1); Theodore II, Emperor of Ethiopia (d. 1868) (f. 3^{v}); Ras Ali, Ethiopian minister (f. 6); Aleka Fanta, of Debre Birhan (f. 8).

Also letters from Sahle Dengel, Emperor of Ethiopia, to Bishop Oragos of Jerusalem (f. 10); to the Bishop of Rome in Jerusalem (f. 12); to Sultan Abdel Mejid (f. 14^{v}); to Pope Kirubeal of Jerusalem (f. 17); to all Christians in Armenia and Palestine.

Given by Mrs. Mary Tufnell Barrett, 1961.

22 ff.

1748. STATUTES OF THE COURT OF THE ARCHES

A collection of statutes of the Court of the Arches by Daniel Dun, (1598) Dean of the Arches, entitled, 'Statuta omnia et singula almae curiae Cantuariensis de Archubus Londoniense, quae in antiquo libro statutorum eiusdem curiae inscripta. . .', 1590.

Index of contents (ff. ii–vi^{v}).

The volume contains the following items:

Statuta by Archbishop Winchelsey, 1295. (*Concilia*, ii, 204–13) (ff. 1–19).

Statuta by Archbishop Stratford, 1342. (*Concilia*, ii, 681–95) (ff. 19–48^{v}).

Confirmation by Edward II of the Articles of the Clergy, 1317. (*C.P.R., 1313–17*, 607) (ff. 49–53).

Ordinances made by the Archbishops of Canterbury:

Concordantia duorum statutorum quae contraria videbantur, 1309. (*Concilia*, ii, 303–4) (ff. 53^{v}–54).

Certa declaratio super computatione anni concessi ad appellationem prosequendam in tuitoriis, 1303. (*Concilia*, ii, 274–5) (ff. 54^{v}–55^{v}).

Ordinatio pro decenti regimine et gubernatione tam advocatorum quam procuratorum et caeterorum ministrorum curiae Cantuariensis, 1423. (*Concilia*, iii, 427–8) (ff. 55^{v}–57^{v}).

De modo et forma interponendi sequestrationes fructuum cum occasio postulaverit, 1320. (*Concilia*, ii, 497–8) (ff. 57^{v}–59).

Ordinatio demonstrans iura separata spectantes ad officia registrarii principalis et actorum scribae curiae Cantuariensis, 1378 (ff. 59–61^{v}).

Ordinatio de forma iuramenti ab omnibus curiae Cantuariensis ministris praestanda, 1390. (*Concilia*, iii, 212) (ff. 61^{v}–62^{v}).

Ordinatio super augmentationem feodorum registrarii curiae Cantuariensis pro scriptura attestationum, testium et exhibitorum in eadem curia, 1392. (*Concilia*, iii, 217–18) (ff. 62^{v}–64).

[**1748** *cont.*]

Ordinatio ne extranei sed solummodo advocati et procuratores Cantuar. admittantur ad postulandum seu procurandum in eadem [curia], et ut nullus huius curiae minister alteri inferiori mancipetur, 1401. (*Concilia*, iii, 263–4) (ff. 64–6).

Ordinatio ut procuratores non assumant nec prosequantur causas inconsultis advocatis; deque habitu procuratorum gestando, 1403. (*Concilia*, iii, 273–4) (ff. 66–7).

Ordinatio limitans iura ad officium registrarii principalis curiae Cantuariensis spectantia, 1397. (*Concilia*, iii, 233) (ff. 67^{v}–68^{v}).

Alia ordinatio describens iura registrarii principalis curiae Cantuariensis separata ab officio actorum scribae dictae curiae, 1397. (*Concilia*, iii, 233–4) (ff. 68^{v}–70).

Tenor commissionis ad exercendum iurisdictionem sede Cantuariense vacante, 1313 (f. 70^{r-v}).

Prescriptio iuramenti tam ab advocatis quam procuratoribus curiae Cantuariensis praestandi (ff. 70^{v}–71^{v}).

Statuta et ordinationes in curia audientiae apud Lambeth . . . de consensu omnium advocatorum et procuratorum eiusdem curiae, 1508. (*Concilia*, iii, 650–1) (ff. 71^{v}–74).

Ordinatio super confirmatione statuti alias editi de numero procuratorum curiae Cantuariensis, 1528. (*Concilia*, iii, 710–11) (ff. 74–7).

Statutum de numero procuratorum curiae Cantuariensis, 1542. (*Concilia*, iii, 858–9) (ff. 77–9).

Oath of supremacy (ff. 79^{v}–80).

Statuta quaedam per Revd. Dom. Matthaeum Parker . . . edita, 1573. (*Concilia*, iv, 273–5) (ff. 81–86^{v}).

Statuta per . . . Johannem Whitgift . . . publicata, 1587. (*Concilia*, iv, 328–34) (ff. 89–100^{v}).

Purchased, 1961.

vi+104 ff.

1749. LETTER FROM POPE JOHN XXIII

Letter from Pope John XXIII to Archbishop Fisher, 14 January 1961, with a copy of a letter by the latter, written on Archbishop Fisher's return to England after his visit to the Pope in 1960.

Given by Archbishop Fisher, 1961.

6 ff.

1750. LETTERS TO BENJAMIN WEBB

Letters to Benjamin Webb (1819–85), Prebendary of St. Paul's, 1850–85.

Among ecclesiastical subjects mentioned are ritualism (f. 11 seq.); communion wine (f. 59); the name 'Jehovah' (f. 78); hymnals (f. 118); reunion with eastern churches (f. 139). There are also references to the restoration of Chester (f. 54) and Salisbury (f. 153) cathedrals; the National Association for Freedom of Worship (f. 162 seq.); Oxford University reform (ff. 85–94, 105–7); St. Paul's cathedral (f. 155); W. H. Mill, his father-in-law (f. 38). Also letters to Mrs. Webb, mostly of condolence on the death of her husband, 1872–92 (ff. 182–192ᵛ). See also MS. 1751, ff. 1–4. The names of the writers will be found in the index.

Purchased, 1961.

196 ff.

1751. MISCELLANEOUS

Guardbook containing miscellaneous letters and papers, 1820–1932, including letters and papers of Lord Bexley, P. C. Claughton, Bishop of Colombo, T. J. Rowsell, Canon of Westminster and Deputy Clerk of the Closet to Queen Victoria, and letters concerning the coronation of George IV.

Correspondence of Nicholas Vansittart, 1st Baron Bexley, 1826–44, as follows: letter from Lord John George Beresford, Archbishop of Armagh, to the Warden of St. Columba College, 1845, about the progress of the college (ff. 1–2ᵛ); Charles James Blomfield, Bishop of London, to Lord Bexley, 1830, about the English church at Buenos Aires and clergy for North America (f. 3); Philander Chase, Bishop of Illinois, to the same, 1835, about the religious needs of his diocese (ff. 6–7ᵛ); George Isaac Huntingford, Bishop of Hereford, to H. T. Symonds, Vicar of All Saints, Hereford, 1826, advising on procedure for erecting new church (f. 8); Charles Lindsay, Bishop of Kildare, to Sir Charles Flint, 1833, about Irish church revenues (ff. 11–13ᵛ); George Murray, Bishop of Rochester, to Lord Bexley, 1844, about presentation to the living of Sidcup (ff. 15–16); Daniel Wilson, Bishop of Calcutta, to the same, 1839, about the erection of a cathedral at Calcutta (ff. 18–20) (ff. 1–20).

Given by Lady May Louisa Thornton, wife of Sir Hugh Cholmondeley Thornton, 1962.

Letter from Sir George Gilbert Scott, architect, to William Hodge Mill, Regius Professor of Hebrew, Cambridge, 1853, about a proposed architectural museum (ff. 21–2); the same to [James] Neale, 1875, concerning the latter's measured drawings of St. Albans cathedral (ff. 23–4) (ff. 21–4). Purchased, 1961.

Letter from John Henry Hobart, Bishop of New York, [to Archbishop Howley], 1830, congratulating him on his appointment (f. 25).

Letters from bishops to Archbishop Manners Sutton about attendance at the coronation of George IV, 1821. Also a letter from Archbishop Manners Sutton, 1820 (f. 46), and order of the Privy Council approving the form of service for the coronation of William IV, 1831 (f. 47). The names of the writers will be found in the index (ff. 26–48).

Letters and papers of Piers Calverley Claughton, Bishop of St. Helena (1859–62) and of Colombo (1862–70). The names of the writers will be

[1751 *cont.*]

found in the index. Other papers are: Claughton's letters of deacon's orders, 1837 (f. 111), and priest's orders, 1838 (f. 112); subscription by same to Thirty Nine Articles, 1842 (f. 113); institution of same to rectory of Elton, Hunts., 1845 (f. 114), and subscription and declaration of conformity (ff. 115–16); address from the clergy of the Deanery of Yaxley to John Bowen, Bishop of Sierra Leone, 1857 (f. 117); *Order of Ceremonial for the consecration of the Bishops of Bangor, St. Helena, and Brisbane,* 1859 (f. 119); hymn for use at the College of St. Thomas, Colombo, 1853. Begins: After long days of storm and showers. *Printed* (ff. 121–2); address to Claughton from N.C.O.s and men of the Royal Artillery and Bombay Engineers, 1862 (ff. 123–124^{v}); form of licence for curate used by Claughton as Bishop of St. Helena. *Printed* (f. 125); address by the clergy of Ceylon to Claughton, with his reply, 1870 (ff. 126–128^{v}); pass for Claughton to travel to England, issued by the Governor of Ceylon, 1871 (f. 130); collation of Claughton to archdeaconry of London, 1871 (f. 132), with account of fees (ff. 133–5); cutting of sermon by Claughton on Practical Sympathy, from *The Christian World Pulpit*, 1873 (f. 136); appointment of Claughton as Chaplain-General, 1875 (ff. 137^{v}–138); photograph of Claughton (f. 137); arms in colour of Claughton (f. 140), diocese of St. Helena (f. 141), and diocese of Colombo (f. 142) (ff. 49–142).

Given by the Revd. B. J. Wigan, Rector of Edenbridge, 1962.

Letters and papers of Thomas James Rowsell, Canon of Westminster and Deputy Clerk of the Closet to Queen Victoria, 1871–86. The names of the writers will be found in the index (ff. 143–87).

Given by the British Records Association (deposit 140), 1937.

Miscellaneous letters: J[ohn] Cave-Browne, Vicar of Detling, to Archbishop Benson, 1895, accepting appointment as honorary curator of Lambeth Palace Library (f. 188); William Scott Moncrieff, assistant minister of St. Thomas, Edinburgh, to the Revd. Randall Thomas Davidson, 1875, on the liturgy of the Scottish Episcopal Church (ff. 190–2); Beatrice Webb, wife of Sidney Webb, [to Archbishop Temple], 1902, enclosing a copy of *The Case for the Factory Acts* (ff. 193–194^{v}); correspondence on Lambeth Degrees between Sir Charles Dalrymple, 1st Bt., member of the Scottish Universities Commission, and Arthur Hamilton Baynes, chaplain to Archbishop Benson, and (1931) Provost of Birmingham, 1891 (ff. 195–201) (ff. 188–201).

201 ff.

1752. WORLD CONFERENCE ON FAITH AND ORDER

Minutes of a committee appointed by the Archbishops of Canterbury and York in connection with a proposed World Conference on Faith and Order, 1913–26. The Conference was held in 1927.

Formerly in the possession of the Revd. Tissington Tatlow, secretary to the committee. Given by the British Council of Churches, 1960.

i+196 ff.

1753. NOTEBOOK

Notebook in various hands, written from both ends, and containing:

Sermon on Proverbs 8, v. 15, preached by John Sargenson, Rector of St. Mildred, Canterbury, in Canterbury cathedral on Charles II's birthday, 29 May 1683 (ff. 1–17).

'A true Relation of the wrongs done by Coll: Wren and his Forces to me, Richard Burton, of Dufton Church in the County of Westmorland, Clerke', 1644 (ff. 18–24).

Copies of deeds relating to the family of Baker of Crook, co. Durham, 1696–1736.

Marriage settlement of George Baker of Crook, co. Durham, esq., and Elizabeth, only daughter and heiress of Thomas Conyers of Elymore Hall, co. Durham, esq., 1717 (ff. 25–60).

Marriage articles of the same, 1716 (ff. 61–67v).

Settlement of six exhibitions at St. John's College, Cambridge, founded by George Baker of Crook, co. Durham, 1710 (ff. 113v–102v).

Extract from the will of George Baker, 1698 (f. 101v).

Will of George Baker, of Crook, co. Durham, esq., son of the last, 1723 (ff. 100v–97v).

Will of Thomas Conyers of Elamore Hall, co. Durham, esq., 1728 (ff. 96v–86v).

Will of Elizabeth Baker, late of Durham, subsequently of York, widow, 1736 (ff. 84v–76).

Purchased, 1960.

ii+115 ff.

1754. LETTERS TO ARCHBISHOP AND MRS. HOWLEY

Letters to Archbishop Howley and his wife from members of the royal family, 1819–48. They include references to: the building of St. Paul's church, Malta (ff. 5–6, 9–10v, 19–20); preferment for George Davys, tutor to Queen Victoria, 'my interesting child', later Bishop of Peterborough (ff. 32–3); a visit to Lambeth by Queen Victoria, 1842 (f. 42); a cushion invented for use in labour at childbirth (f. 46); 'the Catholic Question', 1819 (f. 47); the appointment of the Revd. R. W. Jelf as tutor to Prince George of Hanover (ff. 48–9), and the confirmation of the Prince (ff. 52–9); preferment for the Revd. George Glover, Rector of Southrepps (ff. 64–6); a tutor for the Duke of Cambridge (f. 68); George IV's proposal to appoint the Revd. H. C. Cust, Canon of Windsor, to the see of Rochester (ff. 98–101v); condolences on the death of Archbishop Howley (ff. 137–138v, 145–146v).

Purchased, 1960.

164 ff.

1755. ESSAY ON DE PAUPERIE SALVATORIS

Helen Campbell Hughes: 'An Essay Introductory to the De Pauperie Salvatoris of Richard FitzRalph, Archbishop of Armagh'. Thesis for the degree of Ph.D. of Manchester University, 1929.

Inserted (ff. ii–iii) an offprint of an obituary in *The Bookseller*, 1944.

Given by Miss Margaret Hughes, sister of the author, 1961.

Typescript copy. xii+221 ff.

1756. JOURNAL

Journal of a journey through Cheshire and Staffordshire [by the Revd. Henry Delves Broughton, Perpetual Curate of Haslington, Cheshire], 1829. At f. 3^v is a sketch of the Sandbach Crosses.

Given by A. E. Jones, 1960.

42 ff., of which ff. 23–41 are blank.

1757. *REFLECTIONS ON DEATH*

'Reflections on Death', [by William Dodd, Rector of Hockliffe), 18th century. This manuscript contains chapters I–XVIII of the text as printed, from which it differs in some particulars.

At pp. 126–44 a copy of two printed sermons, 1862.

Given by the Revd. Christopher Perowne, 1960. Bookplate of Christopher T. Perowne.

ii+178 pp.

1758. SERMON

Sermon on Acts 20, v. 32, 'preached by the Revd. Mr. Clark at Chesham Bois [Bucks.] on March the 21st 1762'. At the back of the volume some verses 'on death', 'on judgement', etc.

Given by the Revd. Christopher Perowne, 1960. Bookplate of Christopher T. Perowne.

i+31 ff.

1759. MANUAL OF DEVOTIONS

Manual of devotions by George Skene, Scottish episcopalian minister at Forfar, Angus, 18th century. It includes devotions for the sick and morning and evening prayers.

Given by Dr. A. C. Don, formerly Dean of Westminster, 1960.

iv+140 pp.

1760. COMMUNION OFFICE

'An Office for the Sacrifice of the Holy Eucharist,' written by a Scottish episcopalian minister, possibly Arthur Petrie, minister at Meiklefolla and (1776) Bishop of Moray. It is bound in a printer's advertisement, dated Edinburgh, 1765. The text differs from the Scottish Communion Office published in 1764 (ff. 1–33).

Also included are a reprint of the Office from *The Scottish Chronicle*, [1929], annotated by the Revd. Frank Edward Brightman, Fellow of Magdalen College, Oxford (ff. 34–49^{v}), and letters from Brightman and Arthur John Maclean, Bishop of Moray, Ross, and Caithness, to Dr. A. C. Don, 1926–30 (ff. 52–4).

On the front cover is written 'Nº 4th', and at f. ii a note by A. C. Don that the manuscript was found 'in the Library at Inshewan in 1926'.

Given by Dr. A. C. Don, formerly Dean of Westminster, 1960.

iv+54 ff.

1761–4. REGISTERS

Registers of baptisms, confirmations, burials, and marriages in the diocese of Shantung, China, 1906–50.

1761

Register of baptisms, 15 March 1906–9 March 1940.

ii+52 ff.

1762

Register of baptisms, 11 November 1934–29 September 1950; confirmations, 11 March 1928–29 September 1950; burials, 8 September 1934–25 December 1946.

i+61 ff.

1763

Register of marriages, 15 April 1912–14 June 1942.

12 ff.

1764

Marriage certificates, 24 October 1945–6 November 1948.

6 ff.

Given by the Foreign Office, 1960.

1765. LETTERS FROM ARCHBISHOP WILLIAM TEMPLE

Letters from William Temple, Archbishop of Canterbury, to his elder brother Frederick Charles Temple, 1894–1944.

Given by the Revd. F. S. Temple, 1960.

Typescript copies. 319 ff.

1766. THESIS ON ARCHBISHOP LAUD

Katharine McElroy: 'Laud and his Struggle for Influence from 1628 to 1640.' Thesis for the degree of D.Phil. of Oxford University, [1943].

Given by the Bodleian Library, Oxford, 1960.

ii+337 ff.

1767. HORSLEY PAPERS

Letters and papers of Samuel Horsley, Bishop of St. Asaph, and of his son Heneage Horsley, Dean of Brechin, 1785–1904. The papers were used in H. H. Jebb, *A great bishop of one hundred years ago*, 1909.

1. Letters to Bishop Horsley, 1785–1805. The correspondents are:

Baron Arundell of Wardour, 1800, about the education of Roman Catholics (ff. 1–2).

Weldon Champneys, Precentor of Westminster, 1802, on Horsley giving up the Deanery of the same (f. 3).

George Gaskin, Rector of Stoke Newington, London, 1804, concerning London incumbents (ff. 4–5).

[Bishop Horsley], 1790, on the repeal of the Test Acts. *Copy* (ff. 6–8).

Robert Hamilton, physician, 1785, concerning the controversy with Joseph Priestley (ff. 9–10^{v}).

George Avery Hatch, Rector to St. Matthew, Friday Street, London; President of Sion College, 1804, concerning London incumbents (f. 11).

Sir John Coxe Hippisley, 1st Bt., 1805, enclosing (ff. 15–16^{v}) a copy of a letter to himself from W[illiam] W[indham], 1805, on the Catholic Question in Ireland (ff. 13–16^{v}).

William Pitt, Prime Minister, 1796, about the appointment of a High Bailiff of Westminster, with (f. 19) copy of reply (ff. 17–19).

The same, 1798, inquiring whether the Lord Chancellor's permission was obtained to hold a prebend of Gloucester in commendam (f. 21).

The Duke of Portland, Home Secretary, 1801, about the dedication of *Hosea* to George III. (4) (ff. 23–6).

Joseph Stock, Bishop of Killala, and (1810) Waterford, 1804, about his intended book *Critical remarks on . . . the Old Testament* (ff. 28–9).

Lord Thurlow, 1797, on his classical studies (ff. 30–1).

The same, n.d., on the Lambeth Parish Bill (f. 32).

Congratulatory letter from Trinity Hall, Cambridge, n.d. *Latin. Seal* (f. 34).

Thomas Witherby, 1804, enclosing observations on a sermon by Horsley (ff. 34–9).

2. Letters from Bishop Horsley to Frances Emma Horsley, wife of Heneage Horsley, 1801–6. (25) (ff. 41–74).

3. Papers of Heneage Horsley (1776–1847), son of Bishop Horsley, Dean of Brechin, 1797–1847. The letters mainly concern the writings of Bishop Horsley, but also include (ff. 97–137) letters from the Bishop to Heneage as an undergraduate at Christ Church, Oxford, and (ff. 95–96^{v}) a copy of

a letter by Heneage Horsley about the making of an episcopal residence at Dundee for the Bishop of Brechin. The names of the writers will be found in the index (ff. 75–162).

4. Miscellaneous notes, probably copies by Heneage Horsley of writings by Bishop Horsley. They include metrical versions of passages in the Bible [cf. Bishop Horsley's *Sacred Songs*] (ff. 83–90^{v}); notes on Genesis and St. John (ff. 163–70, 174–7); 'Thoughts upon Civil Government and its relation to Religion,' 1790 (ff. 198–203); on liberty (ff. 214–15) (ff. 163–215).

5. Miscellaneous papers, 1732–1904. They comprise: letters from E[lizabeth] Horsley, half-sister to Bishop Horsley, to Mrs. Chapman, 1802 (ff. 216–17); John Horsley, half-brother to Bishop Horsley, to his niece Sarah Horsley, 1819 (ff. 218–19); William Ewart Gladstone to the Revd. A. Irwin, 1847 (ff. 220–1); the vestry of St. Paul's Church, Dundee, to Samuel Horsley, son of Heneage Horsley, 1847 (ff. 222–3); Francis Roberts to — Whiteman, 1846, on the first Sikh War (ff. 224–227^{v}); Henry Cleaver, registrar of St. Asaph, to the Revd. Heneage Horsley Jebb, great-grandson of Bishop Horsley, Rector of Potsgrove, 1904 (f. 228); Beaupré Bell, antiquary, to Edmund Law, Fellow of Christ's College, Cambridge, and (1769) Bishop of Carlisle, 1732 (f. 229); family tree of Horsley (f. 233) (ff. 216–33).

Given by Miss E. M. Jebb, 1960.

233 ff.

1768–9. HORSLEY PAPERS

Letters on family and domestic affairs to Francis Horsley and his wife, 1785–1818. Horsley was proprietor of the first independent English newspaper in India, and half-brother to Bishop Horsley.

Given by Miss E. M. Jebb, 1960.

1768

Letters to Francis Horsley from his sisters, Anne Horsley, 1785–1806 (ff. 1–123^{v}), and Elizabeth Horsley, 1785–1804 (ff. 124–241^{v}).

241 ff.

1769

Letters to Francis Horsley from Sarah Horsley, his sister, 1785–1818 (ff. 1–79); Elizabeth Anne Palmer, daughter of William Palmer of Nazeing Park, Essex, merchant, his niece, 17[88]–94 (ff. 80–91); R. Cunyngham, 1799 (ff. 92–94^{v}).

Letters to Mrs. Horsley, wife of Francis Horsley, from Anne Horsley, her sister-in-law, 1793–1804 (ff. 95–176^{v}); Elizabeth Horsley, her sister-in-law, 1795–1800 (ff. 177–98); Mary Horsley, daughter of John Horsley, 1801 (ff. 199–202); Sarah Horsley, her sister-in-law, 1796–1802

[1769 *cont.*]

(ff. 203–18); Elizabeth Anne Palmer, daughter of William Palmer of Nazeing Park, Essex, merchant, 1794–8 (ff. 219–25).

225 ff.

1770. DIARY OF ARCHBISHOP WAKE

Diary of William Wake, (1705) Bishop of Lincoln, and (1716) Archbishop of Canterbury, 7 March 1705–25 January 1725.

Given by the Hon. George Dawnay, 1960.

xv+270 ff.

1771. DIARY OF LORD NORTHBOURNE

Diary of Sir Walter Charles James, 2nd Bt., (1884) 1st Baron Northbourne, 1851.

An index of subjects (pp. 376–86) has been added in another hand.

Given anonymously, 1960.

iv+387 pp.

1772. PHOTOGRAPHS

Photographs of Archbishops and Bishops of the Church of England, *c.* 1905. The names will be found in the index.

Given by Miss B. E. Clementson, 1959.

61 ff.

1773. LETTERS

Letters to the Revd. Walter Hobhouse, editor of *The Guardian*, Mervyn George Haigh, Bishop of Coventry, and to the Revd. Christopher Cheshire, 1901–42, as follows:

Letter to the Revd. Walter Hobhouse, editor of *The Guardian*, from Archbishop Davidson, 1904, about the appointment of suffragan bishops and the problems facing the Archbishop (ff. 1–4^{v}).

Given by Miss Dorothy Hobhouse, 1963.

Letters to Mervyn George Haigh, Bishop of Coventry, 1927–42, concerning Prayer Book revision (ff. 5^{v}–6), a commission on the relations of Church and State (ff. 11–12^{v}), and the Lambeth Conference, 1930 (ff. 13–15^{v}). The names of the writers will be found in the index. Also included is a letter from Herbert Hensley Henson, Bishop of Durham, to Archbishop Davidson, 1927, about opposition in Parliament to the Revised Prayer Book, 1927 (ff. 19–22^{v}) (ff. 5–22^{v}).

Given by Mrs. M. Blackman, 1963.

Letters to Christopher Cheshire, Warden of Liddon House, and Rector of Holy Trinity, Chelsea, from Henry Scott Holland, Regius Professor of Divinity, Oxford, 1901–31. Also a sermon by Scott Holland on John 14, v. 6 (ff. 66–99v) (ff. 23–108).

Given by Elizabeth Cheshire, widow of the Revd. Christopher Cheshire, 1959.

108 ff.

1774. DIARY OF BISHOP WILLIAMS, 1689

'A Diary of the Proceedings of the Commissioners appointed by K. William and Q. Mary to revise the common Prayer, 1689. Taken by Dr. [John] Williams, now Bishop of Chichester, one of the Commissioners, every Night after He went home from the several Meetings.'

This manuscript is a copy made by Richard Terrick, Bishop of London, of a further copy of the original diary made by Edmund Gibson, later Bishop of London, and John Garnett, [Rector of Cowlam], 1708. The diary was published by W. H. Black from the transcript by Gibson as a Parliamentary Paper in 1854.

At ff. i–iii a letter [from the Revd. Anthony Hamilton, Archdeacon of Taunton, grandson of Bishop Terrick], 1834.

Given by Robert Hamilton Moberly, Dean of Salisbury, 1960.

iv+87 ff., of which ff. 58–87 are blank.

1775. THEOLOGICAL NOTEBOOK

Prayers and meditations, apparently by an incumbent in co. Durham, including (ff. 63–83v) a sermon preached at Stranton, 1690. At the front and back a few entries of offertory collections, 1685–9.

Given by Dr. E. S. de Beer, 1962.

118 ff.

1776. COMMUNION SERVICE

The Communion Service as it might be, by Lord Hugh Cecil, (1941) 1st Baron Quickswood, 1935. With corrections by the author. See also MS. 1777, ff. 1–7.

Given by the Earl of Selborne, 1963.

1777. THE APPARITOR-GENERAL OF THE PROVINCE OF CANTERBURY

Papers of William Wake, Archbishop of Canterbury, concerning a dispute about the fees and jurisdiction of the Apparitor-General of the Province of Canterbury, 1727. They consist of the following:

Statement of case concerning a dispute about fees between the Apparitor-General and the registrar of the P.C.C. (f. 1).

Statement of the case and judgement by Archbishop Wake, with (ff. 7–10) a draft of the same and summary of depositions in previous disputes by Wake (ff. 3–10).

[1777 *cont.*]

Notes mainly by Archbishop Wake concerning the early history of the office of Apparitor-General, including copies of the patents of some 15th-century Apparitors-General and of the patent of William Folkes, 1725. Also a copy of Archbishop Parker's orders for the office of apparitor of the P.C.C. and a list of Apparitors-General, 1551–1641 (ff. 11–26).

Letter from Henry Farrant, registrar of the P.C.C., to [Archbishop Wake], n.d., enclosing clause proposed to be added to his patent (ff. 28–9).

Patent of George Body as apparitor in the dioceses of Bristol, Bath and Wells, and Exeter, 1573. *Copy* (ff. 31–2).

Settlement of a dispute between Philip Jacob, Apparitor-General, and Everard Exton, registrar of the P.C.C., by Archbishop Sancroft, 1683. *Copy* (ff. 33–34^{v}).

Extracts and notes, partly in the hand of Archbishop Wake, from records of the P.C.C. concerning the office of apparitor (ff. 35–8).

Letter from the registrar of the Prerogative Court of York to [William] Ward, Commissary of the same, 1726, describing the duties of the Apparitor-General in that Province and of his deputies. Also the patent of William Haselum as Apparitor-General of York, 1717. *Copies* (ff. 40–41^{v}).

Letter from George Paul, Vicar-General, to Archbishop Wake, [1726] (f. 42).

Opinion of Humphrey Henchman, civilian, 1726 (ff. 44–45^{v}).

Letter from Hugh Boulter, Archbishop of Armagh, [to Archbishop Wake], 1726, concerning a dispute with the Archbishop of Dublin about uncanonical marriages; and about his Apparitor-General (ff. 46–7).

Correspondence between Archbishop Wake and John Bettesworth, Dean of the Arches and Judge of the P.C.C., 1727, concerning a dispute between the latter and William Folkes about jurisdiction (ff. 48–65).

At ff. i–ii a list of contents, one of them annotated by Archbishop Secker. Some of the papers bear endorsements by A. C. Ducarel.

ii+65 ff.

1778. BAILIFF'S ACCOUNTS

Bailiff's accounts for estates of John Tatlocke at Alton, Holybourne, and Worldham, Hants, 1745–61.

38 ff.

1779. ACCOUNTS FOR STANGATE ESTATE, LAMBETH

Accounts of William Bent to Christopher Hodgson, Receiver-General of the Archbishop of Canterbury, for the Stangate estate, Lambeth, 1826.

18 ff.

1780. PRAYER BOOK OF THE CHURCH OF IRELAND

The final draft of the revised *Book of Common Prayer* of the Church of Ireland as approved by the General Synod, 1877.

Given by Samuel Moore Kyle, Archdeacon of Cork, and member of the revising committee, 1888.

vi+138 ff.

1781–2. CHURCH CONGRESS PAPERS

Papers of the Church Congress, 1864–1932. The Church Congress was an unofficial meeting of Anglican Churchmen held annually from 1861 to 1913 and then at less regular intervals.

Given by Mrs. J. Cahn, 1962.

1781. CHURCH CONGRESS PAPERS

Minutes of the committee of the Church Congress, 1877–1928.

iii+100 ff.

1782. CHURCH CONGRESS PAPERS

Miscellaneous papers of the Church Congress, 1864–1932.

Account of William Emery, Archdeacon of Ely. Reprinted from the *Cambridge Chronicle*, 11 June 1864 (f. 1).

Standing rules for regulation of Congress, 1865 (f. 2).

Standing rules of the Church Congress, 1881. *Printed* (ff. 3–4).

Object and standing rules of the Church Congress, 1905. Reprinted from the *Church Congress Manual* (ff. 7–8^{v}).

The object and standing rules of the Church Congress, 1905 (ff. 11–12).

List of congresses, 1861–1904 (ff. 13^{v}–14), and a further list with additions to 1908 (f. 15).

Notice of Annual Meeting of standing committee of the Church Congress, 1906. *Printed* (f. 16).

List of members of the advisory and standing committees of the Church Congress, 1915–19 (ff. 18–20).

Notes on the history of the Church Congress. *Typescript* (ff. 21–3).

Notice to members of the standing committee concerning proposed meeting of Church Congress at Toronto, 1928. *Printed* (f. 24).

Letter from G. F. Emery, honorary permanent lay secretary to the Church Congress, to *The Times* about the location of the Congress, [1930] (f. 25).

Extract from *The Times* about the future of the Church Congress, 1932 (f. 26).

[1782 *cont.*]

Letter to Walter Godfrey Whittingham, Bishop of St. Edmundsbury and Ipswich, 1932, about meeting place for Church Congress. *Copy* (f. 27).

List of Church Congresses, 1861–1930 (f. 28).

28 ff.

1783. NOTES ON ARCHBISHOP HERRING

Genealogical notes on the family of Herring, with particular reference to Thomas Herring, Archbishop of Canterbury, by Herbert T. Herring, 1913. Included are copies of letters to the author from Walter Rye, Norfolk historian, 1912 (ff. 8–12); Francis Henry Baring, formerly partner in Baring Brothers & Co., 1912–13 (ff. 14–27), and Sir Algar Howard, Rouge Dragon Pursuivant, and (1944) Garter King of Arms, 1912–13 (ff. 30–1). Also copies of the wills of Gerrard Herring, of Cambridge, draper, 1701 (f. 35); William Herring, of Cambridge, draper, 1722 (f. 36); Archbishop Herring, 1756 (ff. 37–43), and William Herring, Chancellor of the Diocese of York, 1763 (f. 44).

Given by Mrs. M. Herring, 1962.

Typescript. iii+44 ff.

1784. SERMONS OF JOHN CALVIN

'Sermons de M. Jehan Calvin sur le premier livre de Moyse, dict Genese', containing 25 sermons preached almost daily in alternate weeks, 4 September–31 October 1559, and (f. 125) an incomplete sermon on Genesis 18, 26 April 1560. The sermon preached on 31 October is incomplete.

A contemporary transcript in French in a neat and uniform hand, perhaps copied from the official transcription formerly at Geneva. The manuscript contains signatures A1 to Q2, but does not appear to be a copy of a printed text. For the history of the manuscripts of Calvin's sermons see T. H. L. Parker, *Supplementa Calviniana*, 1962.

Size 20×30 cm. Bound in quarter red leather enclosing old vellum covers. Some damage by damp, but text not affected.

The name Henry Sulger, no. 10 Nevill's Abbey, appears on f. 128^v. At the front the bookplates of Andrew Gifford (d. 1784) and of the Bristol Baptist College, and the old shelfmark of the latter, Z.c.21.

Purchased, 1963.

ii+131 ff.

1785. PERAMBULATION OF PARISH OF LAMBETH

Perambulation with maps of the boundaries of the parish of Lambeth, including (pp. 61–4) the extra-parochial district of Lambeth Palace, [by

Charles Alexander Craig, district surveyor of Lambeth and Newington], 22 May 1811.

Given by William Tiffin Iliff, M.D., 1872.

vii+70 pp.

1786. LAMBETH ENCLOSURE

'Minutes of proceedings of the Commissioners appointed under an Act of Parliament, 46th Geo. 3rd, for Inclosing lands within the Manor of Lambeth', 1808–10. At the back of the volume (ff. 108^{v}–125^{v}) copies of letters from Forster Cooke and Frere, clerks to the Commissioners, 1808–12.

v+131 ff., of which ff. 35–108 are blank.

1787–8. WESTMINSTER ASSOCIATION

'The Westminster Association for the further relief of the sufferers by the war in Germany' was founded in 1814, and received a Parliamentary Grant of £100,000. The joint secretaries were Joshua Watson and Rudolph Ackermann.

See also MS. 1789, ff. 3–96.

Given by Canon Charles Inge through A. B. Webster, 1950.

1787. WESTMINSTER ASSOCIATION

Minute book of the committee of the Westminster Association, 26 March 1814–1 May 1816.

i+58 ff.

1788. WESTMINSTER ASSOCIATION

Report of a subcommittee of the Westminster Association on the distribution of funds, containing accounts of sums already remitted and proposals for the distribution of the Parliamentary Grant, with remarks on the condition of the localities in Germany, 1814.

ii+16 ff.

1789. MISCELLANEOUS PAPERS

Guardbook containing miscellaneous papers, 1812–95.

List by the Revd. H. J. Todd of presentation copies of his *Catalogue of the archiepiscopal manuscripts . . . in Lambeth Palace*, 1812. Removed from a copy of the catalogue (ff. 1–2).

Papers of the Westminster Association for the relief of the sufferers by the war in Germany, 1814–16. They include letters of thanks from local committees in Germany for the distribution of relief to Joshua Watson and Rudolph Ackermann, joint secretaries of the Association, and the

[1789 *cont.*]

following miscellaneous papers: minutes of a meeting of the committee of the Society of Merchants Trading to the Continent, 1814. *Extract* (f. 59); minutes by Archbishop Manners Sutton of a meeting of the committee of the Westminster Association, 1816 (f. 61); table of the appropriation of the Parliamentary Grant for the relief of sufferers and orphans, with instructions for its distribution, 1814. *German. Printed* (f. 63); audited account of the Parliamentary Grant, 1814–16 (ff. 65^{v}–66); audited account of the Westminster Association, excluding the Parliamentary Grant, 1814–16 (ff. 67^{v}–68); account of grants made from the Parliamentary Grant, 1815 (ff. 69–71); seating plan for a concert in the Whitehall Chapel in aid of the Westminster Association, with account of receipts and expenditure, 1814 (ff. 73–4); vouchers for expenses incurred in administering the Parliamentary Grant, 1814–16 (ff. 76–90); diploma awarded to Joshua Watson by the King of Saxony, 1815. *German* (ff. 95^{v}–96). See also MSS. 1787–8 (ff. 3–96).

Notebook containing (1) 'A schedule of certain writings and papers at Lambeth Palace left in Archbishop Moore's study' (ff. 99–108). (2) 'Schedule of books and papers relating to property belonging to the See of Canterbury which were found in the Receiver's Office when the same was taken for a Record Office' (ff. 109–14). (ff. 99–114).

'Schedule of books and papers relating to property belonging to the See [of Canterbury], delivered to Mr. [Christopher] Hodgson by the R. Honble. Charles Manners-Sutton, Speaker of the House of Commons, executor of the late Archbishop of Canterbury', 1828 (ff. 118–127^{v}).

Letter from 'A Husband' to Archbishop Howley, 1843, on reforms of the consistory court (ff. 131–132^{v}).

Papers about the baptism of Archbishop Tait. They include a letter from Randall Thomas Davidson, Dean of Windsor, and (1903) Archbishop of Canterbury, to Archbishop Benson, 1890 (ff. 133–4), enclosing a declaration by James Campbell Tait, Writer to the Signet, of the baptism of his brother Archbishop Tait, 1874 (ff. 135–6); death certificate of Thomas MacKnight, minister of the Old Church, Edinburgh, in 1836 (f. 139); letters to Davidson from J. and F. Anderson, Writers to the Signet, 1890 (ff. 137^{v}–138, 140–141^{v}, 143); certificate of the baptism of Archbishop Tait in 1811 (f. 142). Also a certificate of the baptism of Archbishop Davidson in 1848 (f. 146), and a letter from A. Pitman to the same, 1911, sending the Tait family Bible (f. 147) (ff. 133–147^{v}).

Given by Randall Thomas Davidson, Dean of Windsor, 1890.

'Report on the Higher Organisation of the Anglican Communion, presented to the Bishops Meeting', 1895. Annotated by John Wordsworth, Bishop of Salisbury, chairman. *Printed* (ff. 149–152^{v}).

Transferred from Lambeth Palace, 1963.

152 ff.

1790. DORSET DURING THE COMMONWEALTH

Dorset entries extracted by Edward Alexander Fry from the Augmentation Books in Lambeth Palace Library (MSS. 966–1021), [1915]. ff. 99–130 and 181–209 are printed in *Proceedings of the Dorset natural history and antiquarian Field Club*, 1915, 55–105.

Given by the author.

Typescript. ix+245 ff.

1791. SERMONS BY THE REVD. FRANCIS WILMOT

Sermons by Francis Wilmot (1760–1818), barrister-at-law and Rector of Trusley and Pinxton, Derbyshire, including (ff. 116–18) notes on a sermon by Brownlow North, Bishop of Winchester, to the House of Lords, and (ff. 119–21) by [Richard] Prosser, [(1808) Archdeacon of Durham], to the House of Commons, 1801.

An incomplete index (f. iii).

At the back of the volume are legal notes and (ff. 193–5) three State Lottery tickets, 1786.

Given by Roger Ellis, 1963.

iii+197 ff.

1792. ACCOUNTS OF THE S.P.G.

Audited accounts on parchment of the Society for the Propagation of the Gospel, presented with the auditor's report in January of each year. The accounts are dated 1721, 1723, 1725, 1731–4, 1737, 1739–40, 1759–65, 1791, 1793–4, 1796–7.

26 items.

Purchased, 1963.

1793–4. JOINT CONFERENCE ON FAITH AND ORDER

Papers of the Revd. Tissington Tatlow, secretary of the Joint Conference of the Archbishops of Canterbury and York's Committee on Faith and Order and representatives of the Free Churches, and of the subcommittee appointed to draw up subjects for discussion, 1912–39.

Given by the Revd. Floyd Williams Tomkins, 1962.

1793. JOINT CONFERENCE ON FAITH AND ORDER

Minutes and miscellaneous papers of the Joint Conference and subcommittee on Faith and Order, 1914–19.

Minutes, 1914–19. Mostly duplicated copies of the minutes, but with draft minutes of three meetings (ff. 1–148).

[1793 *cont.*]

Miscellaneous papers principally concerning the drafting of the First and Second Interim Reports of the subcommittee, 1916–17.

Also included are a report by a committee of Bishops to the Archbishop of Canterbury on the proposed Conference on Faith and Order. *Duplicated* (ff. 149–54); list of members of the Archbishops of Canterbury and York's Committee (f. 155); extract from the corrected draft report of the Joint Commission of the Protestant Episcopal Church in America to the General Synod on the progress of Faith and Order, [1914]. *Typescript* (ff. 156–61); memorandum about a visit of representatives of denominations in the United States to Great Britain. *Typescript copy* (ff. 162–4); *Statement concerning the World Conference of all Christian Churches, by the deputation from the American Churches,* [1914] (ff. 165–6); report of a private conference on Christian Unity convened by Canon George Harford, Vicar of Mossley Hill, Liverpool, reprinted from the *Liverpool Courier*, n.d. (ff. 167–8); *A Statement of the Quaker position in regard to the document entitled* '*Towards Christian Unity*', 1916 (ff. 183–8); statement by Harold Francis Hamilton, formerly Professor of Pastoral Theology, Bishop's College, Canada, of 'The Anglican Position with Regard to Reunion'. *Typescript copy* (ff. 213–18); *Reply from the Society of Friends to the Second Interim Report issued by the Jerusalem Chamber Conference,* [1917] (ff. 219–221^{v}); findings of a conference of the Anglican Fellowship on Intercommunion, 1919. *Duplicated* (ff. 222–3); memorandum by A. E. Garvie, Principal of New College, Hampstead, 1919 (ff. 224–5); memorandum by William Temple, Rector of St. James, Piccadilly, and (1942) Archbishop of Canterbury, for the Joint Conference, [1917]. *Typescript* (ff. 226–32), and a memorandum by the same for the subcommittee, n.d. *Duplicated* (ff. 233–7) (ff. 149–237).

237 ff.

1794. JOINT CONFERENCE ON FAITH AND ORDER

Correspondence of the Revd. Tissington Tatlow concerning the Joint Conference and subcommittee on Faith and Order, 1912–37. The names of the writers will be found in the index.

292 ff.

1795. ORDER OF HOLY COMMUNION

'The Order of the Administration of the Lord's Supper or Holy Communion', written and illuminated on vellum for Archbishop Davidson, 1928.

The following inscription appears on f. 28, 'Hunc Librum Randallo T. Davidson. Archiepiscopo Cantuarensi. 1878–1928. D.DD. Amici et Cognati Concelebrantes. Exscripsit Barbara et pinxit Hallam Murray.'

iv+30 ff.

1796. STATISTICS FOR WESTMINSTER

'Statistics of St. Margaret's and St. John's, Westminster', 1846, and (ff. 31–52) *A few words on the state of Westminster*, 1847, by Alfred Jones, (1872) Vicar of St. John's, Kenilworth.

The statistics, which are arranged by localities, are for the numbers of houses, families, individuals, children under 12, children at Infant, Day, Church, Dissenter, and Dame schools, churches, attendance at church, chapels, attendance at chapel, shops open on Sunday, gin and beer shops, adults unable to read, unmarried couples, brothels, prostitutes, beggars, thieves and 'smashers', lodging houses, city missionaries, meeting-rooms, missionary schools, uninhabited houses.

Given in memory of Archbishop Tait, 1883.

i+79 ff.

1797. AUTOGRAPHS

Autographs of Bishops of the Church of England, taken principally from letter-covers, 1802–39.

74 ff.

1798. LETTERBOOK OF FREDERICK TEMPLE

Letterbook of Frederick Temple, Principal of Kneller Hall, Isleworth, and subsequently Archbishop of Canterbury, December 1850–June 1851. Kneller Hall was a training college for workhouse schoolmasters.

Most of the letters are addressed to the Committee of Council on Education, but other correspondents include: [Matthew] Arnold (ff. 54, 70); Henry Petty-Fitzmaurice, 3rd Marquess of Lansdowne, President of the Council (ff. 64–5); Gerald Valerian Wellesley, chaplain to Queen Victoria, and (1854) Dean of Windsor (ff. 3, 12–13, 29–30); H. F. Zaba, inventor of a system of mnemonics (ff. 59, 68–9).

97 ff.

1799. REPORT ON SCHOOLS IN DERBYSHIRE, 1841

Copy of a report by the Revd. John Allen, Inspector of Schools, to the Committee of Council on Education, 1841, on 59 schools inspected in Derbyshire. There are detailed reports on the following schools:

Fairfield (ff. 19–30^{v}); Matlock (ff. 31–42^{v}); Ironville (ff. 43–54^{v}); Hathersage (ff. 55–66^{v}); Derby (National) (ff. 67–78^{v}); Ravenstone [now Leics.] (ff. 79–90^{v}); Derby (Trinity Church) (ff. 91–102^{v}); Stanton Ford (ff. 103–114^{v}); Dore [now Yorkshire] (ff. 115–126^{v}); Chesterfield (ff. 127–138^{v}); Pentrich (ff. 139–150^{v}); Youlgreave (ff. 151–162^{v}); Derby (Infant) (ff. 163–174^{v}); Chapel-en-le-Frith (ff. 175–186^{v}); Darley (ff. 187–198^{v}); Bamford (ff. 199–210^{v}); Radbourne (ff. 211–222^{v}); Newhall (ff. 223–234^{v}); Buxton (ff. 235–246^{v}); Edale (ff. 247–258^{v}); Cromford (ff. 259–270^{v});

[1799 *cont.*]

Bakewell (ff. 271–282^{v}); Norton [now Yorkshire] (ff. 295–306^{v}); Castleton (ff. 307–318^{v}); Greenhill (ff. 319–330^{v}); Edensor (ff. 331–342^{v}); Denby (ff. 343–354^{v}); Hope (ff. 355–366^{v}).

Covering letter from Harry Chester, assistant secretary to the Committee of Council on Education, to Archbishop Howley, 1842 (f. 1).

366 ff.

1800. LIST OF PARLIAMENTARY SURVEYS, 1650–8

List of parochial surveys made by virtue of Ordinances of Parliament with a view to the union or division of parishes. The surveys were used by the Trustees for the Maintenance of Preaching Ministers during the Commonwealth. The volume contains (*a*) list of the contents of the surveys made in 1650 (now Lambeth Palace Library COMM./XIIa/1–19) (pp. 1–325); (*b*) 'abstracts' of the original surveys in the order in which they were received, 1655–8 (pp. 533–675).

Index of counties (p. 1157).

1163 pp.

1801. CORRESPONDENCE OF CADELL AND DAVIES

Correspondence and papers of Cadell and Davies, of London, booksellers and publishers, 1799–1830. The names of the writers will be found in the index.

204 ff.

1802. LETTERS OF THOMAS HORNSBY

Letters of Thomas Hornsby, Sedleian Professor of Natural Philosophy, Oxford, to F. Wingrave, of London, bookseller, mainly concerning the settlement of the estate of Sir Charles Nourse, 1789–95.

81 ff.

1803. LETTERS FROM ARCHBISHOP LANG

Letters from Archbishop Lang to the Revd. Richard Atherton Rawstorne, Rector of Croston, Lancs., 1915–47.

Given by the Revd. R. A. Rawstorne, 1963.

97 ff.

1804–11. CORRESPONDENCE OF THE REVD. C. P. GOLIGHTLY

Correspondence of the Revd. Charles Pourtales Golightly (1807–85), mainly concerning opposition to the Tractarian Movement in the university and diocese of Oxford. The correspondence also relates to Woodard

Schools, *Essays and Reviews*, charges of heresy against Benjamin Jowett, the appointment of Frederick Temple to the see of Exeter and A. P. Stanley's appointment as Select Preacher. The names of the writers will be found in the index. See also MS. 1946, ff. 9–34^{v}.

Given by Major F. Kennedy, 1920.

1804 Acworth–Burgon. 204 ff.
1805 Cameron–Fremantle. 296 ff.
1806 Garbett–Greene. 337 ff.
1807 Guillemard–Hume. 260 ff.
1808 Jeune–Pusey. 251 ff.
1809 Ranking–Thirlwall. 161 ff.
1810 Trower. 300 ff.
1811 Tucker–Wynter. The following miscellaneous papers are also included in this volume:

advice for her son by Adelgonda Margarett Dodd, wife of the Revd. Richard Dodd, *c.* 1768 (ff. 253^{v}–256); informal will of the same, 1768 (f. 258); notes by Golightly on the Martyrs' Memorial at Oxford (f. 260); fragments of an account by Golightly on the early years of the Oxford Movement (ff. 261–4); newspaper cuttings (ff. 265–6); *To the Church-Wardens of the Diocese of Oxford*, [1867] (ff. 267–8); print published by T. Shrimpton of leading churchmen, with key (f. 269); print of J. H. Newman, 1841 (f. 270).

270 ff.

1812. MISCELLANEOUS LETTERS AND PAPERS

Guardbook containing miscellaneous letters and papers, mainly ecclesiastical, 1820–1921. They are as follows:

Correspondence between Archbishop Howley and Lord John Russell concerning the Tithe Act, Pluralities and Residence Bill, church rates, the Report of the Commission on Cathedral and Collegiate Churches, etc., 1834–46 (ff. 1–33^{v}).
Purchased, 1963.

Miscellaneous letters of Archbishops of Canterbury and of Bishops of London, 1820–65. The names of the writers will be found in the index (ff. 34–53).
Purchased, 1958.

Letter from Leonard Harding Squire, Curate of St. Paul, Maidstone, to Lucy Tait, daughter of Archbishop Tait, 1880, about the customary rent of Addington Park (ff. 54–8).

Letter from Sir Thomas Barlow, 1st Bt., to his brother John Barlow, 1921, containing reminiscences of the Benson family (ff. 59–63^{v}).
Given by Miss Helen Barlow, 1964.

Letters from Henry John Todd, Rector of Coulsdon, Lambeth Librarian, to John William Whittaker, Fellow of St. John's College, Cambridge,

[1812 *cont.***]**

1820, about the translators of the Authorized Version of the Bible (ff. 64–9).

Letter from the Revd. Edward Irving, founder of the Catholic Apostolic Church [Irvingites], to C. E. H. Orpen, M.D., 1831, on faith healing (ff. 70–1).
Given by Augustus Theodore Wirgman, Rector of St. Mary, Port Elizabeth, South Africa, 1893.

Letter from John Henry Newman, Fellow of Oriel College, Oxford, to [William] Palmer, [Fellow of Magdalen College, Oxford], 1840, on the political situation between Russia and Turkey (ff. 72–3).
Given by the Earl of Selborne, 1964.

Letters from Arthur Penrhyn Stanley, Dean of Westminster, to Frederic William Farrar, Canon of Westminster, (1895) Dean of Canterbury, 1861–81, and (f. 102) a note by Farrar of Stanley's last words (ff. 74–102^{v}).
Purchased, 1963.

Correspondence of John Wordsworth, Bishop of Salisbury, about the trial of Edward King, Bishop of Lincoln, the consecration of Thomas Lancaster, Archbishop of Armagh, etc., 1889–93. The names of the writers will be found in the index (ff. 103–21).
Removed from MS. 1396.

Letters from Prime Ministers offering episcopal appointments, 1867–96: the Earl of Derby to George Augustus Selwyn, Bishop of New Zealand, 1867, offering the see of Lichfield (f. 122); Benjamin Disraeli to William Connor Magee, Dean of Cork, (1890) Archbishop of York, 1868, offering Peterborough (f. 123); W. E. Gladstone to James Fraser, Rector of Ufton Nervet, 1870, offering Manchester (f. 124); the same to Edward White Benson, Bishop of Truro, 1882, offering Canterbury (f. 125): the same to William Stubbs, Regius Professor of Ecclesiastical History, Oxford, (1889) Bishop of Oxford, 1884, offering Chester (f. 126); the Marquess of Salisbury to the same, 1888, offering Oxford (f. 127); the same to William Dalrymple Maclagan, Bishop of Lichfield, 1891, offering York (f. 128); the same to Mandell Creighton, Bishop of Peterborough, 1896, offering London (f. 129); the Earl of Rosebery to John Percival, headmaster of Rugby, 1895, offering Hereford (f. 130). *Typescript copies* (ff. 122–30).

Correspondence of George Ridding, Bishop of Southwell, about the work of the Association for the Furtherance of Christianity in Egypt, 1898–9. The names of the writers will be found in the index. Also included are *Report of Journey to Jerusalem and Cyprus, October and November*, 1898, by Arthur Cayley Headlam, (1923) Bishop of Gloucester, for the Eastern Church Association (ff. 159–71); extract from the *Church Missionary Intelligencer*, 1898 (f. 173); appeal for funds to erect a school and church at Assouan, [1898] (f. 174) (ff. 131–74).
Given by Dame Laura Ridding, n.d.

Correspondence between Randall Thomas Davidson, Bishop of Rochester, (1903) Archbishop of Canterbury, and Thomas Kelly Cheyne, Oriel Professor of Interpretation of Holy Scripture, Oxford, Canon of Rochester, concerning criticisms of the latter's sermons in Rochester Cathedral on the Old Testament, 1891–2, including (ff. 207–215ᵛ) letters from Samuel Reynolds Hole, Dean of Rochester, to the Bishop of Rochester (ff. 175–215ᵛ).

Account of the opening of the tomb of Hubert Walter, Archbishop of Canterbury, by J. Brigstocke Sheppard, LL.D., with two letters from Robert Payne Smith, Dean of Canterbury, to Archbishop Benson, 1888 (ff. 216–223ᵛ).

Letter from Sydney Smirke, architect, to J. Huggins, 1860, apparently about the appointment of a curator of the Soane Museum (ff. 224–5).

Papers of Piers Calverley Claughton, Bishop of Colombo, as a pupil and subsequently Governor of Repton School, 1841–85. They include a letter from W. B. Steath, master at Repton, 1841 (f. 226); letter from the Revd. Henry Robert Huckin, headmaster of Repton, 1874 (f. 228). Also the following printed papers: form of service for tercentenary celebrations, 1857 (f. 229); verses, prize poems, and list of prizes, 1869 (ff. 230–46); miscellaneous school lists, 1834–6, 1869, 1884–5 (ff. 247–84); lists of cricket matches, 1885–6 (ff. 285–8); programme for speech day, 1881 (ff. 289–90). Also copies of names carved on tables in hall (ff. 291–2). Election leaflet of George Nathaniel Curzon, (1921) 1st Marquess Curzon of Kedleston, [1885]. *Printed* (f. 293). Appeal for funds for restoration of St. Wystan's church, Repton, 1938. *Printed* (ff. 294–5) (ff. 226–95).
Given by Alan O. Claughton, n.d.

Sale catalogue of property of E. B. Vigurs, 1849. It includes stained glass removed from Lambeth Palace by Archbishop Moore in 1803. *Printed* (ff. 296–300ᵛ).

Prospectus for *Punch, or The London Charivari*, [1841]. *Printed* (ff. 301–302ᵛ).

302 ff.

1813. SERMON

Sermon on Philippians 2, v. 5, by Frederick Denison Maurice, later Professor of Moral Philosophy, Cambridge, 1865.

Given by John Victor Macmillan, Chaplain to the Archbishop of Canterbury, (1934) Bishop of Guildford, 1912.

i+25 ff.

1814–16. SERMONS

Sermons by [William Skinner, Vicar of Sunbury, Middx. (1676–1717)].

1814: Sermons preached, 1686–98, and (ff .30–33^{v}) a list of texts and places at which sermons were preached, 1690–1716.

Covers stamped 'W.S.' and on the inside of the back cover the signature 'Gulielmus Skynner'. Some leaves have been torn out.

38 ff.

1815: Sermons, 1696–1704. All preached several times up to 1716.

220 ff.

1816: Sermons, 1705–10. Most preached several times up to 1711.

154 ff.

1817. ACCOUNTS OF STUDENTS AT OXFORD UNIVERSITY, ETC.

Notebook bound in vellum containing accounts in the hand of William Skinner, Rector of Didmarton, son of William Skinner, Vicar of Sunbury [q.v.], mainly for the residence of himself and his sons at Oxford University, 1711–52.

Accounts of William Skinner, (1725) Rector of Didmarton, at Oriel College, Oxford, 1711–23 (pp. 1–31, 196–8).

Accounts of his son William Skinner, (1769) Prebendary of Hereford, at Pembroke College, Oxford, 1744–51 (pp. 32–5).

Accounts of his son Richard Skinner, — Rector of Bassingham, at Corpus Christi College, Oxford, 1745–52 (pp. 39–45).

Accounts of his son Benjamin Skinner, (1766) Rector of Purley, and Rector of the second portion of Waddesdon, at Pembroke College, Oxford, 1748–52 (pp. 49–50).

Accounts of his nephew Robert Eden, 1720–1 (pp. 140–1).

Accounts of William Skinner, the elder, 1722–35 (pp. 142–65).

List of books bought by the same, 1711–54 (pp. 190–5, 199–206). Also a catalogue of his library, 1717 (pp. 208–25); extract from his will (p. 228); inventory of his goods (p. 229).

ii+235 pp.

1818. ACCOUNTS OF THE REVD. BENJAMIN SKINNER

Accounts [of the Revd. Benjamin Skinner, Rector of Purley and Rector of the second portion of Waddesdon rectory], 1770–2.

9 pp.

1819. REGISTER OF ATTENDANCE AT LECTURES

Register of attendance by members of Oxford University at lectures perhaps by John Randolph, Regius Professor of Divinity, (1809) Bishop of London, 1784–9.

30 ff.

1820. ACCOUNTS

Notebook and accounts of John Edridge, of Aspenden, Herts., yeoman, 1666–90. Also accounts of his son John, 1692–1703, and a few miscellaneous accounts, 1724 and 1759.

71 ff.

1821. HISTORY OF SALTWOOD PARISH CHURCH, KENT

History of the parish church of St. Peter and St. Paul, Saltwood, Kent, by Oliver G. Villiers, 1963. Illustrated with photographs and drawings.

Given by the author, 1963.

v+50 ff.

1822–4. WORDSWORTH CORRESPONDENCE

Correspondence of Christopher Wordsworth (1774–1846), Master of Trinity College, Cambridge, and of his sons Charles Wordsworth (1806–92), Bishop of St. Andrews, John Wordsworth (1805–39), Fellow of Trinity College, Cambridge, and Christopher Wordsworth (1807–85), subsequently Bishop of Lincoln. Some of the correspondence has been used in Charles Wordsworth, *Annals of my early life, 1806–1846*, 1891, and *Annals of my life, 1847–1856*, 1893. The names of the writers will be found in the index.

Purchased, 1964.

1822. WORDSWORTH CORRESPONDENCE

Correspondence of Christopher Wordsworth, Master of Trinity College, Cambridge, 1803–45.

327 ff.

1823. WORDSWORTH CORRESPONDENCE

Correspondence of Charles Wordsworth, Bishop of St. Andrews, 1825–91 (Anderdon–Manning).

281 ff.

1824. WORDSWORTH CORRESPONDENCE

Correspondence of Charles Wordsworth, Bishop of St. Andrews, 1831–91 (Merivale–Wright) (ff. 1–173).

[1824 *cont.*]

Miscellaneous letters: William Ewart Gladstone to Sir Roundell Palmer, (1882) 1st Earl of Selborne, 1870 (f. 174); the same to the Revd. John Wood Warter, Vicar of Heene with West Tarring and Durrington, 1847. *Copy* (ff. 176–177^{v}); George Moberly, headmaster of Winchester College, (1869) Bishop of Salisbury, to Edward Twisleton, barrister, 1835 (ff. 178–179^{v}).

Letters testimonial to the Warden and Fellows of Winchester College commending Charles Wordsworth for the post of second master, 1835 (ff. 180–92).

Correspondence of John Wordsworth, Fellow of Trinity College, Cambridge, 18[25–39] (ff. 193–208).

Correspondence of Christopher Wordsworth, Bishop of Lincoln, 1836–74 (ff. 209–33).

233 ff.

1825–7. SERMONS

Sermons [by William Skinner, Rector of Didmarton, Glos.], with the dates and places in Gloucestershire, Wiltshire, and South Wales, etc., at which they were preached, 1725–53. Some of the sermons appear also to have been preached by [his son, Benjamin Skinner, Rector of Purley, 1768–76].

i+181 ff.; i+231 ff.; i+242 ff.

1828–9. SERMONS

Sermons [by Benjamin Skinner, Rector of Purley, Berks.], with the dates and places in Berkshire, Buckinghamshire, and Oxfordshire, etc., at which they were preached, 1749–76.

i+232 ff.; i+198 ff.

1830. FASTI CICESTRENSES

'Fasti Cicestrenses. A copy of the notebook of Mackenzie Walcott, sometime Precentor of Chichester, containing a list of Dignitaries, Canons and Prebendaries of Chichester Cathedral to the year 1714', transcribed with an introduction by W. D. Peckham, 1940. Index nominum.

Given by W. D. Peckham, 1945.

Typescript copy. x+115 ff.

1831. DIOCESE OF CHICHESTER

A calendar of institutions and collations for the diocese of Chichester by W. D. Peckham, entitled, 'A Calendar of the Register of Richard Fitzjames (1504–1506), of the entries sede vacante in the Provincial Register [of Archbishop Warham], and of part of the Register of Robert Sherburne (1508–1536), Bishops of Chichester.' Index nominum.

Water-stained and slightly scorched, perhaps when the library was bombed in 1941.

Given by W. D. Peckham, n.d.

Typescript copy. iii+81 ff.

1832–3. SERMONS

Sermons by William Sherlock, Dean of St. Paul's and Master of the Temple, preached at the Temple and elsewhere in London and at Therfield, Herts., 1687–1705. The sermon on 2 Timothy 2: vv. 1–2 (MS. 1833, ff. 1–22) is printed in *Sermons preached upon several occasions*, 1755, i, 353–77.

Purchased, 1964.

ii+195 ff.; i+186 ff.

1834. MISCELLANEOUS LETTERS AND PAPERS, 1572–1802

Miscellaneous letters and papers, 1572–1802.

Letter from Archbishop Parker to John Boys, steward of the liberties of Canterbury, 5 December [1572], requiring the court of the liberties to be held yearly. *Seal* (f. 1).

Purchased, 1963.

Will of Edward Coker, of London, grocer. Proved in the Prerogative Court of Canterbury, 9 June 1631. *Copy* (f. 2).

Order of the Commissioners for Ejecting Scandalous Ministers in the Northern Counties that the Triers to the Commissioners in Cumberland and Westmorland pay the salary of John Fawcett, their registrar, 27 January 1658 (f. 4).

Petition of the churchwardens and overseers of St. Margaret's, Westminster, to — Fairfax for relief of the poor, 17th century (f. 6).

Petition of James Harmon, Esq., only son of the late Sir William Harmon, to the Lord Treasurer for the next vacancy for a landwaiter's place (f. 8).

Enclosing:

Petition from the same to the King setting out his sufferings during the Civil War, and an order of the Privy Council granting him a place as landwaiter, 1673. *Copy* (ff. 8–11).

Given by F. C. Eeles, 1954.

Bond of John May of Worting, Hants, yeoman, to Christopher May of Basing, yeoman, in £100, 30 January 1677 (f. 12).

[1834 *cont.***]**

Letters from Henry Compton, Bishop of London, [1677–90], as follows:
To Sir William Coventry, secretary to the Duke of York, 2 October [1677], asking for the Chancellorship of St. David's for [Andrew] Saull (f. 13).

To Sir Robert Southwell, 7 November [1687], on the removal of his son from the university and objections to education abroad (f. 15).

To the Earl of Danby, 2 December [1688], describing the removal of Princess Anne to Nottingham, a conference between James II, the Marquess of Halifax, and others, and the resolve of the City of London to welcome the Prince of Orange (f. 17).

To Sir Robert Southwell, 14 July [1690], on the battle of the Boyne (f. 19).

To [Henry] Savile, [envoy in Paris], 8 February [1682], apparently on the treatment of foreign Protestant refugees (f. 21).

To —, n.y., on domestic matters (f. 23).
ff. 13–23).

Purchased, 1964.

Advertisement for a four-day coach service between London and York, 1678. *Copy* (f. 24).

Francis Bugg, former Quaker, [to Archbishop Sancroft], 12 August [1680], concerning the 'mallis of the Leaders of the Quakers', and mentioning George Keith and George Whitehead (f. 25).

John Paterson, Bishop of Edinburgh, to the Earl of Winton, 13 June 1682, about the patronage of Tranent (f. 26).

Royal licence to Obadiah Walker and his assigns to print and sell named books for 21 years, May 1686. *Copy* (f. 28).

Petition of Archbishop Sancroft and 'divers of the suffragan Bishops' to James II, refusing to publish the Declaration for liberty of conscience in the churches, [18 May 1688]. *Copy*. Printed D'Oyly, *Life of Sancroft*, i, 262–4 (f. 29).

Also the draft of part of an Act of Parliament for exercising the dispensing power in favour of Dissenters, temp. Chas. II (ff. 31–3).

Also a protest against a resolution of the House of Lords that the Church was not in danger, 6 December 1705. *Two copies*. Printed *Journals of the House of Lords*, xviii, 43–4 (ff. 34–36v) (ff. 29–36).

Given by the British Records Association (deposit 206).

Public letter by James II, from Rochester, 22 December 1688. *Copy. Mutilated*. Printed Echard, *History of England*, ed. 1720, 1134 (f. 38).

Letter from Elizabeth Porteen to 'Mr. Pelcome, His Grace the Archbishop of Canterbury's Gentleman', 6 September 1705, about a dispute over her widow's pension (ff. 40–1).

Letter from David Baillie, prisoner in Newgate, to Archbishop Tenison, 6 April 1708, asking him to intercede for him (f. 42).

Letter from John Bettesworth, Principal Official of the Court of Arches, [to Archbishop Wake], 28 November 1727, about disputed jurisdiction on the appointment of William Folkes to be Apparitor of the consistory court of Canterbury, joint registrar and actuary of the Court of Arches (ff. 44–45^{v}).

Will of Robert Eden, of the parish of St. Mary de Crypt, Gloucester, 1736 (f. 46).

Removed from MS. 1814.

'Inventory and schedule of the books and papers belonging to the Commissioners for Building 50 New Churches, and which are deposited by order of the said Commissioners in his Grace the Lord Archbishop's Palace at Lambeth by Edward Sleech, agent to the said Commissioners, 10th February 1759' (ff. 48–50^{v}).

Note by Archbishop Secker of the number of houses at Bersted, East Lavant, Pagham, Slindon, and Tangmere, Sussex (f. 52).

Circular letter from the Society of Antiquaries addressed to Andrew Coltee Ducarel concerning an edition of Domesday Book, 8 December 1757. *Printed* (f. 53).
Also a report from the President and Council of the said society to the Commissioners of the Treasury submitting estimates of the cost of a facsimile of Domesday Book, 23 January 1769. *Copy* (ff. 55–6).

Names and places of abode of the constables, beadle, engine keepers, and turncocks, belonging to Castle-Baynard Ward, 1781 (ff. 57–9).

'A Sermon preached in the church of Alnwick on Sunday the 13th day of February 1785, after the funeral of the Revd. Thomas Knipe, by Percival Stockdale' (ff. 60–72^{v}).

Letter from Samuel Peters, formerly Anglican minister in Connecticut, to Arthur Petrie, Bishop of Moray, 20 February 1786, describing the affairs of the American Episcopal Church. *Copy* (f. 73).

Letter from Edmund Malone, Shakespearian scholar, [to Archbishop Moore], 7 July 1797, asking for permission to study the Bacon and Carew manuscripts at Lambeth (f. 74).

Statement of the affairs of the Society of Patrons of the Anniversary of the Charity-Schools, addressed to [John] Nichols, 15 April 1802. *Printed* (f. 75).

Order regulating wearing gowns by the sheriffs of London, 18th century (f. 77).

An account of a system of shorthand, entitled 'La Plume Volante or the Art of Short Hand', 18th century (ff. 78–82^{v}).

87 ff.

1835. DIARY OF THOMAS LEGH CLAUGHTON, BISHOP OF ST. ALBANS

Diary of Thomas Legh Claughton (1808–92), Bishop of St. Albans, kept at irregular intervals while Fellow of Trinity College, Oxford, and then as Vicar of Kidderminster, 1837–63, with (f. 96) a few entries for 1887.

Given by Francis Steer, 1964.

v+218 ff., of which ff. 97–218 are blank.

1836. DIGEST OF ACT OF PARLIAMENT

'Digested abstract of an Act 3 & 4 Victoria Ch.: 113 (11th August 1840), intituled "An Act to carry into effect with certain modifications the fourth Report of the Commissioners of Ecclesiastical duties and revenues", arranged in 13 parts.' The Act implemented recommendations made by the Ecclesiastical Commissioners in their Fourth Report, dated 24 June 1836, concerning cathedrals and collegiate churches.

Also included are a copy of the Act 6 & 7 Will. IV, cap. 77, establishing the Commissioners, and of the Act 3 & 4 Vict., cap. 113.

On p. i the following inscription 'John Hassard [secretary to A. C. Tait, Bishop of London] from Christopher Hodgson [Secretary and Treasurer to Queen Anne's Bounty], March 1857.'

ii+204 pp.

1837. MISCELLANEOUS PAPERS

Miscellaneous papers as follows:

Instrument of Thomas Henricke, Vicar-General of the Bishop of London, on appeal by Thomas Newberye of Hornchurch from the court of the Archdeacon of Essex, 6 February 1562. *English draft* (ff. 1–2).

Given by Miss W. Myers, 1961.

Contemporary copy, but incomplete, of the will of John Caius, Doctor in Physick, of the parish of St. Bartholomew the Less, London, 14 June 1573. The sections of the will have been numbered in red chalk (query: by Archbishop Parker). The will is printed in *Works of John Caius*, ed. E. S. Roberts, 1912, 73–8 (ff. 3–4).

Inquisition by order of Cromwell 'for the unitinge of parishes etc.' of parishes in Shropshire in the Hundreds of Bradford North and South, Pimhill, Oswestry, Ford, Condover.

The parishes mentioned are:

Whitchurch (f. 5); Ightfield (f. 5); Prees (f. 5); Wem (f. 6); Shawbury (f. 7); Stanton-upon-Hine-Heath (f. 7); Lee Brockhurst (f. 7); Moreton Corbet (f. 7); Wrockwardine (f. 8); Rodington (f. 8); Ercall Magna (f. 8); Waters Upton (f. 8); Leighton (f. 8); Eaton Constantine (f. 9); Buildwas (f. 9); Dawley (f. 9); Stirchley (f. 9); Wroxeter (f. 9); Uppington (f. 9); Wellington (f. 9); Wombridge (f. 10); Preston (f. 10); Eyton (f. 10); Upton Magna and Withington (f. 10); Uffington (f. 10); Atcham (f. 10);

Edgmond (f. 10); Chetwynd (f. 10); Lilleshall (f. 11); Longdon-upon-Tern (f. 11); Newport (f. 11); Longford (f. 11); Bolas (f. 11); Kinnersley (f. 11); Drayton in Hayles (f. 11); Stoke-upon-Tern (f. 11); Hodnet (f. 11); Childs Ercall (f. 11); Cheswardine (f. 11); [Preston-on-the-Weald Moors] (f. 12); Norton in Hales (f. 12); Adderley (f. 12); Ellesmere (f. 12); Cockshutt and Crosemere (f. 12); Hampton (f. 12); Dudleston (f. 13); Hordley (f. 13); Loppington (f. 13); Ness (f. 14); Shrawardine (f. 14); Montford (f. 14); Myddle (f. 14); Fitz (f. 14); Petton (f. 15); Baschurch (f. 15); Bicton (f. 15); Whittington (f. 16); Halston (f. 16); Ruyton of the Eleven Towns (f. 16); West Felton (f. 16); Hordley (f. 16); Melverley (f. 16); Kinnerley (f. 17); Knockin (f. 17); Llanymynech (f. 17); Blodwell (f. 17); Oswestry (f. 18); Selattyn (f. 18); St. Martin's (f. 19); Pontesbury (f. 19); Westbury (f. 19); Habberley (f. 20); Alberbury (f. 20); Ford (f. 20); Cardeston (f. 20); Condover (f. 21); Frodesley (f. 21); Longnor (f. 21); Leebotwood (f. 21); Smethcott (f. 21); Woolstaston (f. 21); Stapleton (f. 21); Pulverbatch (f. 21); Berrington (f. 21); Pitchford (f. 22); Acton Burnell (f. 22); Ruckley and Langley (f. 22); Kenley (f. 22); Church Preen (f. 22); Harley (f. 22); Cound (f. 22); Cressage (f. 22); Sutton (f. 23); Shrewsbury (f. 24).

Endorsed, 'This is a type-written copy of the transcription made by Rev. N. E. Evans of a 1655 Inquisition found at Cadoxton-juxta-Neath, Glam., by Mr. Glen A. Taylor, F.S.A., Neath, Glam.' (ff. 5–25).

Given by the Revd. C. Jenkins, 1959.

Treaty of Breda. *Publication of the Peace between England and the United Netherlands*, August 1667. Printed terms of the treaty with seals and signatures of the parties (f. 26).

Petition of the Dean and Chapter of Chichester to Archbishop Wake concerning disputed election of Proctors to Convocation, 1728. *Seal* (f. 27).

Citation to attend visitation by George Newell, Commissary of the Peculiar and exempt jurisdiction of the manor of Groby, Leics., March 1729 (f. 29).

Given by the British Records Association (deposit 125). See also MS. 1488.

Petition by residents of Lambeth to Archbishop Herring for taking down the wall of the Archbishop's laundry for widening Church Street, July 1752 (f. 30).

Diploma of the Hamburg Patriotic Society for the Encouragement of the Liberal and Useful Arts to Joshua Watson, Secretary of the Westminster Association, 1814 (f. 31).

Given by A. B. Webster, 1954.

Letter from Frederick Holmes, Professor at Bishop's College, Calcutta, to Joshua Watson, 1826, describing the layout and progress of the college. Partly printed in A. B. Webster, *Joshua Watson*, 1954, 157–8 (ff. 32–33^v).

Given by A. B. Webster, 1954.

[1837 *cont.***]**

Proofs of minutes of committees on Church Unity appointed by the Lambeth Conference, 1897 (ff. 34^v–40).

Brass rubbing of part of a memorial to the Revd. John Thomas, sometime Lambeth Librarian, at All Hallows-by-the-Tower, London, 19th century (f. 41).

Drawings of furniture in Lambeth Palace [by L. B. Peircey, 'publicity artist'], made for publication in the *Furniture Record*, August 1921 (ff. 42–6).

Given by A. J. Clements, 1963.

Drawing by Spy [Leslie Ward] of Cosmo Gordon Lang, Bishop of Stepney, and (1928) Archbishop of Canterbury (f. 47).

Given by the Revd. A. C. Don, 1959.

Photographs of: (f. 48) Archbishop Benson; (f. 49) Archbishop Fisher; (f. 50) Miron Cristea, Patriarch of Roumania, 1936; (f. 51) Joint Theological Commission for discussions with the Orthodox Church proposed by the Lambeth Conference, 1930. With key. Given by the Revd. A. C. Don, 1959 (ff. 52–5); Lambeth Palace and parish, 1883 viz. (f. 52) the Great Hall, Lambeth Palace; (f. 53) Morton's Tower from inside Lambeth Palace; (f. 54) Lollards Tower and the chapel of Lambeth Palace; (f. 55) old house in Palace Yard, Lambeth. Given by Miss Annie Cockerell, 1961; (f. 56) boys of Westminster School, 1893 (ff. 48–56).

56 ff.

1838–45. LONGLEY PAPERS

Papers of Archbishop Longley and other members of the Longley family, 18th century–1892.

Given by Gregory Rowcliffe & Co., 1964.

1838. LONGLEY PAPERS

Letters from Archbishop Longley to his son Henry Longley, 1848–64.

129 ff.

1839. LONGLEY PAPERS

Letters from the same to the same, 1865–8.

134 ff.

1840. LONGLEY PAPERS

Letters from the same to his sister Catharine Longley, 1858–67.

89 ff.

1841. LONGLEY PAPERS

Miscellaneous letters and papers, 1804–68.

Family letters.

Letters from Archbishop Longley to his wife, Caroline Sophia Longley, [1853] (ff. 1–47).

Letters from Elizabeth Longley, wife of John Longley, Recorder of Rochester, to her daughter Catharine, [1804] (ff. 48–51ᵛ).

Letter from the same to her daughter Martha, [184] (ff. 52–4).

Letter from Anna Maria Lloyd, wife of John W. Lloyd, Commissioner of Chatham Dockyard, to her mother Elizabeth Longley, [1836] (ff. 55–56ᵛ).

Letter from Catharine Longley to her sister Martha Longley, 1817 (ff. 57–61ᵛ).

Letter from Rosamond Longley to her sister Catharine Longley, 1839 (ff. 62–63ᵛ).

Letters from the same to her sister Martha Longley, 19th century (ff. 64–68ᵛ).

Miscellaneous papers of Archbishop Longley.

Letters from Robert Gray, Bishop of Capetown, to Archbishop Longley, 1868 (ff. 69–72); letter from Earl Grey to the same, 1859 (ff. 73–5); verses by J[ames] A[rthur] Wilson, entitled 'on leaving Westminster School', 1812 (ff. 76–77ᵛ); request 'veniam abeundi' by John Matthews, undergraduate at Christ Church, Oxford (f. 78); leaflet *To restore the apparently drowned* (f. 80); proceedings at the enthroning of Archbishop Longley, 1862 (ff. 81–2); list of curates seeking preferment (ff. 83–84ᵛ); proofs of newspaper article on the Lambeth Conference, 1867 (ff. 85ᵛ–86); list of Bishops attending the Lambeth Conference, 1867. *Printed* (ff. 87–8); agenda and arrangements for the Lambeth Conference, 1867. *Printed* (ff. 89–90); abstract by Longley of income and expenditure for 1868 (f. 91); newspaper cuttings about memorials to Archbishop Longley (f. 92) (ff. 69–92).

Biographical account of Archbishop Longley for the years 1794–1829 by his son Henry Longley. Copy of MS. 1842. *Typescript* (ff. 93–155).

155 ff.

1842. LONGLEY PAPERS

Biographical account of Archbishop Longley for the years 1794–1829, written by his son Henry Longley in 1884. See also MS. 1841, ff. 93–155.

i+187 pp., of which pp. 128–87 are blank.

1843. LONGLEY PAPERS

Genealogical collections for the Longley family, 18th–19th centuries.

31 ff.

1844. LONGLEY PAPERS

Papers of Sir Henry Longley, son of Archbishop Longley, 1834–92.

They comprise: letter from Henry Longley to his sister Caroline Longley, 1853 (ff. 1–4); letter from the same to his sister Mary Longley, 1853 (ff. 5–7); correspondence between the same and his brother George Longley, 1853–9 (ff. 8–13), and death certificate of George Longley (f. 14), and letters of administration for the estate of the same, 1892 (f. 15); certificate of baptism of Henry Longley, 1834 (f. 16); summons of Longley to the bar of Lincoln's Inn, 1860. *Copy* (f. 17); licence for the marriage of Longley and Miss Diana Eliza Davenport, 1861 (f. 18); orders of the Poor Law Board concerning the appointment of Longley as Legal Inspector, 1870. *Printed* (ff. 20–1); appointment of the same as inspector for the Local Government Board, 1872 (f. 22); appointment of the same as Third Charity Commissioner, 1874 (f. 24); appointment of the same as Second Charity Commissioner, 1879 (f. 26); appointment of the same as Chief Charity Commissioner, 1885 (f. 28); appointment of the same to be C.B., 1887 (f. 30); appointment of the same to be K.C.B., 1889 (f. 32); account by Henry Longley of the administration of the Poor Law in New York and Boston, U.S.A., 1872. *Copy* (ff. 34–104); newspaper cuttings about Longley's *Report to the Local Government Board on Poor-Law Administration*, 1874 (ff. 106–9).

109 ff.

1845. LONGLEY PAPERS

Gamebook of Sir Henry Longley, 1852–92.

147 ff.

1846. HOXTON CHURCH

Wash drawing by Francis Edwards (1784–1857), architect, of the church of St. John the Baptist, Hoxton, London, designed by him for the Commissioners for Building New Churches, 1825. The drawing depicts the west and south elevations. It is dedicated to Archbishop Howley.

Some damage by damp. Size 16 × 20 inches.

1847–60. PAPERS OF THE BISHOP OF FULHAM

Papers of the Bishop of Fulham concerning English Churches in Europe. Apart from the papers relating to the church at Danzig, which cover the period 1706–1939, all other papers date from the 20th century.

1847. BISHOP OF FULHAM PAPERS

Danzig. 'A Register of the marriages and baptisms which have happened from the year of Our Lord 1706 in the English Church (or chapel) in Dantzigk, built for the use of those of the nation of Great Britain who reside there', 1706–1811 (ff. 1–15). Also lists of communicants compiled annually at Easter, Whit-Sunday, and Christmas, 1723–1806 (ff. 33–72).

A copy by William Pewson, delivered to Alexander Gibson, Consul in Danzig, 5 April 1817.

iii+87 ff.

1848. BISHOP OF FULHAM PAPERS

Danzig. Articles of an association for the relief of British residents in Danzig, consisting of:

Revised statutes of a corporation for the maintenance and relief of Scottish residents, 1708. With German translation. Signed by the members of the corporation (ff. 1–4^v^).

Act of a convention of the English and Scottish corporations for the relief of their respective residents uniting their resources, 1711. With German translation. Signatures of members of the joint corporation, with in some cases dates and places of death, to 1883 (ff. 6–8^v^).

11+44 ff.

1849. BISHOP OF FULHAM PAPERS

Danzig. 'Statute of the British Poor and Chapel Funds in Dantzic,' 6 April 1871.

i+43 ff., of which ff. 8–43 are blank.

1850. BISHOP OF FULHAM PAPERS

Danzig. Historical notes on the English church by William Pewson, entitled, 'History of the British Chapel established according to the rites and ceremonies of the Church of England at Danzig, from its establishment in 1707 to 1807, when it closed on account of a French army besieging the garrison; more particularly since the re-establishment thereof on Whit Sunday 1822.'

The contents are:

Chronological lists of services on Sundays and holidays, with the psalms sung, the numbers of the congregation and of communicants, and a column of observations, 1822–44 (pp. 1–13).

Appendix containing:

Extracts from E. Praetorius, *History of the Danzig clergy*, with a list of the clergy, 1692–1898 (p. 38).

Printed card for reopening the chapel, 26 May 1822. Extract from letter from the Chief President of Danzig to Alexander Gibson, British Consul, 6 November 1822, about the right of the English clergy to officiate (p. 39).

Note by Kuffs, Counsellor of Police, requiring discontinuance of notice of the English church in *Intelligenz-Blatt*, 23 April 1823 (p. 41).

[1850 *cont.*]

Letter from the churchwardens [to the chaplain], 1 July 1823, concerning lack of funds for the chapel. *Copy.* Seal of the chapel (p. 42).

Account of obtaining authority for a baptism, 1823 (pp. 43–4).

Letter from the churchwardens to the Revd. Julius Tucker, 31 December 1823, discontinuing his appointment as chaplain owing to lack of funds. *Copy* (p. 45).

The same to the same, 25 February 1824, on the undesirability of appointing a successor. *Copy* (p. 46).

Account of windows and new panes, [1835] (p. 46).

Hymn sheet, [1838]. *Printed* (pp. 47–9).

Advertisement of divine worship in *Intelligenz-Blatt*, 1 August 1844 (p. 50).

xiii+63 pp.

1851. BISHOP OF FULHAM PAPERS

Danzig. Account book of the Offertory Fund, 1923–35, and of the Stipend Fund, 1923–32, of the English church.

i+72 ff.

1852. BISHOP OF FULHAM PAPERS

Danzig. Account book of the Special Fund, 1929–39, and of the Stipend Fund, 1933–9, of the English church.

i+47 ff.

1853. BISHOP OF FULHAM PAPERS

Danzig. Receipts and other documents relating to payments from the Offertory Fund, 1878–1939, including (ff. 311–16) an account of the various funds at the disposal of the English church.

331 ff.

1854. BISHOP OF FULHAM PAPERS

Danzig. Bank statements and vouchers for the Stipend Fund of the English church, 1923–39.

130 ff.

1855. BISHOP OF FULHAM PAPERS

Danzig. Correspondence of the churchwardens of the English church with English residents at Danzig concerning payments to the Stipend Fund, with some vouchers and bank statements, 1923–39.

265 ff.

1856. BISHOP OF FULHAM PAPERS

Danzig. Miscellaneous vouchers for repairs and maintenance of the English church, 1929–39.

159 ff.

1857. BISHOP OF FULHAM PAPERS

Danzig. Papers concerning the English church, 1706–1939.

A. Miscellaneous papers, including: agreement of subscribers for erecting the English church at Danzig, with the signatures of the subscribers and the amounts subscribed, 29 March 1706 (ff. 1–2^{v}); agreement of the English community at Danzig to purchase a house and establish a rotation in the appointment of ministers. Signed and sealed by John Robinson, Envoy Extraordinary, 19 October 1706 (f. 3); correspondence of the Revd. H. Lawrence, minister at Danzig, with J. S. Stoddart, concerning taking up residence, 1879 (ff. 6–11); expenses of the church, 1862–80 (ff. 18–20); papers concerning the claim of the English church to exemption from taxation, *c.* 1930 (ff. 29–34).

B. Correspondence and papers of C. Jeffrey and J. Bligh, churchwardens, 1928–39, mainly concerning the finances of the English church. Also included are an account of the history of the church by Mrs. Martha Dunsby, wife of the Revd. F. S. N. Dunsby, minister at Danzig, [1932]. *German. Printed* (ff. 57–62^{v}); inventory of the property of the church, [1936] (ff. 148–9); list of some books belonging to the church library, [1936] (f. 157); photographs of an antique table, of the royal arms, and of the pulpit in the English church, [1936] (ff. 158–60).

C. Minutes of general meetings of the English church community at Danzig, 1935–7 (193–209).

209 ff.

1858. BISHOP OF FULHAM PAPERS

France. Dinan. Record compiled by the Revd. G. P. Irby, incumbent of Christ Church, Dinan, of services, parish and vestry meetings, etc., 1903–9. At f. 114 a note of marriage banns, 1905, and at f. 115 the dimensions of the church.

115 ff.

1859. BISHOP OF FULHAM PAPERS

Historical notes and photographs of English churches in Europe, 20th century.

A. Brussels. List of chaplains at the church of the Augustines and the Chapel Royal, 1815–73. *Printed* (f. 1).

Biarritz. *Short history of St. Andrews church (Anglo-American), Biarritz*, [1940] (ff. 2–6^{v}).

[1859 *cont.***]**

Frankfurt-am-Main. The Bishops of London and of Northern and Central Europe thank the French Reformed Church for the use of the latter's church for 82 years, 1907. *Copy* (f. 8^{v}).

Hamburg. Notes on the English church, including: *Translation of the concessions granted to the English Episcopal Congregation at Hamburgh*, 1834. *Copy* (ff. 11–13); notes on the English house in the Gröninger-strasse and the Bosselhof, with a list and biographical notes of English ministers at Hamburg, 1612–1934 (ff. 14–24); notes on the history of the church (ff. 25–6); account of the church of St. Thomas Becket at Hamburg, by Lt.-Col. C. G. Phipps. Printed in the *Royal Engineers Journal*, March 1949. *Copy* (ff. 27–35); report of the annual general meeting of the English church committee, 1949 (f. 36); various printed notes (ff. 37–9).

Ruthleben. Account of a Y.M.C.A. hut used as a chapel in the Ruthleben Internment Camp, 1915–16. The papers include hymn sheets and kalendars of services (ff. 40–73).

Antwerp. *The mission to seamen. Annual report and balance sheet*, 1949 (ff. 74–9).

Copenhagen. Note on the English church (f. 80).

Elsinore. Note on the English church (f. 81).

Davos. *St. Luke's church, Davos. A short history*, 20th century (ff. 82–3).

Lausanne. Note on the church (f. 84).

B. Photographs of and notes about English churches in Europe, *c.* 1950.

AUSTRIA. Vienna, with a note on the church (ff. 85–8).

BELGIUM. Antwerp with a note on the chaplaincy (ff. 89–93).
Bruges, with a note on the church (ff. 94–100).
Brussels (Christ Church), with a note on the church (ff. 101–11).
Brussels (Church of the Resurrection) (ff. 112–14).
Ghent (Mission to Seamen) (f. 115).
Knocke (ff. 116–19).
Ostend (ff. 120–1).
Poperinghe (Talbot House) (f. 122).
Ypres (f. 123).
Chart of services in English churches in Belgium (f. 124).

CZECHOSLOVAKIA. Karlsbad (f. 125).

FINLAND. [Helsingfors], with a note on the chaplaincy (ff. 126–9).

FRANCE. Arcachon, with a note on the church (ff. 130–1).
Biarritz, with a note on the church (ff. 132–7).
Bordeaux, with a note on the church (ff. 138–40).
Dieppe, 1950 (ff. 141–2).
Dinard (ff. 143–5).
Dunkirk, with a note on the church (ff. 146–8).
Le Touquet (ff. 149–50).

Paramé, 1950 (ff. 151–2).
Paris (ff. 153–61).
Pau (ff. 162–4).
St. Jean de Luz (ff. 165–6).
St. Lunaire, 1950 (f. 167).
Versailles, with a note on the church (ff. 168–70).

170 ff.

1860. BISHOP OF FULHAM PAPERS

Photographs of and notes about English churches in Europe, *c.* 1950.

GERMANY. Baden-Baden (ff. 1–5).
Bad Ems (f. 6).
Bad Homburg (f. 7).
Bad Nauheim (ff. 8–9).
Berlin (St. George), with historical notes (ff. 10–26).
Berlin. Commonwealth chapel, 1947 (f. 27).
Berlin. Cumberland House chapel, 1946 (f. 28).
Berlin. Church Centre chapel, 1948 (f. 29).
Berlin Crypt church—Kreuzkirche, 1947 (f. 30).
Cologne, with historical notes (ff. 31–2).
Düsseldorf, with historical notes, 1951 (ff. 33–43).
Flensburg (Danish Church) (ff. 44–6).
Frankfurt[-am-Main], with historical note (ff. 47–54).
Hamburg, with historical note (ff. 55–67).
Hanover, with historical note, 1948 (ff. 68–71).
Herford, [1949] (ff. 72–4).
Holtenau garrison church, *c.* 1945 (ff. 75–7).
Lübeck (ff. 78–9).
Minden (f. 80).
Plön (f. 81).
Schleswig (f. 82).
Stuttgart, 1950 (ff. 83–5).
Wiesbaden, with historical note (ff. 86–91).

HOLLAND. Amsterdam, with historical note (ff. 92–7).
Haarlem (f. 98).
The Hague, with historical note (ff. 99–115).
Rotterdam (ff. 116v–121).
Utrecht (ff. 122–3).

NORWAY. Balholm, with historical note (ff. 124–5).
Oslo (f. 126).

POLAND. Danzig (ff. 127–8).
Warsaw—statue only (f. 129).

RUSSIA. Moscow (ff. 130–3).

SWEDEN. Göteborg, with historical note (ff. 134–8).
Stockholm, with historical note (ff. 139–41).

[1860 *cont.*]

SWITZERLAND. Berne (f. 142).
Château d'Oex (f. 143).
Davos, with historical note (ff. 144–6).
Geneva (f. 147).
Grindelwald (ff. 148–9).
Les Avants (ff. 150–2).
Lucerne (f. 153).
Montana (ff. 154–5).
Villars, with historical note (ff. 156–7).
Zermatt (ff. 158–9).
Zürich (ff. 160–2).

Miscellaneous photographs as follows: chaplains' conference at Fulham Palace, 1937 (f. 163); chaplains' conference at Bedford College, London, 1950 (f. 164); chaplains' conference at Bedford College, London, 1951, with many of those present, including the Bishops of London and Fulham, named (ff. 165–8).

168 ff.

KA 432/1 item 39

Letter from Jeronimy Clifford, merchant and planter of Surinam, to Archbishop Tenison, 1711, concerning his losses due to a breach of the treaty with Holland in 1674.

INDEX

Note. N. R. Ker's 'Archbishop Sancroft's re-arrangement of the manuscripts of Lambeth Palace' is not included in the index.

Buckingham (*cont.*):
— Water-colours of churches by G. Samuel, 18th cent.: **1456,** *passim.*
— Sketches of churches, 19th cent.: **1457,** ff. 47–68.
Buckingham and Chandos, *Duke of.*
v. Grenville (Richard Plantagenet Campbell Temple Nugent Brydges Chandos).
Budham (T. L.). Letter to Revd. C. P. Golightly, 1874: **1804,** ff. 135^{v}–136^{v}.
Buenos Aires.
v. AMERICA.
Bugg (Francis), *former Quaker.* Letter [to Archbishop Sancroft, 1680]: **1834,** f. 25.
Buildwas, *Salop.* Survey, 1655 (*copy*): **1837,** f. 9.
Bulkeley (Benjamin), *Vicar of Withycombe.* Letter to the Bishop of London, 1735: **1741,** f. 115.
Buller-Yarde-Buller (John), *1st Baron Churston.* Letter to Baroness Burdett-Coutts, 1866: **1381,** f. 113.
Bullock (*Revd.* William Thomas), *secretary to the S.P.G.* Correspondence with Baroness Burdett-Coutts, 1859–73: **1380,** ff. 118, 124; **1385,** ff. 142, 186; **1386,** ff. 206, 214, 218–20.
— Correspondence with W. J. Farrer, 1865–6 (*copy*): **1378,** ff. 50, 63, 114.
Bulwer-Lytton (Edward George Earle Lytton), *1st Baron Lytton.* Correspondence with Baroness Burdett-Coutts, 1866–7: **1377,** f. 131; **1380,** f. 110; **1381,** ff. 183–5.
Burch (Arthur), *Registrar of the Diocese of Exeter.* Letters to L. T. Dibdin, 1891–6: **1586,** ff. 34, 119–120^{v}, 126.
Burchfield (Robert W.), *philologist.* Letters to Revd. C. Jenkins, 1952–6: **1634,** ff. 23–4.
Burdett-Coutts (Angela Georgina), *Baroness*; *philanthropist.* Letters; and papers, 1847–75: **1374–88.**
— Memorial from Province of South Australia, 1847: **1385,** f. 9.
— Memorial from diocese of Grahamstown, [1849]: **1383,** ff. 5–6^{v}.
— Address from clergy and laity of Graaff, South Africa, 1848: **1386,** f. 49.
— Address from residents of Colesberg, South Africa, 1848: **1386,** f. 43.
— Letter to Earl Grey, 1848 (*copy*): **1385,** f. 44.
— Letter [to F. Robe, Lieut.-Gov. of South Australia], 1848 (*copy*): **1385,** f. 47.
— Letter from inhabitants of St. Helena, 1851: **1386,** f. 387.
— Correspondence about schools, 1858–76: **1387.**
— Benefaction to St. Andrew's chapel, Great Yarmouth, 1859–61: **1388,** ff. 151–93.
— Correspondence about miscellaneous charities, 1859–70: **1388.**
— Letter to the Bishop of London, 1862 (*copy*): **1385,** f. 164.
— Letter to Ven. J. Sinclair, 1862 (*copy*): **1385,** f. 173.
— Letters to Archbishop Longley, 1862–8 (*copies*): **1374,** ff. 1, 7, 17, 25, 39, 45; **1381,** f. 245; **1383,** ff. 24–5; **1385,** f. 82.
— Letters to the Bishop of Oxford, 1864 (*copies*): **1374,** ff. 178–84.
— Legal cases submitted to Sir T. Twiss, 1865–6: **1382,** ff. 1–13, 20–8.
— Letters to Earl Russell, 1865–6: **1380,** f. 122; **1383,** ff. 38–9.
— Address at prize-giving, 1866: **1388,** f. 92.
— Letter about status of colonial bishoprics, [1866] (*draft*): **1383,** ff. 83–6.
— Letters to the Bishop of Capetown, 1866: **1383,** f. 81; **1386,** ff. 193, 201–3.
— Letters to Lord Romilly, 1866 (*copies*): **1381,** ff. 165, 171.
— Letter to —, 1866 (*copy*): **1381,** f. 34.
— Petition to Queen Victoria, 1866 (*printed*): **1383,** f. 96.
— Questions submitted to counsel about British Columbia, 1866: **1383,** ff. 73–4, 92–4.
— Letters to the Earl of Derby, 18[67]–8 (*copies*): **1378,** f. 141; **1381,** f. 194.

Ely Chapel.
v. LONDON: Holborn.
Embey (Richard), *of Bibury, Glos.* Probate of his will, 1722: **1488**/21.
Embleton, *Northumb.* Drawing of church, 19th cent.: **1459**, f. 64.
Emery (G. F.), *secretary to the Church Congress.* Letter to *The Times*, [1930] (*printed*): **1782**, f. 25.
Emery (William), *Archdeacon of Ely.* Account of, 1864 (*printed*): **1782**, f. 1.
Emmet (Cyril William), *Vicar of West Hendred.* Letters to *C.Q.R.*, 1910: **1619**, ff. 25–28ᵛ.
Englefield, *Berks.* Sketches of church, 19th cent.: **1457**, ff. 14–15.
Entwistle, *family of.* Stamp of arms, 17th cent.: **1372**.
Epping, *Essex.* Water-colour of church, 18th cent.: **1456**, f. 15.
Epsom, *Surrey.* Water-colour of church, 18th cent.: **1456**, f. 16.
Ercall Magna, *Salop.* Survey, 1655 (*copy*): **1837**, f. 8.
Ernest Augustus, *1st Duke of Cumberland and King of Hanover.* Letters to Archbishop Howley, 1819–38: **1754**, ff. 46–59.
— Letter to Revd. Christopher Wordsworth, 1835: **1822**, f. 31.
Escalger (G. A.), *priest.* Letter to Revd. F. Meyrick, 1878: **1482**, f. 113.
— Letters [to F. A. White], 1878: **1482**, ff. 104–12.
Escomb, *co. Durham.* Drawing of church, 19th cent.: **1458**, f. 22.
Esher, *Surrey.* Water-colour of church, 18th cent.: **1456**, f. 17.
Espin (Thomas Espinelle), *Professor of Theology, Queen's College, Birmingham.* Letter to [N.] Castle, 1854: **1725**, ff. 139–140ᵛ.
— Letter to Revd. C. Wray, 1867: **1604**, ff. 148–9.
Essays and Reviews.
v. Golightly (*Revd.* Charles Pourtales).
Essex, *County of.* Water-colours of churches by G. Samuel, 18th cent.: **1456**, *passim.*
— *Soke of.* Probate of will by, 1809: **1488**/39.
Essex, *Earl of.*
v. Devereux (Robert).
Eston, *Yorks.* Drawing of church, 19th cent.: **1460**, f. 36.
Ethelbert, *King of Kent.* Grant by (*copy*): **1226**, ff. 47–8.
Etherley, *co. Durham.* Drawing of church, 19th cent.: **1458**, f. 23.
ETHIOPIA.
v. Dengel (Sahle), *Emperor.*
Theodore II, *Emperor.*
Ali (Ras), *minister.*
Fanta (Aleka).
Evans (Francis), *of parish of St. Mary, Shrewsbury, gent.* Probate of his will, 1703: **1488**/13.
Evans (John), *Bishop of Meath.* Letter to Revd. W. Beauvoir, [1716]: **1554**, f. 31.
Evans (*Revd.* John), *secretary to the S.P.C.K.* Letters to Revd. C. P. Golightly, 1841–5: **1805**, ff. 161–181ᵛ.
— Letter to Revd. W. Stubbs, 1865: **1680**, ff. 24–25ᵛ.
Evans (Robert Wilson), *Vicar of Tarvin*; *Archdeacon of Westmorland* (*1856*). Letters to Revd. Christopher Wordsworth, 1830–9: **1822**, ff. 33–6.
Evanson (*Revd.* William Alleyn), *Lecturer of St. Luke, Old Street, London.* Translation of J. M. Goeze, *Vertheidigung der Complutischen Bibel . . .*, 1829: **1305**.
— Translation of J. M. Goeze, *Ausfuhrlichere Vertheidigung des Complutischen Griechischen Neuen Testaments*, 1830–1: **1300–1**.
— Translation of J. M. Goeze, *Fortsetzung der ausfuhrlicheren Vertheidigung*, 1830–1: **1302–3**.
— Translation of J. B. Lüderwald, *Anmerkungen über I. Joh. v. 7*, 1832: **1304**.
Eversley, *Viscount.*
v. Shaw-Lefevre (Charles).
Ewell, *Surrey.* Water-colour of church, 18th cent.: **1456**, f. 18.
Ewing (Alexander), *Bishop of Argyll and the Isles.* Account of Scottish Episcopal Church, 1848 (*printed*): **1597**, ff. 1ᵛ–4ᵛ.

Fremantle William (Henry), (*cont.*):
— Letter from Revd. R. T. Davidson, 1880: **1477,** f. 133.
— Letters from Lady Durand, 1880: **1480,** ff. 82–92.
— Letter to the Bishop of Edinburgh, 1880: **1480,** f. 143.
— Letter from Sir W. R. Farquhar, Bt., 1880: **1480,** f. 113.
— Letter from Lord Hatherley, 1880: **1480,** f. 437.
— Letter from Sir W. C. James, Bt., 1880: **1480,** f. 192.
— Letter from the Bishop of Lichfield, 1880: **1480,** f. 243.
— Letters from Mme E. Loyson, 1880: **1481,** ff. 337–40.
— Correspondence with Revd. F. Meyrick, 1880: **1479,** ff. 101, 248–53.
— Letters to F. A. White, 1880–1, 1886: **1480,** ff. 115–42.
— Letter from the Bishop of Winchester, 1880: **1480,** f. 22.
— *Fund for the support of M. Loyson* . . ., 1886: **1472,** ff. 329–32.
— Letter to Revd. S. A. Barnett, 1886: **1466,** ff. 11–13ᵛ.
— Letter to Mrs. Hatch, 1889: **1467,** ff. 112–113ᵛ.
— Letter from Lord Mount-Temple, 19th cent.: **1480,** f. 363.
— Letter from Very Revd. A. P. Stanley, 19th cent.: **1480,** f. 350.
French (Alfred Henry Laurence), *schoolmaster*; *godson of Revd. C. P. Golightly*. Letters to Revd. C. P. Golightly, 19th cent.: **1805,** ff. 182–187ᵛ.
French (Thomas Valpy), *Bishop of Lahore*. Letters to Revd. C. P. Golightly, 1846–80: **1805,** ff. 188–228ᵛ.
Frere (Walter Howard), *Superior of the Community of the Resurrection, Mirfield*; *Bishop of Truro (1923)*. Letters to *C.Q.R.*, 1906–15: **1617,** ff. 258–9; **1618,** ff. 52, 185; **1619,** ff. 32–33ᵛ; **1620,** ff. 15–17.
— Letter to the Bishop of Exeter, 1912: **1642,** f. 49.
— Memorandum on alternative forms of service, 1912: **1642,** ff. 50–62, 204–9.
— Letters to Revd. C. Jenkins, 1915–18: **1630,** f. 97; **1642,** ff. 3–4.
— Letter to Revd. T. Tatlow, 1916: **1794,** f. 38.
— Testimonial for Revd. C. Jenkins, 1918: **1630,** f. 102.
Freshwater, *Isle of Wight*. Sketch of church, 19th cent.: **1459,** f. 27.
Fressingfield, *Suff*. Estate business, 1727: **1373,** f. 50.
Friderike Louise Karoline Sophie Alexandrine, *wife of Ernest, Duke of Cumberland*. Letter to Mrs. Howley, 1833: **1754,** f. 147.
Friends, Society of.
v. Quakers.
Frodesley, *Salop*. Survey, 1655 (*copy*): **1837,** f. 21.
Frodsham (George Horsfall), *Bishop of North Queensland*. Letter to *C.Q.R.*, 1907: **1618,** ff. 53–54ᵛ.
Frost (Abigail), *daughter of Archbishop Secker's nephew*. Letter to Miss [Ann] Frost, after 1760: **1719,** f. 1.
— Letter from Revd. B. Porteus, 1772: **1719,** ff. 5–6.
Frost (Ann), *daughter of Archbishop Secker's nephew*. Letter from Miss A[bigail] Frost, after 1760: **1719,** f. 1.
— Letter to [T.] Frost, 1764: **1719,** ff. 2–3.
Frost (John), *Rector of Bishop's Court*. Letter to his brother and sister, 1760: **1719,** f. 4.
Frost (Thomas), *nephew of Archbishop Secker*. Letter from the Bishop of Oxford, 1751: **1719,** ff. 13–14.
— Letter from Miss Ann Frost, 1764: **1719,** ff. 2–3.
— Letters from Miss C. Talbot, 1768–9: **1719,** ff. 19–27.
Frost —, *wife of T. Frost*. Letter from the Bishop of Oxford, 1748: **1719,** f. 16.
Frost (*Mrs.*). Letters from the Bishop of Chester, 1779: **1719,** ff. 7–10.
[Frost —]. Letter from Revd. G. Stinton, 1779: **1719,** f. 18.
Frosterley, *co. Durham*. Drawings of church, 19th cent.: **1458,** f. 25; **1461,** f. 22.

Froude (James Anthony), *historian.* Letter about his undergraduate days, 1839: **1680,** ff. 63–4.
— Letters to Revd. B. Webb, 1866: **1750,** ff. 42–4.
— Letter to Very Revd. A. P. Stanley, 19th cent.: **1680,** f. 216.
Froude (Robert Hurrell), *Archdeacon of Totnes.* Letter from W. Froude, 1839: **1680,** ff. 63–4.
Froude (William), *brother of J. A. Froude.* Letter to Ven. R. H. Froude, 1839: **1680,** ff. 63–4.
Fry (Edward Alexander). Extracts from Augmentation Books by, [1915]: **1790.**
Fry (John), *Pastor of Rondebosch, South Africa.* Letter to Baroness Burdett-Coutts, 1852: **1386,** f. 78.
Fulford (Francis), *Bishop of Montreal.* Letters to Baroness Burdett-Coutts, 1858: **1385,** ff. 245–8.
Fulford (Mary), *wife of Francis, Bishop of Montreal.* Letter to Baroness Burdett-Coutts, 1858: **1385,** f. 249.
Fuller (John), *headmaster.* Letter to Baroness Burdett-Coutts, 1875: **1387,** f. 264.
Fulmer, *Bucks.* Sketch of church, 19th cent.: **1457,** f. 54.
Furneaux (William Mordaunt), *Dean of Winchester.* Letters to Revd. J. N. Dalton, 1917: **1680,** ff. 9–12.

G [ ]. Letter to *C.Q.R.*, 20th cent.: **1620,** ff. 155–156v.
Gadderar (James), *Bishop of Aberdeen (1724).* Letter to Bishop J. Falconer, 1713 (*copy*): **1536,** pp. 164–72.
— Letter from Revd. T. Brett, 1721 (*copy*): **1536,** pp. 151–3.
— Letter from J. Smith, [1721] (copy): **1536,** p. 151.
Gainford, *co. Durham.* Drawings of church, 19th cent.: **1458,** f. 26; **1461,** f. 23.
Gallican Catholic Church.
v. France.
Galway, *Earl of.*
v. Ruvigny (Henri de Massue de).
Garbett (Cyril Forster), *Archbishop of York.* Letters to Revd. A. C. Don, 1946: **1469,** ff. 172–3.
Garbett (James), *Rector of Clayton cum Keymer; Archdeacon of Chichester (1851).* Letter to Revd. C. P. Golightly, [1841]: **1806,** ff. 1–2.
Garden (George), *episcopalian minister at Aberdeen.* Note on, 19th cent.: **1541,** p. 18.
Garden —, *Scottish Presbyterian.* Letter from Archbishop Secker, 1767: **1727,** f. 102.
Gardiner (Dorothy), *historian.* Letter from Sir S. E. Downing, 1930: **1726,** ff. 116–18.
— Letter to Revd. C. Jenkins, 1936: **1634,** f. 80.
Gardiner (Robert Hallowell), *secretary of advisory committee of World Conference on Faith and Order.* Letter to Christian brethren, 20th cent. (*copy*): **1794,** ff. 286–8.
Gardiner (Thory Gage), *Canon of Canterbury.* Correspondence about table presented to Lambeth Palace, 1909. **1729,** ff. 250–4.
— Letters to Revd. C. Jenkins, 1932–4: **1633,** ff. 74–5, 78–80, 85–9.
— Letter from Very Revd. Hewlett Johnson, 1932 (*copy*): **1633,** ff. 72–3.
— Letter from Miss D. W. Russell, 1933 (*copy*): **1633,** ff. 82–4.
Gardner-Waterman (Waterman), *Vicar of Loose.* Notes on churchwardens' accounts, 1929: **1468,** ff. 77–9.
Garrett (Lindsay S.), *author.* Letter to *C.Q.R.*, 1908: **1618,** ff. 186–7.
Garvie (*Revd.* Alfred Ernest), *Principal of New College, Hampstead.* Letters to Revd. T. Tatlow, 1914–19: **1794,** ff. 39–54v.
— Memorandum on Faith and Order 1919: **1793,** ff. 224–5.
Gascoyne-Cecil (Hugh Richard Heathcote), *1st Baron Quickswood (1941).* Letter to *C.Q.R.*, 1906: **1617,** ff. 210–11.
— *The Communion service as it might be*, 1935: **1776.**
— Notes on revision of Communion service, 20th cent.: **1468,** ff. 181–7.

Harley, *Salop*. Survey, 1655 (*copy*): **1837**, f. 22.

Harlington, *Middx*. Water-colour and engraving of church, 18th cent.: **1456**, ff. 28–9.

Harmer (John Reginald), *Bishop of Rochester*. Photograph of, 20th cent.: **1772**, f. 24.

Harmon (James), *son of Sir W. Harmon*. Petition for landwaiter's place, 17th cent.: **1834**, ff. 8–11.

Harmondsworth, *Middx*. Water-colour of church, 18th cent.: **1456**, f. 30.

Harnack (Adolph von), *theologian*. Letters to Revd. E. Hatch, 1885–7 (*German*): **1467**, ff. 34–5.

Harness [William], *Perpetual Curate of All Saints, Knightsbridge, London*. Letters from E. Harrison, 1865: **1380**, ff. 14–17.

Harper (James Walker), *Canon of Perth*. Copy of Nonjurors' offices by, *c*. 1905: **1528**.

— List of some liturgical books belonging to, 20th cent.: **1543**, ff. 347–8.

Harper (William), *Scottish episcopalian minister*. Letter to —, 1729: **1543**, f. 11.

Harpsden, *Oxon*. Drawing of church, 19th cent.: **1459**, f. 89.

Harris, *Baron*.
v. Harris (George Robert Canning).

Harris (George), *lawyer*. Letter to the Dean of Arches, etc., 1781 (*copy*): **1560**, f. 8.

Harris (George Robert Canning), *4th Baron Harris*. Memorandum about proposed memorial to, 1932: **1633**, ff. 76–7.

Harris [Walter], *historiographer*. His edition of *De praesulibus Hiberniae*, 1734: **1373**, f. 109.

Harrison (*Mrs*. Adeline M. Barker). Letter to Baroness Burdett-Coutts, 1875: **1387**, f. 266.

Harrison (Benjamin), *Archdeacon of Maidstone*. Letters to Baroness Burdett-Coutts, 1846–7: **1384**, ff. 40, 62, 124.

Harrison (*Sir* Edmund Stephen), *Deputy Clerk of Privy Council*. Letters [to Revd. W.] Harness, 1865: **1380**, ff. 14–17.

Harrison (Henry), *Vicar of Kilndown*. Protest by, 1850 (*printed*): **1491**, f. 103.

Harrowby, *Earl of*.
v. Ryder (Dudley).

Harston (Edward), *Vicar of Sherborne*. Letter from the Bishop of Salisbury, 1857: **1543**, ff. 9–10.

Hart, *co. Durham*. Drawings of church, 19th cent.: **1458**, f. 28; **1461**, f. 25.

Hart (John), *member of an advertising firm*. Letter to *C.Q.R.*, 1916: **1620**, ff. 43–4.

— Letter to the same, 20th cent.: **1620**, ff. 162–163ᵛ.

Hartlepool, *co. Durham*. Drawings of church, 19th cent.: **1458**, f. 29; **1461**, f. 25.

Harvey (John C.), *Churchwarden of St. Clement, Bournemouth*. Letters to *C.Q.R.*, 1906–7: **1617**, ff. 276–279ᵛ; **1618**, ff. 58–9.

Haselum (William), *Apparitor-General of York*. Patent, 1717 (*copy*): **1777**, f. 41.

Hass (Ludvig Daniel), *Danish pastor*. Letter to Revd. N. Wade, [1852] (*trans*.): **1543**, ff. 89–90.

Hassard (*Sir* John), *Vicar-General*. Letter to H. A. Darbyshire, 1865: **1380**, f. 28.

— Letters to Baroness Burdett-Coutts, 1866–[8]: **1380**, f. 59; **1381**, f. 22; **1385**, f. 330.

— Letter from Revd. W. H. Fremantle, 1866: **1380**, f. 61.

— Letter from A. F. Kinnaird, 1867: **1381**, f. 222.

— Letter to C. W. Holgate, 1893: **1812**, ff. 120–1.

Hatch (Arthur Herbert), *son of Revd. E. Hatch*. Letter from Revd. R. W. Dale, 1889: **1467**, ff. 25–26ᵛ.

Hatch (*Revd*. Edwin), *historian*. Correspondence, 1865–89: **1467**, ff. 1–96.

— Obituary notice, 1889 (*printed*): **1467**, f. 154.

— Letters of condolence to widow of, 1889: **1467**, ff. 97–139ᵛ.

Henchman (Humphrey), *civilian.* Letters to the Bishop of London, 1725: **1741,** ff. 32–5.
— Legal opinion, 1726: **1777,** ff. 44–45ᵛ.
Henley (John), '*Orator*'. Case concerning conventicle kept by, 1726: **1741,** ff. 40–2.
Henley-on-Thames, *Oxon.* Sketch of church, 19th cent.: **1459,** f. 90.
Henricke (Thomas), *Vicar-General of the Bishop of London.* Instrument, **1563** (*draft*): **1837,** ff. 1–2.
Henry I, *King of England.* Charter (*copy*): **1226,** f. 10.
Henry II, *King of England.* Charters (*copies*): **1226,** ff. 12–14.
Henry VIII, *King of England.* Statutes for Christ Church, Canterbury, [1541] (*copy*): **1356,** pp. 1–54.
Henson (Herbert Hensley), *Bishop of Durham.* Letter to Archbishop Davidson, 1927: **1773,** ff. 19–22ᵛ.
— Letter to Revd. M. G. Haigh, 1929: **1773,** ff. 11–12ᵛ.
— Letters to Revd. C. Jenkins, 1930: **1634,** ff. 125–128ᵛ.
— Letter to the Bishop of Winchester, 1944: **1468,** ff. 217–18.
Heraldry. Arms in colour of Archbishops of Canterbury, 1584: **1310.**
— Treatise of nobility, 1598: **1371,** ff. 83–111.
— Stamp of arms of Brudenell family, 17th cent.: **1372.**
— Arms of Claughton family, 19th cent.: **1751,** f. 140.
— Arms of diocese of Colombo, 19th cent.: **1751,** f. 142.
— Arms of diocese of St. Helena, 19th cent.: **1751,** f. 141.
— Genealogical notes of Herring family, 1913: **1783.**
— *v.* Burke (*Sir* Henry Farnham).
Camden (William).
Howard (*Sir* Algar).
Herbert (Henry Howard Molyneux), *4th Earl of Carnarvon.* Letter to Baroness Burdett-Coutts, 1866: **1380,** f. 105.
— Letter to Very Revd. A. P. Stanley, 1878: **1680,** f. 230.
Hereford, *Diocese of.* Formularies used in, 17th cent.: **1590–1.**
— Photographs of Hereford cathedral, *c.* 1873–4: **1744,** ff. 12–13.
— *Bishop of.*
v. Atlay (James).
Hampden (Renn Dickson).
Huntingford (George Isaac).
Musgrave (Thomas).
Percival (John).
Wren (Matthew).
Herford.
v. GERMANY.
Herne (John), *of Lincoln's Inn.* Gift from Archbishop Laud, 1645: **1729,** ff. 147–56, *passim.*
— Correspondence with his brother, 1703 (*copy*): **1729,** ff. 147–56.
Herne (Robert). Correspondence with his brother, 1703 (*copy*): **1729,** ff. 147–56.
Herring, *family of.* Genealogical notes for, 1913: **1783.**
Herring (Gerrard), *of Cambridge, draper.* Will, 1701 (*copy*): **1783,** f. 35.
Herring (Herbert T.). Genealogical notes, 1913: **1783.**
Herring (Thomas), *Archbishop of Canterbury.* Letter [to the Archbishop of York], 1750: **1719,** ff. 63–6.
— Petition from inhabitants of Lambeth, 1752: **1837,** f. 30.
— Will, 1756 (*copy*): **1783,** ff. 37–43.
— Genealogical notes about, 1913: **1783.**
— Photograph of portrait, 20th cent.: **1728,** f. 19.
Herring (William), *of Cambridge, draper.* Will, 1722 (*copy*): **1783,** f. 36.
Herring (William), *Chancellor of York.* Will, 1763 (*copy*): **1783,** f. 44.
Hertford, *County of.* Water-colours of churches by G. Samuel, 18th cent.: **1456,** *passim.*
Hertzberg (N.), *Provost of Ullensvang, Norway.* Letters to Revd. Charles Wordsworth, 1833–5 (*Latin*): **1823,** ff. 181–4.
Hervey (Arthur Charles), *Bishop of Bath and Wells.* Letters to Revd. C. Wray, 1870: **1604,** ff. 259–262ᵛ.

Humphreys (John), *of Shrewsbury*. Letters to Baroness Burdett-Coutts, 1858–60: **1386,** ff. 223–7, 230–6, 241.
Hunt (*Mrs.* Alice). Correspondence with F. A. White, [1880]: **1480,** ff. 180–5.
[Hunt (Brian), *naval chaplain*.] Account of discipline and religion in Navy, 18th cent.: **1742,** ff. 11–14^{v}, 17^{v}–18.
Hunt (John Edward), *Bishop of Northern Rhodesia*. Photograph of, 20th cent.: **1772,** f. 25.
Hunt (Nicholas), *of Canterbury*. Letter from J. Tillotson, 1688: **1719,** f. 69.
Huntingford (George Isaac), *Bishop of Hereford*. Declines some office, 1813: **1727,** ff. 103–4.
— Letter to Revd. H. T. Symonds, 1826: **1751,** f. 8.
Huntingford (*Revd.* George William), *schoolmaster*. Letter to Revd. Charles Wordsworth, [1846]: **1823,** ff. 189–90.
Huntington (Frederic Dan), *Bishop of Central New York*. Letter to Revd. R. J. Nevin, 1879 (*copy*): **1477,** f. 211.
Hunwick, *co. Durham*. Drawing of church, 19th cent.: **1458,** f. 33.
Hurley, *Berks*. Sketch of church, 19th cent.: **1459,** f. 91.
Hurst, *Berks*. Sketch of church, 19th cent.: **1457,** f. 16.
Hurst (*Sir* Gerald Berkeley), *Judge*. Correspondence with Revd. C. Jenkins, 1926: **1634,** ff. 132–4.
Hurworth, *co. Durham*. Drawings of church, 19th cent.: **1458,** f. 34; **1461,** f. 30.
'Husband, A.' Letter to Archbishop Howley, 1843: **1789,** ff. 131–132^{v}.
Hutchings (William Henry), *Archdeacon of Cleveland*. Letter to Revd. C. Wray, 1866: **1604,** ff. 315–17.
— Letters to *C.Q.R.*, 1904: **1616,** ff. 204–7.
Hutchinson (James), *Chaplain at Rome*. Letter to Archbishop Howley, 1839: **1754,** ff. 110–11.
[Hutton (Matthew), *Archbishop of York and (1757) Canterbury*.] Letter from Archbishop Herring 1750: **1719,** ff. 63–6.
Hutton (William Holden), *historian*; *Dean of Winchester (1919)*. Letters to *C.Q.R.*, 1904–12: **1616,** ff. 208–9; **1617,** ff. 81–85^{v}, 290–308a^{v}; **1618,** ff. 68–72, 193–7, 301–2; **1619,** ff. 40–3, 116–18, 206–208^{v}.
— Letters to the Bishop of Salisbury, 1908: **1401,** ff. 30, 34.
— Letter to Revd. C. Jenkins, 1910: **1634,** ff. 136–137^{v}.
— Letters to *C.Q.R.*, 20th cent.: **1620,** ff. 166–176^{v}.
Hyacinthe, *Père, Rector of the Gallican Catholic Church*. Account of fund for, 1878–82: **1474.**
— Correspondence with F. A. White, 1878–89: **1481,** ff. 1–268.
— Letterbooks of F. A. White of correspondence with, 1878–85: **1475–6.**
— Letter from the Bishop of Moray, Ross and Caithness, 1878 (*printed*): **1477,** ff. 170–1.
— Papers about negotiations with Anglo-Continental Society, 1878–1903: **1472–82.**
— *Catholic Reform and the Anglican Church*, 1879: **1472,** ff. 59–72.
— Letter from C. Miel, 1879 (*copy*): **1482,** f. 225.
— Letter to [C.] Roosevelt, 1879 (*French copy*): **1477,** f. 190.
— Lectures on Positive Christianity, 1880: **1472,** ff. 283–304.
— Correspondence with Revd. F. Meyrick. 1880–1: **1479,** ff. 206–14.
— Correspondence with Revd. R. J. Nevin, 1880 (*copy*): **1477,** ff. 237, 242; **1481,** f. 272.
— Sermon, 1880 (*printed*): **1472,** ff. 115–118^{v}.
— Correspondence with the Bishop of Edinburgh, 1881 (*copy*): **1472,** ff. 155–8, 220–221^{v}; **1481,** ff. 269, 345.
— Letter from Archbishop Tait, 1881 (*copy*): **1477,** ff. 13–16.
— Report of American bishops on Old Catholics in France sent to, 1882: **1472,** ff. 308–310^{v}.
— *Simple réponse a une calomnie*, 1883: **1472,** ff. 311–313^{v}.

Johnston (Charles Francis Harding), *Vicar of Headington Quarry, Oxford.* Letter to C. Jenkins, 1903: **1630,** ff. 46–47^v.

Jolly (Alexander), *Bishop of Moray.* Correspondence with the Bishop of Aberdeen, 1784 (*copy*): **1541,** pp. 49–52.

— Correspondence with the Bishop of Moray, 1784 (*copy*): **1541,** pp. 45–51.

— Declaration at his consecration as coadjutor, 1796: **1543,** f. 17.

— Letter to Revd. R. Aitken, 1800 (*draft*): **1543,** f. 18.

— Letters to —, 1812–24 (*copies*): **1543,** ff. 20–1.

— Address, 1835: **1543,** ff. 63–67^v.

— Letter to T. Stephen, 1836 (*copy*): **1538,** f. 20.

— Form of admitting a penitent, [19th cent.]: **1523.**

Jolly (Peter), *Scottish episcopalian minister.* Mentioned, 19th cent.: **1524,** ff. 18–36, *passim.*

— Prayers, 19th cent. (*copy*): **1545,** ff. 101–2.

Jones (Alfred), *Vicar of St. John, Kenilworth (1872).* Statistics for Westminster, 1846: **1796.**

— *A few words on the state of Westminster,* 1847: **1796,** ff. 31–52.

Jones (Matilda). Autograph, 1813: **1594,** f. 1.

Jones (William Henry Rich), *Vicar of St. James, Curtain Road, Shoreditch, London.* Letter from the Bishop of London, 1847: **1812,** f. 51.

Jones (William West), *Bishop of Capetown.* Letter to —, 1878: **1727,** f. 152.

Jortin (*Revd.* John), *historian.* Author of *An enquiry into the rationale of Christianity* known to, 1758: **1350,** f. 31.

Joseph (Horace William Brindley), *philosopher.* Letters to C. Jenkins, 1898–1901: **1630,** ff. 48–51.

Joss (William). Copy of correspondence of the Bishop of Aberdeen, 1804–6: **1542.**

Journals. Of journey through Cheshire and Staffordshire, 1829: **1756.**

— Of tour of Scotland and northern England, 1846: **1600.**

— Of tour on Continent by Bishop A. Ewing, 1855: **1597,** ff. 15–41.

— Of tour in the Middle East by Revd. R. T. Davidson *et al.*, 1872–3: **1602–3.**

— *v.* Diaries.

Jowett (*Revd.* Benjamin), *Master of Balliol College, Oxford.* Charges against, 1856: **1804–11,** *passim.*

— Letters to Revd. E. Hatch, [1880–7]: **1467,** ff. 37–47.

Joyce (*Revd.* Gilbert Cunningham), *Warden of St. Deiniol's, Hawarden.* Letters to *C.Q.R.*, 1906–7: **1617,** ff. 316–317^v; **1618,** ff. 79–80.

Judd (Henderson), *Registrar of the diocese of Los Angeles.* Letter to *C.Q.R.*, 1909: **1618,** ff. 306–8.

Jupp (Reginald Barry), *Provost of Mombasa.* Correspondence with Revd. C. Jenkins, 1955: **1634,** ff. 193–194^v.

Justice of the Peace. Memoranda of Sir R. Twysden as, 1636: **1389.**

Juxon (William), *Archbishop of Canterbury.* Extracts from Register by A. C. Ducarel, 18th cent.: **1351,** f. 118.

Kaehler (R.). Notes on rectors of St. Margaret, Canterbury, *c.* 1930: **1468,** ff. 48–72^v.

Karlsbad.
v. CZECHOSLOVAKIA.

Kay (*Sir* Edward Ebenezer), *Lord Justice of Appeal (1890).* Letter to Baroness Burdett-Coutts, 1866: **1380,** f. 150.

Kaye (John), *Bishop of Lincoln.* Letters to Revd. C. P. Golightly, 1843–5: **1808,** ff. 12–24.

— Letter to —, 1849: **1727,** f. 153.

Kebbel (T. E.). Letter to *C.Q.R.*, 20th cent.: **1620,** ff. 179–81.

Keble (John), *Vicar of Hursley.* Letters to Revd. Charles Wordsworth, 18[31]–47: **1823,** ff. 198–220.

— Letters to Revd. W. H. Mill, 1849: **1491,** ff. 13–19.

Macmillan (John Victor), *Chaplain to the Archbishop of Canterbury*; *Bishop of Guildford* (*1934*). Correspondence with the Bishop of Exeter, 1911–12: **1642,** ff. 32–34v, 69–71.
— Letter to Revd. C. Jenkins, 1936: **1634,** f. 109.
— Letter from the same, 20th cent. (*copy*): **1642,** f. 5.
Maddock (*Revd.* Henry John). Letter to Revd. C. Wray, 19th cent.: **1604,** ff. 389–390v.
Madras, *Bishop of*.
v. Spencer (George Trevor).
Mafeking.
v. AFRICA.
Magee (William Connor), *Bishop of Peterborough*; *Archbishop of York* (*1890*). Letter from B. Disraeli, 1868 (*copy*): **1812,** f. 123.
— Letter to Revd. C. Wray, 1870: **1604,** f. 391.
— Photograph of, 19th cent.: **1744,** f. 24v.
Maitland (*Revd.* Samuel Roffey), *Lambeth Librarian.* Letters to Revd. Christopher Wordsworth, 1837–9: **1822,** ff. 108–111v.
— Letter to Revd. C. Wray, 1840: **1604,** ff. 393–4.
— Letter to the same, 19th cent.: **1604,** ff. 395–6.
Majendie (Henry William), *Bishop of Bangor.* Letter to Archbishop Manners Sutton, 1821: **1751,** f. 38.
Malone (Edmund), *Shakespearean scholar.* Letter [to Archbishop Moore], 1797: **1834,** f. 74.
Malpas (Elizabeth), *of Canterbury, widow.* Lease to, 1701 (*copy*): **1250,** pp. 249–53.
— Lease to, 1724 (*copy*): **1250,** pp. 378–81.
MALTA. Transcript of marriage registers, 1801–92: **1470–1.**
— Proposal to establish diocese of, 1840–44: **1754,** ff. 5–6, 9–10v, 19–20.
— Transcript of Presbyterian marriage register, 1843–92: **1471,** ff. 60v–69.
— Transcript of Wesleyan marriage register, 1869–92: **1471,** ff. 55v–59v.
Man (Miles), *of the Town Clerk's Office, Guildhall.* Letter to the Bishop of London, 1737: **1741,** f. 136.
Manchester, *City of.* Letter about synod at, 1881: **1586,** ff. 15–17.
— Thesis for degree of Manchester University, 1929: **1755.**
— *Bishop of.*
v. Fraser (James).
Knox (Edmund Arbuthnott).
Lee (James Prince).
Moorhouse (James).
Temple (William).
Manners (John James Robert), *7th Duke of Rutland* (*1888*). Letter to the Bishop of St. Andrews, 1880: **1823,** f. 233.
Manners Sutton (Charles), *Archbishop of Canterbury.* Letters to Revd. Christopher Wordsworth, 1804–24: **1822,** ff. 112–26.
— Letter from the Earl of Liverpool, 1813 (*copy*): **1727,** ff. 103–4.
— Letters [to J. Watson], 1814: **1789,** ff. 5–7.
— Letter from Revd. W. Knatchbull, 1816: **1258,** f. i.
— Minutes, 1816: **1789,** f. 61.
— Letters and papers, 1820–1: **1751,** ff. 26–46.
— Letters to —, 1820: **1751,** f. 46; **1812,** f. 35.
— Draft coronation service for George IV, 1821: **1312.**
— Schedule of papers belonging to, 1828: **1789,** ff. 118–127v.
Manners Sutton (Charles), *1st Viscount Canterbury* (*1835*). Letters to Revd. Christopher Wordsworth, 1804–25: **1822,** ff. 127–31.
— Schedule of papers delivered by, 1828: **1789,** ff. 118–127v.
Manning (Henry Edward), *Cardinal.* Letters to the Bishop of St. Andrews, 18[25]–91: **1823,** ff. 234–281v.
— Letter to the Warden and Fellows of Winchester College, 1835: **1824,** ff. 189–190v.
— Letters to Revd. Christopher Wordsworth, 1840–5: **1822,** ff. 132–148v.

Manning (Henry Edward) (*cont.*):
— Letter to Revd. C. Wray, 1846: **1604**, ff. 397–8.
— Letters to Revd. W. H. Mill, 1849–50: **1491**, ff. 11, 27–30, 33, 84, 119.
— Extract from address, 1865: **1383**, f. 36.
Manning (William T.), *chairman of advisory committee of World Conference on Faith and Order*. Letter to Christian brethren, 20th cent. (*copy*): **1794**, ff. 286–8.
Mansfield, *Notts*. Probate of will in court baron, 1667: **1488**/4.
Mansfield (*Miss* M.). Letter to *C.Q.R.*, 20th cent.: **1620**, ff. 220–221v.
Mant (Richard), *Bishop of Down and Connor*. Letter to Revd. C. Wray, 1846: **1604**, ff. 399–400v.
— Letter from Revd. W. Presslie, 19th cent. (*copy*): **1545**, f. 102v.
Mapledurham, *Oxon*. Sketch of church, 19th cent.: **1459**, f. 94.
Marcet [Alexander John Gaspard], *physician*. Account of public education at Geneva, 1814: **1309**.
Marcus (Moses), *teacher of languages*. Calligraphic specimens in Hebrew, etc., 18th cent.: **1742**, f. 160.
Maria Louisa Victoria, *Dowager Duchess of Kent*. Letters to Archbishop Howley, 1828–33: **1754**, ff. 30–4.
— Letters to Mrs. Howley, 1829–33: **1754**, ff. 139–43.
Marjoribanks (Dudley Coutts), *1st Baron Tweedmouth (1881)*. Letter to Baroness Burdett-Coutts, 1866: **1381**, f. 159.
— Memorandum of conversation with [Sir T. Twiss, 1866]: **1381**, f. 161.
Marjoribanks (Edward), *banker*. Letter to Baroness Burdett-Coutts, 1866: **1381**, f. 59.
Marlborough, *Suffragan Bishop of*.
v. Earle (Alfred).
Lancaster (Thomas).
Marquette, *Bishop of*.
v. Williams (G. Mott).
Marriage registers.
v. REGISTERS.
Marriott (*Revd*. Charles), *Fellow of Oriel College, Oxford*. Letter to Revd. C. Wray, 1855: **1604**, f. 401.
Marriott (*Revd*. Wharton Booth), *schoolmaster*. Letter to Revd. C. Wray, 1853: **1604**, f. 403.
Marshall (J. W. M.), *of Handsworth, nr. Birmingham*. Letter to Revd. C. Wray, 1846: **1604**, ff. 404–5.
Marshall (Thomas), *Vicar of St. John the Baptist, Peterborough*. Letter to the Bishop of London, 1736: **1741**, ff. 123–4.
Marske, *Yorks*. Drawings of churches, 19th cent.: **1460**, ff. 48–9; **1462**, ff. 34–5.
Marten (R. T.), *secretary of the City Association for German relief*. Letter to J. Watson and R. Ackermann, 1814: **1789**, f. 3.
— Letter to J. Watson, 1816: **1789**, f. 47.
Martin (*Revd*. Francis), *Fellow of Trinity College, Cambridge*. Letter to Revd. Christopher Wordsworth, 1841: **1822**, ff. 149–150v.
Martin (H.), *of Buckland-in-the-Moor, Devon*. Letter to Revd. C. P. Golightly, [1840]: **1808**, ff. 73–74v.
Martin [(Mary), *wife of Sir W. Martin, Chief Justice of New Zealand*]. Letter to —, 1845 (*extract*): **1562**, ff. 36–39v.
Martin (Stephen), *Captain in the Royal Navy*. Certificate issued by, 1703: **1557**, f. 192.
Martin (*Sir* William), *former Chief Justice of New Zealand*. Remarks on Ecclesiastical Discipline Bills, 1862: **1727**, ff. 64–5.
Martineau (James), *Unitarian divine*. Letter to Revd. E. Hatch, 1889: **1467**, f. 77.
Marton, *Yorks*. Drawings of church, 19th cent.: **1460**, f. 50; **1462**, f. 33.
Mary, *Queen of England*. Commission to the Bishop of Winchester and others, [1554] (*copy*): **1742**, f. 81.
Mary, *Queen of England, wife of William III*.
v. William III.

Monk (James Henry), *Bishop of Gloucester and Bristol*. Letters to Revd. Christopher Wordsworth, 1827–34: **1822**, ff. 163–165v.
— Letter to Revd. C. Wray, 1853: **1604**, f. 435.
Monkwearmouth, *co. Durham*. Drawings of church, 19th cent.: **1458**, f. 38; **1461**, f. 33.
Monro (David Binning), *Provost of Oriel College, Oxford*. Letter to Mrs. Hatch, 1889: **1467**, ff. 130–1.
Montana.
v. SWITZERLAND.
Montfaucon (Bernard de), *scholar*. Letter to Revd. W. Beauvoir, 1720 (*French*): **1554**, f. 70.
— Letter to the same, 18th cent. (*French*): **1554**, f. 72.
Montford, *Salop*. Survey, 1655 (*copy*): **1837**, f. 14.
Montgomerie (Archibald William), *13th Earl of Eglinton and 1st Earl of Winton, Lord-Lieutenant of Ireland*. Letter to the Bishop of Meath, 1852: **1727**, f. 33.
Montreal.
v. CANADA.
Montrose, *Angus*. Photograph of plate at, 20th cent.: **1546**, p. 233.
Monuments. Inscriptions in London churches, *c.* 1638: **1485.**
— Report and papers on ornaments of the church and its ministers, 1907–8: **1398**, ff. 18–145; **1401**, ff. 20–68.
— *v.* Ancient Monuments (Churches) Committee.
Moodie (William), *Professor of Hebrew, Edinburgh*. Letter to Revd. H. Horsley, 1812: **1767**, f. 155.
Moore (*Revd.* Aubrey Lackington), *tutor at Keble College, Oxford*. Letters to Revd. E. Hatch, 18[88]–9: **1467**, ff. 79–82.
Moore (*Revd.* Henry Kingsmill), *Principal of the Church of Ireland Training College, Dublin*. Letter to *C.Q.R.*, 1912: **1619**, f. 223.
Moore (John), *Archbishop of Canterbury*. Letters to R. Mylne, 1790–8: **1489**, ff. 69, 78, 84.
— Note, [1795]: **1373**, f. 33.
— Letter from J. Sealy, 1796: **1726**, ff. 134–5.
— Letter from E. Malone, 1797: **1834**, f. 74.
— Report by committee of the Board of Bishops about Land Tax, 1799 (*copy*): **1373**, ff. 135–8.
— Autograph, 18th cent.: **1222**, p. i.
— Genealogical notes concerning, 18th cent.: **1736.**
— List of stained glass removed from Lambeth Palace by, 1803: **1726**, ff. 28–30; **1812**, ff. 299v–300.
— Schedule of papers in his study, 19th cent.: **1789**, ff. 99–108.
Moore (William Robert), *lawyer*. Letter to L. T. Dibdin, 1896: **1586**, f. 122.
Moorhouse (James), *Bishop of Manchester*. Photograph of, 20th cent.: **1772**, f. 39.
Mopinot (E[mile]), *secretary to the Council of the Gallican Catholic Church*. Letter to Mme E. Loyson, 1880 (*copy*): **1482**, f. 228.
Morant (Philip), *Vicar of Broomfield; historian of Essex*. Letter to the Bishop of London, 1737: **1741**, f. 129.
Moravians. Publication of hymns in England, 1755: **1373**, f. 37.
— Account of episcopate of by the Bishop of Oxford, 1888 (*printed*): **1397**, f. 55.
Moray, *Bishop of*.
v. Jolly (Alexander).
Petrie (Arthur).
Moray, Ross and Caithness, *Bishop of*.
v. Eden (Robert).
Maclean (Arthur John).
Wilson (Piers Holt).
Moreton Corbet, *Salop*. Survey, 1655 (*copy*): **1837**, f. 7.
Morgan (Henry Thornhill), *Vicar of St. Margaret, Lincoln*. Letters to *C.Q.R.*, 1908–9: **1618**, ff. 208–9, 316–317v.
— Letter to the same, 20th cent.: **1620**, ff. 224–5.
Morgan (William Moore), *Prebendary and Librarian of Armagh*. Letter to the Bishop of Salisbury, 1908: **1401**, f. 46.

Parker (Matthew), *Archbishop of Canterbury*. Statutes for Hospitals at Canterbury and Harbledown, 1560–74 (*copy*): **1355**, ff. 1v–11.

— Letter to J. Boys, [1572]: **1834**, f. 1.

— Annotations perhaps by, 1573: **1837**, ff. 3–4.

— Injunctions for Christ Church, Canterbury, 1573 (*copy*): **1356**, pp. 56–70.

— Arms in colour, 1584: **1310**, f. 4.

— Extracts from Register by A. C. Ducarel, 18th cent.: **1351**, ff. 89–94v.

— Orders for apparitors, 18th cent. (*copy*): **1777**, ff. 24–5.

— Photograph of portrait, 20th cent.: **1728**, f. 1.

Parker (S.). Letter to Baroness Burdett-Coutts, 1866: **1381**, f. 169.

Parker (Wilfrid), *former Bishop of Pretoria*. Letter to Very Revd. A. C. Don, 1960: **1469**, f. 209.

Parkinson (*Revd.* Richard), *Principal of St. Bee's College*. Letter to Revd. C. Wray, 1853: **1604**, ff. 485–488v.

Parliament.
v. GREAT BRITAIN.

Parochial libraries. Catalogues of Tenison's library at St. Martin-in-the-Fields, *c.* 1693: **1707–8.**

Parochial Mission Women's Association. Minute books, 1862–82, 1887–1916: **1682–93.**

Parry (Oswald Hutton), *Vicar of All Hallows, East India Docks, London*; *Bishop of Guiana* (*1921*). Letter to *C.Q.R.*, 1911: **1619**, f. 140.

Parry (Thomas), *Bishop of Barbados*. Letter from the Bishop of Jamaica, 1867 (*copy*): **1385**, f. 306.

Paterson (John), *Bishop of Edinburgh*; *Archbishop of Glasgow* (*1687*). Letter to the Earl of Winton, 1682: **1834**, f. 26.

Patrick Brompton, *Yorks*. Drawing of church, 19th cent.: **1460**, f. 53.

Patrixbourne, *Kent*. Lease of lands, 1561 (*copy*): **1226**, ff. 142–3.

— Presentment of court leet, 1820 (*copy*): **1226**, ff. 150–1.

Patterdale, *Westmor*. Sketch of church, 19th cent.: **1460**, f. 14.

Patterson (*Revd.* Melville Watson), *Fellow of Trinity College, Oxford*. Letter to C. Jenkins, 1902: **1630**, ff. 55–57v.

Patullo (George), [*Nonjuror*]. Letter to Bishop J. Falconer, 1722 (*copy*): **1536**, pp. 156–7.

Pau.
v. FRANCE.

Paul V, *Pope*. Mandate to Vicar-General of Bishop of Pistoia, 1609: C.M. XIV, no. 8.

Paul (George), *Vicar-General*. Letter to Archbishop Wake, [1726]: **1777**, f. 42.

Payne (Richard), *Vicar of Downton*. Letter to Revd. Charles Wordsworth, 18[42]: **1824**, ff. 95–97v.

Peacock [*post* Cust] (Daniel Mitford), *Vicar of Sedbergh*. Letter to Revd. Christopher Wordsworth, 1803: **1822**, ff. 179–180v.

Pearce (Zachary), *Bishop of Rochester*. Correspondence with Archbishop Secker, 1763: **1349**, pp. 167–75.

Pearson (Alfred), *Suffragan Bishop of Burnley*. Photograph of, 20th cent.: **1772**, f. 42.

P[earson] (J[oan] C[inetta]). Form of service for marriage of, 1932 (*printed*): **1726**, ff. 143–6.

Pearson (Richard), *of Aylesbury, Bucks., the elder, victualler*. Probate of his will, 1795: **1488**/36.

Peck (F.), *Nonjuror*. Letter to Bishop J. Falconer, 1718 (*copy*): **1536**, pp. 136–9.

Peckham (John), *Archbishop of Canterbury*. Extracts from his Register by A. C. Ducarel, 1755: **1358.**

— Extracts from his Register by A. C. Ducarel, 18th cent.: **1351**, ff. 2–5v, 54.

Peckham (W. D.), *antiquary*. Calendar of institutions and collations for diocese of Chichester, 1504–23: **1831.**

— Transcript of Revd. M. Walcott's *Fasti Cicestrenses*, 1940: **1830.**

Peckover (Alexander), *Quaker*. Letter to Baroness Burdett-Coutts, 1870: **1387**, f. 118

Webster (Laurence). Dispute with Symon Pecock, clerk, arbitrated, 1589: **1727**, f. 100.

Weekes (*Miss* E. L.). Notes on copy of statutes of Canterbury cathedral, 20th cent.: **1729**, ff. 87–91.

Welby (Thomas Earle), *Bishop of St. Helena*. Letter to the Bishop of St. Helena, 1861: **1751**, ff. 103–104v.

— Correspondence with E. M. Syfret, 1873 (*copy*): **1378**, ff. 158–61.

Welch (C. E.), *archivist*. List of contents of formulary, *c.* 1952: **1729**, ff. 92–109.

Wellesley (Arthur), *1st Duke of Wellington*. Letter to Revd. Christopher Wordsworth, 1835: **1822**, f. 320.

Wellesley (Gerald Valerian), *Dean of Windsor*. Letters from Revd. F. Temple, 1850–1 (*copies*): **1798**, ff. 3, 12–13, 29–30.

— Letters to Baroness Burdett-Coutts, 1866: **1380**, f. 95; **1381**, ff. 1, 19, 72.

Wellington, *Salop*. Survey, 1655 (*copy*): **1837**, f. 9.

Wellington, *Duke of*.
v. Wellesley (Arthur).

Wells, *Som*. Photograph of cathedral crypt, *c.* 1900: **1728**, f. 34.

Wells (Herbert George), *author*. Critique by Bishop C. Gore of *God the invisible king*, [1917]: **1468**, ff. 208–14.

Welton, *Yorks*. Drawing of church, 19th cent.: **1462**, f. 52.

Wem, *Salop*. Survey, 1655 (*copy*): **1837**, f. 6.

Wendey (Titus), *Vicar of Stebbing*. Letter to the Bishop of London, 1733: **1741**, f. 102.

Wentworth (*Sir* John). Star Chamber proceedings against, 1615: **1252**, ff. 164–87.

Wesley (*Revd.* John), *founder of Methodism*. Letter to —, 1755: **1373**, f. 37.

West (Arthur George Bainbridge), *Vicar of Essendon*. Letter to *C.Q.R.*, 1906: **1617**, ff. 386–7.

West (Benjamin), *painter*. Photograph of portrait by, 20th cent.: **1728**, f. 26.

West (George John), *5th Earl De La Warr*. Letter to the Warden and Fellows of Winchester College, 1835: **1824**, f. 180.

West (John), *of Banbury, Oxon*. Probate of his will, 1729: **1488**/25.

West (John), *Chaplain to Archbishop Whately*. Letter to the Bishop of Meath, 1850: **1727**, ff. 41–42v.

West Felton, *Salop*. Survey, 1655 (*copy*): **1837**, f. 16.

West Horsley, *Surrey*. Judgement in Court of Arches concerning, [1923]: **1586**, ff. 295–311.

West Indies. Returns to Governor H. Hamilton, 1790 (*copy*): **1543**, ff. 27–8.

— Correspondence of Baroness Burdett-Coutts about, 1865–8: **1385**, ff. 257–326.

— *v.* Courtenay (Reginald), *Bishop of Kingston*.
Knight (Alan John), *Archbishop of the West Indies*.
Parry (Thomas), *Bishop of Barbados*.
Rigaud (Stephen Jordan), *Bishop of Antigua*.
Spencer (Aubrey George), *Bishop of Jamaica*.

West Molesey, *Surrey*. Water-colour of church, 18th cent.: **1456**, f. 54.

West Thurrock, *Essex*. Water-colour of church, 18th cent.: **1456**, f. 55.

West Witton, *Yorks*. Draw ofing church, 19th cent.: **1460**, f. 64.

Westbury, *Salop*. Survey, 1655 (*copy*): **1837**, f. 19.

Westbury, *Baron*.
v. Bethell (Richard).

Westcott (Brooke Foss), *Bishop of Durham*. Notes on the critical study of Holy Scriptures, [1897] (*printed*): **1401**, ff. 5–6v.

Western New York, *Bishop of*.
v. Coxe (Arthur Cleveland).

Westminster Association. Papers, 1814–16: **1787–8**; **1789**, ff. 3–96.

LIST OF OWNERS AND DONORS

Atlay (*Miss* Agnes): gave **1680,** ff. 239–248^{v}.

Ayerst (*Revd.* William): owned **1357.**

Barlow (*Miss* Helen): gave **1812,** ff. 59–63^{v}.

Barnet, *Herts.*: St. Andrew's Library owned **1501.**

Barrett (*Mrs.* Mary Tufnell): gave **1746–7.**

Barrington (Shute), *Bishop of Durham*: gave **1721.**

Beauvoir (Osmund): bookplate, **1359; 1552–8.**

Benson (Arthur Christopher): gave **1403.**

Benson (Edward White), *Archbishop of Canterbury*: gave **1415.**

Blackman (*Mrs.*): gave **1468,** ff. 208–20; **1773,** ff. 5–22^{v}.

Blakeney (T. S.): gave **1727,** ff. 105–84.

Blore (W. P.): gave **1486–7.**

Boyveau et Chevillet, *of Paris, booksellers*: label of, **1549.**

Brechin Diocesan Library: owned **1522; (1523); 1524–5.**

Bredgar, *Kent*: Bible belonging to the parish of, **1362**/1–2.

Bright (Benjamin Heywood): gave **1365.**

Bristol Baptist College: owned **1784.**

British Council of Churches: gave **1752.**

British Records Association: gave **1488; 1495; 1559–60; 1751,** ff. 143–87; **1834,** ff. 29–36; **1837,** f. 29.

Cahn (*Mrs.* J.): gave **1781–2.**

Carboni (Gaetano), *of Vetralla, Italy*: owned **1504.**

Cheshire (*Mrs.*): gave **1773,** ff. 23–108.

Church Commissioners: gave **1561.**

Church House Library: bookplate, **1682–93.**

Claughton (Alan O.): gave **1812,** ff. 226–95.

Clements (A. J.): gave **1726,** ff. 140–6; **1728,** ff. 31–2; **1837,** ff. 42–6.

Clementson (*Miss* B. E.): gave **1772.**

Coates (Ronald): owned **1501.**

Cockerell (*Miss* Annie): gave **1837,** ff. 52–5.

Collins (William Edward), *Bishop of Gibraltar*: owned **1499.**

Comité pour la Défense des Droits des Israélites en Europe Centrale et Orientale: gave **1716–1716B.**

Cornwallis (Frederick), *Archbishop of Canterbury*: owned **1256.**

Cottenham, *Countess of*: gave **1719,** f. 69.

Crisp (Frederick Arthur): owned **1389–94.**

Cure (*Lady*): gave **1405.**

Davidson (Randall Thomas), *Archbishop of Canterbury*: bookplate, **1737; 1789,** ff. 133–47.

de Beer (*Dr.* E. S.): gave **1775.**

Dibdin (L. G.): gave **1586–9.**

Dickinson (Francis Henry): owned **1515.**

Don (Alan Campbell), *former Dean of Westminster*: gave **1468,** ff. 188–207; **1469,** ff. 166–202, 205–46; **1728,** f. 27; **1759–60; 1837,** ff. 47, 50–1.

Douglas (*Revd.* John Albert): gave **1468,** ff. 221–82.

Ducarel (Andrew Coltee): bookplate, **1703–4**: owned **1351; 1358; 1371; 1705.**

Eeles (Francis Carolus): gave **1501–51; 1719,** ff. 71–99; **1834,** ff. 8–11.

Ellis (Roger): gave **1791.**

Elwick (*Revd.* Robert): owned **1362**/1–2.